T0369695

THE FLETCHER JONES FOUNDATION
HUMANITIES IMPRINT

· The Fletcher Jones Foundation has endowed this imprint to foster
innovative and enduring scholarship in the humanities.

The publisher and the University of California Press Foundation gratefully acknowledge the generous support of the Fletcher Jones Foundation Imprint in Humanities.

A Party for Lazarus

A Party for Lazarus

SIX GENERATIONS OF ANCESTRAL
DEVOTION IN A CUBAN TOWN

Todd Ramón Ochoa

UNIVERSITY OF CALIFORNIA PRESS

University of California Press
Oakland, California

© 2020 by Todd Ramón Ochoa

Library of Congress Cataloging-in-Publication Data

Names: Ochoa, Todd Ramón, 1969– author.
Title: A party for Lazarus : six generations of ancestral devotion in a Cuban
    town / Todd Ramón Ochoa.
Description: Oakland, California : University of California Press, [2020] |
    Includes bibliographical references and index.
Identifiers: LCCN 2019049795 (print) | LCCN 2019049796 (ebook) |
    ISBN 9780520315976 (cloth) | ISBN 9780520315983 (paperback) |
    ISBN 9780520974111 (epub)
Subjects: LCSH: Babalúaiyé (Afro-Caribbean deity) | Fasts and feasts—
    Orisha religion—Social aspects. | Fasts and feasts—Social aspects—Cuba. |
    Ancestor worship—Cuba.
Classification: LCC BL2532.S5 O24 2020 (print) | LCC BL2532.S5 (ebook) |
    DDC 299.6097291—dc23
LC record available at https://lccn.loc.gov/2019049795
LC ebook record available at https://lccn.loc.gov/2019049796

Manufactured in the United States of America

28 27 26 25 24 23 22 21 20
10 9 8 7 6 5 4 3 2 1

For Erika Samoff, Gabo Ochoa Samoff, and
Marcos Ochoa Samoff, with gratitude and love

CONTENTS

ACKNOWLEDGMENTS

This book would not have been written without the loyal support of the Department of Religious Studies at the University of North Carolina at Chapel Hill. Funding for research in Cuba is hard to come by, and the Department of Religious Studies made visits to Cuba possible when there was otherwise no path forward. I could not have undertaken this work without the confidence inspired in me by my colleagues in the department. To the leadership and staff of UNC's Institute for the Study of the Americas, I am grateful for the unwavering commitment to keep Cuba research a central part of its mission.

Two writing fellowships made this book possible. In the spring of 2012, I received a semester leave as part of a faculty fellowship at the Institute for the Arts and Humanities at UNC–Chapel Hill. Many thanks to my cohort of fellows that semester for the conversations, critiques, and insights that came to frame this book. The book was drafted under the atrium of the National Humanities Center and the auspices of a faculty fellowship during the 2017–18 academic year. The cohort of fellows brought together in that singular place affirmed me and gave me the courage to give this book new directions. I am especially grateful to Libby Otto, Laura Murphy, Rian Thum, Kimberly Jannarone, Shahla Talebi, and Hilde Hoogenboom, along with the center's director and its extraordinary staff.

Many colleagues at UNC–Chapel Hill supported me in the decade it took to write this book, and their thoughtful attention lifted me time and again. In the Department of Religious Studies, I am grateful to Laurie Maffly-Kipp, Randall Styers, Ruel W. Tyson Jr., Jonathan Boyarin, Zlatko Pleše, Brandon Bayne, and David Lambert. Barry Saunders, in UNC's Department of Social Medicine, has inspired and encouraged me countless times. Graduate students in the Department of Religious Studies and Anthropology, along with undergraduate students in several seminars devoted to Black Atlantic praise communities, are too numerous to list. I am left with the insights gained into the skilled embodiment and imaginative performance of "orisá mounting" from two seminars in which Andrew Ali Aghapour led workshops in "everyday ancestor performance."

In Cuba, I am indebted to many friends and conversation partners. In Havana, where my group of friends thins by the year as more and more Cubans seek lives abroad, I am grateful to Caridad Acosta Acosta for twenty years of generous and inspiring friendship. Cary has oriented me and enlightened me so many times. Dannys Montes de Oca y Moreda has been a radiant conversation partner and friend for twenty years. Sergio Rajiv Gómez Sáez has become a friend and guide in all things "new" in Cuba's ever-shifting economy. Margarita Sáez Sáez has been a teacher and guide in worlds of African-inspired praise for twenty years. Without Margarita's imagination, instruction, and insistence, this book would not exist.

In Sierra Morena, I am grateful to countless people, who for the sake of protecting them from unwanted and unexpected consequences of this book must remain unnamed. I regret this deeply, but the wisdom of research protocols should be heeded. There is not a word of what is written in the pages that follows that is not touched by multitudinous insights provided me by interlocutors major and minor over twenty years. Decades-long friends and passing strangers contributed to my understanding of the scintillating poetry of Cuba's Creole praise forms. The richness, texture, and taste of in-town *santo-orisá* praise was ultimately beyond my grasp. I thank the many friends and conversation partners who extended their time and confidence with incalculable generosity even as I fell short of understanding their lives as fully as they might have wished.

Comments from two reviewers for UC Press were invaluable to me as this book was revised. The energy poured into the reviews was humbling and inspiring. Insights drawn from the critiques will continue to inform me long after this book is in print.

The contributions of these reviewers, colleagues, confidants, and conversation partners were central to this writing, but the book's errors and excesses are mine alone.

My energy and self-esteem were lifted by the confidence of friends who quietly assured me I should proceed. In Chapel Hill, a heartfelt thank-you to Linda Green and Maria Wisdom. In New York, I am in debt to and in awe of Daniella María Gandolfo and Michael Taussig. In Palo Alto, Rachel Samoff and Joel Samoff have been steadfast. I am deeply grateful to my family, Christiana Mutzl Zilke, David Zilke, Christiana Ochoa, Max Ochoa, and David Ochoa. Christiana Mutzl Zilke, my mother, read the manuscript many times. This book owes more than I can express to Erika Samoff, Gabo Ochoa Samoff, and Marcos Ochoa Samoff.

This is an account of *santo-orisá* praise in a small town in Villa Clara Province, Cuba. It is based on twenty years of on-and-off visits of various lengths, none more than two weeks, always in December. This is the research program of a midcareer professional anthropologist with a teaching job that keeps me from doing "real" fieldwork for extended periods. It may be something as fortuitous as the December date of the feasts I write about that made this book possible. By chance, the party hosted by my teacher of santo-orisá praise happens during the three weeks I am regularly afforded as a break between the fall and spring semesters.

Santo-orisá is a term of my making, which I use throughout the book to gesture at the briskly recombinant quality of the praise scenes I describe. *Santo* invites associations with Catholic saints. It also means "holy," or "dear" in a devotional sense. *Orisá* refers to an African-inspired sovereign entity who presides over a discrete dimension of human life, such as love, illness, or struggle. These sovereign entities, "African gods and goddesses," populate Caribbean and mainland religions throughout the Western Hemisphere and Atlantic basin, where they are known as *orisha, oricha, orixa,* or *òrisá*. In Havana, *oricha* is the preferred spelling and consequent pronunciation. In the feasts at the heart of this book, in songs and also in local speech, the pronunciation in Spanish is "orisá," with both the "s" and "á" clearly pronounced. I have chosen to use the latter spelling for this reason alone, and not to signal proximity to African sources or authenticity derived therefrom, which would be a reasonable interpretation. I use the compound term *santo-orisá,* then, to express how the people who shared their lives with me often use both words to refer to the same entity, be it a Catholic santo or an African-inspired orisá. A prime example of this is the santo-orisá at the heart of this book: San Lázaro–Babalú Ayé. Invariably, I will be undisciplined in maintaining my artificial coupling and often simply use *santo* or *orisá,* as did the people with whom I worked.

In the pages that follow, I portray santo-orisá praise as it has been lived by an extended family over six generations. My teacher of African-inspired praise in Cuba, Isidra Sáez, introduced me to her hometown of Sierra Morena in 1999 and persuaded me, after several years, to write about the feasts hosted there for the santos-orisás. As a result, the family I write about is her own, and the genealogies I write about are her own. That said, to safeguard against any unintended consequences of writing this book, I have chosen to use pseudonyms for all the living people who could be identified, including Isidra. I use the names of the dead, as I was steadfastly encouraged to do.

In fact, there was no learning about praise feasts, called *bembés,* without also learning about the ancestors who hosted the santos-orisás in the past. With the help of many interlocutors, some with no more than a few words to offer, these ancestors and the santos-orisás they served came into focus. Stitching together Isidra's family history over many years revealed astonishing resilience and creativity on the part of people who were enslaved in Cuba during the second half of the nineteenth century, earned their freedom at the end of that century, and who along with their descendants cultivated a community of ancestor and santo-orisá devotion during the arduous first decades of the twentieth century.

Nor was there any learning about bembés and santo-orisá devotion without entering into the dramas befalling Isidra's family as these were refracted and intensified through property disputes, kinship fissures, and triumphs and losses, big and small. These dramas surrounded and suffused the bembé this family hosted yearly for more than fifty years. I hope that writing about kin relations, with their assumptions about loyalty and love and consequent potential for betrayal, will help readers connect to the scenes I describe while the rudimentary shape of bembé feasts comes into view. An important part of this book is capturing how Isidra's family and their collaborators, the ancestors they hold dear, and the santos-orisás they praise have fared in all their convolutions over fifty years of socialist revolution. This is described over the course of the book, and readers who are curious about Cuba and its revolution will find this account of interest.

So, the story I tell here is about a family and the feast they have historically hosted, which repeats yearly. For decades, the same community has hosted the santos-orisás, and for decades the same dancers take upon themselves the same santos-orisás. The santos-orisás preside over a bembé, a year passes, and the santos-orisás preside again. But it would be a mistake to assume that feast scenes are ever the same. Bembé dates repeat, hosts repeat, music repeats, dancers repeat, and the santos-orisás who mount them repeat, but the scenes are remarkably different. Difference-in-repetition is, in fact, what bembés and the santos-orisás promise. The exceptional turns of life, or fate, that only santos-orisás can bring to engrained struggles are the "difference" that people who host and attend bembés seek, over and over. To make the differences felt, I have tried to accent the everydayness of praise life in town, and to some degree what predominates in the book are descriptions of bembé routines. It is only in the midst of the repetitive, redundant, mirrored, and replicated actions of a bembé that the extraordinary fate-shaping, healing gestures of the santos-orisás can be appreciated.[1]

The unsettled reader will have noticed my use of the term *praise*. The alert reader will have noticed that I am using it in place of the term *religion*. I make this choice because *praise* better connects to the action of bembé feasts than does the term *religion*. The term *religion* tends to connect the reader to books, structures, and organizations, which are not the point of bembé feasts. *Religion,* as a term, wants to elevate the action of feasting—the dancing, singing, drumming (and sweating and laughter and eating) of communal encounters—to realms of value more abstract and beyond the sensual action itself. In orienting the reader to the worldly sensuality of bembé lives, I join a chorus that for thirty years has agreed that religion does not emerge from some place other than the routines of everyday life, its foibles, its power, and its profuse, incomprehensible minor situations.[2] Religion does not come from above but rather from within social life. Neither does religion make sense of life situations any more than situations vitalize religion. So, rather than use an all-too-familiar term that deceptively gives readers a handle on bembé feasts, I choose descriptions upon descriptions of the feasts so as to hand readers over to bembé life. Words that sit tight against the action are preferred, like *praise*. It comes closest to the activity of celebration and the Spanish term by which the feasts are called—*fiestas* [parties]. *Praise* adds to the casual associations readers might construe in the English word *party*. *Praise* is not the only word I use to communicate the activity of gathering in celebration of the santos-orisás, and as the narrative advances, I will use more terms.

Conscious that praise is imbricated with mundane experience, this book also portrays rural life in socialist Cuba in the first two decades of the twenty-first century. It draws from my experiences in Havana over thirty years to depict the arrangements, problems, and provisional solutions that make living in Cuba so unique. Life is meaner in the countryside, especially because access to hard currency and hard-currency goods, which are the lifeblood of the cities, is much more difficult. This is not to say that country life is not without enjoyments, and occasionally dairy and fish show up, which are so lacking in a city like Havana.

Not since Pope John Paul II visited Cuba in 1998 have gatherings to praise the orisás run the risk of being shut down by the police, but hosts must still register their gatherings with local authorities. This is even more the case in a small town like Sierra Morena, where the capacity of the police to keep an eye on things is great. Still, unlike countless feasts that disappeared in the Stalinist heyday of the Cuban Revolution in the 1970s, never did feasts for the santos-orisás cease to be celebrated in Sierra Morena. This was the case with the bembé hosted for San Lázaro–Babalú Ayé by Isidra's mother. I still don't know how she did it, but through some combination of vision and political savvy, for which revolutionary fervor was essential, she managed to keep her feast going. This is remarkable, because in the 1970s the revolution valued things exclusively for their political usefulness, and the activity of hosting the santos-orisás has never served exclusively utilitarian ends. This is not because orisá praise feasts are above the worldly affairs of the revolution, but rather because bembés materially exceed its utilitarian values.[3] Year after year, bembés succeed in making life new for people in part because they are too much for the revolution to encompass. Let there be no mistake: the revolution is central to everyday Cuban life, and it is therefore central to hosting scenes of orisá praise. Just how these two coexisting, apparently discordant domains of Cuban life bear on one another is an important part of what this book is about.

Isidra eventually persuaded me to pursue this project in part because she showed me how bembés in Sierra Morena differed from African-inspired praise scenes in Havana. In the last twenty years, as more ethnographies have appeared, praise scenes from Havana and Santiago have come to stand for African-inspired religion in Cuba as a whole.[4] If this project has a basic contribution to make, it is to hint at the great diversity among Cuba's African-inspired communities.

The principal differences between African-inspired praise in Sierra Morena and that of the cities can be found in the ways each handles the cultural resources at its disposal. It is a question of how West African and Central African cultural resources are combined, played with, and recombined. In Sierra Morena, the West African resources are from Ewe and Fon peoples, and together they are called Arará. The Central African cultural resources are from Congo people.[5] In Sierra Morena, Arará and Congo inspirations are combined and feasted together, along with robust Spanish Catholic and Spiritualist resources. In Havana, Central African inspirations are also Congo, but the West African cultural resources are principally Yoruba. Perhaps for this reason, West African and Central African inspirations in Havana became two very different praise communities, Ocha and Palo, which never feast together, although a diplomatic code allows individuals to practice both.[6] From the point of view of Havana ritual masters, the bembés of Sierra Morena lack ritual discipline, combine what should remain separate, and in the end are good healthy bumpkin stuff.

One especially difficult thing for Havana practitioners to value about Sierra Morena praise scenes is that in town there are no priests or priestesses, so no initiations or initiates. These are crucial to African-inspired communities in Havana. In fact, one of the arguments I'm making about praise in Sierra Morena is that without these roles there is little beyond the action of individual bembés to call a "religion." Which brings me back to the choice of "African-inspired praise" to describe bembés—this allows me to talk about social and communal lives that are at once more particular, more dynamic, and more partial than the concept of religion would predispose us to expect.

My strategy, then, for writing about bembé praise in Sierra Morena has been to write about tiny forces—teeming, nearly imperceptible forces, that together produce many sensations, mine and those of the people kind enough to share their lives with me. In this book, these sensations are piled up, agglomerated, and allowed to become felt as encounters to be shared with the reader. Such felt encounters are what philosophers are today calling "affect." In the course of this book, the forces presented here are meant to affect us through their collective intensity. This is the principal aspiration of this book—to move forces into the reader, however tiny such forces might be. We might call this movement "import"—of forces into the life of reader.

"Importance," then, is forces made felt across a distance, be it in time or space, even if the distance is as small as that between two people facing each other—perhaps an orisá and a devotee. But this book aspires to achieve importance between African-inspired praise in rural Cuba and ethnographic writing in the United States. I do not understand this book to mediate the forces it presents so much as participate in an entanglement with them. My objective is more to mobilize forces than it is to communicate or translate them. In fact, I would like the book to mediate as little as possible. To import the liveliness of the santos-orisás into the social life of the reader—that is the point of this writing. Then, to precipitate a minor event for the reader, if only by changing a single social nucleotide. The goal of this writing is simply to make social life felt anew.

PART ONE

_____

ONE

The Ring and the Altar

EVERYONE WANTS THE HOUSE IN TOWN. Ten half siblings have claim to it, and the fight goes back a long time now, to 1998. A deed to the house would help, as would a will from their deceased mother, Vicenta Petrona Sáez, but the house has neither. Vicenta Petrona, whom everyone, including her children, called Cucusa, bore ten children to five common law spouses over her lifetime. The third of these spouses was Orfilio Ruíz, the love of her life, with whom she had five children. By the standards of her day this was Vicenta Petrona's most successful relationship, lasting over a decade and including the acquisition of the house in which she lived the rest of her life. Cucusa and Orfilio's five children consider the house theirs, purchased by their mother and father in 1940, but their half siblings see it differently.

One of them has lived in the house as a squatter for a decade. Getting her out will be very hard. This is revolutionary Cuba, where housing is guaranteed and tenants have rights to the spaces they occupy, even when their status is poorly documented. Furthermore, the missing deed and lack of instructions from Cucusa give the squatting half sister a unique opportunity to call the place her own. Housing in Cuba is very tight, adding to the difficulty of coaxing someone to voluntarily leave a spacious ranch house. It would be possible to sell the house with a new deed, but revolutionary housing regulations don't allow one to be issued without the consent of the squatting half sister. House sales in Cuba are incredibly complicated anyway, so things are stuck.

The house is in the town of Sierra Morena, on Cuba's north coast, between touristy Varadero Beach and the town of Sagua la Grande, to the east. A highway called the North Circuit travels this coast, which is mostly fallow sugar country. Sierra Morena has the good fortune to sit on the North

Circuit, and all around are farmers trying to figure out how to make the best of the quickly shifting economy. The only thing happening there is the highway itself, and even that is pretty dead.

Local dump trucks, tractors, and other diesel vehicles, most of them government property, are what rattle along the North Circuit today. But when I first visited in 1999, at the end of a decade of crushing shortages, you could spend most of a morning sitting on the side of the road and not see a single vehicle. There were horses and horse-drawn carts and plenty of people walking, but no vehicles. Nearly twenty years later, maybe ten cars go past in an hour, most of them "company cars" ferrying people midway up the ladder at the Ministry of Agriculture (MINAG) or the Ministry of the Interior (MININT). The MINAG guys, dressed in snappy polo shirts and artificially distressed jeans, chase elusive government quotas for grapefruit and pineapple production at repurposed sugar cooperatives. The MININT people, in their two-tone olive uniforms, hunt among the coastal mangroves for the equally elusive, though more frequently found, would-be inner tube refugee. Gas is short in Sierra Morena, but these days you can hire a local driver to take you to Havana for $80, which is madness only a foreign visitor like me could afford. Locals have a hard time getting farther than three kilometers west, to the municipal seat of Corralillo, because bus tickets anywhere else have gotten so expensive over the last decade.

Sierra Morena sits on a little steppe on a low hill, for which the term *mountain [sierra]* is tongue in cheek, the joke long lost. The town overlooks a lagoon twelve miles wide, on the far side of which are sandy keys and the open sea of Cuba's north shore. At Sierra Morena, the North Circuit seeks high ground as it dodges farmland that was once swampland and still goes under when a hurricane hits, which is pretty regularly. Hurricane Irma blew through in 2017, causing serious damage. Hurricane Michelle was significant in 2001, and Kate, in November 1985, is remembered with dread. Hurricane after hurricane is remembered before that. Climbing the low hill, the highway runs straight at town before veering back toward the sea, ultimately acknowledging Sierra Morena at but a glancing point. The town is just out of view.

Cucusa's house is close to the highway, with only a row of structures and a playground separating it from the rattle of the road. It sits on a paved street and has a red tile roof and long front veranda. Tall windows dressed in painted iron bars run the length of the veranda, and in their midst is the double front door. Inside this door is the central room of the house, which is both a dining room and living space. The ceilings go right up to the rafters, which are bare. In the corner facing the street is an altar devoted to San Lázaro–Lazarus the Beggar. The inside walls have no paneling, and you can see the siding is rough-milled wood. Bedrooms lie to either side of the great room. At the back is a kitchen that is attached to the house and enclosed; many in town are not. The cement floor, an important in-town detail, made Cucusa's daughter, Isidra, especially proud. An ample yard, with fruit trees and an open well once topped with a winch, is beyond the kitchen. Sitting on its hill, the house has suffered little lasting harm from hurricanes over the eighty years the family has owned it. Ultimately, the house couldn't withstand the storm that followed Cucusa's death.

The house was probably built between 1910 and 1920, though I do not know for sure. Sierra Morena itself was established in 1888, when a hurricane wiped out settlements on the shore of the lagoon.[1] The house was decades old when Cucusa and Orfilio bought it in 1940, shortly after the birth of their fourth child, Isidra. They were thirty-some years old, and it was the year Orfilio won a huge purse in the numbers game. "He loved gambling of all sorts," said Isidra. "If he could have, he would have bet us children on the numbers game. My father, Orfilio, bought the house with the winnings. He paid cash." Orfilio wasn't alone in his love of gambling, and even today, despite government persecution, the numbers game thrives in revolutionary Cuba. It is called *la bolita,* or *charada china,* and its numbers runners work in every neighborhood of every town and city in Cuba. Their daily rounds take them to nearly every house in the country. Orfilio bought the house because it was in town, close to the highway, had a solid roof, a well, and room for his growing family. "But more than anything," said Isidra, "he bought it for the cockfighting ring behind the house. He loved cockfights more than he loved the numbers game."

On fight days, back before the revolution came and the cockfighting went underground, the house became an appendage of the ring. Orfilio would preside, betting and drinking, while Cucusa, her mother, and her children, sold concessions. "It was the 1940s," said Isidra, "and Sierra Morena was socially segregated, with separate social clubs in town. The Lyceum was there for whites, and Union and Brotherhood for Blacks." Orfilio was one of the lightest people anyone could imagine calling "Black," so he was called *mulato.* He was light even for those called mulato, and so he was referred to as *mulato claro,* or "light mulatto." This is the way Cuban people racialize one another, adding to "Black" and "white" a palette of browns, whites, yellows, reds, and even blues. These are then mixed with shadings of great variety, from "dark" to "light" to "light-light." A person is eyed from head to foot, and in a breath's time their skin, hair, lips, eyes, and nose are combined into a racialized description like "a reddish-white guy with bad-ish [frizzy] hair and a *nose that, well, you know . . .*" [*un blanco rojizo con pelo medio malo y una nariz que ya tu sabes . . .*]. That is how I am generally described. Lighter, slender features are valued, and darker, fuller features are denigrated in a vocabulary at once explicit and rich in the powers of insinuation.

In this hyper skin-conscious and feature-conscious world, the cockfights were special. "They were one of the few gatherings in town where people of all shades could mingle," said Isidra. "Some with linen suits and shined shoes, others with muddy boots and clothes from working their fields." Better-dressed folks would have come from nearby Corralillo, the municipal seat, while the others would have come from the surrounding hills. In the 1940s, the Corralillo folks would have lined the street with Buick Roadmasters, Chrysler Highlanders, and Dodge Coronets, while locals would have tied their horses to the veranda posts. The Corralillo folks would have been lighter, if not to say whiter, while folks from town would have been darker, if not more Black. "Everyone talked, played, and mingled," she said.

"Orfilio left my mother and five young children for a lover he had in Havana. He left us the cockfighting ring." Isidra remembers it in the middle of the yard. To one side was the well, to the other a wing comprising two rooms and an outhouse. Banks of bleachers, four seats high, surrounded the ring. "The fruit trees you see there now? My mother took care of those trees, so the ring was shaded, and during most of the year there was food: oranges in spring, mangoes and guavas in summer, tangerines in fall, *fruta bomba* [papaya], and coconuts all year round.

"Orfilio left her in 1943, and Cucusa made the most of it. Sundays would roll around and the yard would fill up, first with the men who brought their roosters, then with betting fans, and finally the spectators." As a child, Isidra remembers running around playing tricks on her siblings and mother and, when she got older, on the bettors themselves. "I was a handful! The smartest of us all! I was as fast as anyone. I had a runaway [*traviesa*] streak and loved messing with people. I was too much for my mother and my grandmother, Ma' Isidra, and I did what I wanted. They needed my help, but did I care?" She would use the crowd to vanish. "I would run to visit cousins or friends, or simply hide. Once, I made it all the way to the beach and played a trick on one of Batista's bosses. Once, from one of my hiding places, I saw my father at the ring, with his lover from Havana. After he left us, he came back once or twice, to bet." In my years of listening to Isidra, I have pictured this wild little girl many times.

Her sister, Eulalia, was two years younger and followed Isidra loyally. They were the two youngest, the girls. Their brothers were formidable figures; the eldest, Orfilito, had traveled as far as Camagüey looking for work in the *zafra* [sugar harvest] and eventually settled there. During the late 1950s, when the anti-Batista struggle was in full swing, the next two oldest brothers got involved. Máximo and Roberto were militants in the local clandestine organization. They talk about it now, as do their sisters; in fact, they boast about it, because in Cuba the clandestine movement came to power. After 1959, Máximo and Roberto were town heroes for their roles in supporting Fidel Castro's 26th of July Movement and toppling Batista and his local bosses.

Cucusa and Ma' Isidra worked the concessions that made a chunk of money when the ring was open. "They sold sandwiches, whatever was on the fruit trees, and sips of aguardiente [cane liquor]. Otherwise, they watched the ring, the couples, the people from far away, and us kids.

"They needed my help, but I was always on the loose. Cucusa was pulled away by visitors who wanted her attention in the living room, at the altar to San Lázaro [Lazarus the Beggar]. They would ask her permission to approach it and ask her for the proper way to address San Lázaro, or ask if they could make a donation. These were people who had come a distance to the fights, who couldn't drop by whenever, people from Corralillo, or farmers on horseback from farther inland or from the next hill over, which everyone in town considered far enough to be *monte* [wild]. My mother helped all these people who were looking for comfort in times of illness. She healed them.

"Local folks were here all the time because Cucusa left the door to the house open so that people could drop in. This town knew Cucusa's San Lázaro, and she would find them any time of day kneeling right there, where you see the altar today." These people knew Cucusa's San Lázaro from his appearances at feasts Cucusa held for him, where they also called him Babalú Ayé.

On the altar were two statues of San Lázaro. The Catholic-inspired figurines show Lazarus the Beggar as a scraggly-haired pauper with spindly limbs. His legs are bloodied with open sores, which also mar his chest, Jesus-like. Dogs gather around him, to lick his wounds. His shoulders are hunched over crutches, and he leans weakly to one side. He wears only a tattered purple tunic tied around his waist as a loincloth. In other versions of this figure the tunic is made of burlap sackcloth. Despite his privation, his expression is serene. His eyes stare forward blankly, focused not on his discomfort but on the future that awaits him, which is at the side of Abraham the Father in heaven. A halo sometimes crowns his head. Those who keep statues of Lazarus the Beggar sometimes make little purple capes for them, to emphasize the exalted status of the saint.

Cucusa's altar had two statues of San Lázaro. The smaller one was nearly hidden in the back corner of the high shelf of the altar, surrounded by a frill of paper flowers. This little San Lázaro was the shabbier of the two, though this was hidden by a homemade cape of purple satin.

The larger statue of San Lázaro was on the lowest shelf. Both figurines were dressed in burlap pants, chests bare, their capes covering their shoulders. Their faces were losing their contours, blurred as if corroded, and whatever paint might have once defined eyes, lips, cheeks, and beards now ran in brownish streaks.

The two San Lázaro statuettes shared the altar with other Catholic-inspired figurines. On the lowest shelf next to the figure of San Lázaro was a statue of the Virgin of Charity—La Virgen de la Caridad del Cobre—Cuba's patroness. She was dressed in homemade capes and shawls of light blue and golden satin and lace. On the middle shelf, in a place of honor, was a statuette of Santa Bárbara—Saint Barbara—with her crown, her red dress, and her white lace shawls, her chalice and her sword. Santa Bárbara's place alone in the middle of the altar spoke to the central role she occupied in Cucusa's healing, especially when she feasted San Lázaro and her other santos.[2] Each shelf was set with lace cloths and outlined by plastic and paper flowers.

For many years after meeting the two San Lázaro figurines, I figured they were redundant, the older and more deteriorated one replaced by the newer, larger figurine; the older then removed to the top shelf. That was before I could see the two statues as "doubled," that they were versions of more than one saint. The New Testament gives us two Lazaruses. There is Lazarus the Beggar, who is sick and pleads at the gate of a rich man while dogs lick his sores. The beggar dies, but angels carry him to the side of Abraham the Father in heaven, while the rich man dies and goes to hell. This is the Lazarus pictured in the statues—crippled, afflicted, and wretched, along with his dogs. The New Testament depicts another Lazarus, one who dies but is then resurrected by Jesus after four days in the tomb. This is Lazarus of Bethany, who was himself wealthy enough to turn beggars away. The crucial difference between the two stories for Cubans—not just those who frequented Cucusa's altar but Cubans all over—is that Lazarus the Beggar overcomes death by going to heaven, while Lazarus of Bethany overcomes death by being resurrected to life on earth. In Cuban popular religion, the beggar Lazarus does not go to heaven but survives death to return to life on earth.

The statues on Cucusa's altar were a compound of these two biblical figures, a resurrected beggar who overcame death twice (once by going to heaven, then once by returning to life on earth). In Cuban popular praise for San Lázaro there is never any mention of Lazarus of Bethany, the resurrected. The inflection is emphatically on the adversity of poverty and illness, and the tenacity to survive shown by the beggar Lazarus. Lazarus of Bethany disappears in Cuba, and so does the rich man who goes to hell in the story of Lazarus the Beggar. In Isidra's understanding of San Lázaro, it was all about life in the here and now—no one goes to heaven, no one goes to hell, and San Lázaro was a power to help people thrive in life. The Cuban version is the braiding together of the two stories, the combination of poverty, illness, death, and return—to this life. But these two Lazarus stories are not the reason there were two statuettes on Cucusa's altar. As I said, no one ever speaks about Lazarus of Bethany.

This doubled resurrected santo, triumphant over illness and the grave, was added to yet again in Cuba and made more. The doubled santo became a "compounded" entity, because to the resurrected beggar was added the magnificent and forbidding person of Babalú Ayé, sovereign of illness and healing. Babalú Ayé commanded illness and healing for people who came to Cuba as slaves from West Africa, especially for the Ewe and Fon peoples of Old Dahomey from whom Cucusa and her neighbors were descended. Babalú Ayé bears the title *orisá,* meaning "law giver" or "sovereign." He presides over illness and healing and decides exceptions to the rules of sickness and recovery.

Babalú Ayé came to Cuba with people who were enslaved in what are today Benin, Togo, and Nigeria. In the eighteenth and early-nineteenth centuries, these were lands known for great cities and royal courts that impressed European navigators, explorers, traders, and slavers. These were the city-states and kingdoms of Allada, Oyo, and Dahomey, the latter of which is sung about energetically in Sierra Morena. The city-states were rivals, and each sold the other's people as slaves to Europeans, who only exacerbated their enmities.[3] Allada, Oyo, and Dahomey provided Spanish Cuba with over three hundred and fifty thousand enslaved people over three centuries, most of them forcibly brought to Cuba late in the European trade, in the 1800s.[4] The fall of Oyo in 1834, for example, led to thousands of refugees and defenseless people being enslaved and shipped to the Western Hemisphere, especially

Cuba and Brazil.[5] In Cuba in the nineteenth century, these people and hundreds of thousands of others were enslaved on the vast sugar plain just to the south of Sierra Morena.[6] To these people, and their descendants, Babalú Ayé was also known as Asojano and Sakpata, names used today in Sierra Morena.

In Cuba the West African god of mortal illness—be it smallpox, leprosy, or cancer—became Babalú Ayé, sovereign of illness and healing, master of pestilence and recovery. Babalú Ayé can deploy illness, and he can withdraw it. Babalú Ayé is pestilence itself, and also the sovereign power to overcome it. By commanding illness inside and out, he decides exceptions to the incontrovertible course of disease and suffering. For this Babalú Ayé bears the title *orisá*.

"But Babalú Ayé doesn't ask for much," said Isidra. "A yearly feast, pennies in alms, and that you never forget, or look aside, from the afflicted and ill. Not a lot to ask. But if you do forget illness, yours or the illness from which your parents suffered, or from which your own children suffer, forget so that you turn away from the ill around you—for *that* Babalú Ayé will bring illness to you again. And who will you turn to then? Back to Babalú Ayé. So why suffer the long way around? Stay with Babalú Ayé, with the ill, with illness, and he will always be at your side."

A compound santo, now adding the orisá Babalú Ayé to San Lázaro the Doubled. The santo who overcomes death is joined to the orisá of illness and healing. A beggar sovereign, a santo-orisá: San Lázaro–Babalú Ayé. It was this compound entity of which the two statues spoke, but I was able to arrive at this view of things only with time spent in orbit of that altar, in stories and as he appeared at parties thrown in his honor in Sierra Morena every December 17. These parties are called *bembés,* and Cucusa started hosting one in honor of San Lázaro–Babalú Ayé in 1943. Those who attended Cucusa's bembé hoped for a face-to-face encounter with San Lázaro–Babalú Ayé, to place their worries personally at his feet.

Broken, infested, worn down to a pair of sackcloth pants, the Beggar Sovereign is whom visitors sought at Cucusa's altar. They sought the leper-orisá humbly, lowly, as low as the Pestilent One himself, with his sores and dogs. His leprosy endears him to those afflicted with less terrible illness. In 1950, when Isidra was a child running past the altar, children were dying in their first months of life; the whole island was sick with malaria, worms, toothaches, arthritis, and leprosy itself. Nine years later the revolution would set out to change all that.

Visitors to Cucusa's house could encounter San Lázaro–Babalú Ayé at the altar, perhaps on their way to bet on a bird or have a few sips of cane liquor with acquaintances from the town over. They might be moved to leave a penny at the altar, perhaps with the thought of an ill parent or child back home. If Cucusa tended to them, which meant bringing them close to the assurances only San Lázaro–Babalú Ayé could provide, she would invite them to her bembé on December 17, San Lázaro's Day. If they accepted, they might promise a bottle of aguardiente or a cake for the bembé. More serious cases promised a goat or ram to offer the santo-orisá or one of his peers on his day. On December 17, they would be brought face to face with the santo-orisá and his healing touch.

Her children, her cockfighting ring, and tending to people at her altar kept Cucusa busy. But it was the bembé she hosted for San Lázaro–Babalú Ayé that she worked for the year through. It was a promise she made to the sovereign of illness one day in 1943 when she almost lost a second child to fever and asthma. Every year on December 17 she would gather her community to sing his praises, and from that year forward she never missed a December 17 as long as she lived. The party grew until it became the only bembé for San Lázaro–Babalú Ayé worth attending in town. The fate of her household, of her children, of her community, rode on the love and discipline Cucusa brought to tending San Lázaro–Babalú Ayé and those who sought him every day.

The year Cucusa died, 1998, there was no bembé for San Lázaro–Babalú Ayé at her house, but the next year, 1999, her daughter Isidra successfully hosted the feast there. Notwithstanding Isidra's best efforts since then, over the next decade other feasts sprang up on December 17 to fill the void left by Cucusa in Sierra Morena, and by 2009 the feud between Cucusa's children had their bembé teetering on the brink of collapse. Isidra was determined to keep the bembé going, and she often turned to memories of Cucusa and those who came before her to help steer the bembé forward. She recalled specific bembés from her childhood, and time and again sought a figure alongside her mother. This was Tomasa Cairo, Sierra Morena's beloved hostess of bembé parties. It was Tomasa Cairo who brought bembés out of nineteenth-century slavery and gave the santos-orisás a twentieth-century life.

TWO

La Sociedad Africana, 1880–1940

CHACHA CAIRO AMONG THE DEAD
AND THE SANTOS-ORISÁS

CENTRAL CUBA ALONG THE NORTH COAST, with its keys, inlets, and shallow bays, was known in the nineteenth century and into the twentieth as Región Sagua. This, after the town of Sagua la Grande, the metropolis for the region fifty kilometers east of Sierra Morena. In the nineteenth century it was a wild part of Cuba, with its protected lagoons and mobility for small boats and their contraband. The hamlet of Santa Rita was several miles east of where Sierra Morena stands today, down on the water. There was a plantation and sugar mill there by the same name. Most people in Sierra Morena understand that Santa Rita preceded Sierra Morena as a community, and that people from there moved in one fell swoop to the town's present location on the hill overlooking the lagoon. Those who remember will tell you that Santa Rita was wiped out by a hurricane, date uncertain, and that Sierra Morena came after, up on the hill. Atlantic hurricane records tell of a terrible storm that raked Cuba's north coast in 1888, and Catholic Church records date the founding of Sierra Morena to that year.[1] Other records tell of a small settlement in present-day Sierra Morena as far back as the 1830s.

The weather event of 1888 came at the end of another storm, one more convulsive, that blew through central Cuba starting in 1880. This was the emancipation of Cuban slaves, which started systematically in 1880 and progressed, piecemeal, until 1888.[2] It transformed Cuban society absolutely and led to the present-day community of Sierra Morena, with its santos-orisás and its bembés. The people who fled the 1888 hurricane and headed up the hill were emancipated slaves, free to move in Cuba.

Many of the freed slaves from the Santa Rita exodus used the last name Cairo, likely borne from the owner of Santa Rita or another before him. They were joined in Sierra Morena by emancipated people from other nearby sugar mills and plantations along the coast: the Farrés and Sáez people came from the Horizonte plantation, the Portilla folk from Las Dos Marías plantation, and the Alfonsos from the Santa Lutgarda plantation. These four plantations were responsible for the bulk of people in Sierra Morena and the last names common in town today. In the town over, Rancho Veloz, emancipated people came from yet other plantations, and other last names predominate.

Tomasa Cairo was a latecomer. She stayed in Santa Rita after Emancipation and the 1888 storm to care for her beloved husband, Guadalupe Cairo. When she arrived in Sierra Morena sometime around 1900, she was a widow and had no children. Sierra Morena was growing in two places at once: the central plaza with the newly constructed Catholic church, and a neighborhood east of this called El Río [the River]. It was up on a creek and where most of the Santa Rita, Horizonte, Dos Marías, and Santa Lutgarda emancipated plantation people lived. She settled on the outskirts of El Río and got to work building what she would call her Sociedad Africana. Everyone called Tomasa Cairo "Chacha."

Chacha Cairo might have been a late arrival, but that didn't slow her down. People in town knew her from Santa Rita, for the feasts she hosted there. In Sierra Morena she met Ma' Josefa Sáez, a freed slave from the Horizonte plantation exodus. Ma' Josefa Sáez was a first-generation *criolla* [Creole]; like Chacha, she was the formerly enslaved Cuban-born daughter of enslaved Africans. Chacha saw herself in Ma' Josefa and drew on her and other first-generation children of enslaved Africans to build her Sociedad Africana. Kimbito Sáez, from the Horizonte group, was also one of these. Kimbito was born in Cuba sometime in the 1860s and lived the first twenty years of her life as a slave. The three of them, Chacha Cairo, Ma' Josefa Sáez, and Kimbito Sáez, were contemporaries, born shortly before or after 1865. Despite their common last name, there was no relation between Ma' Josefa and Kimbito. Their African parents are remembered but spectrally today.

Lázaro M. lived in Sierra Morena all his life. Born in 1920, he was eighty-nine years old when I met him in 2009. I visited him on several occasions up to 2018, when I last saw him. Lázaro was named after San Lázaro–Babalú Ayé. The orisá of well-being and affliction has a part in every birth, when the health of mother and her newborn realize their full codependence in the drama of their separation. Born on December 17, San Lázaro's feast day, thirty-some years after the end of slavery in Cuba and being the tenth of eleven children, Lázaro M. had very little chance of being named anything else.

Lázaro M. is the person who knew about the plantations and the last names that came from them. He told me, "Chacha, Kimbito, Ma' Josefa, those women, they were Cuban-born slaves. The last generation born in slavery. They were the children and grandchildren of Africans brought from Africa. The Africans called their children *criollos* [Creoles] because they were different from themselves. They were Cuban."

The Africans were Ewe and Fon people from Allada and Old Dahomey, Yoruba people from Oyo, and BaKongo from the Congo River basin. Their children took on different speech, different tastes, and different horizons. They kept some of the language of their parents only with difficulty. Spanish was the lingua franca among the enslaved and their masters even before they were born. In Sierra Morena these African parents and grandparents, the "old ones" [*los viejos*], Lázaro M. said, were called Lucumí. They had names like Ma' Catarina, Ma' Merced, and Ma' Yaguá. Lázaro remembered only one Lucumí man, Ta' Teodoro. The Lucumises, as Lázaro referred to them in the plural, "had ritual scars on their cheeks. They were interested in life's big questions, and not afraid of death, debt, or betrayal." People like Chacha and Lázaro would lend the old Lucumises a hand and along the way learned what they could of African songs and ways of life. "The old Lucumises kept to themselves," said Lázaro. "You would think our bembés would be something they would like, but they weren't. Our parties were too new for them, the music included Castilian words, they were too different from the lives they knew in Africa before they were enslaved. But they had lots to teach, so people did what they could to learn from them." The old Lucumí people did not figure as prominently in the making of Chacha's Sociedad Africana as the Cuban-born Creoles, though you can feel them coming forward now and again in community talk.

As the twentieth century began, Chacha Cairo could look behind on her childhood of enslavement and look ahead to a future of her own making. The world she sought to build was modest in terms of Cuban aspirations for the time. The island had just concluded a decades-long independence struggle from Spain, and the country looked ahead to a new century. People who just a decade before were enslaved or indentured now joined their fates to a new economy and a new nation. Cubans moved throughout the island in the first decade of the twentieth century, looking for prosperity in the cities. But emancipation and independence brought with them social strife as Cuban whites reacted to the opportunities of newly free Cuban Blacks with campaigns of intimidation and terror reminiscent of those of the Jim Crow South.³

In this context, Chacha Cairo's choices were at once humble and brave. She did not move to Havana, Santa Clara, or even Sagua la Grande, down the coast. She did not even move to Corralillo, five kilometers west. She settled in Sierra Morena, a few kilometers from the plantation where she had been a slave. Her goal was to knit together a community that could feast the santos-orisás, peers to San Lázaro–Babalú Ayé, with righteousness and dignity. She would need musicians—drummers and singers—who could "call" the santos-orisás to her feasts with their rhythms and lyrics. With solid musicians, a chorus of dancers would assemble. Among the dancers she would cultivate "mounts," or "steeds": people who offered their bodies to the santos-orisás, like a steed offered to a sovereign rider, who could then parade about in the flesh among the gathered chorus. "Embodied" in/on their mounts, or steeds, the santos-orisás could enter the broader community with their healing and their counsel. At the beginning of the twentieth century, in the wake of slavery, Chacha Cairo sought to assemble a stable of such mounts, seven in total, one for each of the santos-orisás. Together, the seven mounts would lead her Sociedad Africana into the twentieth century. It was among the emancipated Santa Rita, Horizonte, Dos Marías, and Santa Lutgarda people and their descendants that she found her stable.

Ma' Josefa Sáez was her contemporary, born on the Horizonte plantation on the coastal plain of Región Sagua sometime around 1865. According to Lázaro M., she was a great dancer and, though it is unclear, was probably Chacha's "lead mount" for Yemayá, sovereign of the sea, tides, and maternity. Ma' Josefa was partnered with Jorge Sáez, also from the Horizonte exodus. Church-avowed marriage was rare among the emancipated people living in Sierra Morena. The terms *marido* and *marida,* meaning long-term or common law partner, were used to refer to those coupled but not formally husband and wife [*esposo y esposa*]. Jorge Sáez was Ma' Josefa's marido. Jorge Sáez became Chacha's mount for Changó, orisá of masculinity, warfare, and music. As Lázaro M. specified, he was Chacha's "second" mount for Changó. The first was her husband, Guadalupe Cairo, deceased in Santa Rita, whom she missed terribly as she built her community.

Lázaro M. said, "Jorge Sáez was hard to get along with. He and Ma' Josefa lived out of town and kept a small farm. He was a respected steed for Changó at Chacha's Sociedad Africana, but he was also a feared *palero* [stick worker, root man, or sorcerer]." Jorge Sáez's stick knowledge was attributed to Central African people enslaved in Cuba, especially BaKongo, "Congo," people. Their aggressive practices of healing and harming, and their ethos of cultivating close relationships with the dead, set them apart from the Ewe, Fon, and Yoruba-descended people who praised the santos-orisás and anchored Chacha's society. But Chacha respected Congo knowledge and practices and those devoted to them. Jorge Sáez surrounded himself with Congo substances, one of which, a stone capable of commanding the dead to do errands on his behalf, was said to birth other stones. His descendants still care for it and feed it in Sierra Morena. Jorge was one of those who learned from the old Lucumises and was known as the disciple of Ma' Yaguá.

Ma' Josefa and Jorge Sáez brought a great many resources to Chacha's Sociedad Africana. They were the mounts for Yemayá and Changó, and were thus central to any bembé. Jorge could be counted on to work Congo sorcery should people in the community need that kind of aid. Their greatest contributions to the Sociedad Africana, though, were their children, Digna Sáez and Loreto Sáez. Born free in the decade after Emancipation, they would each become "lead mounts" in Chacha's Sociedad Africana.

Ma' Josefa gave birth to Digna sometime in the 1890s or early years of the twentieth century. By the time she was in her late teens, around the First World War, she had replaced her mother as the lead mount for Yemayá in Chacha's Sociedad Africana. They say Digna was a beautiful mount for the orisá sovereign of the sea. Digna was pretty and strong, capable of carrying Yemayá's beauty, strength, and tidal determination with grace. Yemayá is sovereign over all of the sea's movements, including its surges. Hurricanes, like Irma in 2017, and Kate in 1985, and the 1888 storm that wiped out Santa Rita and the other coastal plantations, establish beyond a doubt that Yemayá is to be respected. A mount for Yemayá will ably move her body in dances that mimic waves, both calm and fierce. Digna was a steed for Yemayá through storms big and small at the Sociedad Africana, and her dancing is remembered more than a hundred years after her birth.

Yemayá's realms of command extend beyond the sea. She also rules over the tides of fertility. She is the mother's keeper, sovereign over menstruation, pregnancy, birth, and maternity. Yemayá adores children, whom she protects but also steadily corrects. Her relationship with children is always maternal; when she is consulted, Yemayá sides with parents in feuds and questions of discipline. The weight of motherhood's worries makes Yemayá a beloved orisá of hard choices. She is imagined with dark skin. In this regard, Yemayá reminds people of the African mothers who birthed lighter-skinned Creole children.

Digna Sáez became the mother of twins, a blessing from Yemayá and yet another argument for her readiness as Yemayá's steed. She quickly rose among the town matriarchy, soon standing alongside Chacha, Ma' Josefa, and Kimbito. Today, Digna's twin daughters are aged matriarchs themselves and preside as revered guests at one of the feasts that sprang up for San Lázaro–Babalú Ayé after Cucusa died.

Digna is also remembered to this day for her propensity to shift into Congo styles of dance. She would shake Yemayá from her back so as to receive the Congo dead, who mounted up in Yemayá's place without skipping a beat. Her Congo dead intervened forcefully where her Yemayá might have chosen a more moderate path. Those unable to satisfy their worries about fertility or child rearing with Yemayá would seek out the Congo powers Digna bore.

There were other mounts for Yemayá at La Sociedad Africana, though none as brilliant as Digna. One was Cucusa, a generation younger and remembered as a hesitant steed who carried Yemayá only a handful of times. Cucusa's daughter, my teacher Isidra, is the same.

Ma' Josefa and Jorge Sáez brought their daughter Digna to Chacha's Sociedad Africana. They also brought their son, Loreto, who would come to replace his father, and even the memory of Guadalupe Cairo, as La Sociedad Africana's lead mount for Changó.

"Digna's little brother was Loreto Sáez. He was a great Changó, but he wasn't the one Chacha loved best," said Lázaro M. "She never forgot her husband, Guadalupe Cairo. That was back in Santa Rita, where Guadalupe Cairo was the lead mount for Changó. He died before Chacha came over to Sierra Morena. Loreto Sáez eventually rose to prominence as her prime mount for Changó. It was his mother, Ma' Josefa, who set him and Digna on their paths, but he got his Changó from his father, Jorge Sáez.

"Loreto was a strong man, but not big," said Lázaro M. A black-and-white photograph of Loreto shows him with a square jaw, high cheek bones, sharp almond-shaped eyes in large sockets, and a button nose with prominent round nostrils. The mouth below these is closed tight, pursed almost, and under the flared cheek bones it is small, like his nose. Loreto leans forward in the photograph, as if he were coming close to you. He seems calm, if stern. "He was one of the younger people who took time to learn from the old Lucumises, while they were still around. In this he took after his father. Loreto went less for Congo knowledge than either his father or sister, though.

"Loreto had so many women!" said Lázaro M., himself renowned as a ladies' man. "In this he was just like Changó—virile. He was the town watchman, and maybe this contributes to his reputation. Watchman was out at night, and in a little town like this he knew everything. Who was getting along and who was fighting, who was late getting home, and who wasn't home at all. He didn't have to be home at night. He was out saving lonely women from harm. He was with women whose men were out of the house, and Loreto knew where. The only one he didn't fool was his *marida,* Quintina, who had her ways of scaring his lovers off."

Night watch in a town that hosted bembés was a complicated job after Emancipation. Fear of Blacks gathering to feast their santos-orisás drove white reprisals throughout the first decade of the twentieth century and beyond.[4] In those days a paramilitary organization called La Guardia Rural [the Rural Guard] made it a priority to shut down bembés. Later, in the 1950s during the revolutionary uprising, the Rural Guard served the dictator, Fulgencio Batista, and looked for people listening to the radio and getting involved in leftist politics. It broke up suspected revolutionary meetings and continued to target bembés. The town watchman sometimes knew exactly who the Rural Guard was looking for but kept his mouth shut. Loreto and Quintina's youngest daughter, Pica, told me he was a good watchman, which in Pica's enigmatic style of speech could mean all sorts of things, including that he turned a blind eye to insurgents. This was important, because he was one of the few people in town allowed to have a gun. Carrying a gun also put Loreto under Changó's care, as warfare and belligerence of all kinds are Changó's to foment and control. Pica said he never fired it. In the twenty years I have visited Sierra Morena, stories about guns are very rare. I credit that to the revolution and its systematic control of firearms. One story does circulate in Sierra Morena, and it is from the 1950s, before the revolution.

During Batista's control of Cuba, the Rural Guard was respected in Sierra Morena, and I gather that men in town composed it. One night, before Fidel Castro came to power, there was a party at Chacha Cairo's Sociedad Africana, on the eastern fringes of town. Loreto was by this time Chacha's mount for Changó; he was the finest "horse," steed, that Chacha kept for Changó in her stable. Loreto took Changó up like a horse mounted by a royal personage. Changó is sovereign over drums and therefore over the feast, where drums compose the world of sound so loved by the santos-orisás. Loreto was also Chacha's finest drummer—another indication of Changó's favor. Loreto's skill at beating the drums is fondly remembered. Changó is master over beatings of all sorts, and fighting is naturally under his domain. He loves a good fight and doesn't shy away.

"This is a story Chacha told me," said Isidra. "I didn't see it. Loreto was mounted by Changó and presiding at the Sociedad Africana, playing the drums while mounted, which only Loreto could do. Changó himself was seated before his great drum. Can you imagine? I can't remember if the bembé was for Changó or Yemayá or which orisá, but the Rural Guard showed up. The Rural Guard considered bembés to be out of bounds, too noisy, too much disorder, and maybe mixed up with revolutionary activity. They showed up with their guns and everything. Pistols. When they arrived at Chacha's, the crowd was up around the door. They marched right up until they reached the threshold. They were ready to shut things down, but instead they froze. Everyone could see their hesitation. There was Changó, master of war, sitting at the drum they were about to bring to a halt. Wouldn't you hesitate? Then they stepped inside, and just like that they buckled, taken in one stroke by Changó, who mounted both at once. Loreto was already mounted, so now there were three Changós. Count them—" She laughed.

Loreto's Changó was so fierce, so compelling, so absolute, that the two men had no chance of not being similarly mounted. Changó takes what he wants. This is the privilege of the santos-orisás, who effortlessly rule over people's lives. Santos-orisás are elements of life; they discharge forces that play in life, change it, and overflow it. They claim life as theirs. Changó the sovereign took his steeds firmly in hand and commanded their every move.

When the santos-orisás mount up, be it at a country bembé like Chacha's or at a Havana Ocha (Santería) celebration, their first request is usually to be adorned with clothes befitting a sovereign. When they mount up, they find themselves in the clothes of their steeds. To a santo-orisá they are rags. A sash, a cape, a satin cap displaying their preferred colors and insignia makes them happy. Shoes, among the prestigious things of everyday life in Cuba, look to the mounted sovereigns like symptoms of frivolous colonial refinement and therefore debased. "Please remove my shoes," an orisá will ask.

"You can imagine, then," Isidra said, "these two Changós, looking down at what they were wearing, gesturing to have them removed. Old Chacha carefully took off their boots, which they allowed. Then she removed their pistols. She placed them on the altar she kept at her house, next to the figurine of Santa Bárbara, who you know is matched with Changó. The pistols were replaced with Changó's red sash, which she tied across their hips. You can't imagine how pleased those Changós were. They were mounted until the party was over." The two Changós, in the company of Loreto's Changó, presided over the gathering, counseling the afflicted and talking at length. It was the 1950s, and nothing else is remembered about that particular bembé, but the scene says a lot about who was sovereign in Sierra Morena during Batista's reign. What the santos-orisás advised is forgotten, but knowing Changó, we can assume they talked about revolution and war.

Other steeds for Changó came up in Chacha's Sociedad Africana, but none challenged Loreto's lead role. One was his daughter, Pica, and so compelling was her father's take on Changó that Pica didn't start mounting him until after Loreto died. Before that, she mounted only the fiery orisá Oyá. But when she started to take up the formidable presence of Changó, people said, "That is her father's Changó, exactly like him. Loreto's Changó has chosen a new mount, and it is Pica, his daughter." Isidra said this time and again: "You want to know what Loreto's Changó was like? Look at Pica when she is mounted."

That Loreto's daughter became a mount for Changó is normal in Sierra Morena, where people "inherit their santos" from parents or others in a family line. This is different from Havana Ocha, in which santos-orisás are received through initiation. Pica inherited her Changó from Loreto as Loreto inherited his Changó from Jorge Sáez and Digna inherited her Yemayá from Ma' Josefa. Counting themselves, that pair of "old mounts" [*viejos caballos*] gave Chacha and her Sociedad Africana two generations of Yemayá mounts and, counting Pica and Pica's daughter, four generations of mounts for Changó.

. . .

Ma' Josefa and Jorge Sáez were not the only ones to bring new mounts to Chacha's Sociedad Africana. Kimbito Sáez also brought her children, grandchildren, and great-grandchildren under Chacha's care. Her daughter and granddaughter became Chacha's lead mounts for the sovereigns Obatalá and Oyá.

Kimbito was born sometime before 1865 and bore the last name of a group of slaves bound to the Horizonte plantation: Sáez. Whether she was born at Horizonte or was purchased at the dock on the lagoon or from another slave owner I do not know, for no one remembers. Who her parents were is lost to memory. Kimbito grew up during three hard decades of Cuban independence struggles from Spain, as abolition was openly debated and ultimately achieved. Isidra, my teacher and guide in the world of Sierra Morena bembés, asserted that Kimbito was African, trafficked to Cuba as a little girl. Kimbito was her great-grandmother, and it meant a lot to Isidra to be able to name an African in her family. She tied her claim to Kimbito's name, which she said was an African name proper, "probably a Congo one." Isidra was unambiguous and said Kimbito was from Congo and didn't like the suggestion that she might have been *criolla*, or Cuban-born.

"Listen to that *K* at the beginning of her name," she said. "Could she be anything but Congo? And we only ever called her Kimbito. Where do you think that *ito* is from? It's Spanish. It's the diminutive that we Spanish speakers put on everything endearing. But it cuts off a piece of her name. Kimb— something. That was her name. How is that not Congo?"

Kimbito was skinny and short and had very dark skin. The fame of her dark skin, which persists three generations after her, contributed to Isidra the great-granddaughter's appraisal of her ethnicity, though she did not know for sure. "Congos were short and dark," she said, repeating ethnic stereotypes inherited from Cuban slavery.

Lázaro M. knew Kimbito. "She was dark, it's true, and itty-bity. But she was pretty, and one hell of a dancer and flirt, even as an old woman. You would never have guessed her age. Kimbito wasn't her given name, though. That was Petrona. Kimbito was Cuban born, the daughter of Africans, just like Chacha Cairo and Ma' Josefa Sáez were the daughters of Africans. Those old ladies were all slaves once, but they were *criollas*—they were born here."

"Then, the nickname Kimbito?" I asked Lázaro in 2012.

"Like I said, she was a hell of a dancer. Her nickname came from her dancing, which was fast and slick—like the fluid [*babita*] inside of *quimbombó* [okra]. You should have seen her."

Quimbombó is a Cuban Spanish word for okra, certainly of Congo-inspiration, *kingombo* being Kikongo (the language of BaKongo, "Congo," people). Following Lázaro's interpretation, Kimbito's nickname was a contraction of *quimbombó*, with the added diminutive *-ito* to speak endearment. Kimbito was a nickname, Lil' Okra.

Kimbito's *maridos* are not remembered, except for "Abuelito" José María Sáez, by his last name also one of the Horizonte enslaved. She had seventeen children, and three with Abuelito José María are remembered: Florencia, María La Paz, and Ma' Isidra.

Florencia is lost to memory, except for her name, because she did not play a role in Chacha's Sociedad Africana. María La Paz didn't either, but she entered the Congo-inspired practice of cultivating the dead and healing through forces capable of harm. María La Paz was known as a *palera* and *ngangulera,* as a "stick worker" or "root worker," and feared in Sierra Morena, like Jorge Sáez was. Lázaro M. said, "Tremenda bruja [great witch]. She left here a full-grown woman with a serious reputation for witchcraft [*brujería*]." María La Paz ended up in the port city of Caibarién beyond Sagua la Grande, a hundred fifty kilometers east along the coast.

It was through her daughter, Ma' Isidra, that Kimbito gave an orisá mount to Chacha's Sociedad Africana. Kimbito is remembered not because of her unique name or because of her own role in Chacha's Sociedad, because it does not appear that she was a mount for the santos-orisás. She is remembered mostly because she was the mother of Ma' Isidra, who was a compelling mount and central to Chacha's community.

Kimbito gave birth to Isidra Sáez on the Horizonte plantation in 1880. Her father was José María Sáez. Cuba was then a Spanish colony, one of the last left after a century of Latin American freedom struggles. A decade-long (1868–1878) independence and abolition war waged by Cuban Creoles ended in defeat shortly before her birth, and its principal leaders—José Martí, Máximo Gómez, and Antonio Maceo—were all in exile. Despite decades of debate and a decade of warfare, slavery was a fact in 1880. That year, Cuba began an eight-year emancipation process to finally rid itself of the nearly four-hundred-year-old practice. Little Isidra and her sisters were born on the precipice of freedom and knew it as girls. It must have been sweet for Kimbito to see her girls emerge into adolescence and adulthood as a free people despite the hardships of life in post-Emancipation Cuba. As a teenager in the 1890s, Isidra witnessed the excitements and terrors of war as the independence struggle again picked up steam and its leaders returned from exile. The last push in the Cuban fight for independence from Spain was fought on horseback with rifles and swords, and in December 1895, Antonio Maceo charged west toward Havana within a half a day's walk of the new town of Sierra Morena. Isidra's story, or those of her parents or siblings, say nothing explicit about how they felt about Maceo's fight, if they joined or supported it. Isidra was a fifteen-year-old girl, after all. Her story does say that she went on to become the lead mount for the santo-orisá Obatalá in Chacha Cairo's Sociedad Africana.

Isidra was famously quiet—a perfect mount for the taciturn, wizened Obatalá. When folks remember Isidra's Obatalá, they evoke a discreet elder, thoughtful and serious, and a trustworthy judge in tricky situations. The one photo that exists of her shows a petite woman with white hair, dressed in white, trim and tidy. When people in Sierra Morena remember her, they call her Ma' Isidra, in recognition of her seniority in Chacha's Sociedad Africana and as a term of endearment. "Ma' Isidra was tiny, smaller than Kimbito, and you know she was small," said Isidra, her granddaughter. "So you can imagine the impression she made, petite as she was, being a steed for so serious and imposing an orisá as Obatalá."

When people talk about Ma' Isidra's Obatalá, they always refer to the santo-orisá as "she," as in, "Obatalá, she is very precise. She likes things to be clean and ordered. She is the most formal of the orisás." Obatalá can be thought of as feminine or masculine, he or she. Yemayá uses feminine pronouns, and Changó masculine ones. Obatalá's gender oscillates between feminine and masculine. Men and women can be mounts for any orisá, and the orisá they carry need not correspond with their sex. Men serve as dancer-steeds for matronly Yemayá, for example, and women for manly Changó. Loreto's daughter, Pica, inherited his Changó. When a person is mounted, the gender of the orisá determines the pronouns used when referring to the steed, so Pica, when mounted with virile Changó, was always referred to as "he." When mounted by Oyá, Pica was referred to as "she." The same applies for the male steeds of female orisás, like Yemayá, Ochún, and Oyá. This does not apply to the steeds of Obatalá. "Obatalá has sixteen paths," I was told, "eight male, and eight female." So the steeds of Obatalá are referred to not by the gender of the santo-orisá, but by the gender of the mount. In Havana, Obatalá is sometimes suggested to be androgynous, intersex, or trans. In Sierra Morena, the image of Obatalá is more dichotomous in a cis-gender manner, male or female depending on the mount.[5]

"Ma' Isidra's Obatalá wanted to be treated carefully, with great respect," said Isidra. "My grandmother loved the color white, and she kept her clothes perfectly clean. When she was at Chacha's bembés and there was a chance she would be mounted, she needed to be dressed in her finest whites, bleached and pressed from head to toe. That is what Obatalá wants, and Ma' Isidra would never risk being mounted by her santo and not be ready for her." White is understood to be cool in Sierra Morena: it keeps heads cool in tricky situations, especially those that require healing by the santos-orisás. The cool of white is also essential in countering Congo-inspired works of sorcery. Mounts for Obatalá keep steady. Ma' Isidra, like her santo-orisá, is remembered for her calm mind and sound counsel.

Ma' Isidra's preference for crisp white clothes, neatness, and coolness, all of it was in recognition that Obatalá is the sovereign of heads. She is the orisá who makes thinking possible and keeps it clear. Obatalá rules over the intellect, thought, and ideas. As such, she presides over all decisions and is responsible for sound judgments. Among her santo-orisá peers, Obatalá is a scholar and an interpreter of orisá law. Ma' Isidra's Obatalá, when she was mounted at a bembé, was sought for her counsel in decisions people found impossible to make, and her Obatalá healed those suffering afflictions of the head, like anxiety, depression, epilepsy, and madness. So like her santo-orisá was Ma' Isidra that she was sought out to heal these afflictions even when she wasn't mounted.

Over her life, Ma' Isidra had fourteen children, three fewer than her mother, Kimbito. Two of her maridos are remembered. The first of these was Lino Sáez, who was a sweet man and considered a good match for her. With Lino she had four children, the youngest of whom was Vicenta Petrona—Cucusa—named after her grandmother, Kimbito, if Lázaro M. is to be credited. Ma' Isidra and Lino fell apart, and she took up with Ernesto Portilla. By his last name, Portilla likely descended from the exodus of emancipated people from the Dos Marías plantation. People credit Ma' Isidra's cool with allowing her to be with Portilla, one of the most feared Congo-inspired healers in town. His healing was active and sometimes involved lurking forces among the dead used to intimidate others, including those responsible for ill will. This made him a *brujo,* a *palero,* a sorcerer, and his work was considered "hot." Ernesto Portilla did not serve as a mount for any santo-orisá, and he kept to the margins of Chacha's Sociedad Africana. He died a young man (as brujos will) and left Ma' Isidra with fourteen children and "a pile of Congo things." This included the fearsome twin healing bundles, which he called Mariana Congo and Chakuaná. Once in her care, Ma' Isidra always kept these two powers in separate white porcelain bowls wrapped in white cloth. Ma' Isidra loaned Chakuaná to one of Ernesto Portilla's sisters, who took it to Havana. Word is, it is kept by Portilla's descendants in Havana to this day. Ma' Isidra passed Mariana Congo down to Cucusa when she died, and it came to rest not far from her altar to San Lázaro–Babalú Ayé. The Congo heat Ernesto Portilla left behind would have been impossible to handle without sovereign cool on her side, and that is just what Ma' Isidra found each day in her devotion to Obatalá. In fact, because she lived with all that Congo-inspired heat with such aplomb, those in town considered her counsel especially cooling against Congo-inspired sorcery.

Ma' Isidra gave herself wholly to Chacha's Sociedad Africana, and when the time came she brought her own children into the care of that community.

Two of her daughters are remembered clearly: Cucusa, who was Ma' Isidra's last child with Lino Sáez, and Albertina, her fifth child with Ernesto Portilla.

Cucusa's contributions to Chacha's Sociedad were not those of a santo-orisá steed. She was a child of Yemayá, but she rarely bore the sovereign of the seas on her back. Cucusa's role in the Sociedad was to help organize Chacha's yearly feast, especially as Chacha got older. In time, when Cucusa broke off to start her bembé for San Lázaro–Babalú Ayé, this experience would be invaluable. Cucusa also devoted herself to her younger Portilla half siblings and had a hand in raising all ten of them. Albertina in particular became her great friend and companion throughout most of her life. It was Cucusa who nicknamed Albertina "Chucha." Under the care of her mother and older half sister, Albertina Portilla came up strong in Chacha's Sociedad Africana and became the lead mount for Oyá, santo-orisá of tumultuous change.

Oyá brings change intensely, like a storm. She is a dangerous force, and like a storm-churned wind, she drives change before her. On the coast you could confuse Oyá and Yemayá because so much strong weather comes off the sea. Oyá's accent is on the wind, Yemayá's on the water. Oyá differs from Yemayá also in that Oyá has no children, whereas Yemayá presides over motherhood. Perhaps because of this, Oyá is relentless when she comes. Her winds kick up scenes of merciless devastation. Nothing can withstand her when she brings her force to bear. Such is her fervor for transformation that she claims two places of great change as her own: the cemetery and the marketplace. Oyá stands vigil at the cemetery gate and decides who will be buried and who will remain standing. Her command over the transition between life and death is her greatest curse and gift. At the marketplace she presides over every exchange and the stakes tied to these. The path from the market to the grave is hers. A steed for Oyá must have the strength to carry the tempest of dire words. She is everything Obatalá is not.

Often, mounts seem in life like the orisás who mount them. Loreto was like Changó in his role as the town's weapon-wielding, law-keeping watchman, and in his renown for having many lovers. Ma' Isidra was a calm, cool healer of heads despite being surrounded by Congo fire. Cucha Portilla was an exception. She is recalled as a joyful person, in contrast to Oyá's tempestuousness and severity. Lázaro M. remembered her as having "a beautiful voice to match her jovial way." Her bouncy nickname matched her upbeat spirit.

Chucha Portilla the mount had an effect on Oyá, her santo-orisá rider. Chucha's Oyá was careful, more placid than blustery. The winds of change she brought were no tempest. Truthfully, in Sierra Morena I have rarely seen the "classic Oyá" as you might see her at Ocha-Santería parties in Havana, with its circuit of paid dancer-mounts. I have hardly seen her come wild and frightening. In the bembés of Sierra Morena, the santos-orisás are more spontaneous, playful, and more person-like. People from town say, "Our saints work. If a saint isn't working, then the mount is faking it." This work is compassionate, public, and personal, and what is meant is that the mounts address people directly, cleanse them of misfortune, and advise them on what must be, what can be avoided, and what is to come. Chucha Portilla's Oyá worked in this manner, directly, intimately. She is remembered for the deep concern she showed the afflicted when the change she brought was hard to bear.

Oyá's temperament did affect Chucha in one way. The orisá of storm fronts and transformations marked her politics. "The problem of the revolution gripped her," said Lázaro M. "She was very revolutionary. When that storm came, she was swept right up." Tumult and fervor were the social rules of the day. She got as far as being a party militant in the neighboring province of Matanzas, Isidra told me. In her revolutionary enthusiasm Chucha was nearly matched by her older half sister, Cucusa. The half sisters would go on to play roles in building the revolution in its first decades.

Chacha Cairo, Ma' Josefa Sáez, and Kimbito Sáez gave their lives to La Sociedad Africana of Sierra Morena for forty years. They introduced their children and grandchildren to Chacha Cairo's wisdom, and they nurtured and cared for generations of santo-orisá mounts so that the larger community could savor santo-orisá praise and know santo-orisá healing. Ma' Josefa, and her children Digna and Loreto, brought Yemayá and Changó to Chacha's bembés. Kimbito, through her daughter, Ma' Isidra, and her granddaughter, Chucha Portilla, brought Obatalá and Oyá. They were the heart of Chacha's praise and of the feast life of her Sociedad Africana.

* * *

Chacha Cairo needed yet more steeds for other orisás. These figures were peers to Yemayá, Changó, Obatalá, and Oyá. They were santos-orisás who were indispensable to the healing accomplished at her Sociedad Africana. Without them, Chacha's accomplishment in the first half of the twentieth century would not have been so resounding and may not have succeeded at all. Chacha needed more than anything a mount for La Caridad–Ochún, sovereign of charity, love, and all sweet things.

Chacha's Sociedad Africana was dedicated to the Virgin of Charity, the Catholic patroness of Cuba. This figure is beloved in Cuba as the protector and patron of the island nation. The Virgin of Charity emerged in Cuba's east, a little statuette found miraculously bobbing in the sea by three fishermen. Salvaged, she became a patroness to slaves toiling in mines in the town of El Cobre, in Cuba's east. La Virgen de la Caridad del Cobre, as she came to be known, then became a patroness to fighters in Cuba's long struggle for independence. The success of that struggle in 1898 led to her apotheosis as a national icon. After Emancipation, the three fishermen who found her came to represent Cuba's Creole mixture (European-African-indigenous), and their little boat expanded voluminously to stand for the storm-battered island itself. That Chacha Cairo maintained a shrine to the Virgin of Charity and hosted a feast for her on her church-appointed day each year is not surprising given what Chacha and her community lived through in the second half of the nineteenth century. Surviving slavery, decades of war, eight years of gradual emancipation, another war, then finally achieving both freedom and national independence—these were more than sufficient reason to pay tribute to the Virgin of Charity with the decorum suited to the santos-orisás.[6]

Chacha kept an altar for the Virgin of Charity in her home, which was also the meeting place for the Sociedad Africana. On September 8, "her day," Chacha's house would raise the statuette of the Virgin of Charity onto a bier, and, accompanied by trumpets, they would sally forth from El Río on the outskirts of town, singing Catholic hymns of praise. "We would come from El Río and wind through town. The procession was long, and everyone was welcome to join," Isidra told me. Her memories were from the mid-1940s and 1950s, when she was a little girl, before the revolution came. "Along the way we picked up neighbors and children and people in town who had nothing to do with the Sociedad Africana. White people, everyone. We reached the center of town, and the priest would come to the church door and bless our Virgin of Charity. He blessed our procession.

"We would march back to La Sociedad Africana, and the crowd got bigger and bigger. The procession would spill around Chacha's house, and then the drums would break the feast open [rompimos]. The white and Black social clubs—the Lyceum and Union and Brotherhood—along with the segregation they maintained, were left back in town, and, like Orfilio's and Cucusa's cockfights, everyone was welcome." Chacha's bembé for the Virgin of Charity momentarily broke down those socially treacherous lines of distinction and exclusion that we call "race," and that Cubans prefer to call "color." A few other houses in town held feasts on important days, and there, too, lighter and darker people gathered together.

The drums broke the afternoon, and in a rush of sound Chacha gave the Virgin everything. Over the years, hundreds and hundreds of animals were slaughtered for the annual feast, which fed anyone who came. The animal offerings coaxed the Virgin of Charity to come to the party in person. This she did as Ochún, orisá of sensual love and sweet femininity. Ochún feasts on golden chickens and young goats, and if these were offered, and the songs to her were sweet, then Ochún could be expected at the feast. Everyone fed, the singers and drummers would break the crowd into song and dance, readying for her arrival. It was for her, for La Caridad–Ochún, that the Sociedad Africana met. For three days they would play and dance and sing for her.

The alliance between the Virgin of Charity and Ochún is known throughout Cuba. It is intimate, and in places like Sierra Morena the two names are often interchanged. La Caridad–Ochún is a compound santo-orisá, like San Lázaro–Babalú Ayé. The Virgin of Charity and Ochún share a love of shiny metals, like copper, brass, and gold. Cubans look for these colors, and where they spot them they see the live potentials of La Caridad–Ochún. She is imagined to have golden yellow skin, and often her mounts will be racialized as *mulato* and have light brown skin. La Caridad–Ochún displays herself flirtatiously and is unashamed of her beauty and sensuality.

"Otilia," Isidra said, "had beautiful light skin and delicate eyes—she was the daughter of a slave woman and an indentured Chinese man from Canton." She was the Sociedad Africana's prime steed for La Caridad–Ochún. Mounted upon Otilia, La Caridad–Ochún loved everything light colored and tending toward gold—yellow cloth, sunflowers, golden squash, and yellow fruit, like pineapple and mango. Those who aspire to be a mount for La Caridad–Ochún, to carry her on their backs, will be excellent dancers, and Otilia Sáez was. Santos-orisás mount their steeds in the course of dancing, and because dance is so important a part of human sensuality, of flirting and seduction, it belongs to La Caridad–Ochún. She presides over dance, she judges it, and she gives it as a gift. To be her mount, you must dance fluidly and sensuously, like a winding river. La Caridad–Ochún is consequently the sovereign of rivers and their sinuous transits through the land. River water is "sweet" compared with the water of the sea, and this sweetness further binds Ochún to the powerful, winding movement of rivers. Those rivers inevitably water the cane that is ubiquitous in Cuba. La Caridad–Ochún presides over the pull of sweet water into its roots and capillaries, and over its mixture with the golden light of the sun to produce the sweetness of sugar itself. La Caridad–Ochún loves sugar in all its forms: as candied fruit, as cake, and especially as meringue frosting. She loves not only sweetness on the tongue but also sweetness as it runs through life, and she is sovereign over sweet romance and young vulnerable love, before the seriousness and responsibility of parenthood begins. They say Otilia was lovely, sweeter than Chacha, and kind to everyone in the Sociedad Africana—the men, the women, the children.

The drums and chorus at Chacha's bembé for La Caridad–Ochún called the santo-orisá to her steed, Otilia. Together, musicians, singers, and dancers, who replied to the singer's prompts, called the santos-orisás. At her feast her santos-orisá peers were expected, and a great bembé would see all seven sovereigns take mounts. Chacha would not have been satisfied with a bembé for La Caridad–Ochún until she welcomed Ogún, master of the forge and the strength needed to control it.

Ogún is a smith, sovereign over metal, iron tools, and weapons by virtue of being their maker. He claims metal for himself, as his, despite the noises his war-making peer Changó might make with his thunder ax. With the machetes and axes born of his craft, he clears the roads that bring settlers and farmers to establish human rule over the wilderness. In Cuba in the nineteenth century, Ogún's command came to rest on the machinery of the Industrial Revolution, the iron of railroad tracks and the steam engines that carried sugarcane to the mills, presses, cauldrons, and furnaces. Ogún is the patron of makers and innovators of all kinds—of conquerors and their machines of war and commerce, including guns, cannons, and trains.

At La Sociedad Africana, Ogún's mount was Gobierno Cairo, a descendant of the Santa Rita evacuation and a generation younger than Chacha. Gobierno Cairo was a huge man, both muscular and rotund. Ogún's mounts spin with machete-wielding gestures as they dance him onto their backs. They mimic this prized attribute by swinging their arms in a whirl of blows. Each swing is a sovereign strike against the untamed wilderness that humanity tirelessly domesticates into agriculture with Ogún's shovels and hoes. Like Changó, Ogún is admired as a warrior and considered an ally in struggles of all sorts. His enormous size made Gobierno Cairo a perfect mount for Ogún, who actualizes raw strength.

Lázaro M. remembered Gobierno's Ogún. "He was enormous, shirtless, and sweating from every pore. Gobierno's Ogún was fury contained. You could see it on his face. He would hold forth, he imposed himself, he swung a machete. Chacha's bembés were serious affairs, and there was no fooling around. If others were mounted by Ogún, she would never allow them to actually swing a machete, but Gobierno's Ogún demanded it and she consented. He would slap the flat of it against his chest until great welts appeared. That Ogún was so fierce, it was practically Congo."

In a fight it would be good to have both Ogún and Changó on your side, but they rarely see eye to eye. Ogún likes his mounts shirtless and barefoot, cigar in mouth and machete cocked, with a sip of *aguardiente* quick to hand. Changó likes his mounts dressed as regally as possible, if only with a band of satin around their waists, and he hates aguardiente. In Sierra Morena, Ogún is a farmer, not a city slicker, which is more or less what Changó is. Ogún presides over the country, over tamed wilderness and agriculture, while Changó presides over the city-state, its politics, and its armies. Ogún is raw strength; Changó is the calculated application of power. Gobierno Cairo was a farmer, perfect for his part. Ogún and Changó are rivals for feminine attention, too, both that of Oyá and Ochún. Past dramas circling on the protracted love tangles of these four orisás have soured the relationship between Ogún and Changó. When he wasn't mounted with the furious master of the forge, people say Gobierno was a gentle person, sweet and quiet. Loreto Sáez, who mounted Changó, was his good friend. When Cucusa started her feast for San Lázaro–Babalú Ayé, in 1943, Chacha "loaned" her Loreto to help with the work of slaughtering the animals, not to mention managing the musicians and santos-orisás. When Loreto died, Chacha sent Gobierno. He was a figure of authority, renowned for his meticulous, righteous handling of the knife in the moment of animal offerings.

Finally, Chacha could not host a bembé for her beloved La Caridad–Ochún without praising one last orisá, who in fact she always praised first. This was Elégua, or Elégba, as some singers in Sierra Morena call him. You cannot start a bembé without first laying praise for this orisá, and neither can you end one. Elégua is master of all beginnings, be these real or metaphorical. He is also master of all endings. He presides over starts, inceptions, conceptions, and openings, just as he does over ends, completions, terminations, and closings. All thresholds, doors, and portals are his—he opens them and closes them. Elégua presided over the door of Chacha's house, and thereby decided who came and went from La Sociedad Africana, including his orisá peers. In homes all over Sierra Morena, Elégua appears as a coconut, rock, or little rag doll near the front door. He presides over life thresholds, too, like the passage from fetus to newborn, from child to adult, and life to death. The only threshold over which he does not have full command is the cemetery gate, which he shares with Oyá. Together, they decide who will cross from one world into another. He is sovereign over crossings, like the crossing from everyday concerns to the effervescent play of a fully lived bembé.

In Chacha Cairo's Sociedad Africana the prime mount for Elégua was Santiago Linares. He is remembered as a large man, graceful, and formidably strong. He was of Chacha's generation, the child of Africans and a slave himself as a boy. Along with Loreto, who was two decades younger, Santiago Linares was a force in La Sociedad Africana and one of the members of its leadership circle.

Santiago's Elégua was played to the limit. Elégua sometimes confuses those who praise him because thresholds are multidirectional places, and you can't always tell whether Elégua is coming or going, or whether he is opening passages or closing them. Elégua revels is this murky quality and is known to play in ambiguity. He is imagined as a child, just the one to play in doorways. He opens them, he slams them, and runs irreverently through them. This link to children entangles Elégua with the little Catholic Pilgrim Saint, El Niño de Atocha [the Child of Atocha]. Elégua eclipses his Catholic ally almost entirely, and only rarely is a statuette of El Niño de Atocha seen on any altar. But Elégua is a great advocate of children. Yemayá and the parents who follow her will be stern with children, favoring maternity and parental authority. Elégua is steadfast in letting them be. He revels in their play and tricks. Santiago's Elégua communicated the joy of childhood while he was mounted up, and he played in all sorts of ways. Those who remember seeing him mounted with Elégua, even as an older man, remember him full of tricks and smiles. "He was the most beautiful dancer," said Lázaro M. "He was a huge man, tall and robust, but you should have seen him move; he skipped and spun like a little boy. He loved to heal with a clever trick, right in the middle of the bembé. He could bring laughter out of a chorus, which is not easy to do."

Elégua's claim to thresholds and crossings includes street crossings. In town, candies for the child orisá are regularly seen at the corners, especially on feast days for his peers. In a place where sugar is abundant but candy is rare, the little offerings go untouched by all but the most spirited children. Clever children are privileged in his realm, avatars themselves of the master of transgressions, so when they snatch it, it is Elégua who gets the sweets.

Elégua claims all portals, doors, thresholds, and crossings. He claims all limits. This includes the limit between town and forest. Because he presides over the entrance to the forest, he is sovereign there. He is a scout, a pathfinder, though not a path breaker. That is the business of his orisá peer and co-sovereign of the forest, Ogún. Elégua finds the path when the wilderness closes in. This is a dangerous threshold, as anyone who spends time in the wilderness knows. The forest can play tricks on even the best trekkers and hunters. Loreto's daughter, Pica, and I were on a hike south of town once, before she went blind. We were looking for sticks for Congo-inspired remedies. On our way home we got lost, not in a pathless forest, but in a maze of cow paths in a countryside overrun by the thorny *marabú* bush. It was to Elégua she appealed then, singing his songs, old songs she didn't sing at bembés because they were too old and the chorus would get lost and drop the song. Elégua saw us home.

Elégua is a scout, a young sovereign with the courage of children when their moxie is up: a child-scout, the one to know where the game is, and the one to bring it on. You see this in Elégua's dance when his mounts appear to peek over bushes, shading their eyes to get a better look before ducking to part the underbrush with a little crook as they skip along. Santiago Linares danced like this. Elégua, because he is close to trees and roots, has alliances with the Congo side of life, where the mass of the forest and the mass of the dead tangle indistinguishably. Santiago Linares was among those in town, like Digna Sáez and her Yemayá, who could "turn Congo" when strong remedies were needed. When Santiago Linares died, it was Cucusa's son, Roberto, who most brilliantly replaced Santiago as Elégua's preferred steed. He did this not at Chacha's feast for La Caridad–Ochún, but later, in the fifties before the revolution came, at his mother's feast for San Lázaro–Babalú Ayé.

These were Chacha Cairo's mounts, which she cultivated and cared for at the heart of her Sociedad Africana from 1880 to 1940, so that the santos-orisás would grace her feasts. Ma' Josefa Sáez and her children, Loreto and Digna; Kimbito's daughter Ma' Isidra Sáez and then her daughter Chucha (Albertina) Portilla; Otilia Sáez, Gobierno Cairo, and Santiago Linares. These people, the prime mounts of the Sociedad for the seven sovereigns, composed the leadership of the community, and Chacha called them her Comisión Africana. They were paid attention to, helped when in need, and made comfortable. They gave themselves to be taken and mounted by the santos-orisás, they were the steeds the sovereigns took possession of so that they might have bodies at Chacha's bembés.

Chacha's Society, with its African Commission and its stable of orisá mounts, with its elders, was also a house of children. Chacha la Vieja [Old Chacha], as they called her, was a very large, very dark-skinned woman who had no children of her own. But she took in three girls at least—Ingo, Nene, and Eugenita. Ingo became a lead caller at the Sociedad Africana, replacing the great singer who had the role before her, Reina Collín. Chacha also took in two of Ingo's children, Zenón and Gonzalo, who today sing and drum up bembés in Sierra Morena. Ma' Isidra's daughter, Cucusa, came up in the care of Chacha's Sociedad, and then her children, too. Three of Cucusa's five children with Orfilio Ruíz received orisás on their backs by the time they were ten years old: Máximo took Changó, Roberto took Elégua, and Isidra took Yemayá. Of the three, Roberto's Elégua is remembered fondly to this day. Little Eulalia never received an orisá.

Chacha's Sociedad Africana gathered within its walls some of the most knowledgeable and talented people to leave the coastal plantations of the Sagua Region of Cuba. Meticulously, she cultivated these people and their children over several generations to be mounts for the seven orisás, seven sovereigns to reign over the lives of the community, to mount exceptions to the laws of fate by which life must abide. Chacha's Sociedad Africana cultivated these seven orisás through music, songs, dance, and inspired orisá revelry in order to suffuse the world with the possibility of change and lift people from the pall of ubiquitous affliction. Seven orisás to look up from the darkness of slavery and stage a horizon of possibility in a new century. Seven orisás and their mounts at the heart of Chacha's Sociedad Africana and its bembés. Cucusa would extend this community when she inaugurated a bembé for an eighth santo-orisá, beloved but rare. This was San Lázaro–Babalú Ayé.

THREE

Cucusa Sáez and Her Children

IN 1900, MA' ISIDRA SÁEZ WAS TWENTY YEARS OLD. She lived in Sierra Morena with Lino Sáez, a descendant of the Horizonte exodus like her. More than a decade had passed since Emancipation. The first years of the twentieth century they spent having children, three sons. At twenty-seven, Ma' Isidra gave birth to their fourth and last child together, a girl she named Vicenta Petrona after her mother. This was Cucusa, born free in 1907.

After Cucusa was born, Ma' Isidra left Lino for Ernesto Portilla, who must have been part of the Dos Marías plantation exodus. Ernesto kept to the margins of Chacha's Sociedad Africana but was respected for the Congo-inspired sorcery he worked with the bundles Mariana Congo and Chakuaná. Together, Ma' Isidra and Ernesto Portilla had ten children. Ma' Isidra's fourteen children, the Sáez children and the Portilla children, were the first generation born out of slavery. Ma' Isidra was the mount for Obatalá at Chacha Cairo's Sociedad Africana, and all her children participated in the bembés held there, especially the feast for the santo-orisá La Caridad–Ochún. As Cucusa grew older, Yemayá claimed her as a mount, but she rarely took the sovereign of tides onto her back. Rather, she spent bembés at Chacha's Sociedad looking after her younger Portilla siblings. Many of them became bembé musicians, singers, and mounts, like her beloved half sister Albertina, whom she nicknamed Chucha. In time, under the watchful eyes of Chacha Cairo, Ma' Isidra, and Cucusa, Oyá claimed Chucha as a mount.

Cucusa started to care for her own children when she was nineteen, in 1926. Her first child was Mirella, and no one seems to know who her father was, except that he was a Cairo. Cairos were ubiquitous in Sierra Morena at this time, most of them descendants of the Santa Rita exodus, then thirty years in the past. Cucusa folded Mirella into the care she gave to her Portilla half siblings and raised her close to Chacha's Sociedad Africana.

Three years later she gave birth again, to a daughter by a new *marido* named Yeyo Cairo. They named the girl Sara Hilda. Mirella was three and nicknamed her new half sister Cuba. It stuck. Mirella and Sara Hilda were not more than eight and five years old when Cucusa and Yeyo split, more or less when she took up with Orfilio Ruíz.

Cucusa was twenty-seven when their first child was born in 1934, a boy named Orfilito, after his father. Her next two children with Orfilio were also boys, each born two years apart. Mirella was twelve and helped her mother with these Ruíz boys along with Cuba. Mirella became a beacon for Cucusa and helped her as Cucusa had helped Ma' Isidra with all the Portilla children in her day. Two years later, Cucusa was thirty-three and expecting her fourth child with Orfilio. It was 1940.

Mirella hoped her mother's new baby would be a girl. She loved Cuba and wanted there to be some Ruíz girls to balance the Ruíz boys. Close to the birth of the baby, Mirella got sick. She was asthmatic, and a terrible cough had set in. Because of her asthma, people aren't sure exactly what the illness was, but it is possible she contracted typhus. In a very short time she died from a "problem with her lungs."

Mirella was a fast-moving, playful kid whose death was a shock to the community. Cucusa mourned Mirella's death as her pregnancy came to term. The new child was a girl whom Cucusa named Isidra, after her mother. This child wriggled so much that Ma' Isidra said her namesake granddaughter had caught some of Mirella's spirit. As the child grew, Cucusa came to agree with her mother's appraisal and taught little Isidra that her unstill, irreverent attitude came from her deceased sister.

After Mirella died, Cucusa was left with Cuba, by her second husband, Yeyo Cairo, and the three little boys and the new baby girl with Orfilio Ruíz. Orfilio was betting on cockfights with his meager winnings from the numbers game, then betting his cockfight winnings on the numbers, in an endless cycle of numbers and cocks, cocks and numbers. Shortly after little Isidra was born, one of his numbers hit the jackpot, and with the winnings he bought the cockfighting ring, house and all. Orfilio found in the ring a dream come true, but Cucusa didn't share his euphoria. What consolation is a lottery windfall and new house if your fourteen-year-old child has died?

Cucusa helped Orfilio with the ring and kept house for her growing family. Little Isidra was followed two years later by another daughter, Eulalia.

Cuba was now the oldest, and by the time Eulalia came along, she was helping take care of all the Ruíz brood. She had asthma too, and when she was fourteen, in 1943, she got a cough like Mirella's. Losing one daughter to asthma or typhus, and now the prospect of losing another, panicked Cucusa. She pleaded with the santo-orisá of illness and recovery. She promised San Lázaro–Babalú Ayé that if he kept Cuba and the other children healthy, she would host a bembé for him on his church-assigned day for the rest of her life. Cuba improved. San Lázaro–Babalú Ayé was one santo-orisá Chacha didn't tend at her Sociedad Africana, and that year Chacha "authorized" Cucusa to host her own bembé on December 17. That's the way Chacha's grandson, Zenón, tells the story.

Isidra bristled at the idea that anyone authorized her mother to do anything. She held that Cucusa had no choice, she made her promise, and Chacha supported Cucusa in her new bembé. Cucusa had years of experience at the heart of Chacha's Sociedad Africana, and Chacha assigned Loreto Sáez to join her in preparing the feast. In 1943, Loreto Sáez was in his late forties and the most knowledgeable singer, drummer, orisá mount, and ritualist in the Sociedad Africana. He joined Cucusa's new feast to drum, sing, act as a mount for Changó (sometimes all at once), and to offer the animals, which he knew how to kill correctly.

Cucusa hosted the party for San Lázaro–Babalú Ayé in the house Orfilio Ruiz bought along with the cockfighting ring, and that is where it stayed for the next fifty-four years, until she died at ninety years old. Her bembé was successful for many reasons, but the primary one is that San Lázaro–Babalú Ayé presides over a singular realm of human life, which is illness. Santos-orisás contend with life's troubles in every bembé. Elégua presides over crossings, transitions, and movements of all sorts; La Caridad–Ochún presides over romance, love, sex, and money; Yemayá over maternity and children, and all things having to do with the sea—no small concern on an island like Cuba; Changó and Ogún over fights and struggles of all sorts, so it is not surprising they fight each other; Oyá over life and death risks; Obatalá over all things having to do with the head, including schooling and judgment. Together, the seven are masters of affliction, ameliorating the day-to-day suffering of their mortal children even when this seems impossible to change. Only San Lázaro–Babalú Ayé is master of illness and the suffering that accompanies it, including pain and worry. He is also master of healing and recovery.

San Lázaro–Babalú Ayé steps in when a person's body suffers. There is something deeply disaffecting about having the matter of your person become weak and pained. Pain limits our movements and soon brings us to a stop. It limits our thoughts and soon brings them to a stop too. Physical distress becomes emotional distress. Illness is a dreadful form of fate. Language falters. It affects the matter of our bodies and is thus unavoidable, yet so difficult to express. This is why San Lázaro–Babalú Ayé becomes unavoidable himself, because it is he who commands illness, he who inflicts it, and he who relieves it.

You can be a vivacious, cheerful child, the quickest of the bunch and the light of your home. Neither money, nor love, nor the future are cares of yours. Then one day when you are fourteen, your energy flags and fever overtakes you. A cough sets in. Or you are a mother, and the illness of your children lays you low. Or you encounter illness in the life of your parents, your siblings, or friends. It is over the inevitable event of illness that San Lázaro–Babalú Ayé presides. Because he inflicts it, he can relieve it more than any other santo-orisá.

This is how San Lázaro–Babalú Ayé is different from Lazarus the Beggar. Babalú Ayé isn't only a victim of illness, as is Lazarus the Beggar—Babalú Ayé is also its cause. Thus, San Lázaro–Babalú Ayé is asked to heal in a way that Lazarus the Beggar can't, because Babalú Ayé commands illness and can either impose it or withdraw it. This is one vast difference between the orisás and their Catholic allies: the orisás shape fate both positively and negatively. They rule over adversity in that they not only determine when it leaves but also when it comes. This is an old version of the sovereign, an ancient one, in fact: a divine sovereign who both grants life and ends it. By comparison to Babalú Ayé, Lazarus the Beggar is wretched and a victim of his illness even if he is ultimately rewarded by life in heaven. Babalú Ayé does not wait for heaven. He is an orisá—he rewards and punishes with health and illness and is sovereign over them. Thus, he commands and shapes what is worst in fated life.

Cucusa's feast and day-to-day devotion gave people access to this power. She built her altar to San Lázaro–Babalú Ayé with the statues of the Beggar Saint and kept the door of her house open whenever she was home, from the time she got up until she went to bed. The altar evoked Catholic responses, kneeling, silent reflection, bowed heads, and quiet submission. The figurines of the beggars, despite their elevated place on the altar, ceded to this attention, submitted to it, and made themselves available. This is the beauty of Lazarus the Beggar—his accessibility, humility, and vulnerability, which he shares with those who seek him out.

Hers was the only house in Sierra Morena devoted to San Lázaro–Babalú Ayé in this way, and people would come from all over, from Corralillo, to the west, or Rancho Veloz, to the east. Her house was a block from the North Circuit, and people would veer off the road whether on horseback or a bus. They might come for the cockfights and be drawn in. Cucusa brought them into contact with San Lázaro the Beggar Saint and with Babalú Ayé simultaneously. She kept the doors of the house open for fifty-four years and hosted fifty-four bembés. Not even the revolution, driven with atheist fervor in the 1970s, stopped the feast.

• • •

The doors of Cucusa's house opened onto a wide veranda. The house was in the middle of town, and during her bembés it would overflow with the pile of people reaching the street and the cockfighting ring in the backyard. From the living room, which was also the altar room and where the bembé happened, a barred window as tall as a person opened onto the veranda. People would crowd it to look in at what was happening.

Inside, the drummers sat with their backs to the tall window for refreshment. *La caja* [the box] was the largest drum and was flanked by two attendant drums. These were Chacha's drums, borrowed from the Sociedad Africana. They were barrels with goatskins stretched over the mouth and nailed with upholstery tacks around the rim. At Cucusa's party, as at Chacha's, the drums had to be tightened, or "tempered" [*templados*], over an open flame, so a fire was kept burning in the cockfighting ring.

Loreto Sáez was on the tempered caja. Drummers enjoy competing for a shot at it, the big drum, but Loreto could improvise like anyone's business, rolling his beats like thunder held in the palm of his hands. To challenge him for the drum was folly. Loreto was one of the few, maybe the only one, whom people remember being mounted while he played the drum. It worked because he was mounted by Changó, sovereign of the drum. In general, and this is the case in Havana's versions of African-inspired praise, drummers are not mounted by the santos-orisás. But Loreto played the drums and led the chorus as Changó, keeper of the elemental percussion of thunder, sovereign of all music, and thus of all feasts. Who would take the drum from the hands of its master?

With Loreto's Changó on the caja, and others like Gobierno Cairo and Jorge Sáez on the *quinto* and *mula,* the attendant drums, the santos-orisás took to their mounts as a cavalry. With Chacha Cairo's blessing, the whole of her stable, her Comisión Africana, would grace the feast. There was

Santiago Linares mounted by Elégua, and Ma' Isidra mounted by Obatalá. Digna Sáez was there, mounted up as Yemayá, and Otilia as La Caridad–Ochún. Gobierno was there for Ogún. By the first years of Cucusa's feast in the mid-1940s, her younger half sister, Chucha Portilla, would have come of age to join the steeds for the larger-than-life orisás, to be mounted by Oyá, storm bringer and sovereign of the cemetery gate. Old Chacha Cairo would not have missed it and surely enjoyed all the pleasures of a new bembé for an orisá she did not customarily see at her feasts, and for whom there was no mount among her Comisión Africana: San Lázaro–Babalú Ayé.

A few years after Cucusa hosted her first bembé, her boys started to mount orisás too. Máximo, the second oldest of her children with Orfilio, was a bull of a boy, hotheaded and easily brought to blows. When he was ten years old, in 1946, he was mounted by Changó. By all accounts his Changó was a fury. Older hands wondered how Changó would ever be properly settled on Máximo's back so that he could start healing and be of help to people.

When a santo-orisá first claims a steed, it is common that the person takes it hard. A newly mounted person is much like the horse they are compared to and must be broken. Santos-orisás are keen to mount up on good dancers. They like those who are elegant and fluid in their steps, who mimic the movements of the orisá. Elégua's dances mimic his zigzag hunt for the lost path; Yemayá's steps communicate the ocean's waves; Changó's dances show him carrying his great thunder ax, like Ogún's have him whirling his machetes. The santos-orisás are drawn to a feast by the drums and the properly presented meals of their preferred animals. They are pleased to hear their songs of praise. They delight in the dancers who so subtly and brilliantly imitate their actions and attributes. They watch as a dancer mimics closer and closer until it is the tiniest deed to take the dancer and mount up. A new steed will jerk away and knock about. It takes experienced hands, like those of Chacha and Loreto, to bring the mounts around so that the divine equestrians can ride balanced and steady. If that is impossible, if Changó, for example, can't be properly seated, the old hands figure out how to get Changó off. This can be done a number of ways, some of them simple, but always requiring great confidence if one is going to refuse a steed to a sovereign. New steeds can take years to settle.

Máximo required much handling when Changó came on. He didn't mount up except at Cucusa's bembé, where Máximo was a "licensed mount" [caballo con licencia] by virtue of being her child. Cucusa looked after him, as did all the hands in Chacha's Comisión Africana. Another steed for Changó to join Loreto was welcome in the community and worth the work.

But Loreto and Máximo did not have an easy rapport. Máximo was too impulsive. More, it was Cucusa's youngest boy, Roberto, who took to Loreto. Roberto started to be mounted by Elégua about the same time as his older brother was mounted by Changó. About eight years old is the youngest age at which a child's mounting by a santo-orisá is believable as more than mere play. Children play at being orisá steeds, and it is only after they can be held accountable that their play is taken seriously as the full-on mounting by an orisá—one that must be obeyed. Roberto was mounted by Elégua, and Loreto stepped up to handle the new steed.

Slowly, Máximo and Roberto grew into the Sociedad Africana, which now gathered for bembés at Chacha's and Cucusa's. There was pleasure in watching the boys come along, watching as they developed their capacity to mount these two powerful figures. Changó, on Máximo's back, leaned toward displays of masculine virility and physical force more than toward the mastery of the drum shown by Loreto's Changó. Changó is too much for a child, unbelievable on the back of a child until he grows strong enough to confidently sustain this sovereign aloft. Máximo, understandably, developed as mount more slowly than his younger brother.

Roberto was a good dancer, even as a child, and his Elégua moved beautifully. He came on as a cheerful prankster more than as the stubborn guardian of thresholds he can sometimes be. Elégua is like a child, so Roberto was a natural fit. He danced as a child brave in play, and joined the Elégua saddled atop Santiago Linares, the Sociedad Africana's prime mount for this orisá. People remember Roberto and Santiago dancing together, both mounted by Elégua, Santiago the aged steed and Roberto the dancing child-sovereign, loose in space, his step as much on the ground as above it, somehow getting a foothold on the air and lifting his growing body up.

The boys were in their early teens and carrying their sovereigns more often when little Isidra was mounted by Yemayá, in 1950. She was ten years old. She was down by the river playing with Eulalia. Her mounting was violent and sent Eulalia running back to town for an old hand to come sweep Yemayá off. By the time they returned, Yemayá had departed on her own. The mounting happened out of public view, an affair between children. She did not mount Yemayá many times after that. As with her mother and Chacha, Isidra's affinity for her sovereign was more devotional than performative. Eulalia was not mounted by a santo-orisá at all.

The life Cucusa started to lead after her promise to San Lázaro–Babalú Ayé was not for Orfilio. The intensity of hosting a bembé and tending to the ill at her altar appears to have been too much for him. The year of the first bembé for San Lázaro–Babalú Ayé, he left for Havana to join a lover there. It was 1943, and his departure left Cucusa the sole owner of the house and ring. Somewhere in those heady years of gambling, new children, sick children, lovers, a failing relationship, and the new bembé, the deed to the house was lost.

A couple of years after Orfilio left Cucusa, she took up with Lupercio Cairo. He was her fourth marido, and in 1946 they had a child. Their girl was Zulia, who was thick boned like Lupercio. Cucusa and Lupercio split shortly after Zulia's birth, and she then married Eusebio Díaz, a Spaniard from the Canary Islands [isleño]. It was her only documented marriage. Together they had two children, Eliezer, a son in 1948, and Emelina, her tenth and last child, in 1952. The Ruíz boys—Orfilito, Máximo, and Roberto—could ignore the new half siblings from these two unions, but the girls could not, so it fell to Cuba, Isidra, and Eulalia to help care for the new Cairo and Díaz children.

In 1950, Cucusa was forty-three years old. It was ten years since Orfilio won the lottery and bought the cockfighting ring and seven since his departure. It was ten years since Mirella's death and little Isidra's birth. It was seven since Cuba's illness and the promise to San Lázaro–Babalú Ayé. Since then, Cuba hadn't been so sick again. Cucusa's bembé was established, and with the help of Ma' Isidra she healed visitors at her altar daily, bringing them into contact with the relief only San Lázaro–Babalú Ayé could provide.

All through the 1950s, Cucusa hosted her feast, and it continued to grow. Her children joined in the bembés at Chacha's Sociedad Africana. Little Zulia came along too, but her entrance into the world of the santos-orisás was different. When she was ten, in 1956, she was being mounted by indiscernible powers that lurked in the shadows beyond the orisás and the ancestral dead. They were individual "dead ones" [muertos] whose identities were lost in the darkness they inhabited [muerto oscuro]. The dead afflicting Zulia were sent by someone using the skills and knowledge of Congo-inspired stick work [Palo]. They rocked Zulia's body a few times a year and always disrupted Cucusa's feast. Her mountings by muertos oscuros involved screaming and the brusque drop of her body to the floor. Confident hands like Chacha and Loreto were needed to sweep them off her. As they were departing, effort had to be expended to get words from them, to learn who sent them and what secret enmities this revealed. This absorbed much energy that would otherwise have been lavished on the other young people who were rising as reliable steeds for the santos-orisás. Zulia, though she would one day convincingly mount Oyá, never stopped being afflicted by these powers.

The late 1950s were electric in Cuba. Chacha's and Cucusa's feasts were renowned in town and the surrounding countryside. The children were growing up healthy, and their connection to the feasts was full of promise, with the exception of Zulia's dead. Politics in the region were electric too. In November 1956, Fidel Castro, his brother Raúl, and the Argentine physician Ernesto "Che" Guevara, along with seventy-nine others exiled in Mexico, disembarked from the yacht *Granma,* seasick and exhausted, at the foot of Cuba's eastern mountains, La Sierra Maestra. It wasn't long before word of their armed uprising against the US-backed despot, Fulgencio Batista, spread to the north coast, and Cucusa's family was rapt. Máximo was twenty and Roberto was eighteen, and they longed to join the guerrilla fighters. Isidra was sixteen and Eulalia was fourteen, and they were implicitly excluded from such an idea. Still, they were dazzled. The uprising grew and swept across the island, leading to the general strike of April 1958, which was most successful in Sagua la Grande, just down the North Circuit from Sierra Morena, where the radio station was taken by strikers. When Guevara opened a front in the Escambray Mountains just south of their provincial seat of Santa Clara in October of that year, the boys did not go down to join him but redoubled their efforts in town and along the coast.

Underground politics in Región Sagua were thick. There were plenty of Batista's people along the coast to give youthful revolutionaries a way to participate in the uprising. Batista henchmen occupied the beaches and little fishing harbors ostensibly to secure them from invasion. The lagoon was perfect for the movement of weapons and smuggling, as it had been for centuries. Slaves for the Santa Rita, Horizonte, Las Dos Marías, and Santa Lutgarda plantations likely arrived through that lagoon, some of them as contraband late in the trade. Now militants descended from those slaves and identified with Fidel's 26th of July Movement threatened to sabotage the lighthouse on the other side of the lagoon, six miles out.

Batista's people were determined to defend Cuba from the Communist threat, but they also enjoyed the lagoon. They had beach houses and pleasure craft, and in later years Isidra always remembered Batista's people water skiing and sunning themselves on the beach. Isidra and Eulalia, in their desire to join their brothers in their militancy, once played a prank on a Colonel Cornelio Rojas, Batista's police chief for the region. "Together with some friends, we raised a homemade flag for Fidel's 26th of July Movement at the dock where Colonel Rojas, who was later executed by the revolution in Santa Clara, kept his pleasure boats. One of our accomplices was a very young boy who was discovered and beaten by his father to appease the colonel. But he never gave us up." Isidra said this admiringly—sixty years later.

The revolution triumphed on January 1, 1959, when Batista fled Havana. He was prodded by a trusted West African–inspired *babalao,* a master of ritual divination, who on New Year's Eve foresaw Batista's death in the coming year. Cucusa's family was taken by a storm more dramatic than any hurricane to have raked their coast. When the time came to declare loyalties, they joined it fervently. They supported it in its insurgent days, and when the Committees for the Defense of the Revolution (CDRs) came, in 1960, Cucusa did not hesitate. The CDRs were charged with bringing the revolution to every neighborhood in the country and to protect it from enemies, both foreign and domestic. The CDRs needed a physical structure to host meetings and store documents, and this was almost always a volunteer's home or apartment. Cucusa offered, and the house attached to the cockfighting ring bought with Orfilio's numbers winnings nineteen years earlier became Sierra Morena's first CDR.

The north coast was soon hypermilitarized as threats were exchanged between Fidel and Eisenhower, then Kennedy. As with Batista before, the revolution feared the lagoon for weapons shipments and sabotage. Worse, the keys on the far side of the lagoon were the closest the island of Cuba got to the now hostile United States, and with exiles mounting invasions from Miami, the defense of the coast became a genuine concern. The revolution commandeered all fishing boats. Inlets and channels in the lagoon were blocked by railroad tracks driven end first into the coral. The lagoon became impossible to enter or exit except by one route. When the first years of the revolution passed and more people sought to leave Cuba by any means, this also limited small craft departures. On land, the CDR was directly, indirectly, and tangentially connected to every aspect of this new life. The Bay of Pigs invasion, sixty miles to the south in April 1961, led the CDRs to become institutions of national importance.

The revolution shook rural Cuba, and anyone looking to move could ride the storm surge. The once sleepy, stable town of Sierra Morena disgorged its young people. Cucusa's children were sped along. The eldest, her daughter Cuba, went east and did not get involved. Neither did her eldest child with Orfilio Ruíz, Orfilito, who had long before moved to Caibarién for sugar work and was not much heard from. But her four younger children with

Orfilio were swept away by revolutionary currents. Máximo followed the revolution to Santa Clara, two hours by bus from Sierra Morena and the capital of their province. He made Santa Clara his home and began the slow climb into provincial revolutionary leadership. Little Eulalia was carried farther, to Cienfuegos, where she became a worker in the Ministry of Culture (MINCULT). Isidra, by all accounts the cleverest, was lifted even farther, to Havana, where she received a university degree and became a dance instructor employed by MINCULT.

Havana in the 1960s suited Isidra, and she immersed herself in revolutionary culture. As a dancer she was affiliated with Cuba's experimental Conjunto Folklórico, though she never danced for it professionally. She knew its director, the anthropologist Argeliers León, and befriended many of its early musicians and dancers. As a university student she was housed in a room offered in the apartment of a couple whose revolutionary enthusiasms were questionable. When they fled Cuba in the mid-1960s, the apartment became hers.

Of Cucusa's children with Orfilio, Roberto was the one who stayed behind. It must have been because he didn't want to leave. In those days the revolution offered ladders out of the fields and mountainsides of Cuba, elevating the youth into the future of Soviet-style Communism. It gave everyone education and basic health care. Electricity flowed into the foothills, if not the mountains. Soon everyone had a Soviet TV and fridge.

Roberto was trained as a photographer, which was his passion. He also became the first coordinator of Sierra Morena's CDR, which still met in Cucusa's house. He led the CDR as the revolution extended its reach into every corner of political and civic life. He kept a file on every household in town, tracking the participation of the Cairos, Sáezes, Portillas, and Farrés in revolutionary initiatives. After the successful militarization (1959–61) came the literacy campaign (1960–61); then later in the 1960s the revolution, now called the Communist Party of Cuba, turned on religion. The Catholic Church was the principal target, though all religious expression was suspect. Roberto must have been shaken by this, seeing as his family and everyone in Chacha's Sociedad considered themselves religious, even Catholic. Eventually, the party, especially its Communist Youth, went to war against everything religious in Cuba, including the "Black religions." Roberto and Cucusa managed a rapidly moving situation, and in a climate in which African-inspired religion became toxic to revolutionary aspirations, they never suspended the promised bembé for San Lázaro–Babalú Ayé.

By 1962, Cucusa lived in her house with Roberto, Zulia (her daughter by Lupercio Cairo), and the two children, Eliezer and Emelina, by the Spaniard Eusebio Díaz. That her feast for San Lázaro–Babalú Ayé never failed is less a testament to the tolerance of the revolution so much as it is a measure of Cucusa's political savvy. She had always supported her children as their commitments to the revolution deepened, and now Roberto supported her. Praise feasts were ended in countless locales across Cuba as the revolution became a secular military-bureaucratic state, especially at the end of the 1960s. Cucusa's drums played for San Lázaro–Babalú Ayé every December 17. She continued even in the hardline "black decade" of the 1970s. There cannot have been many homes in Cuba in this period that hosted both a CDR and a feast for the santos-orisás.

The 1970s in Cuba deserve their own book, to be written by a clever cultural historian who can capture the mixture of revolutionary hubris, Stalinist orthodoxy, utopian fantasies, and political complacency that defined those years. They are remembered today as tough years when the revolution, supported in full by the Soviet Union, explored the limit of its power and the Cuban people submitted with discipline. They were hard years for nonconformists, including artists of all sorts, writers, gays and lesbians, and anyone queer, as well as those who stood by their promises to the santos-orisás.

The 1980s are remembered with less bitterness. The economy, tied to geopolitics as this was strategized in Moscow, was strong. Glasnost and Perestroika spread from Moscow to Havana, and people often remember the 1980s with a sense of relief and openness. The 1970s were revisited by the party leadership, and revolutionary "excesses" were acknowledged and denounced. But the leadership was also suspicious of all the openness in the USSR, and in the mid-1980s it clipped the wings of those aspiring to a more robust civil society. When the Berlin Wall came down, soon to be followed by the Soviet Union, the Cuban government cracked down and held on.

The 1990s were a decade-long nightmare. The collapse of the Soviet Union meant Cuba was on its own. Fear of immanent invasion by the United States gripped the country early in the decade as the economy collapsed. The country went dark without Soviet fuel to power the grid. Traveling to a place like Sierra Morena became nearly impossible as barely any vehicle moved. Without trucks and buses the country came disconnected from itself. Produce from the countryside could not reach the cities. Food, which the revolution controlled at every level down to what farmers grew on their land, was drastically rationed. Black markets, which had always existed in revolutionary Cuba, exploded in number and scale as hunger and desperation drove Cubans to figure out food on their own. Rumors of insurrections from below and above had their moments, but the decade was politically stable relative to the economic chaos. But all hope for a true socialist future for Cuba died in the 1990s.

By the mid-1990s, the revolution turned itself upside down to address the crisis and decided that tourism, for three decades denigrated by the party and its leaders for prostituting the country during the Batista years, would become the economic engine of the future. Hotels started popping up, literally casting their shadows on crumbling schools. Limited self-employment, which for decades had been synonymous with black market subversion, was allowed. The possession of US dollars, which for years had circulated as a secret currency among "bankers" in the underground numbers game and among corrupt managers in state-run diplomatic shops, was decriminalized. The diplomatic shops, which for decades had been exclusively for foreigners residing in Cuba, were opened up to the Cuban public as hard-currency-only stores as the government sought to pull in the hundreds of millions of US dollars that fueled the underground markets. Economic life became bifurcated between the Cuban peso, with which rationed staples could be purchased at state-run dispensaries, and the US dollar, with which one could buy luxuries like scented soap, cooking oil, and diapers at the newly opened dollars-only "shopping" stores. The problem was that US dollars were rare because the government, which employed everyone, paid in Cuban pesos, the collapsed national currency. The only people with dollars to spend were black market hustlers, numbers runners, and other antisocials like those who had maintained contact with family in exile. After 1994, when possession of dollars was decriminalized, the question on everyone's lips was "How do I get my hands on more?" The 1990s were hard on everyone, but party militants like Isidra and her siblings had the added burden of justifying their revolutionary commitment when confronted with a political and economic reality that laughed in the face of most of what their party had said and done for the past thirty-five years.

Cucusa's children went nowhere during the 1990s. Depression, economic and emotional, gripped the country for an entire decade. A special kind of stagnation descended on Cuba, one in which nothing moved but many things changed. There was nothing with which to foment change, hardly even food, so life seemed stopped. Then again, there was not a feeling, commitment, or expectation—revolutionary or otherwise—that didn't change as a country of ten million people suffered collective heartbreak.

Cucusa's feast, though resilient, was not impervious to the revolution and its political hairpin turns. Nothing was. Cucusa saw her budding orisá mounts, especially Máximo and Roberto, enraptured by the revolution and successfully integrated into its many apparatuses. To climb within the revolution, a person had to achieve rank in the Cuban Communist Party, first through its youth wing. Máximo, Roberto, Isidra, and Eulalia all achieved militant status. They settled in cities, and climbed in their respective professions. This was the new revolutionary reality, but religious expression, though legal, was socially and professionally scorned. For years, Cucusa's kids didn't come home, and her grandchildren were raised away from the santos-orisás.

Just as the revolution pulled the young away from Chacha's Sociedad Africana, so the old became frail and died. Before the revolution, Ma' Josefa and Kimbito died. The first decades of the revolution saw the death of Chacha Cairo and also of her Comisión Africana—the original stable of mounts for the santos-orisás. Ma' Isidra, Jorge Sáez, Santiago Linares, Gobierno Cairo, Otilia Sáez, Digna Sáez, Loreto Sáez, and Chucha Portilla all died during the revolution's first three decades. Only young people who were well into their twenties when the revolution came to power, like Loreto's daughter, Pica, continued to develop as steeds during the first decades of the revolution. Those younger, like Cucusa's Ruíz children, were carried far from Sierra Morena and its bembés.

Perhaps it is predictable that Cucusa's death would draw them back. It was 1998, and the worst of the crisis years was behind them, though it was hard to tell at the time. Pope John Paul II visited Cuba that year, and the beginnings of religious civil society could be felt in the air. His visit solidified intimations made by the revolution that religious expression would no longer be denigrated. Militants like Isidra and her Ruíz siblings could now contemplate open religious expression without fear of career reprisals against them or their children. Isidra was also recently retired, so perhaps she was less concerned about the professional liabilities of openly returning to Cucusa's bembé. It was clear, at least to Isidra, that the feast for San Lázaro–Babalú Ayé would not continue without her participation. The year Cucusa died, the feast was suspended, but the next, 1999, Isidra set out to keep Cucusa's promise to San Lázaro–Babalú Ayé. She would need the help of all of Cucusa's children, her Ruíz siblings along with her Cairo and Díaz half siblings. At a fundamental level, Isidra understood that keeping the feast going meant keeping Cucusa's house. Without it, the bembé would fail. But in 1998, Isidra was settled in Havana, and the revolution did not allow a person to have two homes. Figuring out how to save everything Cucusa had assembled in order to keep her promise to San Lázaro–Babalú Ayé became Isidra's goal. That was the year I met her, and to her I became a piece in the great improvisational work she was unfolding to do just that.

PART TWO

FOUR

————

1999

RETURN

I MET CUCUSA'S CHILDREN BY ORFILIO RUIZ in December 1999, when they were in their late fifties and early sixties. I had been in Havana for three months, and Isidra had become my teacher, guide, and informant for a book on Palo, the Congo-inspired healing-harming craft widely feared in Cuba. That book focused on a Havana-based Palo community, and it wasn't until late in the fall that Isidra suggested I join her on a trip home to Sierra Morena. She had no money and asked if I would fund it. She wanted to host a feast in her mother's stead, to keep a promise to San Lázaro–Babalú Ayé. I was reluctant—this had nothing to do with Havana Palo, and the time away from Havana would be a distraction. Anthropologists should be careful about how they use their money too. She wanted me to cover the travel, which would be impossibly expensive for her. She won me over, and on my dime we made the trip. Once in town, I was her guest. She was working with another anthropologist, Takako Kudo from Japan, and together with Takako, Isidra's son Ulises, who was fourteen, and her friend Teodoro, a master of Congo-inspired healing-harming craft, we headed for Sierra Morena on December 6 of that year.

In 1999 there was no way for our party to get to Sierra Morena except on a state-run bus. Tourist buses were only just beginning to get foreigners to places like Matanzas and Varadero Beach, or across the island to Santiago. The North Circuit and the little towns along the coast were not on the map for these dollars-only dream rides. The fleet of private cars that regularly shuttle people in and out of Havana today had yet to appear. Even in the worst years of the economic crisis, state-run trains and buses kept running, but their schedules were fictions as fuel shortages and breakdowns made any trip a harrowing affair. Ticket prices were fictions too, as black market markups and special favors got tickets into people's hands more than did the official ticket-allocation waitlists [*listas de espera*]. State-organized hitchhiking was a thing in the 1990s, but our little party would never have made it had we thrown ourselves to its serendipitous mercies. Isidra was sixty, after all, and though she was quick and lithe as if she were thirty, she had her standards. She did live a couple of blocks from the bus station, though, and knew just the right people. Eventually, with the help of some serious Cuban pesos paid under the table, and after an all-night delay, we trundled out of Havana on a Hungarian-designed Girón V bus on the morning of December 7.

The trip took us through Jovellanos, a little sugar town known in those years as the home of the great Cuban high jumper Javier Sotomayor. It was less famously a repeat research site for Cuban anthropologists, folklorists, and others doing fieldwork on African-inspired praise on the island, as well as a site of reverence and mystery for historians of African inspirations.[1] Jovellanos is on the western side of the Llano de Colón, historically one of Cuba's most productive sugar plains and, until the late nineteenth century, a major slave market. Jovellanos is known as Arará territory by scholars and practitioners alike.[2] The entire sugar plain received huge populations of people slaved away from Old Dahomey, people who in Cuba came to call themselves Arará, after their longed-for capital, Allada. Cuban Arará styles of orisá praise, which are felt in percussion, lyrics-wisdom, dance, and orisá interpretation, have always distinguished them from Havana styles. Isidra called Sierra Morena style "Ará Oco," or "Country Arará." There was also a "city Arará," which she described as performed by those who praised the santos-orisás around the city of Matanzas. She called them and their praise "Ará Matanzas." "Two different styles," she said. We were through Jovellanos in the blink of an eye. It took us five hours to get to Corralillo, on the northern fringe of the Llano de Colón, and from there we were helped by an acquaintance with a tractor and trailer who happened to be coming by.

Cucusa's house was handsome and welcoming, with its white clapboard siding, its shaded veranda on the street, and its tall barred windows and red double doors to match a red tile roof. I could see immediately why Orfilio didn't hesitate when he won that numbers jackpot in 1940. Eulalia greeted us at the door. She was in from Cienfuegos the night before. Behind her in the living room was the altar to San Lázaro–Babalú Ayé, with its two statues of the Beggar. Roberto was waiting inside, and our arrival jerked their conversation into high gear.

"She is a traitor," said Roberto, his black eyes sharp, his eyebrows raised. "She should be driven out."

"Just wait until Máximo arrives," said Eulalia. She was an upbeat person, and said this with a kind of sunny dread.

"Máximo?" said Isidra. "Where is Máximo? I don't see him. The person I see here right now is me, and I will make Yamilet pay."

"My bus ride was six hours," said Eulalia. "How about yours?"

Isidra glanced at her younger sister, annoyed. "Roberto," she said, "you live here in town, and you just let Yamilet tear through here, let her take everything, and you didn't say a word."

"Say?" Roberto looked away, then back. "It's not my place to say anything. What Yamilet did in this house is unspeakable, so what have I got to say? She knows it will be paid for."

"Listen," said Eulalia.

"Listen to this," said Isidra interrupting, then meeting her brother hard. "You don't need to say anything? Our niece walked in here and stole from our mother. She came in. One year Cucusa is dead. One year. And Yamilet comes in. You live here in town, two blocks away. You don't need to say anything?"

Roberto went to speak, but she cut him off. "You are the person who is supposed to be looking after this house, but instead you gave the keys to old Pica. You've been part of the Committee for the Defense of the Revolution how many years?"

"Don't bring the committee into this." Roberto was looking straight at her. "I'm not going to mix that with my personal business."

"Don't bring it in?" Isidra was incredulous. "Personal business? At least you admit it is your business."

Roberto was caught behind a stutter.

"Don't bring in the CDR?" She continued half aghast, half pondering the situation. "Theft is theft. That it happens at your mother's house makes no difference. What is the CDR for if not to catch thieves?"

"Listen now, this is not the committee's business. Who am I to bring the CDR against someone?"

"You founded the CDR in this town! You were head of it how many years? This is shit eating if I ever heard it."

"Shit eating? It is not my place to drag the committee into this if they aren't already looking at it. It is not a problem for them. We have bigger problems on this coast than stolen silverware and plates, and you know that."

"Not a problem! Not a problem?" Isidra was on her feet. "A stolen refrigerator is not a problem?"

Roberto met her, lowering his voice. "Do you forget where you are? Do you forget where you grew up? You know what is a mile in that direction," Roberto pointed out the front door, toward the lagoon in the distance. "And ninety miles further on? Do you know how many people set off from here? How many speedboats come in to pick people up?"

"Enough!" said Isidra. "If this isn't a problem for the CDR now, it will be soon. Better to deal with it before someone gets hurt."

Roberto kept his voice low and looked at all of us. "Yamilet will pay for this, and it won't be through the CDR. Just wait until Máximo comes. Then we'll see this get resolved."

Isidra was annoyed. "Roberto, you had better be plugged into your Elégua. This house needs him. And Máximo, he'd better have that ram."

"He should be on the bus from Santa Clara in the next couple of days," said Eulalia. "He is coming to pay his debt."

"Next couple of days?" Isidra was crestfallen. "He can't be here sooner?"

Roberto switched to a quieter mode, and the conversation changed. As quickly as it had exploded, it subsided into gossip. Isidra, who had met his bluster with her own frank appraisal of the situation, couldn't resist the juicy bits. The siblings swapped questions and bits of answers for half an hour or so, until the conjectures and stories took so many turns that few except Isidra could keep up.

Yamilet was Cucusa's granddaughter and lived next door. She was the daughter of Isidra's younger half sister, Emelina Díaz, Cucusa's last child. In her eighties, Cucusa ceded half of her ample lot to Emelina, and she in turn gave it over to Yamilet and her husband, who built a house there. They built right up against Cucusa's house, so that only a narrow passage separated them. Raised voices in one house could be heard in the other, and out front their verandas were shoulder to shoulder. They shared fruit trees out back, but not the splendid well, which Cucusa kept for herself.

Cucusa left no will, and all through the revolution she never had a deed to the house reissued. After she died, her children with Orfilio Ruíz—Orfilio, Máximo, Roberto, Isidra, and Eulalia—locked up the house until they could decide what to do with it. They were the largest group of full siblings and the children of the couple who bought the house in 1940. One day Yamilet, whom the Ruíz siblings left out of any decision-making because she was the daughter of their half sibling, broke into the house along with her husband

and took anything that could be carried, including the refrigerator and beds. This was 1990s depression-era "Special Period" Cuba, so they also took the electrical cables and receptacles, light fixtures, and almost everything else that could be yanked free. Yamilet was crucial in caring for Cucusa in her last days and claimed Cucusa had promised her the furniture and refrigerator. Isidra and her siblings were not going to give her what she was due, and she was done waiting for it.

To complicate things, Yamilet was also Isidra's godchild in Havana-based Ocha-Santería. After Isidra was initiated into the Havana-based West African–inspired religion in the mid-1990s, she did not tarry in bringing her own initiate into Ocha, thus becoming an Ocha godmother [iyalocha]. Becoming an Ocha godmother moves a practitioner into the role of teacher and is considered ritually important in and of itself. For the teacher, new realms of ritual knowledge are unlocked. A teacher also begins to explore their potential for building their own praise house. The relationship between an Ocha godmother and their Ocha godchild [iyawó] should be one of confidence, care, and mutual respect. Yamilet was Isidra's first initiate, but their relationship had soured, and it marked Isidra profoundly. She never brought another initiate into Ocha-Santería. In 1999, Yamilet was the only person in Sierra Morena formally initiated into Havana-style Ocha.

Isidra and Eulalia worked into the evening on December 7 preparing the house to receive San Lázaro–Babalú Ayé and the couple of hundred people who would praise him in ten days' time. Between Cucusa's illness and death, the feast hadn't been celebrated in eighteen months, and a lot of excitement accompanied Isidra's arrival in town. They needed to marshal considerable help, especially in the kitchen, and needed to find the animals that would be offered to the santos-orisás. My job would be to help with this and to care for the animals in the backyard once they were acquired. The sisters drifted from gossiping about town happenings to figuring out who could be counted on for what, which could not be separated from gossiping. What were the chances of their half sister, Zulia, coming from Corralillo? Was she still speaking with Yamilet? What about Zulia's son, Ernesto? Could he be counted on to help? And Agripina, a cousin, would she come from Sagua la Grande, thirty miles to the east? Who were the people with regular promises of an animal for Cucusa's bembé? Who had promises to Babalú Ayé they had not been able to keep the year before? Where might they get a young billy goat for Elégua and a white rooster for Obatalá? Did anyone have a large pot for boiling water, and who could they possibly get a refrigerator from? Where was their cousin Justo, and when would Pica come by to share her version of things?

That evening, Teodoro was put to work doing his version of Havana Palo by protecting the door and sealing off the house. Isidra had brought one of her Palo powers with her, a little rock she called Batalla [Battle], which was a traveling version of Palo powers she kept in Havana. Teodoro traveled with his own portable Palo power, a little statuette with four faces he called Cuatro Vientos [Four Winds]. Teodoro was a master of Congo-inspired healing-harming craft, which would benefit us all while we were in town. Havana versions of Congo-inspired and Yoruba-inspired forces did not necessarily translate to the healing of the countryside, but the Congo ones were more likely to. My other job was to tag along with him, fetch his cigars, move things as he instructed, and generally be his apprentice. Together we enlivened Batalla and Cuatro Vientos with aguardiente and white wine. They were placed near the front door, and a candle was lit there to draw near the ancestral dead, like Cucusa, Ma' Isidra, and Loreto. Together, the Congo powers and the ancestral dead of the house would keep watch throughout the night.

Morning in the house was a pleasure. The street outside was quiet, as was the living room, which was still cool. It was a big house, with plank walls and a high rafter ceiling. It was among the bigger houses in town, with an enormous yard in the back. The fruit trees were mature and provided not only delicacies to eat but also shade and birdsong. The well in the yard was enormous, a round, open well you could have jumped into. There was no sign of the cockfighting ring that had brought Orfilio Ruíz and his young family here nearly sixty years earlier, or of the crowds that came to bet. In its unremitting campaigns against social ills, the revolution prohibited the numbers game in 1959 and cockfighting in 1968. This was also the year small businesses were seized. The ring was doomed on two fronts. Only a pile of rotting lumber to one side of the well, the remains of a two-room wing Cucusa built for her growing sons in the 1950s, bespoke the previous lives of the house.

Eulalia prepared breakfast—a small glass of coffee with two tablespoons of powdered milk. Yamilet had emptied the house, so we were essentially camping under the roof with the task of hosting a huge feast in nine days. This was 1999, with the worst of the economic crisis subsiding, but the new-fangled dollars shops had not yet reached Corralillo, let alone Sierra Morena, so there was nowhere to buy staples like cooking oil or laundry soap.

We had brought as much as possible from Havana, including sheets, pillows, light bulbs, cooking utensils, mosquito nets, dishes, and soap. There was a foam mattress that must have been stolen from an army barracks or hospital in Havana before finding its way onto the black market, where Isidra picked it up. We also brought lots of the basics, things you wouldn't expect we would need in the countryside—rice, beans, cooking oil, salt, tomato paste, even onions. Isidra got all this, and two *tumbadoras* [conga drums], loaded onto the Girón V in Havana with a combination of bribes and moral exhortations to the dignity of Cuban socialism that few besides her could pull off. There were still a million things to find, and the quiet in the house told me she was out shaking the trees.

Eulalia liked to wear colorful pants and flowered short-sleeved polyester blouses. She was taller than Isidra and skinny. She never wore heels. A bracelet, necklace, or earrings completed her daily look.

"See?" said Eulalia. "The kitchen table at which you're seated is borrowed. So is the charcoal stove in the yard. So is the bed on which you're sleeping. We've been successful." Eulalia's smile was half doubtful, but I saw no reason to be low. Finding someone who would loan you anything of value in 1999 Cuba was a miracle.

"Isidra is coming. Just wait until she tells you. How did you sleep? Teodoro is loose in the street. May God save this town." Her drooping eyes were simultaneously cheerful and worried. It wasn't five minutes before Isidra came in.

"Love this town! This is a town of religious people who know how a bembé is done!" She was smiling. Ulises, her son, was behind her, loaded with plastic bags bulging with finds. She had a copy of the day's state-run newspaper, *Granma,* in one hand and a rooster by its feet in the other. "Look at this rooster! What do you think? Tremendous rooster! Colored rooster for Changó. I got it from Hendry up the hill on the outskirts of town. He is going to come later with his daughter to thank San Lázaro. Did Eulalia tell you about the fridge [*el frío*]? Doña Lucia up the street is going to rent hers to us. You can't destroy this house just by stealing the fridge! Just wait till you meet the kid who is bringing it."

The refrigerator was the crown on the pile of Isidra's finds. Still to come was a set of china from one neighbor, a handful of silverware from another, and a fifty-gallon barrel to store water from yet another. "I could have gotten a horse to ride all day if I had wanted one. You're going to love Oier, the guy with the horse."

The two sisters huddled at the table. Proudly, Isidra had Ulises withdraw two liters of milk from a plastic bag. His eyes were wide. Eulalia went for a glass, but Isidra scolded her. "Who found this milk? I can't stop to eat. Between now and the feast, only milk for me."

They were prioritizing things to hunt down when a knock came at the door. At first it was faint, then a little louder with a shout. A hunched woman, portly, with short white hair, almond-shaped eyes, her neck scarred, stood at the door. "Well, I'm glad you are going to do this," she said. "I wondered if you would show up. Just the sight of you makes this good already."

Pica Sáez wore a T-shirt, high-water cotton pants, and beat-up flip-flops. She was around seventy years old, a decade older than the Ruíz sisters. She took a look at me and skeptically accepted my formal greetings. "We'll see about this," she said.

For the next while she took little interest in me. This could not be said for Takako. Takako spoke Spanish very well but with a strong accent that people loved. She was slender and pretty, and with the camera, microphone, and notebook, she was straight out of the movies. She was an event in town, and everyone was dazzled by "Isidra's china doll." Pica was enamored, and they quickly developed a productive rapport.

"You like our Japanese anthropologist?" said Eulalia, laughing. "We've got an American one too."

Pica nodded.

"If you think they're strange, just wait till you meet the *brujo congo* these guys brought with them from Havana."

"I met him," said Pica. "He's up and down the street drunker than . . ." she trailed off. "That guy is full of shit as far as I can tell. You would do better leaving that noise back in Havana."

"There are purposes for him, Pica, don't mind," said Isidra, with an uncharacteristically apologetic tone.

"Say that to my daughter, María. She thinks he's really something."

Pica was the daughter of Loreto Sáez, and she watched the house in lieu of the siblings. Roberto lived in town but had relinquished the keys sometime after Cucusa died. His wife, Celia, didn't want him mixed up with the mess Cucusa had left. Pica opened up the house and looked after things. She quickly fell into talking about the goings-on next door, what things of Cucusa's Yamilet had sold off, and who had bought them. Cucusa's dishes were at Eugenia's, and the silverware was sold up the street to Caridad. These were neighbors Isidra hoped would have defended the house and Cucusa's memory.

"You don't think we need those things now?" said Isidra. "Let's see if either of those women is here on the 17th. Let's see if they have the courage to face the santos of this house, to face Babalú Ayé. Is that what Cucusa promised Yamilet, that she could sell her silverware to the neighbors? Is that the kind of promise an eighty-year-old makes? Those neighbors may as well have looted the house along with her."

"That brother of yours is who should be looking after this house," said Pica. "If he cared, you wouldn't have this problem. I'll hold on to the keys, but you know this is not my problem."

"We'll get this sorted out," said Isidra by way of killing the conversation. "Listen, Pica, where can we get a little goat for Elégua?"

"Now, that is another matter."

Over the next several days, the siblings shaped up and provisioned the house, all the while aiming for the feast on the 17th. The underbrush in the backyard was chopped away, and a bucket was rigged to draw water. A door for the double outhouse (a luxury) was hung on hinges made of bent nails. A kitchen was set up, with the cooking and washing happening under a piece of corrugated tin outside the back door. Breakfast was a glass of powdered milk and a slice of cheese. A small fried fish, a cup of rice, and a ripe banana or fried plantain were lunch and dinner most days.

Fish and cheese are two of the few luxuries people in Sierra Morena have. The sea is two kilometers downhill, and men wade into the lagoon all the time. José, who was married to Roberto's daughter, Celita, was our source of fish, and he explained it: "The lagoon is closed to fishing. National security. Coast Guard patrols. Most people wade out. Others, like me, we fish from inner tubes. No poles. Line on a hand reel. I'll float out a couple of kilometers, to where it is deeper. We drag waterlogged chunks of mangrove out there and drop them on top of each other. Fish love structures. Half a day fishing at a structure and we have more than we can eat. Go to sell it and it is against the rules. Are the inner tubes against the rules? Also. You are allowed to fish, see, but you have to be on shore, and you can't sell anything you catch. Subsistence only. Coast Guard or police boats sometimes take our inner tubes and lines, then they fish our structures clean. Same with our lobster traps. You can really get in trouble for lobster. That's jail time if you get caught too bad. Don't let them find you with a couple dozen tails. An agent will confiscate them and fine you in the morning, then sell them back to you on the black market in the evening. *Everything* is against the law, what we do, what they do." José laughed, raising his eyebrows to underscore the absurdity.

Cheese, so common around the world, was rare in Cuba in 1999, especially in the cities. Because milk is a nearly universal source of nourishment, the revolution takes almost a national security interest in its production. The state provides dairy products, usually yogurt and powdered milk, to children under seven. So the revolution keeps a cow census, including data on every farmer and the state-run dairies. Few countries can boast a cattle census like Cuba's. Small farmers, who milk the vast majority of Cuba's cows, are expected to sell the overwhelming share of their milk to state buyers who know pretty well how much they should be providing, according to the census. The buyers offer a state-mandated price, which is a pittance of the milk's worth on the black market. Farmers are loath to sell their milk for a penny less than what they can get, but there is no legal private market, so a dairy black market thrives anywhere there is a cow.

Iván, a teenager who lived across the street from Cucusa and helped his dad on their parcel outside town, didn't mind explaining how farmers earned something from their milk.

"You can call it a black market [*bolsa negra*] if you want. It is true that we're selling our milk where we shouldn't be, and for prices way above what the government pays. How else are we supposed to survive? The government doesn't pay enough to cover feed, or to cover an injection when a cow gets sick. It's not worth it to keep a cow at what the state offers for the milk. It *is* worth it for what people will pay in town. If not for the black market, we would butcher them all for the meat. That is illegal, too, you know. Census keeps you from doing that. Kill a cow without permission and you go straight to prison. We keep milk for our families, but there is more than we can drink, so that goes for sale. We hide what we can from the state buyer."

Iván was a sweet presence in Cucusa's house. When he was little, his parents were spread thin by the economic crisis, and Cucusa took him in. "She raised me. She took me in and fed me, and I spent more time here playing the drums than at home with my parents. They just let me go. Along the way, I got pretty good on the big drum."

"He's Cucusa's youngest child," said Eulalia, smiling.

He continued about the milk, "It won't keep raw. Even in winter it will spoil. I don't know a farmer with a working fridge out there. You've got to get your milk to town, so you turn it into cheese or yogurt. Cheese requires more milk, but it is easier to transport and keeps. Yogurt is faster to make, but you need plastic bottles and they're a pain. What about the government buyers and the census? So, they are a problem, but we all know one another. I've never met a buyer who isn't a dairyman himself. Good dairyman ends up a MINAG [Ministry of Agriculture] buyer eventually. Local buyer knows you, your family, your land, how many cows you have, and how much milk you should be producing. He uses the census, but he's raising dairy cows too, so he knows the exact conditions you're working with and how much milk there should be. What do you do? One option is to hide your milk. You lie on your quotas. There are a million excuses for why you didn't make the target. Cow is sick, cow is stressed, feed is terrible, there is no feed, pigs broke into the feed and ate it, cow is old, milk went sour so you had to feed it to the pig, or you can blame it on the weather. Millions of excuses. Buyers usually leave you alone. They're hiding their milk too. But they're also trying to get their quotas met, and people are watching them up the line. So when they lean on you, or simply beg you so they can meet their quota, then you offer them some yogurt or cheese. That is how they really get paid. A pound of cheese or two and they'll write down that you met your quota. They write down that they bought your milk, keep the money they were going to pay you, then sell the cheese. Up the chain at the dairy plant, you would think they are expecting the milk the buyer has marked down as purchased, but up there what they want is the cheese from the buyers, or the money. What happens up the chain from there? I don't know about that, but the evening news says diary production is at 98 percent of quota. Seems this is working for everyone." There were plenty of dairy farmers in the vicinity of Sierra Morena, so cheese was plentiful if you had the money. Compared to Havana, where regular visits from underground dairy runners were forever delayed and interrupted, having cheese every day was almost as good as having fish for breakfast, lunch, and dinner.

Roberto came around every day. He had his own house in town where he lived with Celia, his wife. He was retired and had time on his hands, but he was not very helpful. It was the morning of December 12, four days from the feast, and he came by with his most important daily bit of news, which was to report on Máximo's movements. His arrival from Santa Clara was now put off for days. The Communist Party's end-of-year planning in Santa Clara kept him away. Maybe he would get a party car to bring him and his wife, Cyrilla, but it wouldn't be until the eve of the feast.

"The eve of the feast?" Isidra was wide eyed. "Four days from now and I don't count today. How will he deal with Yamilet and her disrespect on the eve of the feast? I'm hosting this bembé, and I'm not going to have that fight on my doorstep. That will not do. I don't need that *arayé* [war] stirred into the bembé. Won't do." Isidra soured, saying, "Doesn't he care about his mother's bembé? With her house under attack? The fool. Who is going to pay for his disrespect? All of us? Máximo will pay more. Changó will have his say."

"Changó?" said Roberto.

"Changó eats ram. Máximo promised him a big one for this feast."

"Then he'll deliver," said Roberto.

"Deliver?" said Isidra. "What is he going to do, bring a ram on the bus from Santa Clara? Rams don't appear out of nowhere. He is going to show up here on the eve of the feast and set about looking for a big ram then?"

"Maybe he will bring it in the party car."

"Can you imagine loading a giant ram into the trunk of a party car? Stop talking shit." She paused. "You. You deal with the ram."

"Me? The ram?" Roberto shook his head.

"You. Your brother is going to arrive on the eve of the feast, and there will be no ram for Changó. He is going to show up and pick a fight with Yamilet without a ram to offer Changó? You two are fools. The fight with Yamilet needed to be had months ago, and now you've put it off until the feast. Along the way you disrespect Changó, possessor of the feast, master of fights, and master of war? The ram is your problem."

It was December 12, and the feast would begin December 16, just before midnight. Eulalia counted four full days to prepare and seemed worried, though always easygoing. The days that followed went quickly and saw people come to the door offering to make good on promises to San Lázaro–Babalú Ayé. Some of these were altar promises made with Cucusa as witness, onetime promises and also promises made in perpetuity, like Cucusa's promise to host the feast year after year. A man came to the door with a rooster for San Lázaro–Babalú Ayé for his feast day. He owed San Lázaro from when Cucusa was alive, and he wanted to make good. This is how animals were gathered for a bembé. They arrived as a result of a promise made over the year, or years before, at the moment Cucusa healed people at her altar, calling on the sovereign of illness and healing. Other gifts were surprises, people keeping promises made far from Cucusa's altar, in the dead of night at the side of a sick person, or standing vigil over a hospital bed. While she was alive and attending at her altar, Cucusa's feasts never lacked animals for any of the orisás she feasted together with San Lázaro–Babalú Ayé: Elégua, Yemayá, Ochún, Changó, Ogún, Obatalá, and Oyá, not to mention animals to satiate the ancestral dead and the Congo powers.

The refrigerator showed up on December 13, and Isidra was as delighted with it as with the delivery man. His name was Yunier, and he was about twenty, was done with his compulsory military service, and had time on his hands. His mom had kicked him out, and he slept on the bare ground outside her house. His official state job (everyone in Cuba at this time had an official state job) was as a watchman at a local grapefruit orchard to make sure no one stole the fruit. When the government has no job to give a person, they put them to watch over something. He survived day to day on those grapefruits and all the other fruit trees for miles around. "I don't eat the grapefruits," he assured Takako and me. "Are you crazy! Eat the grapefruits? And get in trouble? Are you crazy! No, I eat the fruit between here and there, lots of fruit, guayabas, bananas, avocados, anones, mangoes, canisteles, and *fruta bomba*." (Fruta bomba is "papaya" in most of Spanish-speaking Latin America, but in Cuban Spanish the latter is nasty slang for female genitals and never used to describe the fruit.)

Yunier got the fridge into the house. Moving it was no problem for him. He was a giant in Cuba or almost anywhere else in the world, well over two meters tall, lanky, and he had a barrel chest that made it look as if he were pushing his shoulders back. With his bony head, temples and cheeks showing, and his prominent, pointed nose, he looked like an enormous plucked bird.

Yunier was *jabao,* which in Cuba is its own kind of racial curse. Jabaos are "neither here nor there" in the vast spectrum of browns, reds, and yellows that make up the palette of racialization in Cuba. Jabao people are "white Blacks," or "Black whites," depending on the skin shade (usually "white" with a reddish or yellowish tinge), color of the hair (usually blond or red), texture of the hair (usually straight but with a touch of curl), and facial features that mix aquiline and full (a thin pointy nose with lips a little full). Jabaos are teased, and their appearance, which confuses Cubans even with their extremely subtle racial vocabulary, is always the butt of jokes. Being jabao was something Yunier lived with every day, and it defined him as much as his enormous size. Takako, who found Cuban racialization fascinating and confounding, took an interest in Yunier's experience, and he felt himself greatly elevated by her attention.

His gigantic shoes were broken, and he had no chance of finding replacements anywhere near town. He would need a trip to Cárdenas, hours away hitchhiking, to find anything. Worse, even if he got lucky enough to find his size, he would need hard currency, and of that he had not even a dime. He wore his shoes as sandals, his toes protruding, the soles tied to his feet.

"Listen here, Yunier. Why don't you go with Takako and Ramón and teach them how to pick guayabas?" asked Isidra. Yunier seemed willing to do almost anything Isidra asked. Parading through town with Takako, the "china doll," was an event.

Ulises, Isidra's son, was fourteen and still solidly under his mother's wing, though here in town his cousins were pulling him farther and farther afield. Anelé was his first cousin once removed, the daughter of Roberto and Celia's second son, Alejandro. She was a cute kid, three years younger, who lived in Santa Clara and was in town for the bembé on the 17th. She got Ulises's goat by suggesting that girls in town liked him, or worse, insinuating his interest in one or another girl. She especially loved doing this in front of his mother, who never missed a chance to unload.

"You go ahead and get a girlfriend from Sierra Morena. See how long that lasts! Anelé, you're fresh for a little kid. You go tell those little hustlers you're hanging out with that Ulises has a mother like none other!"

In the days before the feast they were joined by another cousin their age, named after his father and his father before him, who was Roberto, Isidra's brother. Because his own father had forever been known as Robertico, Roberto in the diminutive, Robertico grandson would have had to go by something like Robertitico, which is not unknown in Cuba but gets a little cumbersome to say all the time. They called him Boby. He was a sweet kid with a shyness that could tend toward brooding. Like Anelé, he was from Santa Clara. He was not as good in school as either of his cousins, and already at thirteen years old he knew that professional tracks within the revolutionary employment apparatus—like being an actuary or clerk in a government ministry—were out of the question for him. His path was vocational and would not include university education. Boby was between his cousins in age, and he and Anelé were always draped over each other. They walked hand in hand, and she sat on his lap. Boby got Ulises out after dark, and together they went to the plaza by the dilapidated church where there was a flirting scene. Boby was determined to get his hands on some alcohol too, to figure out once and for all what that was about. Little by little these kids found space and time to slip out of responsibilities, and their parents indulged them in the freedoms and pleasures of vacation in a country town.

It was the morning of December 14, and the feast was now two days off. Tense words were exchanged with Yamilet's husband next door. Isidra was surrendered to the task of preparing the bembé and spent her days gathering the endless little pieces she needed, like plastic cups for a hundred people (impossible in 1999), like a large pot for boiling water for plucking birds, like more than one knife large enough to butcher the sacrificed animals. There were orisá details to attend to, like fresh flowers for the altar to San Lázaro–Babalú Ayé, and like a massive bunch of green bananas to hang from the rafters for Changó. So many little things to please Changó. The feast was in honor of San Lázaro–Babalú Ayé, but feasts in general, all of them, are the property of Changó, part of his domain, his to give to everyday people so they can then offer them to the santos-orisás.

She had put off an outing to a place she called La Corua. It was a pool in a small river that ran east of town, the same river the early Sierra Morena neighborhood called El Río had grown up around. She needed to gather plants and other substances for the feast ahead. Plants and herbs for cleaning and healing purposes need to be fresh, so there was no point in going to get them earlier, but now the time had come. She had a list of vines and bushes she wanted cuttings from. More than anything, she wanted water from La Corua, which she would use for a variety of activities. She found Ulises in the street, pulled Teodoro away from his bottle, lined up her anthropologists for the minor ritual ahead, and marched us off into the sunny countryside. She left Eulalia in charge of the house.

Our path to La Corua took us past Pica's house, which was down a rocky track leading out from the middle of town. The broken paths were the subject of much conversation as people recalled a recent storm that "lasted twenty-one days." The houses out that way were of mixed vintage. Prerevolution houses were weathered wood-plank affairs that leaned one way or another under the weight of their terra cotta tiles. Those put up by the revolution were cement structures with cement floors and wavy asbestos cement sheets for roofs. Pica's was one of these, up on a little rise. "They gave it to me after years of waiting," she said. "It didn't have a roof for eight months, but I didn't care. Eventually that came."

She was out back. There were two bedrooms in one half of the house, and a living room–dining room–kitchen in the other. Pica's daughter, María, greeted us. "Mom won't make it up these steps much longer. It is a miracle you can!" She was a cheerful person, heavy like her mother, and also hunch-backed. She was a pretty good copy of Pica, who was herself a close copy of her father, Loreto.

"Good luck getting Mom to go with you," she said. "I can't get her to leave that rooster of hers alone. All she wants to do is pet it."

"Let me through," said Isidra. "Pica, let's go. No diddling or dragging. I need you at La Corua, and you know it. Come on. We need to be back by noon, anyway. Don't want to get caught in the countryside at midday when the dead are about."

Pica limped in from the yard with a beautiful rooster in her arms. She looked at Isidra with almost comic frustration. "You won't stop, will you? What time is it? Am I going to make it back by noon, or just you young people? Don't leave me in the forest with the dead milling about."

The pool was a kilometer out of town, close enough to be back by noon but far enough to give a sense of isolation. As we approached it, trees rose up and shrouded it. Entering the stand of trees, I asked Isidra what was special about La Corua. It was a rare moment when I asked a direct question about what we were up to. Her look was astounded and frustrated at once. She shook her head. "It never runs dry, no matter the drought. La Corua is the heart of nature," she said. "Now you don't need to ask any more questions."

The pool was half in shade, half in sun. In one direction, the cool shade of forest called us as the stream crept inland into rockier stretches. In the other, warm morning light lay on fields that stretched to the sea, a couple of kilometers in the distance. On our side of the pool large smooth stones were underfoot, while on the other a high bank rose up, storm eaten by rains. The pool was calm. Isidra invited us to remove our shoes and bathe our feet and arms. I asked if I could go a little farther, to which she replied, "You take your dip. Let's see if you ever come out of there. You won't be the first one *she* takes for their insolence. Light me a candle right there." This I did, and wondered, as I have time and again, at the peculiar atmosphere created by candlelight amid branches, roots, and river stones in daylight. Where daylight couldn't, candles reached into the murky wash of the dead that surrounded us at all times. There in the forest, at the edge of La Corua, the dead burbled forward into concrete shapes, and the shadows of Cucusa, Chacha Cairo, Ma' Isidra, and Loreto Sáez were called near. At a distance, others among the dead rose up like imposing trees and shadows moving below the surface of the pool.

Ankle deep in water, with Pica at her side, Isidra led a song for Yemayá, sovereign of the sea. She accented Yemayá's fierceness in the lyrics she chose. I wanted to ask why it wasn't Ochún we should invoke, she being sovereign over fresh water and therefore over pools like La Corua. But Ochún is a sovereign of love, and Isidra was there to fight. Given what she perceived to be the struggle of the days ahead, to call Ochún would have been a waste of breath. I would later learn that what lay in the depths of the pool was something torqued by Cuban-Congo values, a *madre de agua,* water mother, mother of water, which could be honored in Yemayá's terms but which was neither synonymous nor identical with her. The madre de agua that dwelt in depths at La Corua was one with the raw force of life, the electric vitality of nature, and the capricious indifference of death. The madre de agua was kindred with the life-giving, life-taking, deadly serious power of women.

Isidra's voice became more emphatic by the verse. With stern eyes she implored us to reply as a chorus, all of us determined to invoke the powers of protection and to attack with as much conviction as her. Teodoro was less than enthused to be on hand and had to be goaded. He got it, the mystery lurking in the depths of La Corua, the potential to tap directly into the seething powers of the dead that coursed through that place. But he wanted to be back in town. He had quickly developed a clientele of those who needed healing of the variety he promised. Teodoro bristled anytime he was simply expected to serve.

We concluded our praise for La Corua with one or two more songs. Between us, Teodoro and I carried back a pail of water. We loaded plastic bags with little river stones, pieces of a termite mound, and cuttings from bushes and trees Pica signaled to us. Pica, who was touched to the point of amusement by our interest in the shrubs and vines of the countryside, reached behind her front door once we were back at her house. She held a pair of stones. "Piedra de rayo," she said. "I found these after lightning strikes." In Havana Palo, of which Teodoro was a master practitioner, fulgurites, or "petrified lighting stones," are important in the bundles called *prendas, ngangas,* or *enquisos,* at the heart of the practice. He was stunned. Pica placed them in his hands to examine.

"No, no. You don't see them like this in Havana," he said. "A prenda with a lightning stone like this at its root will never fail." He looked at Pica wondering if she was giving them to him. She reached out gently and took them back.

"You stay sober and don't cause Isidra trouble while you are here. Maybe one of these will go home with you."

Pica's offer could not have been more welcome. Teodoro was spending all his time in the street, and for all his abjection he had sufficient charisma to charm people into buying him shots of watered-down, government-provisioned rum. That particular chemical brew is a yellowish murk and smells of diesel. In his lifetime, Teodoro had drunk hundreds of gallons of it. I have often wondered why the revolution supplies it in corner dispensaries across the country. Those dissolute little holes are frequented almost entirely by drunks, sleepily sunk in state-sponsored stupefaction.

Drunk and all, Teodoro healed those he met. He had picked up a couple of clients who were having him work Havana Palo against their foes. For this they paid him enough to keep drinking and to eat an occasional greasy fritter, the quintessential revolutionary fast food when it could be found. One of his clients was a woman in her thirties, confident in her bearing. She told him she was being cheated on. She wanted children by her husband, but they had been unsuccessful, and now she feared he would start another family. Teodoro suggested aggressive Palo remedies to win him back, and he promised results from one day to the next. Isidra expected him at her side with his Palo craft and considered anything else moonlighting. That night she needed the door secured, and it was all she could do to pull him away from his drinking and consulting.

Evening of the 14th and the sisters could feel the feast right around the corner. In forty-eight hours the house would fill with revelers, and it needed to be protected against any ill will that might come with them. The vast majority of those who would attend the bembé were going to come through the front door, and it could not go unprepared. The door of a house is a portal not only for bodies but also for their intentions, and more, for the dead that crowd around each person. Hundreds of people would cross that threshold, and there was no knowing who or what among the dead would accompany them. Worse, Yamilet was sure to employ Congo-inspired Palo craft to spoil the feast or cause real harm. Anything she intended would come through the door. For this reason alone it was worth the trouble to have brought Teodoro.

Isidra shut the double doors to the house with a long iron bar. She took long strands of *vencedor* [winner] and *vence batalla* [triumph in battle], herbs we gathered earlier in the day, which she hung as garlands over the door. Brackets holding the bar in place were tied with pieces of dark blue cloth, which is Yemayá's accessory. Horseshoes nailed to the doors immediately stood out. Isidra lodged a small tin crucifix in one. Against the door she placed Batalla and Cuatro Vientos, the Congo things she and Teodoro had brought from Havana. She had Ulises fetch Cucusa's Elégua stone from an adjacent room where the santos of the house were kept. Elégua was placed with the other things, and there she stood a machete. A bowl of water from La Corua stirred with hand-minced herbs [*omiero*] was brought out, and she further seasoned it with pinches of roasted dried corn and other substances.

I was sent to fetch a young rooster from among the animals we had gathered in the backyard. "The smallest one, the black one," Isidra specified. Feet away from where we were working, María, Pica's daughter, was sitting with Takako and my camera, laughing at the photos as she scrolled through. Teodoro took the rooster and without a pause started to pluck feathers from its neck.

"What are you doing?" said Isidra, stopping Teodoro short.

"I'm offering this bird to the door and all of the things we have gathered here. What do you want?"

"You're drunk. Are you going to offer that animal to the door without bathing its feet? Without rinsing its beak? Without first cleansing the knife with omiero [cooling herbal water]?"

She was right, and Teodoro immediately moved to remedy the situation. Taking a little clean water from a glass, also placed by the door, he quickly rinsed the animal's feet and mouth. Then, without pausing, he dipped the knife in the bowl of omiero. A quick peek at Isidra and he started to pluck its neck again.

"Stop. What are you about to do? Do you know anything?"

He looked at her in disbelief.

"Aren't you going to present it?" she said. "Go ahead, present it to me before you pull a single feather."

Abashed now, Teodoro followed her command. He went to present it to Eulalia, and Isidra stopped him again. "Only to me. I bought it, and it is me who is leading the fight to defend Cucusa's house." Those of us gathered didn't utter a peep. He touched the young bird to her hands then suspended it over her head, which he wouldn't dare touch. Without being prompted, Isidra began to speak the names of her dead: "Kimbito Sáez, Ma' Isidra Sáez, Cucusa Sáez, Tomasa Cairo, Ernesto Portilla, Loreto Sáez, Gobierno Cairo, Orfilio Ruíz, Ma' Josefa, Ma' Micaela O'Farril . . ." When she was finished, she knelt down, and without her having to say a word, everyone else knelt too, with the exception of María, who kept scrolling through pictures.

Isidra called out a Palo killing song, and Teodoro perfunctorily cut the head off the bird. He gently placed the head on a little plate in front of Cucusa's Elégua stone, then proceeded to let a few drops of blood fall on it. Every one of the gathered powers was fed a couple of drops, including the machete. The animal's blood was nearly exhausted. Teodoro stepped toward the door and with the stump of the rooster's neck drew equilateral crosses on the hinges and brackets, then on the door itself. He lowered the bird to the ground and placed weight on it, ensuring it was dead. Isidra then commanded all of us to pluck its feathers and use them to "dress" any stray drops of blood. Little feathers were placed over resting blood, including that congealing on the door, thus decorating it with little downy bits.

She then turned to divining whether things were set. She used four coconut shells trimmed into disks [*chamalongo*], which were proper to Cuban-Congo divination. The chamalongo coconut disks were "cooling" in a glass of clean water. She took them confidently and let them drop. They fell with a little clap, and all four of their concave sides were facing the floor. "Muerto parado," said Isidra. "One of the dead has taken a stand."

"Let's see," started Teodoro, "should this bird be cooked and split between the powers gathered here?" He moved to pick up the shells and test for an answer.

"Stop that," said Isidra beating him to the shells. "You don't know the first thing. I'm the one who asks in this house." Then, shaking the shells in her hands, she said, "Is the dead one standing here of this house?"

The shells fell all four facing up, a strong affirmative. "Alafia!" said Isidra. She pointed to the floor, picked up the shells carefully stacked, and said, "Kiss them." She extended her hand to each of us. "It's my mother. No need to ask further. Tomorrow we will go to the cemetery with a candle and flowers. We've been here all these days and have yet to visit the cemetery. Will this do?" Again she threw the shells; this time they fell two facing up, two facing down, also a strong affirmative. "Now, let's get that rooster roasted and split into four parts, one for each corner of the block."

A stillness settled over the house as Eulalia went to work on the bird. Ulises and I, both of us children of Elégua, were tasked with dropping brown paper packets with parts of the bird and hard candies at each intersection to prepare the way for Elégua.

In forty-eight hours the house would be filled with partygoers, and the feast would be full on. The earth still had to be fed for the dead. The altar in the corner of the living room had to be dressed, and a Spiritualist mass for the dead of the house had to be arranged. The cemetery had to be visited. And animals were yet to be found.

FIVE

A Meal for the Dead

THE MORNING OF THE 15TH, one of Chacha Cairo's grandchildren came by with news. Zenón had a friend with a car who had scrounged together some gasoline and wanted to make good on an animal he owed San Lázaro–Babalú Ayé. He would be driving into the countryside to find a rooster and invited Isidra to join him. Out there she would easily find whatever animals she still needed. Again, Eulalia was left to mind the house.

The Cuban countryside in Villa Clara Province in 1999 was quiet, fallow land. The roads away from the North Circuit were dead in 1999, dead beyond any travel. The driver, Hugo, took us down paved lanes barely wide enough for his sputtering four-door Russian Lada. Our trek took us south not far from the Palma Sola reservoir. "Can we see it?" I asked.

"Not a chance," replied Hugo. "There is a national security closure on it. Foreign infiltrators could poison it or blow up the dam. I'm not driving anywhere near it with a *yuma* in my car." "Yuma" was slang for someone from the United States.

We neared a village called San Pedro, and Hugo pulled up to a dirt track blocked by a barbed-wire fence. "Jump out. You can see the first house there in the distance. Ask for animals there. Then, have them point you to the next house, then the next. Keep going, I'll meet you in an hour at the road where you'll come out."

Isidra gave him a doubtful look.

"There's no getting lost, trust me. Just keep a rock in your hand for the frisky dogs and cattle!"

There was maybe a kilometer between the homesteads. These were clapboard houses roofed with palm fronds, some with dirt floors. There were cattle to fight off between the ample yards, and the dogs were nervous and fierce. Some yards were fenced by cactus woven through barbed wire. Fence posts were lengths of train rail that had been cut and planted in the ground, five feet high. Similarly, large metal disks were laid down as pavers across soggy spots in the yards. These were from Soviet-era plows, which must have once worked the surrounding land into the vast Cuban sugar economy. In what reality do you have so much leftover train rail and plow blades that they can be used as fence posts and pavers? A house had a roof made not of thatched palm fronds, or of asbestos-like cement sheeting, but of split open tractor tires. The number used was remarkable, but the effect was undeniable: a roof made of inch-thick, treaded rubber. Here was the heavy infrastructure of the Soviet bloc repurposed for life without oil, without the Soviet Union, which had collapsed eight years earlier.

The homesteads had chickens and roosters of various ages and colors, goats and rams of various ages, and finally turkeys. The menagerie of domestic animals, most of which had a place at the table of one or another santo-orisá, thrilled Isidra. She was eager to buy since the prices were a third lower than she could find in town, half the price of animals in Havana. Harder was getting the housewives to sell. Most wanted their husbands to give the final word. When would they be back? Would they be willing to part with the animals without permission if we paid a little more? Hard was also getting the women to part with the bits of string or rope that would allow us to carry or lead the animals back to the road. Eventually, we bought roosters for 50 Cuba pesos apiece, and a goat for 160 pesos. Hugo met us on the veranda of the last house on our itinerary, his car parked not far away. A beautiful *jabao* rooster for San Lázaro was tied between his feet. *Jabao,* as a descriptor for a rooster rather than a person, was still telling of Cuban racialization. It means a rooster with "mixed-mixed" plumage [*plumas remezcladas*], but with the lightest possible color that isn't white around the neck, which turns out to be a creamy white with nearly translucent yellow highlights on the ends of the feathers, with possibly some light gray flecks.

Our return trip took us through San Pedro, a hamlet attached to an agricultural cooperative. It was but a crossing. A desultory ration dispensary [*bodega*] took up one corner. A medical post, a building that housed the local CDR, and a cafeteria for the co-op workers sat at the others. A cloudy, flavorless punch was the only thing on hand at the cafeteria, and we glugged it with relish. Isidra, always a gleaner at the fringes of the centralized Cuban economy, peeked into the medical post. A doctor slept over a desk. Isidra took pleasure in waking her up to ask if she had laxatives (or anything else for that matter). She needed these for a nephew of hers who had a stubbornly entrenched case of giardia. It so happened the doctor had a small box of laxatives, but when she picked up that we were from Havana, she nailed us with a 400 percent markup. This essentially made our "over the counter" purchase a black market one as the doctor pocketed the difference. With a box of very expensive laxatives and a trunk full of very inexpensive animals, including a turkey to spare, we left San Pedro quickly behind.

We were delighted to have made it back to town before noon so we were not in the countryside when the dead moved about. Isidra went immediately to feed the earth, which would establish propitious conditions for the feast. She wanted to honor the earth and Orisá Óko, sovereign over the earth, the soil, and the things that emerge from this. "Babalú Ayé, too, has a pact with the earth," said Isidra. Everything the earth gives, including nourishment, fertility, harvests of all kinds, and tombs for the dead, should be repaid with occasional "feedings." Isidra had a rooster and pigeon ready to offer, along with plates of dried corn, beans, and rice, each of these a "return" to the earth. Complex ceremonial sequences that can last several days, like bembés, are prepared for by feeding the earth, which will propitiate the dead and establish the basic conditions of success: vitality, productivity, increase, and extension.

I was sent to hunt up Teodoro, but Isidra didn't want me moving about on my own. "Go with Ester," she said. "Too many things are afoot in the street. The last thing I need is for you to be taken down the day before this party is supposed to happen." Ester was one of the people who had showed up over the last couple of days to help. She was Zenón's daughter, Chacha Cairo's great-granddaughter, rough cut in her features, trim, and muscular. She had new scars on her face and body. "They are from when I was thrown in prison," she said. "My lover and I almost killed each other because she was sleeping around. I'm jealous, especially if my girls get with men. We had it out right in the street, and she was good with a knife. I was in prison for a year, and all I did there was fuck [*zingar*] women. That fight made it so everyone in town knew I like women. I don't care what anyone thinks. Cucusa understood me, though. San Lázaro always understood." Ester was resourceful and direct. In Isidra's company she was docile and fulfilled any request. Isidra trusted no one who had fallen out with the revolution, but Ester was an exception.

We found Teodoro the first place she thought to look. Ester was familiar with him by now, since she was a denizen of those small-town streets. "We'll find him where the rum is. That's with José." He was the fisherman, husband of Roberto's daughter, Celita. Teodoro had been at their place most of the morning working a cure for Celita, and drinking.

Celita was Isidra's niece, the daughter of Roberto by way of his marriage with Celia M., daughter of Lázaro M. Like her mother, Celita was beautiful, *mulata* by local standards since she had a pointed nose and cinnamon skin. Her hair was a little too dark for a mulata, and in Havana they might have held her to be "Black," but here in town her glowing, reddish, burnished skin was mulata all day. In her youth she was the pride of her family, her town, and ultimately of the revolution.

Along with her two brothers, theirs was the first generation born within the revolution, raised within it, with its horizons set by the aspirations of Cuban socialism. She and her brothers were country kids in the mid- to late sixties, but even as preschoolers they were integrated into the revolution's ambitious education system. Roberto, their father, as director of the CDR, was a figure within the town party apparatus, so opportunities to connect to larger national programs and initiatives did not slip by. When Celita was ready for high school, she was shipped off to study engineering in Havana. Her brothers remained behind. Celita lived in Havana with her aunt Isidra, in the apartment the revolution had given her in the early 1960s. A rising star, Celita was selected for university studies in Bulgaria, then part of the Soviet bloc.

She was there for seven years and learned both Bulgarian and Russian. When the Soviet bloc collapsed with the Berlin wall in 1989, with them went Bulgaria's international cooperation accords, of which Cuba was a privileged beneficiary. Celita was stranded in Sofia and after months began a winding odyssey through post-Soviet Russia that took her to Moscow and eventually Helsinki. An all-or-nothing black market vodka deal on the border between Russia and Finland bought her ticket home.

She returned to a country in crisis, wracked by perilous doubts about the way forward for the revolution. Her generation was committed to the social-ist future in their hearts and bones. The revolution could not have lost a more precious resource than those young people, prepared and trained for a future now laid bare and worthless. She landed back at her aunt's in Havana some-time in 1990, but the city was terrifying for its interminable blackouts and its nearly starving populace. Cienfuegos, where her aunt Eulalia lived, was no better. Besides, Eulalia had nowhere to lodge her. She had never been given housing of her own by the revolution. Celita chose to return home to her town of two thousand people to be with her parents, Roberto and Celia, and maybe follow her brothers into the local party posts they had achieved.

In 1999 she was in her mid-thirties and childless. Her marriage to José, another wide-traveling local spat back onto Sierra Morena's stoop by the crisis, was seen by his family as a step up, but by hers as a defeat. Celita was poised to become someone of rank within the party apparatus, maybe nationally, and now she was back home and married to a laid-off local. José had seen Cuba from one tip to another as a truck driver and had enjoyed Havana on a trucker's wages, which in the 1980s were substantial given the fuel that could be siphoned off and sold on the side. The diesel dried up with the collapse, as did the parts to keep the Soviet-designed Pegaso and Taino semitrucks running. Back home, José took to running numbers in the underground lottery. When I met him in 1999, he brought in 2,000 to 3,000 pesos a day, which was huge money. The money reflected how popular the numbers game was with people in town, who had always enjoyed gambling. Isidra thought the numbers game out of step with the revolution, but José took Eulalia's bets, and she never missed a day. When he wasn't running numbers, José was fishing. His catches attested to his skill and to the richness of the waters. It kept his family fed and also made him one of the town's go-to underground fish purveyors. He worked hard at the wrong things, as far as Roberto and Celia were concerned.

Fresh red snapper was frying on the charcoal fire out back. José greeted us by offering us a sip of rum. In 1999 Cuba, this was lavish. He pointed toward the house.

"Your Congo is with her," he said. "She can't get pregnant. She's tried every specialist from here to Sagua la Grande to Santa Clara. Excellent doctors, but they failed. She's seen every healer here in town. She's crazy for a baby, and now she's getting depressed. Let's see what your big-town *brujo* can do for us." He raised his eyebrows and smiled a perplexed, bitter expression.

Teodoro had her kneeling in her small living room, a candle lit next to a small conch shell in a bloodied terracotta dish. This was her Elégua. His four-faced figurine, Cuatro Vientos, was there too. Celita told me earlier that the little statue made an impression on her. Cuban-Congo Palo cryptograms [*firmas*] were drawn on the floor in chalk. He was throwing the coconut shell chamalongo to discern the path through her affliction, but he was hard to understand because his speech was full of ritual Creole-Kikongo, which he was highly proficient in. She was not the only person in town taken by his "Congo" speech. Young people, like Ester, loved to hear him rattle off Palo phrases as if they were the latest slang from the big city; still others, like Pica, thought it the sure sign of a huckster. I had seen Teodoro work in Havana, and his weakness was that he could be too perfunctory and brusque with clients, blurting out insinuations of cheating lovers or soon-to-be-ill children. With Celita it seemed to me that he was improvising, drawing a perfunctory consultation into an elaborate scene. A meal of fried fish and a glass of rum was set on the table. He was already drunk, but neither Celita nor José seemed to consider this either a character flaw or a fault in the consultation he was imparting. Celita cried quietly as he worked.

"Tremendo brujo," José said with a touch of humor as he sat back, sipping rum. "That's a hell of a sorceror."

"You don't think so?" I asked.

"What do I know? Havana Palo is beyond me. Congo things here in town are perfectly strong. If it works for her, the better."

The government-provisioned rum was vile. José smiled at my dismay as I swallowed.

"I drink two liters of this a day, and I give away a liter a day. Who doesn't come here for a sip? Look at Ester—she's salivating. Two liters a day and a liter of milk—to kill the ulcer." He grinned.

It was only Ester who managed to pull Teodoro away from the sorcery he worked and the spell of liquor he was under. Her tact and intelligence in nudging him away from the bottle were in contrast to Isidra's reaction when she saw him.

. . .

"Don't you know why I brought you to Sierra Morena? Are you that daft?"

"Isidra, what?"

"What? We are out there breaking our backs to make sure we have animals for tomorrow's bembé. To get the things we need in this house, to prepare the altar. Did you think we couldn't use your help with all of that?"

Teodoro looked at her. She continued, "What was the plan for today? Get the earth fed. Get a *misa* [Spiritualist mass] said for my mother. The feast breaks open at midnight tomorrow. Your plan was to spend the day drinking with José and eating like a maharaja. Great, so now I am supposed to work with a drunk *obá*."

"I'm not drunk, and I'm not an obá," he said plainly. An obá is a Havana ritual specialist who has knowledge of a great number of Ocha-Santería works and has the consecrated rights to execute them. Teodoro was very capable and could execute any work better than most obás, but he was a

Havana *palero* without any Havana Ocha-Santería initiations, and he refused its titles.

Isidra looked at him with frustration bordering on disgust. "Well, now you are working for me. Get the hole dug."

We had help with the task. A cousin of Isidra's, Justo, was the local gravedigger and cemetery keeper, and like Ester he had showed up over the last many days to lend a hand. He was mute. Who better to dig a hole for the dead than a mute gravedigger? Every shovelful of earth in the backyard was a dip into the former lives of that house. Shards of tiles and brick, shards of dishware, old nails, bits of metal, a marble, splinters of wood and animal bones and plastic remains. Archaeologists would have easily distinguished the cockfighting strata. What belonged to it, and what to the once lively rooms Cucusa had built for her older sons, Máximo and Roberto? What did we disturb to propitiate the earth now? What previous structures once enjoyed by the living? What previous holes and previous meals to the dead? These questions did not matter. Our hole would propitiate them in the present, would let them know they were not forgotten and that we needed them for our plans to succeed; that from the oceanic expanse of the dead, we wanted them near.

Isidra had everything ready. The young rooster, candles, cane liquor, seasoned cooking wine, the toasted corn, the dried fish, the smoked hutia, and plates of everyday grains. All members of her family had to be present. The benefits of this meal should spread to the whole family. Any one of them could be a vector for ill will or other dangerous potentials to enter the feast. Yet only Eulalia, Ulises, and his young cousins, Boby and Anelé, were on hand. Roberto, a linchpin in the effort to host the feast, was missing, as was Celia, his wife. Máximo and his wife, Cyrilla, still had not arrived from Santa Clara. Celita and José did not show. Zulia, Isidra's half sister from Corralillo, should have come days ago to help and now wouldn't come until the morning. Our meager crew consisted of Ester and her father, Zenón, and Pica and her daughter, María. Takako was there, and her admirer, Yunier. Iván, the kid farmer and would-be drummer at Cucusa's feast, was there.

Teodoro was ready to go straight to the offering of the animal, a young rooster. Isidra stopped him, again correcting him. She wanted to proceed along the lines of Havana Ocha-Santería ritual. Apparently, this particular meal to the earth had been prescribed by Isidra's Havana-based babalao, a well-regarded ritual master and musician named Papo Angarica. Teodoro refused.

"I don't know how," he claimed.

Back in Havana, Ocha and Ifá are the prestige African-inspired societies. They are considered ritually cool and refreshing compared to Palo, which is considered dangerously hot. Teodoro was a master of Congo-inspired Palo healing-harming craft, which these societies tended to fear or denigrate. He was stubborn in rejecting Ocha and Ifá things, styles, and values. He knew them well and thought he knew better. Isidra said that all paleros eventually arrive at Ocha initiations, to cool them from all the hot work they do. He resented being asked to act within those ritual boundaries.

"Do what you know, then," she said.

"Kneel, then," he said.

She did, next to the hole.

"First things first," he said. "I need aguardiente. Give me aguardiente."

It was Eulalia who was holding the bottle of cane liquor. This was a clear, bright liquor from a government chemist whose income came from running an underground still in Havana. She offered him the bottle. He took an enormous mouthful, and proceeded to blow it in a fine mist all over Isidra's face and chest. He repeated the operation on the rooster to be offered, and on the hole itself. Then he took a long swallow for himself. He took the cigar I was smoking, inverted it in his mouth, then proceeded to blow smoke over Isidra, the animal, and the hole.

"Dump that in," he said to Eulalia, pointing at the plates of grains and tubers Isidra had prepared.

Eulalia responded only after noting no protest from her sister.

"Now get me two railroad spikes."

Again looking to Isidra for a protest and receiving none, she quickly shuffled to and from the house. Railroad spikes are basic ritual matter in Palo work. In Palo they are used to goad situations of all sorts. We had pulled a dozen from an abandoned track outside town a couple of days back. "These are worth gold in Havana," said Teodoro.

He took the spikes from Eulalia and inscribed them with egg shell chalk. Then he pulled out a packet about the size of a deck of cards double wrapped in brown paper. He called a song used in Palo for charging works of sorcery. Our meager chorus responded, with the locals mumbling along, seemingly uncomfortable with the direction events had taken. This was no longer a local meal for the dead, or even one inflected by Havana-style ritual. Unfolding one sheet of paper, he asked Isidra and Eulalia to write the names of the people they wanted "buried." While they did this, he held the packet in his hand. Once they had written the intended recipients of the work, Teodoro folded everything back up along with some sawdust and colored powders. "Bilongo," he said, pointing at the work. He liberally sprayed it with aguardiente and allowed himself another swallow before he settled it in the hole amid clouds of cigar smoke. He drove the two railroad spikes on the left and right of the packet. This he did to "goad" [*arrear*] or "nail" [*clavar*] the work, to drive the bilongo home.

Zenón, Chacha Cairo's grandson and Ester's father, was sitting in a chair leaning on the wall of the house, carefully observing while keeping out of the way. He was unimpressed. To his eyes this was Havana shenanigans gone totally off the rails. Minutes before, Iván, the drummer, had left the scene. Later, Iván asked me why Isidra was giving such a fool the lead. Those of us who stayed did so out of a sense of obligation or out of a desire to see things conclude more correctly than not. Some of the locals, like Zenón, appeared to stay out of morbid curiosity. Pica and her daughter, María, were the exceptions, lending the ritual local credence by their dutiful responses to Isidra's calls.

Teodoro again bathed the young rooster in liberal sprays of cane liquor, then a cloud of cigar smoke. He presented the animal to Isidra, who was still kneeling. The only instruction she gave was to cleanse everybody. All present lined up to be swept by the bird, which Teodoro held by the feet. He finally swished the bird over Isidra's body.

A knife had been readied, and as Justo held the animal's wings and feet, he perfunctorily cut the head off. The blood was directed onto the contents of the hole, especially on the packet. Isidra then stood and "took" the song from Teodoro, directing her calls in more aggressive tones toward the house next door. Encouraging the chorus to lift their voices, neighbors on all sides were treated to a litany of accusations, exhortations, and threats that she issued in the verses she sang. We were complicit in the challenges she issued that night.

The rooster was tossed into the hole, and Justo, Isidra's cemetery keeper cousin, was asked to fill it. Isidra directed me to fetch a pair of candles and light them in the loose soil. The work was finished with a small bouquet of local wildflowers. A bottomless garbage can was put over the candles to keep them lit and to keep anything from disturbing the site.

The meal to the earth began as nourishment and communication with the ancestral dead of the house, was torqued by Isidra through Havana Ocha-Santería ritual, and then became a scene of Havana Palo sorcery. That the same hole could serve these purposes, that the various intentions, gestures, and performance genres could be combined, or braided, was taboo in Havana, but signature small-town Isidra. The recombination of the two ritual sequences, the West African–inspired meal, and the Congo-inspired bilongo burial, would be reflected in the bembé to come, where such recombinations were not only acceptable but expected.

The evening of the 15th settled on us. In twenty-four hours the house would fill with family, townsfolk, and people from the surrounding country-side, all devotees of San Lázaro–Babalú Ayé. Eulalia prepared the altar in the corner of the room where the gathering would take place. Each shelf was carefully cleaned. She gingerly pulled the figurines of the santos from their places. She lovingly removed their robes. Between Takako and I, there were gifts of purple satin and beads that she had made into new vestments for the San Lázaro statuettes. She had me wash the plastic flowers of their grime, and together we braided them with Christmas lights I had found in Havana. Pope John Paul II had visited Havana the year before, and the popular under-standing was that Christmas was back after nearly forty years. Lights and little plastic trees did not tarry in arriving in the dollars shops. Eulalia and I hung what purple cloth remained as bunting. A portrait of Fidel Castro, of 1970s vintage, hung in the corner opposite.

The morning of the 16th, San Lázaro's Eve, and the bembé approached. People came by with sheet cakes and other sweets, like brown sugar maca-roons, which were laid on the floor before the altar as gifts for San Lázaro–Babalú Ayé. A woven basket with homemade sugar candies was placed next to these. The grade school was down the street, and in the morning Isidra beckoned children on their way to class to have one. She made a point of complimenting each child—one was pretty, one was tall, one had straight pretty hair, another had light skin. Isidra knew almost all their parents and grandparents and had anecdotes and memories to impart as the children and their families came and went.

After lunch, Roberto came by, huffing.

"Máximo is here. He is coming. Now we'll see!"

Eulalia smiled, "Just now?"

Isidra had just returned from Corralillo, where she had gone to the munic-ipal police to request the necessary permit for the feast. She was still cooling down. "I don't want any acting out. It's too late for that. Where were you and Celia and Celita yesterday when we fed the earth? That was the time to pound your chest. The people next door have been dealt with. Who do you think stepped up for that? You see her talking to you. Our job now is to keep things under control. Whose name is on this permit from the police? You see her talking to you. We're going to keep it cool. Look at this beautiful room. Look at that altar!"

If Roberto was tall, Máximo was broad. The two brothers shared with Isidra that reddish complexion. Their hair was a similar thick, glossy black, with shine before texture. Máximo was stocky, with a good belly hanging over his dollars store jeans. His shoes were sharp and shiny. Those who knew the dress codes of the countryside could not miss the broadcast of a midlevel party functionary, dressing well and eating well. His face was hung with a jowl, and his eyes were discerning and quick. His wife, Cyrilla, stood behind him in the doorway, shorter and broader than he, and much darker. She was already dressed for the feast and looked exhausted.

Isidra's greeting was surprisingly cordial, even deferential. Eulalia joined her in welcoming Máximo, Cyrilla, and their daughter Yancie into Cucusa's house, offering them glasses of cold water. They had in fact made the trip from Santa Clara in a borrowed party car, a well-preserved Lada sedan, that Máximo had to return in two days' time. Cyrilla admired the clean and orderly scene in the living room.

Then Isidra turned from accommodating sibling to bembé host. "And the ram?" she asked.

"The ram?" said Máximo.

"Máximo, the only animal we don't have is the ram for Changó. The feast is *now,* and the ram for Changó was promised by you."

"By me? How am I supposed to arrive with a ram from Santa Clara?" He looked around to gather support for his incredulity.

"You came in a car."

"In a party car? A ram? Shitting all over the trunk? Where would Cyrilla and I have put our things?"

"You didn't have to bring it from Santa Clara. You could have squared it here. Roberto is here. Eulalia and I have been here for a week. The countryside is full of animals."

"Why didn't you just get me a ram, then?"

"Máximo, you promised that ram to Changó. You made that promise, and now you have to keep it. That includes the sweat and tears of finding the animal."

"How many rams have you passed up? I would have paid you."

"Stop bullshitting [*No seas comemierda*]," Isidra said flatly. "If I broke my butt for a ram, on whose behalf do you think I would give that animal? On my behalf. I need Changó's favor as much as anyone, so don't expect me to break my back for you. My currency is sweat and tears, brother. How much of that have you got in your pockets?" She turned away to end the conversation.

Máximo raised his voice, "*Comemierda?* Bullshitter? Sweat and tears? Do you know what I do every day for this revolution? Do you know what I was doing until last night? Do you know what I gave up to be here?"

"The revolution is the revolution, and Changó is Changó," said Isidra. "Money for the revolution, and sweat and tears for Changó. Or is it the other way around?"

With that she left the room, drawing Eulalia behind her.

SIX

Opening

IT WAS NINE O'CLOCK ON THE NIGHT OF THE 16TH, and the feast was prepared: the house was in order, cleaned from top to bottom, dusted, mopped, the walls washed. The street corners had been secured, the door had been worked, the earth fed, and the dead thoughtfully invoked. The animals were gathered, and the kitchen was assembled, with Zulia the half sister from Corralillo and Agripina the cousin from Sagua on hand to cook the animals. There were animals for each santo-orisá invited to join San Lázaro–Babalú Ayé at his party. The altar was lit. The double doors were flung open in welcoming and confidence. Anyone walking though those doors would be safe, and the gifts and blessings of the santos-orisás would rain down.

Women and children arrived first. If you had white to wear, you wore it. People were perfumed, rarely worn jewelry was on, and gardenias adorned splendid hair. Each arrival took a moment to greet the santos on the altar and pay their respects to the statues of Lazarus the Beggar that presided there.

In the "last hour before San Lázaro," Isidra fluttered about, giving orders where things needed doing. Eulalia was her chief of staff, and her minions included Zulia and Agripina from Sagua, Yunier and Takako, Justo, and me. Teodoro was nowhere to be found. The young folks, Ulises and his cousins, were dutifully nearby. Family and friends arrived by the handful. Máximo and Cyrilla were there with plenty of time, and Yancie was with them. Celita and José were present as well. Roberto and Celia arrived last.

Shortly before midnight, musicians crowded around the drums. Isidra had brought two *tumbadoras* [conga drums] from Havana, borrowed from a graduate student in anthropology at UCLA who was taking dance lessons from her. She would later buy those drums and move them permanently to town. A third tumbadora was borrowed from Zenón, Chacha Cairo's grandson, who was on hand.

Isidra was cordial, charming, and attentive. She knew everyone, their parents, grandparents, their children. Her memory for people and their lives was extraordinary. People filled the room to capacity, and groups were on the sidewalk and in the street, crowding the tall barred windows just behind the drummers. Pica and her daughter, María, were there too.

At the stroke of midnight, December 17, Isidra took the middle of the room and knelt. The crowd followed her. Shaking a maraca, she called the gathering to order. She sang:

"Eh bambalu! Eh bambalu! Eh bambalu-bamba-lubeya! Eh bambalu-bamba-lubeya!"

The crowd instantaneously became her chorus: "Bambalu-bamba-lubeya!"

She called, "Eh bambalu! Eh bambalu! Eh bambalu-bamba-lubeya! Eh bambalu-bamba-lubeya!"

We replied, "Bambalu-bamba-lubeya!"

Isidra called this a "reso," or "prayer." It was sung a cappella, without drums. Cucusa's was the only house to start a bembé this way. It was Cucusa's prayer, and together we sang it in her voice. Later, some of those in attendance told me they came just to be present for *that* prayer and all the goodness it could impart.

Isidra rose to her feet and addressed Elégua: "Saluda santo, saluda Elégua!" [Greet the santos, greet Elégua!]

The chorus followed, and only with their response to her did the drums join to "break" the feast open and bring the bembé to life.

With an imperceptible glance, Isidra passed the call to Pica, who took it from her without missing a beat. She called out several more Elégua songs. Elégua is orisá of the threshold and the portal. He is the one to open, the first to cross, the first to enter, so he is first in the repertoire of orisás sung into relevance at a Sierra Morena bembé, just as he is the first invoked and sung into relevance in Havana and throughout Cuba. Elégua is master of beginnings.

"Elégua primero que to'!" Pica sang. "Elégua before everything!"

The crowd, which was on its feet and dancing, took up the Elégua songs with intensity driven by cheer.

"Elégua primero que to'!"

Not a half hour into the opening did the santos-orisás begin to mount their steeds. María, Pica's daughter, was mounted by Elégua, first among sovereigns. Santos-orisás look upon a feast to choose a mount from among those dancing. They like dancers whose movements honor their personalities, stories, or powers. A great dancer is a delightful sight for a santo-orisá, and will likely be chosen. They are easy to mount in that their steps anticipate the steps of the santos-orisás. A dancer like María will be mounted with barely a sign that it is now a santo-orisá who holds the reins. She danced Elégua's songs with verve, subtly performing the actions for which he is recognized, including parting underbrush and lithely skipping forward down the newfound path. It was auspicious that Elégua was the first to choose a mount and visit the bembé. María was a well-known mount for him, and the chorus welcomed the santo-orisá with a new flight of praise songs for him led by Pica, María's mother.

Eulalia put a *guajiro's* [farmer's] wide-brimmed straw hat on the newly arrived Elégua and offered him aguardiente from a little gourd. Elégua received this with a robust hug and a crack of laughter. Santos-orisás love that their devotees furnish them with insignia items, and with the hat and liquor, María's Elégua was pleased. He danced in vibrant, broad, perfectly timed steps and turns, handling the considerable weight of his steed with the grace of a great equestrian master.

María's Elégua was loquacious. A santo-orisá should come to a bembé in Sierra Morena ready to speak. Eulalia had just provided him with his favorite accoutrements, and he turned to her. Through his words, Elégua imparted views on events past and those to come. Old things he saw anew, and things not yet come he saw for the first time. On one side of his words was the past, on the other was the future. The time of the santo-orisá is the immediate present, time out of time, a time of lives in the midst of their midst, nestled in history but still to come. The santos-orisás are just this, embodiments of what is to come, of what can be. They are masters of potential and becoming.

Elégua's words for Eulalia were such that she and Isidra shepherded the great santo-orisá into their bedroom, where his counsel could be more carefully attended and where his wisdom would not escape, or be overheard by others. Elégua is the protector and keeper of boundaries, and zones of uncertainty, which we had been trying to secure since our arrival. He addressed the struggle they faced with Yamilet. His words were prized, and Isidra and Eulalia knew at once that Elégua would aid their struggle to keep their home safe and regain their lost possessions.

When Elégua reemerged from the bedroom, he had a cigar in his mouth and was beaming along with the two sisters at his side. Already, a group was lining up to greet him, to be touched by him, to be spoken to by this great orisá of beginnings and crossings, and of terrain unknown. We are all subjects of his realm—which is all the in-between places and moments in our lives. Elégua is master of the middle ground and of the movement needed to traverse it. He is sovereign over the changes that movement seeks and brings. His realm includes all projects and endeavors, existing as these do in the past and future at once. If the revolution had been smart, or less dogmatically Marxist-Leninist, it would have adopted Elégua as its patron deity. That the revolution accomplished all it has is evidence of his blessings; that it failed in so many of its accomplishments is evidence of his scorn. They were foolish not to claim him. There in Cucusa's living room there was not a person who would disavow him. Everyone wanted a word with Elégua. All around the dancing and drumming continued unabated with the chorus enthusiastically responding to the calls Pica made.

Moments later, Zulia from Corralillo, Cucusa's daughter by Lupercio Cairo and her first child after the five she had with Orfilio Ruíz, felt the shock of receiving an orisá on her back. Orisás are overwhelming to receive. They are enormous personages who draw their power as much from the present-day devotion of countless people as from ancestral authority, which is oceanic in its dimensions. To carry such a personage, to pull it off or achieve it, requires great self-composure and not a little practice. Zulia appeared to have neither.

She was a robust woman, fifty years old, and, like her half siblings Roberto and Máximo, broad jawed and reddish in complexion, though a little darker. Her half sisters regularly remarked on this and reminded anyone listening of Orfilio's light skin compared with the much darker Lupercio. Zulia wore a tight navy blue dress, and her black hair was cut just above the shoulders, which accentuated the directness of her movements. These included attempts to spin in place and to move her shoulder blades rhythmically. But each move was also interrupted by a jerk, a push of energy seemingly too much for her limbs to carry. This was Oyá, orisá of storms and the cemetery gate, trying her as a mount, but she was too much for Zulia. She could not anticipate Oyá in her dancing, so her attempts to carry the santo-orisá and effectively "bring her down" onto her back failed in lunges forward and precipitous back pedaling, which the surrounding mass of chorus bore with aplomb. It was clear she was not going to succeed. Eulalia, who did much of the orisá tending in the house, tried to get a hand on her, but she was nearly bowled over. Zenón had been watching carefully from a spot next to the drummers. He stepped in and almost without touching her drew the writhing Zulia around. He placed his hand on her cheek below her ear and like an equestrian groom with the halter in his fingers gently guided her toward a chair, which was quickly vacated. With select words he calmed her, and with a carefully timed puff of air to each ear, Oyá was gone. Zulia slumped, her head lowered.

María's Elégua presided for a good while, until Pica tired of calling songs. She had gotten some way through the sequence of santos-orisás, singing songs for each. Zenón took the call without being asked. Zenón was fifty years old, and Pica was twenty years his senior. Together they had been calling bembés for a more than a decade, since the death of Ingo, the main singer for Chacha's Sociedad Africana. Ingo was Chacha Cairo's adopted daughter and Zenón's mother. Pica and Zenón were the prized pair of callers for any bembé, and they probably sang together at a dozen feasts a year. Each of them hosted a feast for Changó early in December.

Zenón was a beloved singer. He was younger, louder, more of a showman and consequently more popular. His songs used less *lengua* [language], less terms in Ewe or Fon or Yoruba, which were the languages of the people from which his community descended. Consequently, they were easier to follow, and the response he drew from the chorus was rousing.

Pica's rest was short. She took a sip of aguardiente and sat for a minute before standing up and dancing. Zenón could see Pica tend toward Changó before she was mounted and readily changed his songs, bringing the chorus and the drummers around to calls for her santo-orisá. Changó took possession of her gracefully. Pica knew Changó so well, had carried him so many times, that he required no effort to take on. Readily, the sovereign of warfare was in the room. Changó was Pica's santo, whom she had "received" from her father, Loreto. She inherited Changó from him as she had inherited his square jaw and almond eyes. There had been no initiation as would be required in Havana. As she had received her button nose from Loreto in the nature of her genes, she had received his Changó as "second nature" in the course of hundreds of bembés where she had seen him take on Changó for his community. The chorus greeted him with raised voices, their energetic responses to Zenón a resounding cry of approval.

Changó, sovereign of warfare and victory, is the prime ally of every warrior, every soldier, and every fighter. He is the guide for those who must fight even if they would rather not. In a fight, the party favored by Changó will prevail. His double-headed battle ax is his insignia—with one blade he defends life, and with another he takes it. His prowess in a fight, offensive or defensive, condenses in his ax. He is a law-giving sovereign and life-shielding protector. Pica danced Changó's ax, mimicking his handling of the weapon in the movement of her arms. Sometimes Changó swung it with two arms, sometimes he displayed it in one hand.

Changó wields another weapon, one more fearsome than his ax, which Pica reflected in her dancing. Changó controls lightning, which he generates spontaneously in his core. He wields this with his hands, effortlessly holding the fluid, brilliant energy. Making no apologies for his maximum virility, which Changó also commands and distributes to his preferred children, the lightning is harnessed in his crotch. He reaches down, and from there he throws the lighting at will. Pica danced this, bending over and reaching low into her abdomen to then display the bolt of lightning above her head. With not an ounce of shame, with nothing but pride in the glory of Changó's rule, seventy-year-old Pica threw lightning for the chorus to receive.

"Pica's Changó works hard," said Celita, Isidra's niece. She was dancing next to me, approving of the turn the bembé had taken. "Santos here work. They help people. You won't see the santos dressed up fancy and putting on a dance show like I'm sure you've seen in Havana. Here they *work*." As she said this, she made a gesture for washing against a board, which was her sign for manual labor.

I kept my eyes on Pica as Zenón called song after song. Changó was dancing beautifully and hugging people between ax blows and lightning strikes. Picking up on my befuddlement, Celita continued, "They help people. Watch Pica's Changó. He is going to take care of everyone here. No one leaves here without some attention. He speaks."

Pica, seventy years old, hunchbacked and "lame" [*coja*] in one leg, was a fabulous dancer. She communicated so many of Changó's virtues in her steps. In her feet was his agility, in her calves his readiness, in her thighs his strength, and in her pelvis his virile audacity. In her back was the strength of a spring, in her core the womb of lightning, in her shoulders was Changó's fighting decisiveness. But more, in the tilt of her head, or the eye contact she made, or the touches she dispensed with her open hands, she communicated Changó's benevolence. After dancing among the chorus for a little while, the sisters shuttled Changó into their bedroom for a private consultation with this all-important santo-orisá. He returned barefoot with a red sash around his waist to work the crowded room, taking an interest in anyone in his path.

Pica's Changó conveyed his favor in a simple greeting. The great power would approach a dancer and open his arms wide, communicating his desire to take you into his arms. Simply receiving his eye contact was a gift. To be embraced by him was unambiguous affirmation of his intentions to shield you from anyone who might challenge you or seek to do you harm. His embrace said that in life's great struggles, you had the master of war on your side. From dancer to dancer Changó went, hugging and touching, making clear he was pleased with all gathered.

Pica's Changó was hard to understand, as santos-orisás so often are when they address you. He spoke in broken Spanish with an accent that projected his ancient provenance, that insinuated he was not Cuban but African. Verbs were not conjugated properly, especially those bound to the first person. The orisás come from elsewhere, from "Guinea" and "Dahomey," and the realm of the dead. Those who knew Pica's Changó understood him perfectly.

The house was overflowing with people, and the sidewalk outside was crammed with townsfolk, some watching through the doors, others gossiping and drinking. Everyone wanted a moment with Pica's Changó. He held forth for another hour, and it was not until 2 a.m. that Changó dismounted and left Pica slumped in a chair. The feast for San Lázaro–Babalú Ayé had cracked open brilliantly, and Isidra decided it was time to move on. The drummers were hard pressed to stop since they were just getting going and the chorus was likewise warmed up. It was only because her cousin, Justo the cemetery keeper, was on the big box that she could put her hand on it and stop the music. Without it the house soon cleared. By 3 a.m., Isidra and Eulalia were ready to get on with the feast itself. The santos-orisás would eat first.

SEVEN

Slaughter

CUCUSA'S HOUSE WAS BUILT AROUND ITS MAIN ROOM, with its altar to San Lázaro–Babalú Ayé and ample space for musicians and a chorus of feast-goers. Toward the back was the kitchen, and to the side next to Yamilet's house were two bedrooms. On the other side of the main room, set off by a curtain, was a large room, nearly a third of the house, reserved for the santos-orisás. It was there Cucusa kept her collection of bowls and plates holding river stones, conch shells, pieces of coral, and other things that were synonymous with the santos-orisás. It was there we would spend the early hours of December 17 feeding them. On hand were Isidra's family—her child Ulises; her sister; her brothers and their wives, children, and grandchildren, like Yancie, Anelé, and Boby; her half sister Zulia; her cousins Justo and Agripina; and close friends of the family, like Pica and María. Teodoro was there, as were Takako and I.

La matanza, the slaughter, is what folks in Sierra Morena call the ceremonial killing of animals to feast the santos-orisás. The term applies whether one animal is killed or many. It is preferred over terms like *offering [ofrenda]* (which I heard rarely) and *sacrifice [sacrificio]* (which I heard never), terms that anthropologists or devotees of biblical monotheism might expect. *Slaughter* is at once more graphic and appropriate to describe the event. The term as I understand it in English, which involves at its most basic the systematic killing of many animals, is appropriate for what we were about to do. We prepared ourselves to kill more than twenty animals, including goats, roosters, chickens, pigeons, guinea hens, and a turkey.

At a very basic poetic and at once cosmological level, this slaughter, the very bloodletting about to ensue, *was* the feast. None of us present in the room was invited to partake. The remainder of the night, Isidra and her family would host the santos-orisás, serve them, please them, and praise them.

The santos-orisás would eat among themselves as we provided meal after meal. We prepared the house for them, invited them with entreaty after entreaty in the music we played for them, and offered them steeds to ride. Now we would bring their animals forward and offer them.

People are selective about the animal flesh they eat: which animals are preferred and which are forbidden; what pieces of the animal are preferred and what pieces are forbidden; which organs; then, how the pieces should be cut; finally, we obsess over how the meat is prepared, presented, and served.[1] The santos-orisás are more selective yet. Each sovereign eats only a few animals, which must be of a specified age, size, sex, and color. After this, so choosy are they that all they want to eat is the blood, served directly from the animal, warm and raw. This is the sustenance on which the santos-orisás thrive. They eat it to the exclusion of the people serving them, who taste not a drop. Later, select prepared organs are presented separately to each santo-orisá according to their tastes. People eat the following day, stews and soups that are made from the flesh that remains of the orisás' meal and that they have left behind. This meat, clean and propitious by virtue of having been brought into dear closeness to the orisás, we would cut, chop, slice, spice, marinate, heat, braise, sear, scald, score, truss, steep, steam, and stew into the hallmark dishes of Cuban Creole cuisine.[2]

For their blood meals we had four-legged animals—goats [cuatro patas]. These animals were considered the most robust, healthiest, richest fare, and thus what the orisás preferred. The blood that pours from a goat or a ram is substantial compared to what spills from any fowl, even a rooster in the fullness of its life. The animals must be blemish free, healthy, and cleaned before being handled for the meals. Most of our animals were gifts and were in fabulous condition. It would be odd to fulfill a promise to a santo-orisá with a less than beautiful animal, as if they wouldn't notice. Having received finery since time immemorial and being accustomed to such luxuries, they are exquisite judges of quality. If Babalú Ayé saves you or heals you or your family, and you thank him with a gift of his preferred animal, a mature goat, at his next feast, the last thing you are going to do is offer up a shabby animal. These animals had been carefully chosen, perhaps even raised and cared for, to be meals for the santos-orisás. Before the animals are offered, their faces are washed and their hooves rinsed with water.

Goats and rams do not like to be handled. The minute you touch them, they resist. Goats especially pull back. They don't like being bathed, and when they are pulled onto cement floors and their hooves slip, they become especially panicky. Even a small animal, a young goat, for example, needs a couple of dexterous and ready hands to walk it into the room where it will be offered. To be properly positioned above the bowls and plates that will receive their blood, they have to be lifted. No matter how devoted their handlers are to their ritual bath, they are dirty. They've come from farms outside of town. Their coats are dusty. Their hooves have picked up the dirt, even if it is not raining. Handling them, lifting them, wrestling them as they kick and twist—this is filthy work, and no one really wants to do it. Peripheral people, helpers and assistants, are usually asked to handle the animals. These are almost always young men or the married-in husbands of sisters and daughters.

José, Celita's husband, Ulises, Boby, and I were the principal animal handlers for our feast. We fed and watered them. We made sure they had not been stolen and had not escaped. When the time came, we bathed them and rinsed their snouts and hooves, then dragged them through the kitchen and living room into the room of the santos-orisás. We lifted them and held them for the senior men in the family who had the privilege of killing. After their blood was offered, we carried the animals from the room to the backyard, where they were hung up, skinned, and butchered. José and Justo were expert in this. Zulia, Agripina from Sagua, and other women helping in the kitchen took the meat from there.

No animals are easy to kill. Even a pigeon is strong. They fight, they kick, their feathers are slick, and their talons are sharp. Their horns offer you a purchase on the animal's life, just as they can goad you. The large animals weigh a lot, and men in their fifties and sixties would rather not handle such a load. Injuries to the back, to the legs, to shoulders, to the wrists, loom in the scene of slaughter.

Handling animals larger than a pigeon requires two people. Chickens can be offered by a single person by twisting off the head, but the rest of the body must be skillfully restrained. Roosters require two people. They have enough blood that tearing off their heads won't do. Even if the heads could be easily separated from their bodies, which they can't—their skin is too tough—the blood should be directed to particular objects and surfaces. Roosters have enough blood for santos-orisás to share, so using a knife to direct the blood is essential. Its point is passed between the windpipe and the backbone, where it is held as the blood streams down the blade, the tip of which can direct the blood with delicate movements of the handle. This same operation is used for offering the four-legged animals.

Neither Máximo nor Roberto wanted the role that custom in their house required of them and that their sister, Isidra, now imposed on them. Cucusa had prepared them, but they were in their late teens and early twenties when the revolution came upon them. At that time, it was Loreto Sáez who did the killing at Cucusa's feast. Then it was Gobierno Sáez. The last time the boys had been involved, their role had been in the yard, keeping, bathing, and handling the animals. Since then, they had spent their lives separated from the ceremonial labors of their mother's house—even Roberto who lived in town. Now Isidra held out the knife. A young goat for Elégua, the first to eat, was wrestled into the room and was ready.

Powerful, aggressive, decisive Máximo was averse to handling the blade. He had failed to bring the ram for Changó. "This is not my job," he said. "Look at these clothes." He spread his arms to display his hard-currency jeans and Tommy Hilfiger polo. His wife, Cyrilla, whispered to no one in particular, "You'll never get the blood out. Those clothes are for work."

Roberto, the junior of the two, wanted nothing to do with the blade. "Not me," he said, as ardently as his brother. His dodge was impeded by his stutter, and Isidra had the knife in his hand before he could close it.

"Not me," he said again.

"Who are you?" Isidra said. "The two of you. Who are you? Whose sons are you? Who raised you? In whose house did you grow up? In whose house do you now stand?"

Her brothers, older, larger, more imposing in their carriages, were struck dumb. Their families—wives, sisters, children, grandchildren, nieces, and nephews—sat waiting in anticipation.

"How many times have you been in this room when this work was done? How many times did you handle the animals for Loreto? For Gobierno? Since you were children. Now you say you can't wield the knife. Look at this house. What do you see? Where is your mother? Where is Loreto? Where is Gobierno? Look at these santos here. More than a year without having been nourished. Your mother's santos!"

The room was quiet. Elégua's goat stood between José's legs, held by the horns. Roberto held the knife.

"Bring it over," he said. "Let's go."

Without a signal, Justo the mute gravedigger started drumming up the big drum, and Pica began to sing Elégua's meal songs, which the room repeated with gusto.

Roberto handled the knife ably. Goats are tricky, famously mischievous and clever, like Elégua. They are the ones who will disappear before the feast, who will chew through their ties, who will kick free and sprint through a previously unnoticed hole in the fence, like Elégua. They will wail and kick as they are lifted, and they provoke costly mistakes on the part of the handlers and, in turn, of the one who does the killing. But this little goat was effectively subdued by José and Boby, and soon its blood bathed the shallow bowl holding the collection of stones and shells that received Elégua's blood meal. We sang up Elégua to communicate our praise and obeisance for the sovereign of openings, thresholds, beginnings, and orifices.

Elégua sat feasting on the blood soaking his stones. The carcass was carried from the room by the animal handlers–cum-butchers. Isidra spoke again.

"The two of you," she began, signaling Máximo and Roberto. "This house belongs to us now. Cucusa is gone. And she has left it to us. But look around you. What do you see? They've taken everything." Anyone else would have been exhausted from days of feast preparation and drinking only milk for sustenance, but Isidra was just getting started.

"Who stands for this house? Who shows their face [¿Quién da la cara?] for this house? Roberto, you live here in town. Every day, you see and hear everything. What gets past you? And what have you shown for this house but cowardice?"

Roberto's hands were bloody, blood soiled his pants, and he looked at her despondently. He quietly put the knife down on the rim of the vessel holding Elégua.

"And you," she said turning to Máximo. "You live in Santa Clara. You have status in the party. When don't you have a party car? And you never come? The minute they broke in, Roberto should have called and you should have been here."

Cyrilla pulled herself up. "We don't have to take this," she said plainly, almost softly. "Máximo, let's go."

Without speaking or looking at Isidra, Máximo rose to leave. Isidra stared in disbelief.

Now, Roberto barked in what was part grunt, part muffled shout. "Heh!" he cried. "Heh! Heh! Heh!"

He whirled in place once, twice, three times. His frame was enormous. His was the largest, tallest, broadest body in the room, and he was now up on his toes, though his knees were bent. One arm was thrown behind his back, the other across his head, so that his face was buried in the crook of his arm.

Pica, who had been singing for Elégua, turned to a high-paced song for the sovereign of the crossing, the intersection, and the portal. Justo reveled on the drum. Roberto began to shout.

Roberto's Elégua hadn't been seen in years. How long had it been? When he was a child, Roberto was mounted by Elégua. "Younger than ten, when he was seven or eight," said his sisters. That would have been 1946. As of then, his Elégua was prized by Cucusa, Ma' Isidra, and Chacha. Loreto took him under his wing and nurtured his tendencies toward the santos-orisás. They loved him for his dancing and clever shenanigans. Later, Pica said to me, "His is the most beautiful Elégua." When he was a teenager, with all his flexibility and strength, it was a delight to have him join the other orisás at a feast, mounted as these were on the senior singers and dancers of the Sociedad Africana, like Ma' Isidra, Digna, and Otilia. Some people said Roberto hadn't been mounted since 1958, when he got involved with the clandestine organizations determined to topple the dictator, Batista. When the revolution triumphed, Roberto, like his brother and sisters, was quickly integrated into its ranks. Although he stayed in town and Cucusa kept hosting bembés for San Lázaro–Babalú Ayé, Roberto didn't mount Elégua again.

Now his cries became more anguished as he rose and spun. His face was streaming with tears, and his stare was blank, his eyes half rolled into their sockets. He lunged toward the bloody stones with one enormous step, then, turning on the spot, he lunged close to those seated around.

He stood straight, his legs spread and his hands resting on his hips. "Heh!" he shouted and touched two fingers to his lips. The tiny gesture was the only invitation his sisters needed. "A cigar. Get him a cigar," said Eulalia, as if she had asked for this several times already. Isidra was up and standing behind him, helping him off with his shirt. Elégua allowed himself to be disrobed in this way. With barely a glance or a gesture he pointed to his feet. Isidra knelt behind him and rolled his pant legs over his calves and undid his shoes. Pica and Justo kept up the Elégua songs as Pica reached for a tiny half gourd in which to put some aguardiente, which is Elégua's favorite. Máximo and Cyrilla stared at one another, Máximo downcast and Cyrilla with a look of frustration that she quickly guarded.

Elégua's accoutrements were close to hand, this being a house where Elégua, mounted on other steeds, was regularly hosted. The peasant's hat that had yesterday been used by María's Elégua was hung on the very chair Roberto had occupied before he stood to offer the goat. A little guava-branch crook was there too. Isidra placed the hat on his head and gently laid the crook in his hand as Eulalia placed a lit cigar in his mouth. Sovereign, he could not be expected to do mundane labor like dressing, undressing, or lighting cigars. Orisá "work" is of another character, not lowly or useful in submissive ways. It comprises simple words and gestures that signal the decision of a sovereign, their favor, their attention, or their opposite. Their work is to craft human situations into new shapes and to determine fates.

Elégua, master of all beginnings, was before us, his arms crossed on his bare chest, standing barefoot in the spilled blood of his meal. He blew enormous puffs of cigar smoke and gestured for the little gourd to be brought to his lips. Eulalia reached up to tip the aguardiente into his mouth.

"Unite!" he said. "This house will fall down around you if you don't unite. Too much disrespect. Siblings disrespect one another!"

His voice was high, higher than Roberto's customary tone. Like Pica's Changó, his Spanish was "broken," marked by "errors" in grammar, such as in conjugation and number. He used the formal form of *you* [*usted*]. He looked around the room, pleased at the deference and attention being paid him.

"What is this? Who is this?" he said, pointing at me. "Visitors in this house? What distance have they come? This is a child of mine! Respect this house!" he said speaking around the cigar in his mouth. "Respect your godmother. Do what she says and serve this house. Heh!"

He turned to others in the room. "This house will fall! United or not, only respect will save this house. Respect, or all of you will fall."

"You," he said, turning to Isidra. "You will save this house! This is yours! There will be betrayals. You can count on no one. Your path is a lonely one. Heh! Alone!"

To Eulalia he said, "To your sister's side. Don't fail her. There will be times when only you stand between her failure and her success. Which will it be? Heh!"

So he went, person by person, speaking directly to José, María, Agripina from Sagua, and to the next generation, Boby, Ulises, and Anelé, about the roles they must play and what was needed from them to help Cucusa's house.

Máximo and Cyrilla had given up on leaving. His words for Cyrilla seemed to calm her. Máximo he beckoned near and spoke softly to him. Isidra needed to hear what Elégua said to him, but she was impolite in inserting herself and drew a fleeting look of surprised disgust from Cyrilla. If Elégua wanted a private word with her husband, he would brush Isidra away. His words for Máximo were too spare for Isidra's liking, but she could hardly take issue with what Elégua said last.

"Heh! A ram! A ram is expected! Heh-heh!"

Of the things that were delightful about Roberto's Elégua, his chuckle stood out. Orisás often call to attention those gathered to praise them by offering a hard, diaphragm-deep hucking shout before they begin to speak, "Heh!" Sometimes they will repeat the huck, two or more times, "Heh, heh, heh!" as they prepare to speak or finish a statement. Elégua, in the shape he took on Roberto, turned the huck into a little chuckle. "Heh-heh! Heh-heh!" From the sovereign of play, this little laugh was a lighthearted version of the more imperious salutations of other orisás. The little laugh seemed to say, "It's OK. Whatever my tidings, don't take them too hard. I don't." From the sovereign of the trick played at the crossroads, the little laugh could be interpreted more mischievously. Down the path of the trick, the little laugh could be conveying impish secrets or tidings of surprises ahead. From the sovereign of horizons and new things, his chuckle could be simple delight. In these ways, Roberto's Elégua used his laugh to add layers of meaning, interpretation, ambiguity, and double entendre to many of his statements.

Roberto's Elégua approached Celita. This could well have been the first time his daughter, now thirty-some years old, first encountered the santo-orisá for which her father was remembered. They talked alone for what seemed a long while as she asked direct questions of Elégua and received lengthy answers. Everyone understood that Celita faced momentous decisions in her wish for children in the months ahead, and having Elégua's guidance was imperative. He oversees the transition from maiden to mother, from Ochún to Yemayá, and all women in childbirth are his subjects, as are their babies, who navigate the passage. He presides over children and childhood.

Elégua presided over us for the next half hour. There was not a person in the room with whom he did not converse, if only for a moment. The exception was Celia, his wife, who had slipped out of the room when Roberto received Elégua. When the time came and his work was done, Elégua gave one last speech, calling us to the struggle for the future of the house, which was synonymous with Cucusa's legacy and the integrity of the family.

Announcing his departure with a hearty set of laughs, he sat down, took off his hat, and laid his crook over the chair back. Just like that, Elégua was gone, and Roberto found himself slumped over in his chair, shirtless and covered in sweat. "Huh?" he asked. "What's this? What's going on?" Noticing then that his pant legs were rolled up and that he was barefoot, the realization came upon him that he had just been mounted. "Dear God," he said, "bring me some water."

We were as far behind on the animal offerings as we could be. It was nearly four in the morning and barely had they begun. In good spirits, Pica returned to singing to the santos-orisás, leading us through songs for each orisá, continuing from Elégua to Ogún to Obatalá to Oyá to Ochún, Yemayá, and Changó. No other orisás visited during the night, and we made remarkable speed through the remainder of the slaughter. In this extraordinary night, when twenty-some animals were offered, three things stood out. The first was that Changó made no protest regarding his missing ram. He could easily have chosen to mount one of us present. Máximo, who owed the ram and who was a mount for him, could have "received" Changó but did not. Pica, too, who mounted Changó with tremendous facility, could have received him but did not. Isidra made much of the missing ram; it was crucial to have Changó's favor, but Changó himself had not much to say about the missing offering.

The feeding of San Lázaro–Babalú Ayé was also noteworthy. San Lázaro–Babalú Ayé was the orisá of the house and for whom we gathered to feast. The other orisás were his guests and, being peers, ate their preferred animals. Like other orisás kept by Cucusa, San Lázaro–Babalú Ayé was a collection of river stones in a shallow porcelain bowl wrapped in cloth. Before the large black goat was offered, the two statuettes of Lazarus the Beggar from the altar in the living room were brought in and placed alongside the santo-orisá stones. A compound San Lázaro–Babalú Ayé was thus assembled from orisá stones and the altar statuettes. They feasted on mature black buck goat, the blood of which was substantial. A black rooster followed to "refresh" San Lázaro–Babalú Ayé from the richness of his meal.

The last offering of the night was for the only Congo-inspired power Cucusa kept. This was Mariana Congo, inherited from Ma' Isidra and from Ernesto Portilla before her. Mariana Congo was tied up in a white cloth bundle and had not been fed since before Cucusa's death. Isidra was tentative as she unwrapped her. "Mariana must be handled with utmost care," she said. "Cucusa was very secretive about Mariana and would turn her back when she worked her. None of us really know what to do here, but she can't go unfed. We will have to figure out Mariana as we go." The room was apprehensive, but go we did, as Pica sang up Mariana with old Congo-inspired songs she pulled from memory and from the dead. Later, Isidra said, "You see, Ramón, I had to move forward with Mariana even if I didn't know how. And did you see? Did you see how the songs came out of Pica? She knew Mariana and knew what songs to sing her. Mariana was pleased, or she would have taken one of us right then and there." She drew her index finger across her throat. "You see? These are the risks you take to learn."

We finished the slaughter after sunrise. The animals, each having been carried from the room into the hands of attendants, butchers, and cooks, were already on their way to becoming stews. I could not stay awake and along with the hosts took a morning nap, only to wake when called for lunch.

All afternoon people came and went casually. Each arrival was offered a plate of stew, either goat, rooster, or chicken, each served separately, though not everyone got some of each. Along with a serving of *arroz moro,* white rice cooked together with black beans in their broth, and perhaps a slice of tomato, this was our ritual meal, the feast that followed the feeding of the orisás. To eat what had only recently been offered (and accepted) by the santos-orisás was to bring our bodies near them by consuming animals they approved of, flesh they had themselves consumed. At times, in conversation over lunch, the animal and the divinity were comingled. Elégua's goat was mischievous, full of tricks and unexpected turns; Yemayá's duck beautiful and fertile; Changó's animals replete with virile qualities. One could wonder if it wasn't the flesh of the orisás themselves we ate.[3] Whether it was the remains of an orisá's meal, or the orisá's flesh, to eat of this meal was to bring your body into tune with the energies, forces, potentials, and virtues of the sovereign whose offering you consumed.

You did not need to be an anthropologically curious person to get any of this. You needed only an emphatic teacher like Isidra, who gave careful thought to associations, connections, and relations, and rarely tired of your questions. "Why are the animals handled with such care before the sacrifice, then booted from the room just after?" "After the animal is killed, is its flesh pure or impure?" "Are there benefits from eating it?" "Must you eat of it in order to attend the party later in the day?" "Must you eat of it to be mounted by an orisá? Must you eat of Elégua's meal to be mounted by Elégua, and Changó's meal to be mounted by Changó?" Isidra was patient, and Eulalia, too, was good at fielding my questions.

People came and went, received their plate of food, and didn't ask which orisá's meal they were sharing. There was neither excessive ornament in serving nor excessive obeisance in receiving. The etiquette for inviting, accepting, and eating this food was informal, and if marked at all, it was by a sense of generosity and good cheer on the part of Isidra, who did her best to be present for each guest. It's true, occasionally a person would request "some of Ochún's chicken" or "San Lázaro's goat," but as with most things "religious" in town, people were remarkably casual. For some people, like Pica, Isidra chose a particular stew. In her case it was a plate of the rooster that was offered Changó in lieu of his ram. Zenón, who had called verses alongside Pica the night before, was offered a similar plate, which he declined. "A glass of water with sugar is all I need." To which Isidra replied, "You must eat! Eat this. This is Changó's rooster. It has Eulalia's magic touch to boot! She seasoned this one right on point. Come on." Zenón replied, "No, just water with sugar. And lots of rum for my throat tonight."

Many who came for a plate of food paid their respects to the little statuettes of Lazarus the Beggar, which had been rinsed and returned to their places on the altar. A little basket sat at the foot of the altar, and depositing pennies [*un medio*] was the customary way of showing respect to the sovereign of illness and healing. In all, maybe a hundred people came for lunch during the afternoon.

EIGHT

————

A Bembé for San Lázaro–Babalú Ayé

BY EARLY EVENING ON THE 17TH, the house had recovered from the nightlong slaughter and from the effort of preparing and serving the meals. The sun set, and people started lingering around the living room and standing in the doorway. Boys played the drums, which stood in their corner by the tall window onto the veranda and the street. By eight o'clock men were handling the drums and started calling out to begin. Isidra held off for what seemed like a long while, until around nine o'clock, when she emerged from her room dressed in a long white dress with a light blue satin turban covering her head. She was resplendent and relaxed. She saw Pica sitting on a chair next to the drums ready to sing and launched right in, again calling to the sovereign of openings, beginnings, and starts, dear Elégua.

Isidra called, "Lindo, lindo, eh! Lindo-lindo Elégua, no hay un santo más lindo que Elégua, no hay un santo mas chéche que Elégua!"

The drums picked up instantly, breaking the tension in the room [*rompieron*]. The chorus responded, not missing a beat. It was the only verse Isidra sang, and Pica picked up the call from there. So vivacious was the chorus that the songs she called for Elégua were like a collective cheer.

Pica called, "Lindo, lindo, eh! Lindo-lindo Elégua, no hay un santo más lindo que Elégua, no hay un santo mas chéche que Elégua!"

To which we responded, "Lindo, lindo, eh! Lindo-lindo Elégua, no hay un santo más lindo que Elégua, no hay un santo mas chéche que Elégua!" We sang, Lovely, lovely! Lovely, lovely Elégua, there is no saint so lovely as Elégua, no saint more wholesome than Elégua!

Pica added a verse: "Lindo, lindo, eh! Lindo-lindo Elégua, yo me voy pa' tierra Dahomey, yo me voy pa' tierra de Elégua!"

To which we responded: "Lindo, lindo, eh! Lindo-lindo Elégua, yo me voy pa' tierra Dahomey, yo me voy pa' tierra de Elégua!" We said, Lovely, lovely! Lovely, lovely Elégua, I'm on my way to Dahomey, I'm going to the land of Elégua!

Last night's drumming and dancing was a "call" to the santos-orisás and the opening of the feast, and though things got excited, including the arrival of several of the sovereigns, which was customary, it was all a bit untimely. Santos-orisás should visit after they have been fed and their devotees have eaten of the orisás leavings. At least that is the way things go back in Havana, where time is tighter and things more expensive and scheduled. This would be the second night of festivities, this one more propitious than the last because the slaughter was concluded successfully. This was the bembé for which everything had been prepared.

Pica sang us forward through several cheers for Elégua before she herself was mounted. It was her second mounting in less than twenty-four hours. At seventy years old, she was known to complain about a stiff knee. She stood between the drums and the chorus of guests and moved by shuffling her feet and gently pivoting her hips. As her repertoire of orisá songs came to settle on those for Changó, she lifted her head and sang to the rafters. She spread her arms and raised her voice, a smile on her face. Her head tilting rhythmically back and forth, she sang for the santo-orisá who had presided over her father's fate, presided over hers, and presided over her daughter's. Her shoulders entered the play, reflecting Changó's powerful upper body. No one present doubted whom Pica embodied in her freshened movements. She bent her elbows in sync with her rotating shoulders and flexing chest, invoking Changó's thunder ax, that legendary weapon among the santos-orisás. With her entire torso now mobilized, she bent at the waist and started to rotate on the balls of her feet. It was hard for me to tell when, exactly, she was mounted by Changó. Perhaps it was when she started throwing lightning bolts from her pelvis. But the chorus knew exactly, and his arrival was communicated less by Pica's actions than by the sudden rise in the voices of those gathered. Their beloved sovereign of struggle, of battle, of war and lightning, Changó, was back in the room. Two nights running he had chosen Pica to carry him at the feast. Changó, master of the drum, lightning wielder, master of thunder, paradigm of masculinity, found her perfectly accommodating as he flung himself upon his steed; she was ready for him, and he settled easily.

To great contrast from things in Havana, she did not stop singing as Changó heaved himself onto her back. How odd this would appear back in the capital, where the "orichas" never (never say never in things African-inspired in Cuba) mount the singers who lead the calls. Orichas in the capital don't sing. Once mounted in Havana, a member of an Ocha-Santería chorus will stop singing. But Pica's Changó did not miss a beat and now sang for us. The crowd lifted their voices in approval as Changó now led them in songs of praise.

The thunder that resounds from a blow of his ax, or follows in the wake of his lightning strikes, is the rolling sound of Changó's third great insignia—the drums. They are his by virtue of his prowess in playing them. When Changó plays the drums, no santo-orisá can resist the call to dance, not even the limping, crippled Babalú Ayé. Santos-orisás dance because Changó compels them with the virtuosity of his play. His is the right to give or take the drums, to grant or withhold skill in playing them. The roar and snap of virtuoso drums is his. Nearly all music is his. His command over drums gives him command over bembés, and all parties. They are his to give and withhold, his to favor with a good set of drums and a great group of musicians, or doom to musical torpidity. That he now sang the chorus forward was the finest thing Isidra could have hoped for, and she was exultant.

Between breaths, in the imperceptible pauses between the steps of his steed, Changó spun to face his drums, to acknowledge the men playing them. He spread his arms and cocked his head, singing praises. The drummers now lifted the feast a little higher, louder, more crisp and precise yet with lighter hands. Their faces shone with the grace of having been recognized by their sovereign. Those who stood waiting their turn stirred with impatience. Every musician enjoys their time on a drum at a bembé; every man enjoys the privilege of playing for the feast, of bringing the chorus into sync with the beat, and of elevating the feast to unpredictable heights. Every musician with the confidence to take a seat at a drum also considers himself better than the rest. You have to be pretty confident to sit down at a drum and play for the master of music standing there before you, singing, dancing, threatening with his thunder ax and lightning, and laying his generous, scrutinizing eyes upon you. Despite considerable trepidation, even drummers down the pecking order itch to have a go when Changó is in the room, to play for him, yes, but also because his presence is a blessing, a guarantee that your potential as a musician will achieve its maximum. You will grow in excellence when Changó stands before you.

Pica's Changó finished a set of songs to himself, then sang again for Elégua. He would sing to all his supreme peers before he dismounted. He held the call with fortitude while Zenón sipped aguardiente. "Keeping my throat fresh," he was fond of saying. The chorus closed in on Changó as those who had not had a chance last night, or had not gotten enough of the master of the pitched fight, sought out his words and touch.

Changó was eventually consumed in his consultations, and Zenón took the call. His was a lower voice, less nasal than Pica's. He claimed his songs were the oldest, taught to him by Ingo, his mother, Chacha Cairo's adopted daughter and a lead singer of the Sociedad Africana after the death of Reina Collín. Zenón was prone to goad the chorus with a turn in the lyrics, or the drummers with a shift in time. He even goaded the santos-orisás when they needed handling. He was revered in town for his ability to sing off the African-inspired powers, as he did with Zulia's Oyá the night before. He could sing off *muertos oscuros* and also the Congo dead. Congos are unruly powers of the night and the wilderness; they can wreck a feast unless properly handled. Zenón's calling was more brash and more self-referential.

Zenón's call, full of bravado, combined with the excited chorus and the drummers jamming at full tilt to bring more santos-orisás into the room. María, Pica's daughter, was mounted by Changó half an hour after her mother. Her mounting was more physically demanding and dramatic. Hers was a full-bodied mounting that followed a dance solo in which she held a substantial share of the floor. She spun vertiginously, stopped suddenly, strode forward with enormous steps, and flexed her chest and arms as she lifted Changó's thunder ax. She was corpulent like her mother, and she knew just how to move around her center of gravity, how to use her weight to great effect. Her movements were a display of pure improvisational command but were soon punctuated with occasional losses of balance as Changó mounted her. Last night she had been a steed for Elégua, but now Changó took her with conviction. María had taken Changó on her back many times, but even so it required tremendous effort to bring him on. She fell under the strain of his enormousness, and those in the chorus around her had to hold her up time and again.

María eventually succumbed in the way a wild horse is broken by a skillful rider. Her Changó joined her mother's Changó, and the two now presided over the feast. Isidra beamed. She and Eulalia danced and dashed to and fro, fetching accoutrements that would please the two Changós. Each Changó was offered a sash of red satin for his waist, and each was attended by one of the sisters, who carried a tiny gourd with dry white wine for him to sip and spray as he desired.

María's Changó came ready to work. In what seemed like three giant strides, her Changó was through the kitchen and out the back door. He sought out Máximo, who was out by the well drinking aguardiente and smoking cigarettes. "Eh!" shouted the sovereign when he found his errant subject.

"U'té' no come?" he demanded. "You don't eat?" Changó asked facetiously in his broken Spanish. "U'té' no come? ¡Changó sí come!" He said, "You don't eat? Well, Changó eats!"

Máximo was struck with what appeared a mixture of embarrassment and annoyance. He spoke not a word.

"Eh! Eh!" shouted Changó, affronted. "¡U'té' trae carnero, u'té' debe carnero!" He said, "You bring a ram, you owe a ram!"

Those around Máximo looked away, not wanting to draw Changó's wrath.

"Eh! Palabra son palabra," said Changó. "Next year, keep your word."

Máximo did not reply or offer visible gestures of defiance. But neither did his posture, or his eyes, express contrition. He regarded Changó with the respect he might accord any superior in the Communist Party. Anything other than basic respect would have been puerile. Together with the revolution, Máximo had outgrown the attempt to eliminate the orisás. But it was 1999, and changes in state tolerance for religion had only just begun; Pope John Paul II had visited only last year. Máximo was a member of the party, one with some rank back in Santa Clara. He had been reluctant to come to the bembé, reluctant to bring a ram, and now he was reluctant to play along in orisá praise. He knew, though, that with Pica and María present, Changó was going to make his appearance, and this encounter was bound to happen. His response to the great orisá was adequate. The encounter ended with a stern rebuke from Changó, but nothing more. Some considered this lucky, given that Máximo did not reiterate his promise. Eulalia commented on this later: "That was María's Changó. Did you notice Pica's Changó said nothing to him? That was worse, and I can promise you he noticed. Loreto's Changó would have taken off his head." Isidra was less charitable: "Máximo is a scoundrel [*descarado*]. How dare he not beg Changó for forgiveness? Don't think he got off easy. He will pay for this, and in one year's time you will see him back here with the ram, on his knees, begging Changó for mercy."

María's Changó charged back into the living room to join the drummers, dancers, and those mounting up the santos-orisás. Among the chorus was a tiny woman from the countryside, in her seventies, whom folks in town classified as "white" [*una blanquita*]. We had met her in the previous days as we sought animals. Serena received us warmly, and she and Isidra had an easy rapport. She was an ardent admirer of Cucusa's ability to connect people with the powers of Babalú Ayé, and her gratitude to Cucusa extended across years.

Serena was also a mount for the santos-orisás. It was my first bembé, so I did not know by whom she was mounted, nor did that detail make it into my notes. Perhaps I never asked, with all the santo-orisá dramas afoot. That did not diminish my surprise that even an elderly white farmer lady could be a mount for the magnanimous African-inspired santos-orisás. She did not bear her "santo" long, nor did she bear her santo with sufficient grace to hold forth among those gathered, so she did not heal. But with her body, in the minutes she was mounted, she joined the play of the bembé and added to its considerable energy.

Who among the santos-orisás did not mount one of their steeds that night? Elégua, Changó, Yemayá, La Caridad–Ochún, and Ogún all visited. Oyá, too, chose a mount. She chose no less practiced a steed than Pica herself, who passed from bearing Changó to bearing Oyá almost without skipping a beat. Not everyone who carries a santo-orisá in Sierra Morena is a steed for more than one santo-orisá, but neither was Pica's plural mounting remarkable. This is very different from the practice in Havana, where Ocha-Santería steeds serve one master. That a person can be serially mounted by two or more orisás at one feast is one of the joys of bembés in north-central Cuba.

Oyá is the sovereign of the tempest, of storm-driven winds, and life-shaking change. She mounts her steeds as they whirl and change directions, rise and drop on their legs, and turn suddenly. Her dance steps bring turbulence into a feast scene and remind those present that Oyá presides over that most tumultuous of transformations, death. She makes her home at the cemetery gate and decides who will enter and who will skirt past. It is the only threshold Elégua shares custody over.

Mounted by this personage, Pica's comportment was much like it was under the influence of Changó. In fact, without Isidra's prompting, I would not have noticed the change of rider. Eulalia knew immediately and ran to gather the accessories Oyá prefers. Quickly, she removed the red sash that pleased Changó and replaced this with a hand-pieced wraparound skirt with nine panels of different colors. The number nine is synonymous with the dead in Cuba. As sovereign of the cemetery, Oyá presides over its population; the amassed horde of the dead are her subjects. Atop Pica she now presided, and people sought her counsel to dispel the gloom of looming death, of the dread of losing someone, of mourning, and the fear of cemetery affairs. Oyá is terrifying and dreadful for this reason, but also attractive to those suffocated by the terrible silences of death. She speaks from the speechless reaches of deaths foretold and of unspeakable mourning. She could articulate such concerns for those gathered. Oyá intervenes in life's most harrowing moments, and her proximity to the thing most feared gives her the authority to distance people from it and spare them its shrouds. Pica, in her grace, her expertise, and her steady confidence, was a welcome mount for so tumultuous a power.

Each santo-orisá brought energy and transformation to the feast. Each sovereign changed those they spoke to or touched, cast their lives anew, and thus healed them. The musical energy was at its limits, and the feast seemed as if it could bear no more. Such was the excitement, and such was my status as a novice, that I hadn't noticed we were as yet without the company of the guest of honor, San Lázaro–Babalú Ayé. To me there was no indication of anything missing. The party was full on. It overflowed with sound, and play, and drama, and carried us exuberantly forward.

But what could be more embarrassing for a host than to prepare a feast for an orisá and then be stood up? What could be more disappointing than hosting Cucusa's feast for the first time since her death and not have San Lázaro–Babalú Ayé come? All that effort, all the wrangling and contention to arrive at this night, and where was San Lázaro–Babalú Ayé?

San Lázaro–Babalú Ayé is not an easy orisá to prepare for, nor an easy one for a mount to receive. He can arrive a wretched beggar, sore infested, and compose a portrait of his misery with the body of his steeds. Perhaps for that reason his praise and devotion are so hard to sustain, and why mounts for him are rare. So it was at the first indication that San Lázaro–Babalú Ayé had chosen a steed that a sigh of relief spread through the crowd. Within the song then on everyone's lips a shout went up, joy and pleasure, almost laughter, at the arrival of this most sought-after santo-orisá.

He chose Celita, Isidra's nice. Celita was young, alert, and sensitive. She was obedient, but also intelligent in words and actions. She was Cucusa's granddaughter by way of Roberto, Isidra's brother. She was also a revolutionary like her father and uncle and aunts. She had traveled for years in Bulgaria, and her future in the party had once been bright, except here she was in 1999, washed up in one of the rural backwaters that twentieth-century Communism had left behind. She had never been mounted by San Lázaro–Babalú Ayé before. She wore a patterned purple satin dress in honor of San Lázaro–Babalú Ayé, who greatly esteems that color.

Celita's mounting was rough. Her gestures, her steps, and the movements of her arms and legs were sharp staccato jerks, both violent and restrained. Her mounting had not come in the course of dancing; it had not flowed from her dance. The grace of such a mounting was missing. Rather, it was as if she had been standing there and suddenly her body was asked to bear a great weight. She was pushed to one side, buckled at the knees, jerked back up as the weight was relieved before the rider rose up on her again. Two or three times the rider tried to mount, but she gave way beneath his stature. Those around her took notice and invited her to accept San Lázaro–Babalú Ayé, some leaning in to help her balance through the ordeal. Then her back was ramrod straight, and her arms were down at her sides. Her feet squarely spread. She was frozen except for a trembling in her core that grew into a steady shaking as it reached her shoulders. Her eyes were open wide and reflected both terror and joy.[1]

San Lázaro–Babalú Ayé took some moments to settle his surprised steed, then moved forward. San Lázaro–Babalú Ayé's steps are broken, cut short by the anguish of his open sores and the torment of the fathomless illness that he hosts. His every gesture is cut short by the pain that wracks his body. Sometimes, he cannot move except with crutches, and in some houses these are brought forth as his most important insignia. Celita's San Lázaro–Babalú Ayé limped, and his face bore the distress of his movements. This did not keep him from getting to work.

Eulalia had followed the mounting with concern, and by the time the santo-orisá had settled onto Celita, she was ready with his regalia, which in that country house was a length of purple satin left over from the altar. Eulalia draped this over San Lázaro's shoulders as she joined the orisá at his side. Isidra had also taken in the scene and flanked the new steed on the other side. Together the three moved slowly to regard the chorus, which was ready for the sovereign of pestilence and healing. A line was already formed as the chorus continued to dance and sing for him. As one by one they approached, San Lázaro–Babalú Ayé took the purple satin and rubbed it along their faces, necks, and shoulders. Sometimes the dancer would turn and the santo-orisá would rub them on their backs. One by one, a procession of feastgoers passed before the santo-orisá and received the gift of his cleansing touch. The drummers roared forward, Zenón called verse after verse, and the chorus took the energy higher.

Some wanted to linger with San Lázaro–Babalú Ayé and asked him for more than the simple, powerful touches with which he healed the crowd.

These were people with particular distress, with anxieties that required concrete and directed acts of healing. A pause, a look into his eyes, a whisper in his ear and the santo-sovereign heard the details of the pains they carried. In some instances, the cure was affected at once, as when Babalú Ayé would crouch down to stroke a foot, or a leg, or someone's abdomen. Other cases required the santo-orisá to address a devotee's tough situation rather than an illness. These were cases in which people spoke to the orisá about the illness of someone else, ill at home or far away, or spoke of worries, some real and present, others not entirely concrete. In these instances, a word from San Lázaro–Babalú Ayé means the world. But Celita showed herself to be a new steed for San Lázaro–Babalú Ayé, since while mounted on her back he did not speak.

Orisás in Sierra Morena come to work. Celita had pointed this out to me just the night before. Whether you put more or less stake in one orisá over another, whether you came to a bembé only once in a while, the expectation was that the santos-orisás would attend to you and take on your distress. Orisás, broken though their Spanish might be, work through speech as much as through physical touch. They see into situations, they see beyond current constraints, into realms of things to come, of things to *become,* in ways that people cannot. Likewise, they see into the past, and through their privileged vision they part the shrouds of time, sort the chaos of jumbled events, and peek into the folds of stories that have become so convoluted, they can no longer be made sense of by the afflicted.

But Celita's San Lázaro–Babalú Ayé did not speak. When he tried, his speech was stunted, and all he could utter were little grunts, or snorts of recognition and assent. Orisá communications, even when emitted by the most articulate of the santo-sovereigns, are always cryptic. There is always a matter of interpretation, guessing, and construal that accompanies orisá speech. This interpretive aspect of orisá healing was accentuated in the case of Celita's Babalú Ayé. Her orisá was effectively mute.

This did not keep him from communicating, however. Eyes wide open and a look of surprise on the face of his mount, San Lázaro–Babalú Ayé proceeded to engage in an elaborate pantomime, using hand gestures and facial expressions to communicate his understandings and the things he saw. Some of the healed seemed to understand perfectly what was meant by his grunts and gesticulations; others were more mystified and turned to Isidra and Eulalia for translations and clarifications. These Eulalia provided with more generosity than Isidra, who seemed doubly annoyed: that people asked more of a sovereign who was already giving them so much, and that that San Lázaro–Babalú Ayé, at once so desired and so welcome, had come mute.

The crowd was not annoyed and adjusted their expectations for this San Lázaro–Babalú Ayé. It made sense that the sovereign of affliction, of open sores and unspeakable ills, would come beset with yet another malady. The physical torments of San Lázaro–Babalú Ayé are indescribable, his degradation unutterable, his anguish supreme. It made sense that he was speechless. In fact, by the logic of orisá healing one is effective by virtue of having passed through and overcome an affliction. The greater the affliction, the greater the potential for healing. Celita's San Lázaro–Babalú Ayé was sunken in realms of misery for which there were no words. But his powers of overcoming were patent, and for the gathered multitude his speechlessness made him all the more compelling.

Celita was an apt mount for the sovereign of sickness and healing. Granddaughter of Cucusa, she was the first manifestation of San Lázaro–Babalú Ayé in her family. Her manner was modest and resigned, like Cucusa's, and on her back San Lázaro–Babalú Ayé asked for very little. Thus is the way of the pauper sovereign. The purple cloth Eulalia had draped over his shoulders pleased him greatly. Isidra and Eulalia were at his side as he healed, one with a plate of grains, the other with a little gourd holding the dry white wine that is the only thing San Lázaro–Babalú Ayé drinks other than the water from coconuts. The plate held rice, beans (both black and red), dry corn kernels, and bread crumbs. San Lázaro–Babalú Ayé took pinches to rub over the bodies of those who sought him. Then he would take a tiny sip from his gourd and blow it on the faces or bodies of the cases before him.

Zenón, who carried the call, sang, "Santo, va bajando Babalú Ayé! Santo, trabajando Babalú Ayé!" He sang, "Saint! Here comes Babalú Ayé! Saint at work, Babalú Ayé!"

It was after midnight, and the santo-orisá healed and healed, holding forth for more than an hour of close-quarters touching, rubbing, blowing, staring, and gesturing. The feast reflected the procession of the afflicted through the room, and San Lázaro–Babalú Ayé's triumphant healing of their troubles. The energy in the room was excited and relieved, unburdened of cares, and free.

Eventually, the line of people clamoring for his touch wore down, leaving the orisá-sovereign exhausted but pleased. It was at that moment, standing alone before the altar Cucusa had made for him fifty-six years earlier, before the two little statues of his Catholic likeness, that San Lázaro–Babalú Ayé turned to his own steed. As the chorus sang his praises, San Lázaro–Babalú Ayé took the sweat-soaked purple cloth and started to rub his steed—her face, her arms, and her neck. Slowly, he moved down the body that hosted him, lingering on Celita's breasts, emblems of feminine fertility and motherhood throughout African-inspired healing in Cuba. He held her breasts, then lifted them slightly. Finally, with tears in the eyes of his mount, he placed his hands over her childless womb, cradling her lower abdomen in his hands. Then he swept the purple cloth through the air and threw off the affliction he found there.

Having brought his hands to heal the aching body of his newfound steed, he departed. Celita seemed to falter, her knees buckled, and her aunts, still attending to her, held her by the elbows. She tried to get her feet under her. Isidra and Eulalia gently sat her in a chair next to the altar. She seemed as stunned as her father had been when he recovered from his mounting by Elégua during the slaughter hours before. María was ready for this. She herself had half an hour earlier come out from under Changó, and now she did for Celita what another had done for her. She straddled the exhausted woman's legs and bent over to gently hold her head. Cradling the nape of her neck, she turned her mouth against one ear and then the next, blowing brusquely into each. Celita seemed to relax then. Already a glass of coconut water had been brought, and the bembé moved on.

Pica was mounted by Oyá all through Celita's ordeal. Minutes after San Lázaro–Babalú Ayé dismounted Celita, the orisá of violent storms sought out Isidra. Under her chin she held a candle that sent streaks of light up her cheeks along her scars, its flame singeing the little white hairs of her mount. Oyá took the fatigued host by the hand and headed for the door. The most likely destination on an outing with Oyá is the cemetery, where she presides. That was more than a kilometer away. Isidra was reluctant. An orisá could start a procession, but the permit from the local police did not allow processions. If she and Oyá headed to the cemetery together, it was possible that the drummers, caller, chorus, and all would follow them. Justo, the mute cemetery keeper and Isidra's cousin, was on the big drum and held the musicians and the chorus tight. Shortly, it was just the two of them heading for the cemetery, their path illuminated only by Oyá's candle.

Cucusa's daughter and unrivaled inheritor of her authority was on her way to the cemetery with its keeper and master. What transpired between Isidra and Oyá can only be surmised. Situations of life, death, fate, and enduring consequences are what Oyá determines, and she would have counsel to give.

Cucusa had only just died, and Isidra surely had questions to ask. Oyá was mounted on Pica, one of her mother's dearest confidants. What sweet and heavy words were exchanged?

The drummers were relentless, as was Zenón. The chorus kept going and must have been replenished several times during the night. A bembé comprises hundreds of people who come, dance for a few hours, then leave, only to be replaced by others. Some linger in the street to refresh before returning. It was after 2 a.m. on the 18th when Isidra and Oyá returned. Wax covered the orisá's hands as she pinched a little candle stub in her fingers, its flame still lit. No sooner were they in the door than Isidra stripped Zenón of the call, cutting in with her own verse between the end of a chorus-wide reply and his next call. She was ready to steer the bembé toward a conclusion, which, in the days of the Sociedad Africana, happened only after the Congo powers were called.

At the time, I was working with Isidra and Teodoro on a book about Palo Briyumba, a Congo-inspired society of affliction in Havana. Palo societies in Havana maintain cosmological self-determination alongside Yoruba-inspired Ifá and Ocha-Santería societies, and Catholicism. One of the insights from that book was that in Havana the three laws—Congo-inspired, Yoruba-inspired, and European-inspired—were distinct but diplomatically entangled laws of fate making and fate breaking. Each claimed privileged moments in which exceptions to the rules of the others could be made and in which those claims could be successfully defended against challenges. In Havana, Congo- and Yoruba-inspired forces keep a discreet distance from each other and do not feast together. A single person could be an expert healer under both "laws," but the materials and feasts of each law are maintained physically separate. Havana-based Ocha-Santería and Ifá societies nurture a sense of superiority over Palo societies, to which the latter are largely indifferent.

Isidra sang, "Vamo' cambia' relo', cambia' relo', cambia relo'! Vamo' cambia' relo', cambia' relo', cambia relo'!" She called, "We're going to change the clock, change the clock, change time / We're going to change the beat, change the beat, change the beat, change the beat!"

The chorus replied, with something of a collective stutter: "Vamo' cambia' relo', cambia' relo', cambia relo'! Vamo' cambia' relo', cambia' relo', cambia relo'!"

Isidra repeated the call and the chorus followed, still tentative on the direction she was taking us. Until then, Fon, Yoruba, and Spanish Catholic inspirations had folded together brilliantly. Now, Isidra proposed to add

Congo inspirations that required a major switch of rhythm, time signature, drum roles, lyrics, and dance steps. With her call she drove the entire feast into another style of music, dance, and play that was yet more energetic and newly aggressive. The first couple of calls ground against us, and she insisted, "Vamo' cambia' relo', cambia' relo', cambia relo'. Vamo' cambia' relo', cambia' relo', cambia relo'!"

Some did not like the sudden change. Zulia, the half sister from Corralillo, was standing next to me at the time and said, "I don't like this Congo stuff. It only heats things up. I don't like the way Congos work." She had been mounted by an aggressive Oyá the night before, and as a child had suffered under *muertos oscuros* sent by Congo-inspired *paleros*. "This is not something our mother did. This is from Chacha's Sociedad Africana." Others casually drifted toward the door. Zenón did not think it the right moment to "switch to Congo" and took the opportunity to step outside. Isidra insisted, kept the call, brought the drummers along, and moved the feast over.

Without Zenón to call, and Pica still mounted with Oyá, Isidra was left to carry the Congo turn she had initiated. She knew plenty of songs from the vast local Congo repertoire, and a couple of men who had not called during the feast stepped forward to offer songs. For twenty or thirty minutes we sustained the Congo turn. Pica, who was mounted with Oyá, was instantly mounted with Centella, a Congo power who shares affinities with Oyá. "Sin borrarse," said Isidra later. "Without erasing." Pica's movements under Centella became brusque, her steps more closely tied to the beat, and her turns bolder. Those who remained reveled in the all-out effort she made and the endurance she displayed. These were Cuban-Congo values I recognized from Havana, but the mixture of the orisás and the Congo powers was incongruous. Isidra had advised that we would likely see this mixing, which in Havana is taught as impure even by the Congo-inspired societies. It was Pica's third mounting of the night.

Isidra was visibly pleased. The feast was a success. The opening night had been a raucous gathering. Pica and Zenón had come to sing and held forth the night through. Then they returned to sing the next day on the 17th. The best drummers in town had joined the feast and offered their music for hours upon hours. Responsive, buoyant choruses had gathered both nights. The animal offerings, though not complete because of the missing ram for Changó, had pleased the orisás of the house, as evidenced by their rousing visits. Every orisá, with the exception of Ogún, had mounted a steed. Roberto's Elégua returned after years of absence. Perhaps most important of all, San Lázaro–Babalú Ayé had found a new steed in the beloved and child-less Celita.

Isidra called the feast formally to a close. It was almost 4 a.m. She had Justo fetch a bucket of well water. This she seasoned with what little remained of San Lázaro–Babalú Ayé's staples—the beans, rice, corn, and bread crumbs he preferred. Rousing the drummers to another couple of songs was hardly an effort, as they seemed ready to keep going. With the closing songs in the air, she spun the bucket by its handle, clearing a wide circle among the dwindling but still numerous chorus. She whirled toward the door, showing the balance of an experienced dancer, and arrived there on two solid feet to toss the water into the street. Three steps back across the threshold, she slammed the bucket mouth-down in the middle of the living room. The reverberation that followed brought the drummers to a halt.

The scene dissipated quickly. Four or five drummers wanted to keep going. Iván and his father-in-law, Gonzalo, were among them, as was Justo. Gonzalo was Zenón's younger brother. The sisters gave the house a quick sweep and were fast asleep. What remained of the party now moved to the backyard, where the drinking and drumming continued to well after sunrise. When a bembé was great and the santos-orisás and the Congo powers are gone; when the life-changing forces of a feast are dissipated and the healing potentials spent; when the chorus is left exhausted and the house gone to sleep; still, the music does not stop. The last liter of our Havana aguardiente was passed about more liberally, and the music changed from praise for the orisás and the Congo powers to praise for one another. Also to mischievous denigration of one another. The action shifted from forbidden play meant to host the santos-orisás through divine impersonation to play just for the joy of the music, for fun, to spend the last of what we had. "¡E'tamos rumbeando rico!" laughed Gonzalo. Though Isidra later grumbled about the racket, she also knew that an all-night rumba was a badge of honor for a feast.

Throughout the feast the night before, Teodoro made attempts time and again for a go at the drums. He thought too highly of himself to have taken a seat before the feast was really going, when younger, less experienced drummers were given their chance. When things were properly heated up, he had tried for the big drum. But the *caja* is jealously guarded by those with confidence to play it. He wriggled his way into the rotation and unleashed some searing Havana riffs on which the other musicians looked askance. He was beyond competent, he was excellent in fact, but his drumming was too flashy, too slick for those gathered. Pica's Changó was singing at the time, and he made it clear with a dip of his chin and a raised eyebrow that the riffs were not appreciated. Teodoro was chided off the drum. On his next attempt at the caja he was directed by his fellow percussionists to the *quinto,* the middle drum, which plays backup rhythm for the caja. He proceeded to improvise brilliantly as in a Havana jam session. But at a Sierra Morena bembé the quinto is not used for improvisation. Only on the caja can a drummer improvise. Breaking the middle drum out of its rhythmic constraints went over very poorly, and he was again ragged off the drum. He slipped into the backyard to drink and brag. When the other drummers wanted to goad him, they offered him the little drum, the *mula,* which keeps a simple time. This he refused, exaggerating his disregard. By the time the rumba broke out in the backyard, a scene Teodoro could have contributed to with flair, he was gone.

We spent two days unwinding the feast, cleaning, sorting, and visiting. María, who got around, carried word of a bembé for San Lázaro–Babalú Ayé that was held at a house on the curve in the road on the outskirts of town. The house hosting it had stepped in the year before, when Cucusa's feast was suspended and did not close its doors when Isidra returned. She found this to be an insult as much to her mother's memory as to herself personally. "Pretenders," she said. "Two years is nothing. They won't last. They should stop with their foolishness and let people focus on a truly righteous party for Babalú Ayé." She did not give the rumor more thought. She had the house to worry about and her efforts were geared toward preparing and securing it for her absence.

Pica, who wanted no more to do with house-sitting after the break-in and subsequent works to counter Yamilet and her husband, would nonetheless remain in charge. Roberto, urged by his wife, Celia, refused the keys. There was not a lot left for Yamilet to steal, but Isidra planned to leave a few things and wanted them looked after. More, she was now worried that Yamilet was going to break in and take Cucusa's very santos, or worse, destroy them. Pica was the ideal person to care for them. The simple work of maintaining them between bembés was second nature to her. She knew to sing for them and to show them respect day to day. If Isidra ever needed one or another of them "lit," which is to say activated by lighting a candle, Pica was the only person she trusted.

A Girón V now waited for us in Corralillo for our return to Havana. Isidra's authority to host Cucusa's feast was cemented. Her claim to her mother's mantle was contested by none of her siblings or half siblings, who all deferred to her. The gathering of her full siblings also said that the children of Cucusa and Orfilio had more of a claim on the property than any others, including the people next door. Most importantly, she had a new mount for San Lázaro–Babalú Ayé.

My trip to Sierra Morena in 1999 was a fluke. I was writing about Congo-inspired Palo sorcery in Havana, and Isidra was my teacher and guide in that work. She proposed the trip to the countryside to provide me with important counterpoints to what I was learning about in Havana. She was very good at justifying her wishes in terms that made sense to me. In the end, she was right. What we experienced in Sierra Morena burrowed into me and provided me with an invaluable understanding of how Havana-centric most writing about African-inspired praise in Cuba can be. It also taught me that African-inspired praise in Cuba is hugely diverse and that the ways praise and practice are organized in the capital are not the way praise and practice are organized throughout the island.[2] Sierra Morena praise was refreshingly nonhierarchical compared to that of the Havana societies, be they Yoruba- or Congo-inspired. It had no priesthood, no initiations, no formal godparents, and no initiate godchildren. Havana praise was top heavy and strict by comparison. Most important, the bembé for San Lázaro–Babalú Ayé was fun. I had traveled and lived and done research in Cuba during eight years in the 1990s, without a doubt the grimmest decade faced by that country in the twentieth century. Rarely had I had fun. The 1999 bembé showed me that despite the terrible shortages, the generation-wide exoduses, and the political despair, a threadbare community in the middle of a fallow countryside could praise their ancestors, feast their sovereigns, and mightily enjoy themselves in doing so. I would not return until December 2005, and even then I did not know that I would write this book.

PART THREE

NINE

2005

LOSS

ULISES WANTED NOTHING TO DO WITH THE TRIP to Sierra Morena. It was December 6, and the rest of the month would be full of end-of-year celebrations with his friends. He was nineteen and flourishing.

"Don't look at me like that," said Isidra.

"I have nothing in Sierra Morena, Mom. People to see here too."

"Nothing? You have me, first and foremost. Your mother. You have Ramón here, your friend who has come from California. You have your Aunt Eulalia and your uncles."

Ulises turned his back and headed for his room.

"Turn around," she said, raising her voice just a little. "Look at your mother."

He did what she asked.

"Do not turn your back on me. Look at me. Do you see who is standing here? Who? The mother that raised you, that breastfed you, that carried you in her womb and then on her shoulders your whole life. That is who is standing here."

He lowered his eyes.

"Look at me. You think your nineteen years count for something? They count for nothing compared to the nineteen years I have spent raising you on the straight and narrow." She said these things sternly but not angrily. She had said them to him countless times before.

He stood there quietly, resigned.

"Don't think for another second that you have a choice. You know you don't." A moment of plain, settled silence passed. "Your cousins will be there, Boby and Anelé," she said, and with that closed the conversation.

The visit was not going to be easy. Isidra's nephew, Robertico, the son of her brother Roberto, was dead.

"Fallecido hace poco," said Isidra. "Deceased a little while ago."

Her statement was short and formal, and I was left to ask the obvious questions.

"Let Roberto tell you when you see him. He'll be happy to have your visit."

I looked at her quizzically, motioning with a tilt of my head and a raised eyebrow that more of the story would be welcome.

"Nothing, Ramón. There is nothing else to say. He was not my son. You see my son right there in his room. Nineteen years, and he is alive and on the straight and narrow."

"What about Roberto and Celia?" I asked. How could she not have said anything about them? Perhaps the six years between my visits had eroded our confidence. Every conversation with Isidra was a test of confidence.

"Roberto is being difficult."

"What?" I was put off. "How is Roberto doing? How are he and Celia feeling?"

"I don't have time for their feelings, Ramón, or for Celita's for that matter. That family should have only one goal right now, and that is the success of Cucusa's feast. Everything else is foolishness [tontería]."

I was speechless. This was normal in Isidra's company, but this time she acknowledged my surprise.

"This is the worst thing that can happen to a parent, Ramón. You now have a child of your own, so you know. But there is no point in lifting a finger for them without the aid of my mother's santos. Roberto and Celia will never rise up without the help of Babalú Ayé. You should know that by now. The only thing I have time for, Ramón, is making sure they do what they must [cumplimentan] for the feast for Babalú Ayé."

I knew little about Robertico. He was the eldest of Roberto and Celia's three children. Robertico was a veteran of Cuba's intervention in Angola, sent by the revolution to fight apartheid in southern Africa in the early 1980s. Once back, he worked in government warehouses managed by his uncle Máximo in Santa Clara, the capital of their province. Then the Soviet Union collapsed, and five unbearable years of economic crisis followed. When the revolution chose tourism as the way forward for the Cuban economy after 1994, Robertico moved to Varadero, Cuba's historic, marvelous white-sand beach stretching north off the central coast. It lies halfway between Sierra Morena and Havana. Varadero became ground zero for the government's tourism strategy after 1994. Crucial to its choice as Cuba's tourist engine was its standing infrastructure, which was a lot of five-story modernist hotels from the 1950s and several ten-story Soviet-era workers' hostels. Varadero had a single causeway for access, which made the government's early plans to impose a strict separation between foreigners and locals more feasible. Robertico worked there in the warehouses that supplied the new foreigners-only hotels that accepted only hard currency. Any attempt to learn more about him from Isidra was met with silence.

Several days of gathering supplies in Havana preceded our departure for the countryside, but eventually on December 11, Isidra, Ulises, and I were in a car heading east out of the city. In the six years that had transpired since my last visit to Sierra Morena, the bread tin Hungarian Girón V buses were replaced with proper coaches, tall and air-conditioned, purchased from China. They came complete with higher prices and less flexible under-the-table arrangements. As a result, a fleet of private cars capable of making interprovincial trips appeared and took up residence just outside the bus station—hard currency only. Hiring one of these made new sense for three travelers with a base camp's worth of things. Our route took us past the causeway to Varadero, just east of Matanzas. I looked across the waterway and tried to find a way to bring up Robertico's death, but nothing was appropriate. Isidra said nothing.

Cucusa's house was ready to receive us. It had been cleaned from head to toe by Zulia from Corralillo, who had moved in a few weeks earlier. In the past year, Isidra and Eulalia had decided that someone needed to be in their mother's house full time. The looting by Yamilet in the wake of Cucusa's death was ever present as an insult and lingering fear. Pica had hung on as a house sitter for five years and decided she could take no more.

Zulia lived in Corralillo, the municipal seat five kilometers west of Sierra Morena. She lived in a government-built apartment. It had two rooms—one for her and one for the second of her two sons, Ernesto. Her eldest son was in prison, in Palma Sola, one of western Cuba's most notorious penitentiaries. Zulia's apartment was on a hill facing the lagoon, and in winter the moist breeze coming off the water chilled her to the bone.

"The gusts," she said. "Tropical architecture—worse, the things the revolution has put up—are not made for that wind. The weather was almost as bad as my neighbors, and all the things the CDR wanted us to do. This is quieter—no meetings, requests, or mandatory mobilizations."

Life five kilometers away in Sierra Morena was easier, more private, and more protected from the north wind. Isidra and Eulalia hardly hesitated to offer their Díaz half sister the house. It needed caring for. The roof was in poor repair; the backyard was overgrown. The one condition they imposed was that for the month of December, the house would be handed over to the two sisters who would requisition it for Cucusa's feast.

"A house can't sit empty. It can't sit alone," said Isidra. "This one less so. The santos need attention. They need human warmth. Who knows what Yamilet next door is capable of. Pica did us a huge favor, but she didn't live here. It is time to move on, and Zulia is our option. Can you feel that it is lived in already?"

I could. It was a quiet evening. The living room was tidy, and even the high ceilings were swept of cobwebs. The cracked cement floors were mopped almost shiny, and the shutters on the tall window to the street were open. Zulia's modest, comfortable furniture was inviting. Eulalia had arrived a couple of days earlier from Cienfuegos, and her domestic skills combined with Zulia's hard work had prepared a home capable of matching the expectations of big-city visitors, which in the Cuba of 2005 was a great compliment. There were beds and even a refrigerator to replace the things that were stolen before the 1999 feast. Still, many things were missing or short, and Isidra had come prepared for the nine days we would be in town. A fifty-pound sack of rice, several bottles of cooking oil, bed linens, cooking pots, even onions. Despite the hard work of her sisters, Isidra understood our trip as a campaign and came prepared for hardship. She had packed her Batalla Palo bundle, understood by Cuban-Congo wisdom to have life-shaking powers. Once greetings were concluded, Isidra withdrew Batalla from the vinyl overnight bag in which it traveled and placed it in a corner by the house's big double portal. She lit a candle there.

The next morning, December 12, Eulalia and Isidra were talking in the room off the kitchen, where they had set up their sleeping quarters. "Ramón, come here," said Isidra softly but with energy in her voice. "Listen to this. Tell him, Eulalia."

"What? That Zulia is a slob? You should have seen this house! What a mess! I think if it weren't for Isaías, her boyfriend, living here with her, it would be worse. At least he can fix a hinge or get up on the roof. Still, everything you see here is my work, my sweeping, dusting, mopping. This was a sty."

Eulalia said this under quiet chuckles. She was cheerful, so it was hard to tell when she thought things were actually unpleasant. She was good at comic exasperation, which went with her big eyes and long face. Encouraged by the audience we provided, she went on, "You think that it is funny? You should have seen me up on a chair to sweep out the cobwebs. You should have seen me in the kitchen, and the grills on the charcoal stove. This looked like a *bayú* [flophouse]!"

Isidra found this last expression hilarious and laughed out loud. Eulalia was delighted to have the floor and repeated it, "¡Un bayú! I mean it! What?"

We calmed down, and her tone became more serious, though still bright. "But really. The place looks OK, but we need to work. Don't think you're just going to show up from Havana and party. I know how Ramón likes to party!" Her sarcasm on the last point made Isidra crack up again.

"Listen, right now we're using a chamber pot in our rooms," she said. "We have to get walls put up around the latrine. The outhouse came down, and Zulia hasn't even thought about getting it back up again. What has she been doing, going in a bucket all this time?" Again, she turned her comic dismay to mischievous effect and had her sister laughing.

"Ramón, that's your job. You get the outhouse up tomorrow. Weren't you a carpenter with your dad?" Eulalia hadn't seen me in six years and remembered a detail like that.

"Stepdad," I said.

"Stepdad," she said. "Tomorrow, Justo will be here with a hammer."

Eulalia continued. "You think the fridge is hers? Isidra knows better. Don't be fooled, Ramón. You think we've arrived at bourgeois comfort here in this little town? You think we're a Varadero Beach resort? Zulia could never! That refrigerator is rented from around the block, and we're paying hard currency for it. You think Zulia has any of that? You're the only one who has that, Ramón!" Now she cracked up. "How is she living here without a refrigerator or a proper outhouse? You tell me!"

Ulises had quickly adjusted to spending the end of the year away from Havana. He and his cousins (first cousins once removed—but it didn't matter) were out in the street getting reacquainted and discovering affinities that sprang effortlessly from their childhood intimacies. Anelé was sixteen, and there was nothing about her Havana cousin that didn't matter to her. She had come over to Cucusa's just to look at him, his clothes, his jewelry, his way of speaking, with his Havana accent and his slang. She lived in Santa Clara, the provincial capital, which compared to Havana was a country village like Sierra Morena. Anelé wanted to get to Havana and was still doing well enough in school to dream of attending university there. Her great aunt Isidra had offered her the same room in her apartment she had offered Celita in the 1970s if she could do it. This meant doing brilliantly in school, being exemplary in the party's childhood ranks, and having party militants for parents. Anelé was on her way with all three.

Anelé was a pretty kid, though too skinny for mainstream Cuban standards of feminine beauty. Her charm came from her open disposition and her curiosity, which found ready expression in large, cheerful eyes. At times those eyes dipped, though, and it was then that they reflected the pall that lay over the family. She was Roberto and Celia's granddaughter, the child of Alejandro, their middle child. Robertico was her uncle, and his death troubled her. She showed it, and her first interactions with her aunts were awkward because the topic was unspeakable for them. She was an upbeat kid, though, and soon she and Ulises were lost in gossip about her favorite topic, the girls and boys in town. Both waited with anticipation for the arrival of their cousin Boby, and no one seemed to know if we would come at all. He was eighteen, and it was his father who had died.

It was evening of our second night in town, and I couldn't understand why Isidra hadn't gone directly to her brother and his wife to comfort them or join them in grieving. I went to visit them to offer greetings and express my condolences, but their house was closed up. It being a small town, neighbors offered possible locations for the two. Roberto was drinking a couple of kilometers out of town. Celia had caught a bus to Varadero. Isidra wanted my report when I returned.

"Why didn't you come with me?" I said.

"I know where I belong. They should know where they belong."

That night the double doors were closed, and Batalla was placed on the floor where they met, beneath the two-by-four that barred them.

Morning of the 13th and Justo was there at 6:30, then again at 8:30. A pile of broken and rotted lumber lay where the outhouse had stood. Justo and I were joined by Isaías, Zulia's companion [*su marido*]. He was small by comparison to his lover, who was a bull in size and disposition. Justo had a hammer, itself a recycled head welded to a piece of recycled metal tubing, maybe from playground equipment. There were no supplies in the town's hardware dispensary, so we scoured the rubble for old nails we could pull, straighten, and use again.

Six years earlier, Justo was the town's cemetery keeper. He worked alone opening graves, filling them, then opening them again a year later to move the remains to niches, as is the custom in Cuba. He communicated with me using jabbing hand signals, and jabbed at others to answer for him in our interactions. Being mute was ideal for a cemetery keeper in a little country town, I thought. The bone trade generated by Cuban-Congo healing-harming practices, especially by Havana-based Palo, would make it obvious to raid a little cemetery like Sierra Morena's, sitting as it did on the highway. Easier, bribe the cemetery keeper, who would have a sack of skulls and bones ready to pick up at the roadside, enough to meet any *palero*'s needs, plus a few to sell on the underground market for such things. Justo had the ruddy brown skin of his cousins and a thin, long nose. Despite being more than sixty, he was lithe and muscled, and his hands were big and ready. His cheekbones were prominent, and his inability to speak magnified his already large eyes, so they seemed enormous as you searched them for signs of what he was trying to convey. He was toothless, but that didn't keep him from being vertiginously, uncannily handsome.

Isaías had no tools, so between the three of us we had Justo's hammer. Isaías, who had just come from a night shift in the kitchen at the Ministry of the Interior (MININT) base on the outskirts of town, understood this to mean that he should find a block to sit on and smoke his morning pack.

"Isidra is crazy. She is good and crazy," he said. Isaías's voice was gravely with a bass timbre.

Neither Justo nor I acknowledged the comment.

"Comes from Havana packed as if this town were a guerrilla encampment. I'm in the kitchen at the MININT base. She could have asked me for half the kitchen she brought with her."

The MININT base was there to help control the chain of keys that runs from Varadero to Sagua la Grande. Arching toward Florida, the keys are the nearest point where the territories of Cuba and the United States come to each other. The lagoon on which Sierra Morena sits is shallow and well suited for those attempting an unauthorized outing for an escape attempt [*una embarcación*]. The revolution calls these "illegal exits" [*salida illegal*] and tries to prevent them. People leave on homemade craft, for which Cuba's refugees have become renowned as inventors, mechanics, and mariners. Or they leave on cigarette boats that zip in from Key West to pick up those who can pay the tens of thousands of dollars demanded by Miami's human-trafficking networks. Of the three lights along those keys, the lighthouse across the lagoon from Sierra Morena is the most remote and affords a highly navigable launching and pickup point. The MININT is a powerful state security force charged with keeping order inside Cuba. In Sierra Morena, it was more interested in the cigarette boats and the trafficking networks they exposed than it was in the homemade craft, though that didn't keep it from regularly intercepting solitary fishermen from town and slashing their inner tubes on the argument that they posed a national security risk.

"She might have moved her entire house here," Isaías said, "but she still needs a big pot to boil the water for plucking all those birds. I said that, and do you know what she said to me?" He didn't wait for us to respond. He knew that we would never join him, nor would we egg him on. "She told me I was useless. That I was a parasite clinging to Zulia, and if I wanted to help, I should start out here grubbing through this pile of shit like the two of you. Listen, she's crazy to treat me like that. Doesn't she know Zulia and I live here? No one knows this house like me right now. No one can get her the things she needs to pull off this party like me. Go figure."

Justo looked at him and jabbed a finger at the roof of the house, then swept his open palm across the vista of the overgrown yard. In a split second he pinched his fingertips together and snapped his hand outward once at the wrist, so that his fingers opened again, pointing at Isaías. "Then why is this place a mess?" his gesture asked.

Isaías cracked a smile. "Listen, Ramón," he said, "the only one in this whole circus who will tell you the truth is me. Justo can speak, in case you thought he was a retard. He just doesn't sometimes. Justo, say it so I can hear it, then maybe I'll answer you."

We finished scrounging for nails, and Isaías helped us dig out the collapsed posts so we could brace them back into the frame of an outhouse. It took us the better part of the morning, but credible walls were up and a door hung by lunchtime. As we split up, Isaías said, "Tell Isidra that she can't count on me to butcher on the 17th unless there is at least one big pot for plucking and a decent knife. She knows where to ask."

When Isaías was out of sight, Justo said, plain as day, "He talks shit," then finished his sentence with a shake of his head and a motion of his hand that meant "he doesn't know shit."

"Justo, you can talk." I said it as calmly as I could.

"When it's important," he said.

"Thank you for helping," I said, imagining I had only a few seconds in which I might be understood, as if he didn't understand every word I said. "Do you still work in the graveyard?"

He looked at me directly and closed his mouth tightly. He pointed his bony index finger and shook his whole forearm back and forth once to indicate no.

Late in the afternoon of the 13th, I tried Roberto and Celia again. She was home, sitting in a rocking chair in her living room. She was crying. I hadn't seen her in six years, and then we had only casual, courteous interactions. I wanted to tell her I knew about Robertico and to express my condolences.

"I was here when you came by yesterday, Ramón. It is kind of you. I can't go on. I can't. I don't know how to live anymore. I don't care about anything, not this house, not anything." She looked out the door to the dilapidated church across the street. "Celita has her beautiful boy now, Guillermo. And she is pregnant again. Do you remember how desperate she was to have children? San Lázaro helped her. Before, I took such joy in Guillermo. I was so happy with him. Now nothing makes me happy. The worst is that I'm not happy for her, Ramón. How can a mother not be happy for her daughter when she has a little child and another one on the way?"

"When was it, Celia?"

"This summer. Six months ago. He killed himself, Ramón."

It was late in the afternoon, and there was no sound of a sputtering pressure cooker on the stove, which was not normal for a house in town during the end-of-year season. "I'm alone," she said crying silently. "No one can stand to be around me. Roberto is out drinking and won't come home. Boby will come, and I don't want to see him. My grandson. This house used to be where the party was during end of year. We had so much fun. Now look at me." I stayed with her for a while, but she would no longer speak. Her despondent grief eventually drove me quietly away.

Isidra was curious. "They say she is crazy. What do you think, Ramón?"

"She is not in good shape. Her son is dead. She is really feeling it."

"Did she tell you that Robertico threw himself off a building in Varadero?"

"No."

"Five stories, Ramón. What is a bright kid like him doing throwing himself off a building? Angola veteran. Party militant. He could have had anything. Five stories. You tell me."

"People kill themselves for all kinds of reasons," I said.

"It is what a life in tourism brings. Depression, alcohol, and then they discover that a whole shipping container of air conditioners under your watch has disappeared. They say it was more than one. Do you know how many years of jail he faced if it was true? Temptation. I tell Ulises to stay away. His is the sign of a teacher. That is a noble profession, you know that, and today's Cuba needs to educate the next generation in revolutionary values."

"Isidra," I asked, "why don't you go see her?"

"Her problems are not mine, Ramón. I would be a fool to try, wouldn't I? She needs a doctor. But nothing will work if Babalú Ayé is not with her. She knows her place is here, in support of this feast and this house and that she has to bring Roberto too. You know these things now, Ramón, so don't ask again." I left her where she stood.

It was evening on the 13th when the house was stirred up by a visit from Pica. The singer, who along with Zenón was the heart of the best bembés in town, was happy to see Isidra and Eulalia. As usual she wore a threadbare T-shirt over her hunched back, flour sack pants, and bedraggled flip-flops. The burn scars that reached up from her chest and around her cheeks and ears were as striking as ever. She was shy despite being the center of attention at bembés. Recently she had been in demand for bembés as far away as Rancho Veloz. She preferred to listen to a conversation, which was difficult when everyone wanted to hear from her. She managed to settle in quickly, eager to soak in gossip and spread it when she could do so discreetly.

Pica had lost weight and was looking good with a little spring in her shuffling step. "But don't think I'm in good shape," she said. "I can't see well at all. My sugar. On top of that, I've got my brother living with me. No one to take care of him but me. He's paralyzed after a drinking binge left him with a stroke. The revolution is supposed to be looking after him, but it's just me. Not so much as a diaper. They gave me a bar of soap back in January. Maybe they'll give out something else this coming year. Let's see!"

"Pica, how was your bembé for Changó? I know that is what you live for," Isidra chuckled.

"Good party this year. Lots of people, even from San Rafael and Rancho Veloz some of them. I've been singing it up a lot this year, been getting in carts and going places to sing. People pay me."

"Pay you? We can't pay you, Pica," said Eulalia, joking.

Pica looked annoyed. "I won't be going anywhere on the 16th and 17th but right here. I won't be going up to the party at the Curve, if you were worried." The party on the outskirts of town that had erupted the year Cucusa died was still going strong. Isidra ignored Pica's comment, but a quick furrow of her brow communicated her distaste.

Isidra steered the conversation back to one of her favorite topics in town, which was Chacha Cairo's Sociedad Africana and the generation of elders that comprised it. She drew Pica out, and it was Pica's father, Loreto, who came into focus.

"When my father was the town watchman, before the revolution, there was no crime. Never was there a shot, or a fight, or a thing stolen. Now there is nothing but throw-downs and break-ins and young people getting killed, and no one ever knows who did any of it."

Isidra tried to correct her course. "Is it true about the two members of the rural guard who came to bust the bembé at Chacha's Sociedad, and they were both mounted by Changó?"

"I was there," said Pica. Then she continued on an apparent non sequitur. "Loreto had a *muerto*, one of the dead, who would mount him out of nowhere. His name was Juan Sáez. He had hands the size of flowerpots. Loreto would wake up in the middle of the night with Juan Sáez mounted up on him. My mother, Quintina, it was all she could do to get his clothes on him, and then she would follow him down the street. When he was mounted like that by Juan Sáez, he would eventually end up facedown in the dirt, pounding the earth with those great fists."

"Pica," Isidra said, "why don't you sing some songs from the Sociedad Africana? Ramón can play *mula* now."

"Sing to that?" Pica said looking at me. "I've got standards. No offense, Ramón, but a drum has to carry me at least a little."

"I've heard you sing to yourself, Pica," said Eulalia.

Pica gently shook her head.

Late that night, Isidra could not sleep. Her cousin, Agripina from Sagua, had come, and they were sharing a bed. Isidra was not one to open a book and read quietly waiting for dawn. She was not one to brew herself a cup of coffee and sit thinking about the day ahead. Ever since she was a child in this town, she had been *inquieta,* unstill. She was famous for moving faster, talking faster, and getting more done than any kid in town. Others in town described her speed and energy as "alterada," or buzzed.

To her, sleeplessness in the middle of the night was caused by a disturbance in the ambience of the dead who perpetually coursed around her, moved through her, and in whom she was submerged.[1] For Isidra there was no such thing as insomnia, medicalized and separated from life. Life for her was the irrefutable, ubiquitous, physical proximity of the dead around us. The dead were in the forest at midday, at the crossroads, and in the bend in the river at La Corua. They were in the house, in the air she breathed, and in the very cells of her body.

It was four in the morning, and she had the lights on in the living room and a pair of rattles in her hands. At the top of her lungs she was singing songs to Yemayá, who presided over her head, which is to say over her fate. Yemayá gathers all sorts of songs and powers to her, and Isidra sang one of her war songs. It was a favorite of hers, the same one she sang at La Corua and in countless other instances.

The night was calm and cool before the first calls of the roosters. Zulia was sleeping on the living room couch, where Isidra was now literally singing up a storm invoking Yemayá, sovereign of the open sea, to shake the foundations of the world should her household be disrespected. Along a coast known for its exposure to terrible storms, including the worst hurricanes, this was not a small thing to ask.

Zulia tried to sleep. She ignored her sister and rolled over on the couch, which was already too small.

"Everybody up! Everybody up! There is no point sleeping when the dead are on the march. They marched right through the front door and they've taken the house. It hasn't been cleaned, and that was a mistake. We're all going to clean now!" Eulalia and Agripina were up already, without complaint. Ulises and I had to be pulled out of bed.

She had Eulalia make her an ample broom of *aroma blanca,* which she had collected the day before. Aroma blanca is a plant common in the countryside with small, shiny, dark green leaves and thorns. It is used to aggressively sweep out the ill-boding dead wherever they may cling. Over the next half hour, she beat every surface of the house with the bundle: the furniture, the walls, the door frames. She sang Cucusa's songs as she went. Zulia got up just before she was whacked along with the couch. Isidra declaimed on the fates of every person present as the sweeping progressed, interpreting the issues faced by each person according to their devotion to Cucusa's house. Zulia, who had moved from Corralillo to care for the house, was first.

"Your children say it all. They are a martyrdom for you. One is in jail, and he is not ever going to get out. The other is sick. You know he almost died last year, and if it weren't for the santos in this house, he'd be dead. He isn't out of the woods yet. You straighten up and serve this house as you're expected to!" Zulia kept her head down.

Isidra took up the song again, scolding every one of us between verses.

"Eulalia, where have you been? In Cienfuegos? You can't hide from your responsibilities. Complacency will be the end of us. Look at Zulia here. You yourself told Ramón and me that Zulia is incompetent, that you found the house a pigsty, worse than if no one were living here. But you won't say it to her face, which it now becomes my duty to do. Do you think this is easy for me? To say the things no one else will? Look at Zulia here. She is an imbecile, and you behave as if she can carry the responsibility for this house alone. She can't. No one can, let alone her.

"Agripina from Sagua, you're here. No one can reproach you for that. But where have you been this year? You live right down the road in Sagua la Grande. How many times have you come to open up the house, sweep it out, and let people see that there is life here, that they can come greet San Lázaro at this altar?

"Ramón, you're here now, but how long has it been? Do you think you can show up here after six years and get anything done? Your emails are too short, and when I have asked you for money, you have been slow. Do you think a house like this can be maintained without hard currency? Money would help my brother Roberto, who should be in control here. Where is he? Drinking in the countryside? Do you think I haven't noticed the disrespect?"

Ulises had fallen asleep in a chair that had been swept by aroma blanca. "Wake up! Wake up! Who do you think you are? A king, a maharaja? You're nothing but a foolish child. What are you doing all day in the street with your cousin and the girls from town? Don't you see your mother needs you, that this house needs you? You're becoming a man now. You will be twenty in a few weeks. You can give so much. Don't think I don't know what happens next. One of these little whores you're running around with is going to get you to take her home to Havana. You blink and she'll be pregnant, and don't think I'm going to take her in. She'll have to climb this wall that is your mother. You don't have a clue. Well, I do. Get up. Take this bucket."

Isidra was about to throw the first of many buckets Ulises and I pulled from the well when Zulia spoke.

"Don't. Don't wet my furniture."

Isidra heard her as if she had shouted. "Don't wet your furniture? Don't throw this bucket of water? This house needs to be cleaned of all the malign things you have let in here, and you're worried about the legs of your couch? Get it out. Get it out of here. We don't need it. Everything out!"

Zulia, who was twice Isidra's size, stood still.

"Don't touch it. Don't you touch my furniture. It stays right where it is. You can mop around it. You don't have to go around splashing water everywhere."

Isidra swung the bucket high behind her before she brought it forward. She began to sing and dance barefoot through the water she had splashed around the couch. As if on cue, Eulalia and Agripina from Sagua went to their rooms and returned dressed head to toe in white with white head-scarves. Isidra herself was in a blue gingham dress, her head covered with a light blue headscarf—clothing that pleased Yemayá. After a song or two, during which Zulia stood still, she turned to her younger half sister.

"Your memory is short if what worries you is your furniture. What about when you were worried for your two sons? Let me remind you. A year ago, where was Ernesto? In an ambulance being rushed to Sagua la Grande because a fever was about to kill him. What did you do? You called Eulalia and asked her to rush here from Cienfuegos to open up the saints' room, to light candles, and get down on her knees before Babalú Ayé and beg for your son's life. And she did it. Look at Eulalia here now. Do I need to remind you of what you felt that night? Of what your sister did for you? What pulled Ernesto out of that coma? Was it Eulalia, who will sacrifice anything for this house? No. It was the santos in that room on the other side of that curtain you're looking at right now. And now you whine about preparing this house for Babalú Ayé on his feast day?" She turned without waiting for a reply and began singing again, emphatically and directly.

Zulia bent down to pick up one end of the sofa and signaled to Agripina from Sagua that she should help. Bucket after bucket of water was drawn from the well and poured on the floor. We spent the time until dawn cleaning and singing and beating away ill-portending forces.

TEN

A Hole to Fill

THE MORNING OF DECEMBER 14 SHOULD HAVE BEEN UPBEAT, with the house newly swept of maleficent forces, fears, and insinuations. But Isidra had not slept and continued to brood about Yamilet next door. In the six years since the break-in, her half niece had engaged in countless little acts of unneighborly aggravation but had not entered the house again. Isidra's greatest fear, which was that harm would come to Cucusa's santos, had not come to pass. Still, Yamilet was a constant threat capable of sowing pain and confusion through Congo-inspired sorcery. People did not throw themselves off buildings without someone lending a hand. Isidra credited her early-morning work with safeguarding the house and our bodies from Yamilet's ill will, but she also feared she could strike at any time. Indeed, with the opening of the feast only two days away, Isidra was concerned. After he emerged from his fever-induced coma earlier in the year, Ernesto, Zulia's son, promised San Lázaro–Babalú Ayé that he would assume responsibilities in preparing the December 17 bembé. He would procure all the animals for the feast so that his aunts would be free from this work. But a mature ram that should have been delivered the day before still hadn't arrived.

"Listen here, Ernesto," said Isidra. "That ram is for the dead [*el muerto*], it is for the meal for the dead [*comida al muerto*]. Feeding the dead with a ram needed to happen here at Cucusa's house long ago, and people don't understand. They don't understand that we wouldn't be in the situation we're in if we had offered a ram last year and before. Robertico is dead, and how close did you come? An animal like that one, do you think I'm the only person who wants to offer a mature ram three days from now? Check on it."

Ernesto was unfazed. He had checked, and the animal was on its way. Animals had steadily arrived during the last couple of days, including chickens and roosters of various colors and degrees of maturity and a small male goat that charmed the sisters. Isidra was especially fond of its playfulness. It was an ideal meal for Elégua and would assure a propitious start to the feast. A huge male goat came later that morning. It was the meal for San Lázaro–Babalú Ayé, and Ernesto paid for it himself.

Sometime later, Ernesto came with the news that the man who had brought the goat was the one who should have brought the ram too. "How could it be?" said Isidra incredulously. "How could the man have been here with a goat and not the ram, and you say nothing to me? Do I look like a shit eater? The shit eater is Ernesto, who you see standing right here. It is a little late to come with this news. What does the man say?"

"A truck from Havana is going up and down the highway looking for animals and has bought everything up. They are going as far as Sagua la Grande looking for animals they can take back to Havana for the 17th." Ernesto would not look at his aunt. "He said he would get another by tomorrow morning."

"Another by tomorrow morning?" said Isidra. "Tomorrow is the 15th. I want to feed the dead with it tomorrow morning. Which ram is he going to bring, the one the truck from Havana left behind because it was too expensive? We're supposed to pay for that one? No. No way. Tell the man to shove it. My friend Oier, around the corner, has a cart. Have him here by two o'clock."

Ernesto did as he was told, and after midday we were trundling south out of town to find a big red ram.

"It will appear," said Isidra confidently, "for me."

Oier, the driver, was proud of his cart and horses. He and his son had two carts and seven horses between them. The carts were fifteen years old, and he did all his own maintenance, including the welding. The horses were used in rotation. "I keep them locked in my backyard, or they'll be stolen. It is a huge problem. A decent horse is 2,000 pesos."

Justo was along, commanded by Isidra to join us. Ernesto was left behind amid persistent scolding. Justo had a flask of government-provisioned rum and offered it around. Isidra turned away in disgust. "Don't you start a bender, Justo!" Oier declined.

"Not since Angola," he said. "I was there for twenty-eight months. During my time that is how long the tours were. Two years and more. I left with our four-year-old son having just died of a stroke, or something, and my wife was left alone with our six-month-old, the one who now drives the other cart.

Can you imagine? Twenty-eight months and guess how much leave? Four days. The rest of the time was in the field. You can't imagine what it is like to go weeks without bathing. You can't imagine the dirt, the heat, then the cold. I saw four battles, the worst of which was a four-hour ambush. If I took a drink now, it would be the end of me."

An hour and six kilometers later we were in San Pedro, the same village we had visited six years earlier. It was no more than a crossing of a red dirt lane with the road. A rusting red and yellow Soviet-era agricultural hulk loomed. A few men sat atop motionless tractors or horses, their forearms rippled and their hands gnarled. Women with little children huddled under slivers of shade. The men wore black rubber boots, the women shabby flip-flops. Relations between men and women in the countryside were remarkably clear. Justo, whose eyes were quick, spotted the only thing for sale in the village ration post—rum. He chugged the last of his flask, then refilled it at a black-market price of 10 pesos.

"Justo," I asked, "how is it that the only thing for sale is rum?" I wondered if he would speak or signal.

"Can't survive here without rum," he said. "We can go without cooking oil, without soap, without fuel for tractors, without toothpaste, without medicine. Not without rum."

The roads to San Pedro were desolate. We spent two hours on the road there and back, and in that time saw three trucks and two cars, total. A boxy, Soviet-era tractor rumbled onto the road for a few hundred meters. The roar of its engine as it passed us was bone shaking. Justo smiled and pointed at the machine. The man driving it was shirtless, sunburned, and powerful, with a potbelly. Still in those years anything that moved in that countryside—bike, car, cart, wagon, trailer, tractor—was a testament to human ingenuity and sacrifice, each a heap of gears held together by a chain of provisional fixes, improvised couplings and tenuous black market arrangements that kept it running.

As we went, animals appeared for Isidra left and right: several chickens, two roosters, and a black turkey. With each success she would glow, but the ram would not appear and she sulked.

"Justo," she started during a silence, "what is going on at the Curve?"

"The curve?"

"At the Curve into town, by the cemetery, you know."

"Bembé for San Lázaro."

"Every year?"

"They've been feasting San Lázaro since the year Cucusa died. Just keeps getting bigger."

"They have no business," said Isidra.

"They're not alone. Five or six houses will feast him this year."

"What do they know?" said Isidra. The cart bumbled along.

Justo took a sip. "It used to be just Cucusa's bembé, cousin, but no more. Lots of parties for him this year."

"Well, at the Curve they have no business. That woman is a scammer. She has no idea how to host him."

"The Sociedad Africana is gone, cousin. Chacha is gone. Loreto is gone. Cucusa is gone."

"Shhh!" She stared at him. "They're gone, it's true. Cucusa is gone. She is. But look who is sitting in this cart with you. Look at Isidra talking to you right now. I'm here, and that is enough. The upstarts are committing disrespect. The woman at the Curve is just the worst of them."

We returned home in the afternoon to find Isidra's niece, Celita, waiting for us. She was sitting at the kitchen table with Eulalia. She sat with her forehead resting in one hand, a handkerchief in the other.

"Can you do it, Aunt?" she asked once Isidra was in the door.

Isidra looked around. "I know you want this, but not without your husband and your father. Bring them here."

"Can't we just do it, Aunt? José is fishing, and my father . . ."

"Celita, I could cleanse you now. I could do it, and it would work like Cucusa's cleansings always did. But I'm not here to do things for the pleasure of doing them, and I'm not here to do things more than once. Your husband and your father will make this worthwhile."

Celita was crestfallen. She didn't hear Isidra's willingness to proceed, only her admonition to gather the men.

"Aunt, look at me. I'm at thirty-eight weeks. Guillermo was a C-section, and this baby is coming out the same way. The appointment is set and I'm scared. I can feel what happened to my brother all over me. My baby is being affected. Please?"

"Bring your father."

Celita took a few deep breaths. She was speechless and dazed as she rose and shuffled out the door.

A couple of hours later her husband, José, was sitting in the living room, sunburned. Celita had gotten word to him out on the lagoon. "She sent Yunier, who always knows where to find me." We chatted, and he could not hide that he was annoyed. Soon, Celita appeared at the door with the silhouette of her father lumbering behind her. Isidra and Roberto barely spoke. As far as I knew, this was the first he had set foot in the house since our arrival.

The work for Celita was done behind the curtain of the saints' room. It involved honey, dry white wine, and a bundle of fresh herbs from the fields and forests. Eulalia joined them but no one else. I could hear Isidra singing some of the house's battle songs to Yemayá, and together they sang to San Lázaro–Babalú Ayé. They finished up with Spiritualist hymns, to which José was partial and could dependably lead. It was late afternoon, the air was still, and a swarm of black flies had descended on the house. They were laconic in the heat like the rest of us and sat listlessly on the walls, the window sills, the furniture. When Celita, José, her aunts, and her father, Roberto, emerged from the room, she was wearing shorts and a tube top, her belly protruding, nine months ready. Her hair, nose, and belly dripped from the aspirations of dry wine that had been sprayed over her. Bits of broken herbs clung to her face, breasts, and belly, stuck there by the honey with which she had been covered. Flies swarmed to her, and she was covered by them. She looked surprised and hugely relieved. As she moved toward the kitchen table for a glass of water, she smiled.

"Look at me," she said. "Look at the flies. Like Babalú Ayé, with his wounds and dogs. He has flies all over him too. It is a good work."

And it was. But as afternoon wore on, the work Isidra had performed, which was understood to have cleansed and refreshed her too, wore off. She was focused again on the missing ram. That she gave the ram such importance was odd given that the hole for which it was destined could be properly appeased with but a pigeon. No one understood why she needed so grand an animal. That night, Celita and José returned for a quiet Spiritualist *pensamiento,* or collective focusing of our thoughts, that had been prescribed during the afternoon cleansing. Roberto was supposed to have returned too, but he never showed up. The pensamiento happened in Eulalia and Isidra's bedroom, where the photographs of their parents and other ancestors were kept. None of the dead chose to mount any of the living, and that was a good sign that Cucusa, Ma' Isidra, Chacha, Loreto, and Kimbito, among others, were at ease. Neither did anyone pick up a *muerto oscuro,* which meant that Yamilet next door was being held in check.

• • •

On the morning of the 15th, Justo dug a hole in the backyard. Isidra sent word out to her family that attendance for the feeding was imperative. Boby, Robertico's son, had arrived late in the night and was staying with his grandparents, Roberto and Celia. Isidra insisted that all needed to attend.

After lunch she gave up hope that a ram would be found and pressed forward with a less lavish but still extraordinary offering: an enormous white rooster meant for Obatalá on the 17th. Our gathering included everyone staying at Cucusa's house, but few others. Isidra stood before the open hole, and like the rest of the women she wore a white kerchief over her head.

"I don't know why she does these things, feeding this and feeding that. Doors, the earth, Congo things. I don't like any of it," said Zulia, who was standing next to me, a row back from the hole. She rubbed the back of her arms the way people do when they approach a Spiritualist altar to sweep off negative energies. Ulises was in the company of his cousins yet further back, and it was a source of relief and prestige for Isidra that Boby was among the gathered, along with Anelé. Neither Roberto nor Celia was present, nor were José, Celita, and Guillermo.

"You are my family. You know why I called you," said Isidra. "There is a hole in this family. An open hole we have to fill. We all know the losses we have endured this year, and we are here to put those losses to rest."

Boby stood grim, away from the hole, and she did not call him forward or single him out. His simple presence helped us contemplate the year, cold and clear. She meant to settle his loss. But Isidra was goaded by the absence of her siblings, their spouses, and their children, especially her niece Celita and her family. Her brother Máximo, so important before, was not going to come from Santa Clara at all.

"There is a hole in this family. An open hole that can't be filled. Don't think your aunt Isidra is sure help. I can only do so much, can only hold off disaster so long. Do you think this rooster will fill our hole? A ram was called for, and together we couldn't come up with it. Do you think this hole isn't calling for one of us? Do you want to avoid being the next one in the hole?" She paused. "Then it is a good thing you are here. Those who have better things to do, they had better understand this hole is open, and one of them is going to end up in it next year, if not before the end of this one."

She held forth in these terms for ten dismal minutes. A scene of healing became a scene of despair with fear circling hungrily. The hole, dug to feed the dead, became a threat, gaping. The offering now became a way to appease the hole itself. Finally, she called for the animal to be handed to her. Generous libations of aguardiente were blown over the huge white rooster and cigar smoke surrounded it.

"Everyone for a cleansing," she said. "Everyone forward, the youngest first." The rooster was rubbed over our bodies as we turned clockwise. After each contact with the animal she would shake the bird toward the hole to cast the negative airs, energies, and vibes into its maw. A candle was lit next to it to light the way for the dead of the house, should any want to mount us. She cleansed herself last, then took a knife to the animal's throat. Blood flowed into the hole to join deposits of toasted corn and smoked fish and hutia with which it had been seasoned. Finally, unable to cut through the animal's skin and feathers, she tore the head free with her hands. The animal was thrown into the hole in our stead. With her bloody hands she handled coconut-flesh disks that Eulalia cut to discern the outcome of this meal. These disks, white and cool, are called vistas, or "views"—into the past, the future, and the unknown depths of the dead. They returned a verdict of no. Another animal would be needed, another cleansing undergone. Some of the older hands, like Justo, grumbled. The rest of us went along, allowing her to drag our lives and fates behind her, circling as we were the rim of an open grave.

I had long wondered what the French theater maestro Antonin Artaud had meant when he described his now infamous "theater of cruelty."[1] I thought then, and have thought many times since, that the experience he named could be found there, with us, around the hole. Not because of the animals we killed nor because of the threats Isidra coldly communicated. These were dramatic, but they were background and prop to what Artaud meant. Rather, I was struck by how high Isidra piled the stakes. That the lives of a dozen people could be gathered up and compounded with the suicide of a man, the presence of his mourning son, the struggles between aging siblings, the fate of a family's sense of coherence, and the ultimate control of a piece of property—that these had been gathered and thrown into the air along with four little disks of coconut flesh was overwhelming. That all this had been piled together without a safe ending in sight; that each step was at once toward both healing and death, toward redemption and despair, with no resolution built into the scene—this is what Artaud meant by a theater of cruelty. Isidra had built a scene in which the greatest stakes in life were put into play, put on display, and the dice rolled. A collective space where dread and miracles haunted every act, where strong feelings were evoked with no sure means for domesticating them. It was a scene in which all the participants joined their lives to uncertain outcomes in the hopes of improving their chances, but without guarantees.

We teetered on the rim of the hole together, ready to be profoundly touched, willing, collectively, to be affected.[2] Time and again, the scenes that bembés made possible seemed designed in their broadest staging to allow people to publicly feel strong things and to collectively, which is to say extensively, be affected by the lives around them.

Finally, after a dove was offered, the fresh views were thrown and came back with affirmative statements. The hole could be filled, "closed," in Isidra's terms. Justo was kept waiting long after he had expected. No one in town knew how to open a grave and close a grave more securely than him, having just recently ended a five-year stint in the cemetery. Besides, having opened the hole, he was the only one who could righteously close it. Despite being put out, he was careful, finishing the work with his bare hands.

Isidra spent the rest of the afternoon preparing for tomorrow's opening of the bembé for San Lázaro–Babalú Ayé. For a couple of hours, she and Eulalia dressed in sackcloth and went door-to-door "begging" for alms. San Lázaro–Babalú Ayé is imagined as a wretch covered in sores, perhaps a leper, reduced to begging. It was Cucusa's custom to go out in the days before the 17th to gather alms [*recoger limosna*]. She would go barefoot through the streets. Neighbors would put pennies in her basket. Isidra used this opportunity to connect with neighbors and others she wanted to see at Cucusa's during the next two days. She would remind them of their promises to Cucusa and of their debts to her house. To line up drummers, singers, and dancers, Isidra spent her free moments since arriving in town going to and fro, making genial house calls. Drummers like Justo, Gonzalo, and Iván, who were all excellent, needed to be teased with promises of rum or aguardiente. Isidra, being a dancer before anything else, paid special attention to women and men she thought danced beautifully and would grace the feast, not only because they had great moves, but also because their dancing would delight the orisás who might then mount them. Lastly, she went to great lengths to make sure the best singers would be on hand, Pica and Zenón above all. Isidra was sure Pica would come and with her María, her daughter. They were both pleasing mounts for Changó, Elégua, and Oyá. There were other singers, like Celia's father, Lázaro M., and Pica's nephew, Aneas, but they tended not to come to Cucusa's. She disliked the talk of the bembé at the Curve outside town. That feast appeared to have grown and was on the lips of many people. Isidra extended her invitations and made sure people knew she did not want them going there instead. The thought that any musician of note would choose to attend the upstart feast annoyed her.

Isidra and company were arriving only on the night of the 11th; time was simply too short. The visiting, the catching up, the checking in, and paying heed that built a community and laid the foundations of a great party were too rushed. In years past, Isidra would have arrived two weeks before the feast to gather everything she needed. Cucusa would have spent all year assembling her bembé.

The 16th was spent putting the finishing touches on the feast. A few missing animals appeared, the altar was lit, and the house opened to the public. Noon, and people started to drop by to greet San Lázaro.

The cousins, Ulises, Anelé, and Boby, cruised for fun in the hours before things got serious. All of them were from out of town, and the locals enjoyed seeing them growing up. Boby and Anelé lived in Santa Clara, Ulises in Havana. As far as townsfolk were concerned, they were big-city kids with big-city clothes and tastes. They were the progeny of the youth who were caught up and carried off by the revolution in its first decades. Ulises had a cell phone, and this was huge. Boby's dad had been living in Varadero when he killed himself, and Boby had Varadero clothes, like denim shorts, T-shirts with skulls and flowers on them, and a pair of Adidas tennies. Anelé was still in high school and dreamed of being a commercial translator in the Varadero tourist boom. "Not a tour guide," she specified. "Commercial—for the Ministry of Tourism."

"Dreaming big, Cousin," said Boby, teasing her. "What you've got is your looks, and when the time comes, I don't expect your tongue will fail you."

Anelé ignored the double entendre, which is unrelenting in Cuban talk. Her response was unfailingly positive: "You can dream big too, Cousin."

"You dream for me, Cousin," Boby said. "I'm dying in school, and military service is coming up. We'll see what happens with that. Maybe I'll stay in. I've blown my chance at the university. For now, let's just have a good time, OK? I'm here to party, pick up a girl or two, and have a good time. You can help me with that, right?"

ELEVEN

———

Dear Elégua

TEN O'CLOCK ON DECEMBER 16 AND JUSTO SAT AT THE BIG DRUM,
ready. Pica relaxed at the kitchen table while her daughter, María, gossiped
and socialized outside. Zenón was nowhere to be found, but with Pica on
hand he could come whenever. The altar to San Lázaro–Babalú Ayé glowed
with little lights reflected in sequin, tinsel, and purple satin. Members of
Isidra's family conversed with neighbors in the living room.

At midnight, Isidra moved to the center of the living room and stood
before the drums with Pica at her side. She shook a rattle steadily.

"Come close, everyone," she said over the chattering crowd, her rattle
opening a path for her voice. The guests settled.

"First, let's give thanks that we find ourselves together again this year, a
year like this one, which has been very hard, tough, full of sacrifice and hard
work. Thanks because we're here in this praise house [*casa templo*] for Babalú
Ayé, giving him thanks that we're gathered together again. But, more importantly, to ask him that for what remains of this year and for the coming one,
that we be healthy, that our paths be open, and that we have the strength to
continue onward on our paths. As we learned it from our dead, always, we're
going to sing the prayer held dear in the traditions of this house. Everyone to
the floor. If you can't kneel, well . . ."

As the crowd settled, she turned brusque. "Silence now! Silence! No cigarettes in the house right now! Get out if you are smoking or drinking!"

She handed Pica the rattle and asked her to lead the prayer.

Quietly, Pica sang, "Bamba luca."

The gathered crowd instantly became a chorus to her call, "Bamba luca!"

"Bamba luca," called Pica.

"Bamba luca," the chorus replied.

"Bamba luca lubeya," she added, her voice rising to a melody now.

"Bamba luca lubeya," we replied.

"Bam-bamba luca," she sang.

"Bamba luca," the chorus replied.

"Bamba luca lubeya," she concluded.

"Bamba luca lubeya," we replied.

"Siete casoño va resa' u'te," she continued.

"Bamba luca lubeya," we replied.

"Bam-bamba luca," she sang.

"Bamba luca," the chorus replied.

"Bamba luca lubeya," she concluded again.

"Bamba luca lubeya," we replied.

"Siete casoño va resa' u'te," she continued.

"Bamba luca lubeya," we replied.

"Bam-bamba luca," she sang.

"Bamba luca," the chorus replied.

"Bamba luca lubeya," she concluded again.

"Bamba luca lubeya," we replied.

"Bamba luca lubeya," she concluded again.

"Bamba luca lubeya," we replied.

"Siete casoño va resa' u'te," she continued.

"Bamba luca lubeya," we replied.

"Bam-bamba luca," she sang.

"Bamba luca," the chorus replied.

She switched now, "Onialé, onialé, onialé, bacoso-bacoso Elégua!"

"Onialé, onialé, onialé, bacoso-bacoso Elégua!" we replied.

"Onialé, onialé, onialé, que besa [now kiss] bacoso!" she called.

"Onialé, onialé, onialé, que besa bacoso!" the chorus replied.

"Onialé, onialé, onialé, bacoso-bacoso Elégua!"

"Onialé, onialé, onialé, bacoso-bacoso Elégua!" we replied.

She paused for a second and sang, now with energy and cheer, "Terendenden, saluda Elégua, terendenden, saluda Elégua!"

The chorus rose to its feet, now greeting the orisá of beginnings, fresh starts, and new things, "Terendenden, saluda Elégua, terendenden, saluda Elégua!"

Pica continued and the feast was on its way: "Terendenden, saluda Elégua, terendenden, saluda Elégua!"

The chorus cheered the name of Elégua, first among peers. Pica's seventy-six years of voice and devotion to Elégua and his music led the bembé forward with the energy and favor of the pathfinder sovereign.

"Lindo-lindo, lindo Elégua, no hay un santo más lindo qu' Elégua, no hay un santo más chéche qu' Elégua!" she sang.

"Lindo-lindo, lindo Elégua, no hay un santo más lindo qu' Elégua, no hay un santo más chéche qu' Elégua!" the chorus replied.

Those who felt Elégua deeply and who felt themselves comfortable in his domain were at the front of the choir, which opened a space for them. Their steps were sweet and bright, moving onto one foot, then skipping off it. Those who could feel the orisá of horizons and openings moving near them, considering whether to mount them, would skip and turn on one foot, bending over in a pantomime of the pathfinder, ducking branches and dodging underbrush. Boby was outstanding among these. Now eighteen, he had steps that were fluid and sharp at once, the strength of his calves and thighs evident in the one-legged bends and spins he accomplished so simply. Anelé danced a basic step that would allow her to stay very close to him. If you weren't dancing at this moment in the feast, there was no room for you in the house. The chorus delighted in seeing a young, strong man like Boby give himself to Elégua. Boby intensified his dancing and lifted the opening higher. Elégua, who delights in parties because they are scenes of limit testing, wants nothing more than to mount a dancing body like the one Boby offered him. So strong, so willing where he was not practiced, how could Elégua refuse such a mount?

Elégua wears a broad-brimmed straw hat to communicate his connection with the outdoors and with those who spend time there, like peasants and those who frequent the forest. Cucusa's house kept just such a hat for Elégua, to please him should he mount a dancer. Of the possible mounts for Elégua in Cucusa's house, it was Roberto, Isidra's brother, who was by seniority and public acclaim the first mount Elégua would select. In fact, sometimes the hat was referred to not as Elégua's but as Roberto's. Eulalia, in an act of generosity and acceptance, placed this accessory on my head when the prayer ended. I had been wearing it for the Elégua songs. She knew Elégua presided over me, and in her dreams he would choose me for a mount. But I was a novice dancer and had no practice in performing Elégua's mounting-up. Chances were slim, but his hat did encourage me to dance a little more loosely and sing a little more freely. It was an honor to wear the hat at that moment in the feast.

All this surely pleased Elégua. The feast was well prepared. The door and the corners of the block had been fed and secured, always with attention to his protocols. A small goat was ready to feed him. The chorus sang his praises joyfully, and dancers moved their bodies to entice him. He must have surveyed the scene and had other plans for his hat, comfortable as it might sit on the head of a traveler. Elégua has never expressed even the slightest interest in mounting me. I was like an old bony nag wearing the ceremonial tack of a regal steed. I had been watching Boby as closely as Anelé, and *my* Elégua thought it would be most appropriate if the hat were on Boby instead. Why shouldn't that dancing, skillful, accomplished child of Cucusa's own line not be wearing his grandfather's hat, his orisá's hat? My Elégua danced his way through the undulating chorus, closer and closer to Boby. I was close enough to feel the air disturbed by his excellent, incandescent movements and have his head easily under my arm. I went to relinquish that lovely hat when Oyá screamed. All eyes were at once on the orisá of tumult and keeper of the cemetery gate. How could it be that Oyá was not the first to mount someone this year? There was a suicide and a hole to fill. The only question was *how many* she would mount.

Before Pica could lead us through the basic repertoire of orisá songs to properly hail each and call out our welcome to them, Oyá mounted the old farmer from whom we had purchased the beautiful white rooster for Obatalá that we had offered impromptu to the hole. She was the same woman Oyá had mounted six years before: Serena, Cucusa's old friend, white as the rooster she sold us, except for her peasant's ruddy tan. Serena was writhing, still not at ease taking this santo-orisá on her back, but better. She needed steadying as she screamed and knocked into the dancing chorus, but shortly Eulalia was at her side. She coached her toward the saints' room, where she would be properly tended to. An honor.

Serena's Oyá was settled onto her steed and making the rounds among the chorus when shouting erupted. Zulia was now mounted by Oyá too. She jerked and shocked her way through the chorus, teetering precipitously on one foot, then shaking suddenly in another direction, knocking people around as she went. María, Pica's daughter, was quick to her side. María was adept at caring for orisás and their steeds. She could either help settle the saint or confidently swish the orisá away. Despite María's reassuring hand, Zulia spun her two hundred pounds on a heel and fell facedown onto the ground where she thrashed, her arms at her sides. With help, María soon had her up, and in Eulalia's hands, she was steered toward the saints' room, where this blazing orisá could be properly settled. The drummers never missed a beat; Pica called, and the chorus danced and sang in response as Serena's Oyá made her way through the house.

Zulia's Oyá was out of the saints' room, regal, commanding, and serious. Compared to Serena's Oyá, hers was intimidating. The chorus cleared a path for her to march barefoot through the front door, where she took in the view up and down the street, lingering at her half niece's door. Yamilet's house was quiet. Zulia was very credible as a mount for the sovereign of ominous winds, storms, and bedlam. She was wrath. The danger she condensed and emitted made her all the more attractive to people in need of her counsel. The more dangerous the orisá, the more scintillating its potential to transform reality. Oyá's transformations were the most radical: she could shut the cemetery gate for one about to enter, or open it for someone innocently walking past. People were pleased to be addressed or touched by her. She called for a plate of honey to offer the gathered chorus as one of her blessings. Eulalia attended to her and held the honey as she went person to person offering us the chance to dip our fingers and taste the sweetness of Oyá, which is the sweetness of being alive, tumultuous though life may be.

Pica was fading. She had been at it for more than an hour and needed a break. This was supposed to be an opening, a "short little touch" of the drums to break the silence and call the santos-orisás, to let them know that their preferred animals were soon to be offered and that we were eager to have them. Santos-orisás appear at feasts whenever they please, whether or not songs, animals, and countless other offerings have been made. Oyá, in simultaneously mounting two steeds the instant we started playing, was evidence of that. They are sovereign, after all.

There would have been wisdom in letting Pica's exhaustion let the whole gathering taper down so that we could get on with the slaughter, but no one wanted to stop. The community around Cucusa's house, family, and feast was just too robust and rambunctious for that. Zenón had arrived some time ago but had remained aloof, sipping government-provisioned rum and bullshitting outside. He didn't need to keep an eye on the scene inside to know when he could make the most effective entry. He could hear with every song, with every call-and-response, with every flourish on the big drum, just where the energy was. He knew by how the drum was struck which musician was on at any time. A couple of them had already called out the window for him to come in. Requests like that were compliments in the highly rivalrous community of musicians. Zenón pretended not to hear them and continued an animated conversation. When he finally came inside, the chorus was ready for him, and Pica too. She belted forth a few more songs, these ones marked by the old Ewe-Fon *lengua* [tongue] she used. This she did this to goad Zenón, who, though he might be younger and louder and more popular, was no match for her in the realm of verse wisdom and ancestral righteousness. The chorus, though, had a harder time responding to these calls, and our energy faltered. People fanned themselves and looked for sips of water. Zenón gestured to this drop in energy.

"See? See? That's why I'm here. Without me the chorus can't even sing." Pica didn't mind leaving him a diminished chorus.

He was a little drunk. He wore a blue mesh tank top and snappy light blue polyester slacks, with flip-flops. An empty plastic rum flask was in his belt, and a little plastic cup was tucked under the neck of his shirt, at his collarbone. He tapped this little cup and made aborted licking gestures to display his parched mouth. "For my throat, for my throat," he said coyly. Isidra, who tightly controlled the aguardiente she brought from Havana, could not refuse him and put Ulises in charge of dispensing drips and drams. This was not an enviable job.

Zenón started out terribly, singing incomprehensible songs that ditched the drummers and chorus. He tried two or three without success.

"See! See! I leave them in the dust too. I leave the drummers in the dust," he said with theatrical smugness.

"Because you sing bullshit," Pica muttered within earshot.

Having made his point, Zenón sang from the well-known core of orisá songs any chorus could rousingly respond to. He began moving systematically through a repertoire that included many songs for each santo-orisá, a repertoire he called his *santoral* [list of saints' names]. The first songs were for Elégua, and as he called them, the chorus caught fire and things were quickly rollicking. The chorus formed a conga line encircling him, and I found myself in it with Anelé in front of me and Boby ahead of her. Boby was a spark in the line, his strong, quick Elégua steps and gestures a pleasure for all. Elégua was in me, too, and as the line compressed, I came close to him and almost without thinking lifted Elégua's hat off my head and put it onto his. Anelé saw the hat go past and shot me a grievous look. Before she could do anything, in the instant the hat touched his head, Boby was mounted.

He shot out of the circle with a blast of energy like a horse out of its stall, and bounded into the kitchen. His cousin was right behind, as if she could rescue him from his willing submission to the santo-orisá master of his head. He went straight for Pica, now sitting at the kitchen table, and kneeled in front of her. She casually touched him on the shoulder to acknowledge him and to release him from the gesture.

Into the chorus he came, spinning on one foot, kicking out, bending over, and ducking his head. He extended his arms, then pulled them behind his back. He nodded his head energetically up and down and shot his arms out again, now spinning. When he reached the center of the room, he went up on one foot, leaned back, and fell over flat, where a couple in the chorus broke his fall. Zenón sang on, signaling with his eyes, a nod of his head, and a touch to the cup at his collarbone, that he could be thanked for bringing down the bembé's first Elégua. The chorus re-formed around Boby's now prone body, while leaving a corridor toward the drums open for him. He was then on his belly with his arms at his sides. Without using these, he propelled himself toward the drums, walking, as it were, on his shoulders and hips. He groaned.

Anelé claimed the role of his tender and kneeled next to him. She put her hand between his head and the floor to keep it from getting scraped up as he crept forward. His cries were sharp and rasping. By chance, the hat had fallen back into my hands when he shot out of the circle, and as he approached the big box, Eulalia appeared at my side and took it gently from me. His aunts stood on either side of the center drum. When he touched his forehead there, they lifted him up and put the hat on his head. Not releasing him, they led him away from the chorus to the saints' room as he nodded his head dramatically in assent.

He returned after a while, still flanked by his aunts, who had removed his shirt and shoes and rolled up his pant legs. They had brushed him off and tied a black-and-red sash around his waist. Elégua's hat was on his head. In his right hand was Elégua's principal accessory, a short crook made from guava painted black and red. This modest tool is Elégua's scepter, like the thunder ax is Changó's. He had a cigar in his mouth, and Eulalia held a gourd of aguardiente for him. Tears streamed down his cheeks onto his chest and along his muscular frame. He jerked forward and limped. Each step was mimicked by his shoulders, which responded with a shift like a wince. His pained steps evoked both Elégua and the hobbled movements of the crippled Babalú Ayé.

Sovereign now, Elégua moved into the scene that had been set for him, into his chorus, among his supplicants, and looked around. He could not speak and grunted instead. This was no playful Elégua mounted up to spread mirth through a house. He was not there to play tricks or bless people with blasts of aguardiente or puffs of cigar smoke. He could not talk to people about the paths they tread, about obstacles they faced, and what lay ahead. This Elégua was jagged and raw. He was more "Congo style," becoming "hotter" in his gestures rather than becoming "cool," which is the ethos expressed by the West African–inspired orisás in Cuba. His rattling steps combined with youthful strength to portray a surging, explosive energy. He was shaken and blazing, both dangerous and beautiful.

Anelé squirmed between her aunts and was right with him, tending him by wiping sweat off him and keeping the gourd of aguardiente Elégua loves. His limp became a strut as he moved through the chorus, which never stopped singing his songs. He received hugs and gave them. Elégua held forth for a long time inside the house and in the street. At one point he stood in a gap between the chorus and the drums and held Anelé by the hand. He opened his arms and brought his crook to his chest, pounding it over his heart. He lifted it to the rafters and looked up with his bloodshot eyes. He opened his mouth and grunted and cried. She cried at his side.

His aunts, who had gotten busy with other orisás, took this as a signal and quickly supplied him with a fresh cigar and refilled his aguardiente, as if to calm him with his favorite vices. He took the cane liquor into his mouth in one swig, then blew it in a giant burst over the dancing, singing heads in the room. It was a blessing. At this, Anelé, who was younger, or more sensitive, or more scared, or more hurt by her cousin's ordeal than were any of the rest of us, turned on a heel and strode out of the house.

She must have run straight for her grandparents', because in short time she returned with Roberto. Until I saw him there, I hadn't even noticed his absence, so scarce had he made himself that December. He walked into the house and through the chorus as if it belonged to him. Here was the man who would be master of this feast and of this house if only he claimed them. He went straight for his grandson, to tend him, to bring him out. Boby's Elégua, seeing his great steed standing there, immediately greeted Roberto with a hug. Roberto wrapped dear Elégua around the shoulders with his massive arms and led him away from the chorus, into the saints' room.

I can only imagine what would have happened if Roberto's Elégua had chosen to come on just then. What would it have been to have grandfather and grandson, the heartbroken father and the orphaned son, both mounted with the sovereign of beginnings and endings, of dawn and dusk, of choices good and bad? But just as Boby was more open to the pain of his father's suicide, so Roberto was more reluctant to show it. He knew that if he was mounted by his santo-orisá there and then, he would be laid low, and his Elégua would be something none had ever seen before. His son, a child of the revolution, a Communist Party militant and Angola veteran, fighting depression and entangled in turbid dealings in the Varadero tourism boom in which he was a rising star, was dead. Five stories. Roberto would do one thing at the feast that year, and it was to relieve his grandson of the majestic but terrible burden of carrying Elégua that night. Soon, Boby was back out among the chorus, dressed, his tears dried. Roberto went home.

An uneventful slaughter followed, which was good given the absence of Isidra's family members, especially Roberto, who was designated to kill the animals. Isidra settled with his absence and asked Pica's nephew, Aneas, if he would provide the service. This was not a small thing to ask. The killing would last until dawn, and though wielding the sacrificial knife is full of blessings, it is also full of perils. An animal on the verge of being offered is bursting with santo-orisá potential: it is the nourishment of sovereigns, after all. The animals have been sung and praised into near identity with the santos-orisás. Collectively generated sovereignty is held in the blood of the animal, and the santos-orisás are enlivened by it. No other substance strengthens and brightens them in the same way. To touch the animals on the precipice of sacrifice is a blessing. To be the one who releases their blood is a privilege. At the same time, it is dangerous to be the person, tiny and flawed by comparison to the powers being handled, who interposes themselves between the santos-orisás and the blood that will feed them. Even slight mistakes are paid for. Aneas did not hesitate.

Pica and María joined Isidra's family for the offerings. Aneas's willingness to lead the killings was all the more generous in that we were also short of animals and there were santos-orisás who would go hungry. But throws of coconut flesh disks were affirmative time and again, and this allowed for greater animals to be shared and lesser animals to make do where greater animals were missing. Everyone, meaning all the santos-orisás kept at Cucusa's house, ate. Last was Mariana Congo, Cucusa's formidable Congo power.

Late morning and José and Isaías had butchered the animals (several roosters, several chickens, several ducks, and three goats), and their respective dishes were being prepared. These, along with two kinds of rice, would be the lunch feast offered to anyone who dropped by. To eat of an animal that satiated the santos-orisás is a gift. The flesh is as close to the matter of the sovereigns as one can come, other than being touched by a santo-orisá when it is atop one of its steeds. To eat of it is to bring the vitality of the santos-orisás into your body in order to find a singular intimacy with their potential. The stews and fricassees are delicious, seasoned with flavors of Creole Cuban cuisine, garlic, onions, vinegar, sweetened cooking wine, sour orange juice, and cumin. The one exception to this feast was Mariana Congo's animal, which was prepared but not shared among us. "Mariana Congo eats apart," said Isidra. Mariana's meal was plated privately in the saints' room and wrapped in a white cloth tied off at the top. In the afternoon Isidra, Eulalia, Ulises, María, Celita, and I carried it off amid long shadows.

Pica came by for a plate of food after we returned. No one talked about her performance the night before. We commented on who among the drummers was muddy and who was crisp, and about the job Zenón did as caller.

"Yard rooster [*gallo'patio*]," Pica called him. Then she changed the topic. "I've been waiting to see that boy's Elégua. Needs to calm down a little. I wish I could have seen his grandfather's. I haven't seen that Elégua since he appeared out of nowhere in 1999. I would like to see him again."

Isidra changed the topic, "Did you go out to the Curve after you left here this morning, Pica?"

"Today?" Pica was incredulous. "What do you think, that I'm a kid?" She chuckled. "The Curve . . ." She trailed off as if annoyed by the question.

"They say it's a mess up there, Pica," said Isidra.

"I've sung up there. They've picked me up in a car and I've gone."

Isidra looked at her expectantly.

"What? What do you want me to say?" she took a sip of water. Isidra was silent. Finally, Pica said almost as an afterthought, "Is it a bembé like one of Chacha's? Is it a bembé like Cucusa's? No. But neither is this one."

Isidra didn't reply.

"They say she has a San Lázaro statue that is life-size," said Eulalia with genuine marvel.

"Shhh!" said Isidra.

"It is what it is," said Pica. "Go up there and see for yourself." She was not one to talk at length about anything.

Evening came soft and easy. Everything was done. The house had been prepared, the altar set, the orisás fed, the meals served. Nothing but a party lay ahead, and the drums kicked up in the early evening. Again, a chorus of singers and dancers filled the house. More than the night before the crowd overflowed into the street. The drummers included Justo, Gonzalo, Iván, and Zenón, too, among others. Pica sang, as did Zenón. Santos-orisás who took mounts included Elégua, Yemayá, Ochún, Changó, and Obatalá, and Oyá was back too.

It looked to be a "feast for the books," as Isidra called it, even without an appearance by the guest of honor, San Lázaro–Babalú Ayé. His orisá peers had been among us for hours gobbling up the energies of the gathering, which were lavishly offered. It would have been nice to have San Lázaro–Babalú Ayé there, and now only a few hours of the 17th remained.

Zenón had Celita in his sights even the night before. He had tried then to sing her santo-orisá down onto her back and failed. Celita was thirty-eight weeks pregnant and seemed exhausted. She spent most of the night sitting quietly or sleeping on Isidra's bed with little Guillermo. Now she was dancing, and he was working her again, singing San Lázaro–Babalú Ayé songs directly at her, having the drummers drive harder, getting the chorus to roar their responses. She wore a sackcloth skirt and a lilac shirt, and her belly protruded dramatically forward. She made no eye contact and seemed aloof, if not dazed.

"Iñ-ye-yeo! Eh-h, iñ-ye-yeo! Que lu-cambio bacoso, Que lu-quami Balú Ayé! Y u'te' que dice que soña godona Balú Ayé! Saluda santo Bab'lú Ayé!"

The chorus rose around her. "Iñ-ye-yeo, Eh-h, iñ-yen-yeo, saluda santo Balú Ayé!"

Zenón called, "Iñ-ye-yeo! Eh-h, iñ-ye-yeo! Que lu-cambio bacoso, Que lu-quami Balú Ayé! Y u'te' que dice que soña godona Balú Ayé! Saluda santo Bab'lú Ayé!"

We replied, "Iñ-ye-yeo, Eh-h, iñ-yen-yeo, saluda santo Balú Ayé!"

Zenón switched, "Balú Ayé mi-moseo, Babalú Ayé mi-mofa, Babalú Ayé mi-moseo, Babalú Ayé mi-mofa, awa-la-oma se-o-weh, awa-la-oma-eh-e-qwa!"

The chorus cried a full response, "Balú Ayé mi-moseo, Babalú Ayé mi-mofa, Babalú Ayé mi-moseo, Babalú Ayé mi-mofa, Awa-la-oma se-o-weh, awa-la-oma-eh-e-qwa!"

Zenón carried this song for several identical call-and-responses, and just like that, San Lázaro–Babalú Ayé was on her. She lunged forward as if to fall on her face, only to stop perched on a strong lead leg. Her right arm was across her eyes, and her left extended erect behind her back. She teetered there for a second, her belly hanging close to the floor, then rose up on her toes and tipped backward as if to fall flat on her back. At once, two or three in the crowd caught her, and she let herself fall into their arms. Zenón tapped his chest to claim credit for bringing on Babalú Ayé. Then he brought a new call to which the chorus responded without a pause. Celita was gently lifted onto her feet and led by her aunts to the saints' room.

When she returned to the crowd, she had a purple sash across her belly and a short broom made from thin sticks in her hand. The chorus-crowd rose in appreciation for their beloved santo, San Lázaro–Babalú Ayé, for whom they had gathered and for whom they had given their all.

Zenón called, "Babalú Ayé-eh-eh-eh!"
We cried, "Babalú Ayé-eh-eh-eh!"
Zenón called, "Babalú Ayé-eh-eh-eh!"
We cried, "Babalú Ayé-eh-eh-eh!"
Zenón finished, "Babalú Ayé caraida!"
And we replied, "Babalú Ayé caraida!"

The sovereign of affliction and recovery was mounted on a steed about to give birth, with swollen feet and aching back, days from a C-section, and sunk in a world of sorrow. She stood there in the doorway of the saints' room looking out at the gathered mass singing her up, singing her forward. Her aunts were caught behind her and peeked out from over shoulders. She didn't move. The crowd, always dancing, shuffled into a line that formed before her as one by one they sought out the healing touch of San-Lázaro–Babalú Ayé.

The sovereign of healing and life, who is at once the sovereign of pestilence and death, moved to stand before the altar devoted to him to receive his supplicants. Some members of the chorus just wanted to be touched or rubbed with Babalú Ayé's broom. Others wanted to speak to San Lázaro–Babalú Ayé to tell him of their afflictions and make their case. To these he listened intently and compassionately, but he never spoke. The line stretched out the door, and children had begun to gather outside as parents sent word home that San Lázaro–Babalú Ayé had arrived. Guillermo, who was four, was awake and calmly watched his mother from a chair on the edge of the living room. Other santos-orisás who were present found their way to the periphery and little by little they dismounted.

In time, San Lázaro–Babalú Ayé touched, brushed, hugged, and cleansed the entire line. The whole time the chorus continued on, led by Zenón, who did not let up. There were none but children left to heal, and the sovereign of pestilence moved toward them and their parents. Mounted on Celita, he made stunted steps, and his limp was pronounced. One way Celita communicated San Lázaro–Babalú Ayé's affliction was to bounce in one place as if hesitant to take a step onto raw feet. She opened her arms and received as many as could come around her. She raised her hands and signaled for her aunts to remove the purple sash from around her womb so that she could hold it. She rubbed the children from head to foot, one by one. Isidra chose just the right moment to dance forward to grab one corner of Babalú Ayé's sash and lift it into the air. The others immediately responded, and soon the purple satin was raised as a canopy. The chorus rallied around this, and San Lázaro–Babalú Ayé was now underneath dancing with a group of children.

She reached up to take the satin back and drew it down to her belly, to stroke it there. After a few seconds of bouncing on her toes and rubbing her pregnant belly, she let the sash back up, where the chorus continued to rotate it in the air.

Zenón called a beloved song for this santo-orisá, "Dame chokoro! Dame chokoro! Dame chokoro, Ba'lú Ayé! Dame chokoro!"

In resounding response, the mass cried, "Dame chokoro! Dame chokoro! Dame chokoro, Ba'lú Ayé! Dame chokoro!"

He called again and again, "Dame chokoro! Dame chokoro! Dame chokoro, Ba'lú Ayé! Dame chokoro!"

We cried again and again, "Dame chokoro! Dame chokoro! Dame chokoro, Ba'lú Ayé! Dame chokoro!"

San Lázaro–Babalú Ayé mounted on Celita for another hour as the feast mellowed into a steady, still raucous call-and-response. San Lázaro–Babalú Ayé kept healing latecomers and anyone who came near him. Around midnight, Celita simply sat down and rested. San Lázaro–Babalú Ayé was gone at once.

Isidra gave Zenón and the chorus another couple of songs, then moved the feast toward Congo style. Zenón wasn't up for it, and as in years earlier he let Isidra take the call. We weren't good for more than fifteen minutes, and no one was mounted. She had Ulises draw a bucket from the well. This she danced through the chorus, spinning as she went until she reached the door. She let the water fly onto the sidewalk, marched back into the center of the living room, and in front of the drummers slammed the bucket mouth down with a boom. The feast was over.

The next day as we prepared to leave for Havana, Celita asked me, "How was it last night? They say I was mounted by San Lázaro."

"You were," I said, surprised by the direct invitation to talk about santo-orisá mounting, which I rarely ever got. In general, people do not talk with an orisá steed about their performance, or the ordeals they undergo, while mounted.

"Guillermo told me."

"Is he a child of Elégua?"

"All children belong to Elégua."

"Did he say things to you he shouldn't have?"

"No, he just said 'Mom, San Lázaro rode you all night long.'" She paused, "Did he?"

"All of Guillermo's night. He woke up to see you mounted for a couple of hours."

"Is that how long it was?"

"Like that. A little more."

"I feel better, Ramón. I made it to the feast. The baby can come now."

We did not remain long in town after the bembé. Perhaps this was my fault. I was eager to get back to Havana, then back to Berkeley to see my family for the holidays. Isidra saw no point in missing a ride back to Havana. It often felt brusque to me, the way we departed, but Isidra was always confident. Never during the years we feasted at Cucusa's house did she leave town thinking anything but that our success had been total. She felt that Celita's gradual rise as a mount for San Lázaro–Babalú Ayé was destiny, and she credited herself for creating the scenes in which her niece could grow. "She heals all of us."

Isidra subscribed to a theory of struggle that mirrored in striking ways the discourse of her government. There was a righteous fight, obstacles to be overcome, and hard work to do. Given a virtuous and fearless struggle, she would triumph. She felt she was again victorious against her treacherous half niece and that each year the house, and the bembé for San Lázaro–Babalú Ayé, was more secure. Each successful feast was a step toward securing Cucusa's house and legacy against Yamilet and all false pretenders. She felt that having Zulia and Isaías living in the house was a gain, even though she wanted more work from them. One part of her plan for the house was to get me to commit to writing a book about her feast, her family, and her town. As I left Havana, I could not agree to such a pact. She understood but urged me not to stay away too long.

TWELVE

2006

DECAY

IN 2006, FIDEL CASTRO BECAME ILL. A man who ruled his country for forty-seven years was suddenly, if predictably because he was eighty, laid low. Until that moment, Fidel had ruled over the revolution with singular rebel flair and meticulous control. He had also done so as a quintessential Cuban *macho*—large, loud, and uncompromisingly masculine. His endurance, virility, and size were important parts of his performance as commander in chief of the Cuban Revolution. One of his more popular nicknames was *el caballo,* "the horse." You could say he carried the revolution like Pica carried Changó. Cucusa had been an admirer, and a large portrait of the *comandante* hung in her living room opposite the altar for San Lázaro–Babalú Ayé. It showed him in three-quarters profile. The youthful, trim guerrilla fighter who had changed Cuban history and seduced dreamers and humanitarians around the world was shown settled into barrel-chested middle age. December 17 approached, and the question on lips throughout Cuba was "Will San Lázaro preserve or punish this most illustrious of his subjects?"

It was December 2006, and I was back in town after just a year. I had decided to pursue a book about Sierra Morena, Isidra's ancestors, and her attempt to continue her mother's bembé. I was being deliberate now, taking proper notes and making field recordings.

· · ·

"What's this?" I asked Gonzalo.

He looked at me with feigned surprise. "You know what that is, Ramón."

"It's the *quinto*," I said, referring to second-largest drum in a full-on bembé. You can't always get three drums for a bembé, and you don't need more than one, really, but if you have the luxury of three, then the second one will be the *quinto*. I was sitting at the drum, hands resting on the skin.

"*Re*quinto," he corrected me.

"What's the difference?"

"No difference. You just sound like you don't know what you're talking about if you say 'quinto.'"

"And the big one, it's the *caja,* right?"

"Come on, Ramón, quit pulling my leg. You can't be this dumb."

"I'm just checking," I said.

"Book's a bad idea," said Gonzalo. "Too slow. You need to cut a record, *compadre.* Give me a chance. I'll get two more drummers, and we'll record a disc of the best bembé music in Cuba. That will get you somewhere. It will get me somewhere!" He laughed.

"I don't have the gear. You know this doesn't work." I pointed to the minidisc player we were using to record the lesson. It was a nice machine for field interviews, in 2006.

"It's true. The mix on that is off. But the sound is good, really good. Do you think the microphone has to do with the mix?"

"Microphone, sure. Wouldn't two mics be nice? But the mix is the machine. It balances sounds as they come in, and that is what gets recorded. Serious sound people would never use this for recording music."

"I can also play modern music, you know. Salsa, casino—I got that."

"Why is the little drum called the *mula* [mule], Gonzalo?"

"It does the work, it carries the rhythm, it keeps time. The mule needs to be fresh and crisp, or the whole party goes down. Big load to carry. Plus, it sounds like a mule, right? Clip-clop, clip-clop."

"The requinto," I asked. "What does it do?"

"It calls the orisá. Some of the old folks call it the *llamador,* the caller."

"So it is the most important, then?"

"Not so," said Gonzalo. "You can have a good bembé without a llamador."

"How is that?"

"With a mula and a caja. Those are the only drums you need."

"Does the caja call the saints?" I asked.

"Also, also. With the help of the mula and of a requinto if you can find one. The requinto only calls. It calls and calls."

"What does the caja do, then, when it's not calling?"

"When it's not calling, it is honoring, it is decorating the call. With the caja you decorate the call. The caja makes the call beautiful, makes it unique, gives the *cajero* [caja player] the opportunity to make the call unique. It is all part of the call."

"And the *campana* [bell]?" I asked. "What does it do?"

"The campana here in town is played by whacking a bolt or railroad spike on an old hoe blade," said Gonzalo. "The campana holds everything together—three drums, caller, chorus. Those can drift off and do their own thing sometimes and then come back in on time because the campana never varies, keeps perfect time, outlines the structure of the whole thing. The campana is an open rhythm, open time."

I didn't get it. I still don't. He could tell and tried again.

"You know orchestras, with a conductor and baton and all that? If the conductor were at a bembé here in town, he would be playing the campana, not just waving a baton around. Musicians, dancers, they tune in if they've let their mind wander, and the campana slots them right in."

"Super important, then," I said.

"Important, but not so much. The campana can just drop out and no one will care. What you can't lose is the mula and the caja. With those two and a strong pair of drummers you've got a solid bembé."

"Do the drummers compete with one another?"

"The drums compete," said Gonzalo.

His son-in-law, Iván, was sitting with us just then. "Listen now, Ramón, the drummers compete, but the drums don't compete. I'm a better drummer than Justo, and he is always trying to show me up. He and I compete because I'm thirty years younger and he hasn't beaten me in five years. He can't get over that, but I will never let him show me up. You see, we're people with issues and egos, so we compete. But the drums don't compete. The mula, the requinto, and the caja complement one another."

"True that," said Gonzalo.

"Do the drummers compete with the singer? Sometimes I see Zenón trying to put you guys down, to impose himself on you. Do you ever want to school him or Pica?"

"Zenón is crazy," said Gonzalo. "Who doesn't want to show him up? He knows more than anyone except Pica and Lázaro M. and a few other old folks. Outplay him and you're getting somewhere. He's a hell of a drummer too."

"Give Zenón credit, Ramón. Half the time when he is schooling the drummers, it is because people are off and he knows better," said Iván.

"Then he turns around and tries to school me," laughed Gonzalo. "What do you think he is saying then?" Gonzalo was Zenón's younger brother. They were the grandchildren of Chacha Cairo by way of their mom, Ingo, who was one of Chacha's taken-in children. Ingo became one of the principal callers at the Sociedad Africana, after Reina Collín and before Pica and Zenón.

"Listen, Ramón," said Iván, "your question, do the singer and the drummers compete? Not in a bembé. A bembé is not a rumba where everyone is jostling everyone. Remember the rumba we had sitting right here a few years back? That was a mess, but it was fun. Rumba is only when the bembé is spent. Here in Sierra Morena the caja fills in and decorates. It brings grace to the space between the singer and the percussion, especially between the singer, the mula, and the campana. If there is a requinto in the game, then the cajero has it easier, there is less space to fill. When a requinto is in the game, then it is harder to spot a cajero's weaknesses. Cajeros like Justo like it when there is a requinto because then they can hide their weaknesses and their limited moves."

"What is a 'move,'" I asked. "Is that improvisation?"

Gonzalo looked at me theatrically. "Improvisation like that crazy *brujo* you brought back in 1999? That guy was a great drummer—for Havana. Here he was a clown. Not improvisation like that."

"Like what, then?"

"The cajero's moves have to happen in the space the beat makes possible," said Gonzalo. "You can't improvise over that. What you're calling 'improvisation' is figuring out how to put something different in the space between the instrument and the beat. Only the musician can do that. Not easy."

"There are only so many moves that fit in the space," said Iván. "Everyone knows those moves: some are harder and some are easier. But every drummer in town knows them."

"So," I said, "with limited space and limited moves that everyone knows, then there is no improvisation?"

"Except for me," said Gonzalo.

"Us," corrected Iván. "What you're calling 'improvisation' is a mix of moves. If you know enough moves, you can mix them all kinds of ways."

"True that!" said Gonzalo. "Son-in-law here and I are the only ones with so many moves that no one can keep up with us. I taught this kid everything he knows."

"Can Zenón keep up?" I asked.

Gonzalo looked at me with feigned inquisitiveness, "Now, that's a different story."

It was December 12, four days before the bembé for San Lázaro–Babalú Ayé would break open. We were sitting in the backyard at Cucusa's. Gonzalo was determined to teach me to play, and I was determined to learn. He was a good teacher but could have been more patient. Iván helped a lot. He was younger and could get his head around things at a basic level and break them down into words in way that Gonzalo could not. Ulises, who turned twenty that year, was very fast at picking up bembé rhythms. "Sign of a musician," said his mother, "musician and a teacher." Isidra, too, listened in on the lessons. Eulalia was already a good drummer, a strong *cajera,* in fact.

The backyard was cleaned up, with the underbrush cut back and rings of rocks around the mango, avocado, guava, and tangerine trees. The outhouse had survived a year because Isaías had shaped it up. A new bucket sat on the rim of the well. The house looked better too. Zulia and Isaías were properly moved in and had a refrigerator and beds. Temperatures were unseasonably high that December, and the heat was on everyone's mind.

"This refrigerator I brought over from my apartment in Corralillo," said Zulia. "It is a Russian refrigerator, the kind that came with the fan for defrosting. Back when the Russians sent these in the eighties, the government discovered that each refrigerator came with its own fan. When the icebox built up ice, you opened it up and set the fan in front of it to blow tropical air on it. Sped up the defrosting. Well, the government separated the fans from the refrigerators and gave the fans out as work incentives. I still have the fan next to my bed."

In the world of Cuban refrigerators in 2006, there were three kinds. First, the American fridges from before the revolution, which were then more than fifty years old and had enormous compressors and faulty seals that made them energy sinks. Those that remained wheezed and hulked in kitchens throughout Cuba. They are now prestige items for the historic service they rendered and for the times they recall. Isidra had one back in Havana. Second, the Russian refrigerators that replaced them in the seventies and eighties, which were much smaller and had poor compressors and seals. The iceboxes built up ice quickly and required regular manual defrosting. Thus the fan. In 2006 a third kind of fridge was coming onto the scene.

"Chinese fridge is a rip-off," said Zulia. It was the talk of the town—the revolution was "handing out" Chinese refrigerators across the island as part of an energy-savings program. They had been coming down the North Circuit for months, first in Cárdenas, then in Máximo Gómez, then Martí, then Corralillo, and finally in Sierra Morena.

"They come and take your old fridge," said Zulia of the government energy agents who came ahead of the refrigerators and made sure everyone participated in the program. "They give you nothing for it. Got that, Ramón? Put it in your notes. Not a penny of a Cuban peso. See this Russian fridge right here? Piece of shit. It has never worked well. What is a Russian fridge doing in Cuba, right? Still, it is worth good money under the table. Why won't they pay me what it's worth?"

"Why not sell it on the black market, then grab a Chinese fridge?" I asked.

"They won't give you a Chinese fridge unless you give them an American fridge or a Russian fridge first."

"Trade-in program?" I asked, putting pieces together.

"Maybe the Chinese fridge is better," said Zulia. "That's not what people are saying. Until they pay me for my Russian fridge, even if only a few hundred pesos off the cost of the new one, I'm not giving it up."

"So, you can't buy a Chinese fridge if you keep an American or Russian one?"

"What, and have two fridges? These people," she said, referring to the revolution, "will never let you have two fridges if they can help it. You don't even have a chance at a Chinese fridge if you don't already have an American or Russian fridge. Trade-in, like you said. They're handing them out as replacements. If you're a poor wretch who doesn't have a Russian or American fridge, then forget it."

"And you have to pay for the new one?" I asked.

"Six thousand Cuban pesos," she said, feigning exasperation. This was a huge amount of money in Cuba at the time. Three years' salary for most people.

"How do people pay for them?" I asked. Zulia looked at me, exhaled audibly, and made a sign with two fingers and an eyebrow that said, "I don't know and I don't care."

Later on the 12th, I was over at Zenón's. He had agreed to be interviewed about anything I needed for my book. I wanted to talk about his grandmother Chacha Cairo; his memories of the singers, drummers, and orisá mounts at the bembés of the Sociedad Africana, like Ma' Isidra, Loreto,

Gobierno Sáez, Otilia Sáez, Ma' Josefa, and Santiago Linares; how he inherited the role of bembé caller from his mother, Ingo; what African languages were represented in bembé songs; how bembés had survived the revolution during the 1970s; and, if possible, anything he might know about Congo-inspired healing-harming craft in town. Also, if he thought San Lázaro–Babalú Ayé would favor Fidel in his illness. All he wanted to talk about was the heat and his new fridge.

"Chinese fridge is terrible," he said, "and with this heat. I'm here with my wife, so we got one of the big ones. Still smaller than the Russian one, and that was a size down from the American. Fridges been shrinking for fifty years. Live alone and you got no choice—an even smaller one for you. They've got your household in the census, so you can't bullshit it. Six thousand pesos. Then there is the thousand pesos in interest."

"Interest?"

"Do I look like I have 6,000 pesos to spend on a fridge? I get paid 200 Cuban pesos a month as a night watchman at the new bar they put in there by Cucusa's. Every dime of that goes to rum. Do the math. The 6,000 pesos is a loan from the government. Payment is 60-some pesos a month, straight out of my paycheck."

"They take a third of your paycheck a month to pay themselves back for the fridge they gave you? That's like ninety payments for your fridge," I said.

"Seven and half years," confirmed Zenón, "and you haven't counted the 1,000 pesos in interest yet. I hear it is like eight years to pay for this piece of shit."

"Why not keep the Russian fridge? That is what Zulia is doing."

"Everyone is afraid to give up their Russian or American fridges. But their days are numbered. Soon there will be no parts for them and no one to work on them, at least not here in Sierra Morena. But the Chinese fridge is going to be a problem. Since the Special Period lightened up, they gave us Chinese electric pots and Chinese rice makers. End of the nineties, early 2000s. Great in the kitchen, great on energy. But they break down, and the parts are expensive. I'm worried about that. They'll get the 6,000 pesos out of me, but on the way to paying that off, how much will I spend on parts? This deal sticks us between no parts and expensive parts. I don't care about the debt. Bring it on. I like new things. I'm going to die. Kids can pay it off for me. If they come down the road with another 6,000-peso piece of shit, I'll sign up for that too!"

"So, this is a payment program for a fridge you can't get any other way," I said. "Because in Havana you can buy an LG fridge for $1,000, or 22,000 Cuban pesos."

"As you say. First, that LG doesn't cost 22,000 Cuban pesos because they only sell it in hard currency, right? That's not the currency I'm paid in. LG has to be hard currency and full payment on the spot. Who can afford that? This way I can pay national currency over eight years. Like I said, shitty fridge."

"So, the revolution sends a buyer out to China to buy like five million refrigerators and buys shitty refrigerators?"

"Buys millions of shitty everything. Like you said, from China. Look in the hard-currency stores. Millions of shitty things. People got to clothe ourselves, got to put shoes on our feet, and cook meals. So we buy the millions of shitty things. At least the fridge is on credit!"

The next day, Eulalia woke up anxious. It was the 13th, and over breakfast she said she wanted the feast all set to go by the end of the day on the 14th. We had arrived late on the 11th, same as last year, but we were not on pace to stage the bembé. We were behind on the animals, for one. Isidra sipped her warm milk and honey, which is all she ate once she arrived in town.

"Don't even start with all those meals you did last year," said Zulia.

Isidra looked up. "Meals?"

"You fed the door, you fed the hole in the ground," said Zulia.

"This house is standing because of those meals," said Isidra. "And here you are, reposed like a queen. What hasn't come to roost here because of those meals?"

"I don't want you digging holes . . ."

"Does it matter what you want?" asked Isidra.

"What I want matters because this is my house."

"Your house?" asked Isidra. "Whose house?"

"I don't want you digging holes in the back and bloodying up my door here."

"Digging holes?" Isidra was on her feet. "You're standing here right now because we *filled* that hole last year."

"Do you know how long that hole smelled? And this year it is so hot."

"Smelled? Do you know who would have been the first to fall into that hole? Your son Ernesto, that is who."

"Don't bring him into this," started Zulia.

Eulalia laughed. "Listen to that! And the santos that pulled for him? And the night I spent with the santos praying for him?"

Zulia did not reply.

"You didn't mourn your son this year because of that work," said Isidra. "You're standing here full as you are of disrespect for this house, and for Cucusa, and for me, because *I* filled that hole last year and your son isn't lying in the cemetery right now."

Zulia closed her eyes slowly and went to sit on the couch.

"There will be another meal for another hole. We have to fill it," said Isidra. "Who do you think is standing on the precipice right now? Don't forget you have a son in prison."

Again she was quiet.

Isidra shook her head. "I have been too complacent. Ask Ulises. Ask Ramón. I have been too complacent. We should have fed the door the night we arrived. Now where are we? Two nights have passed. Do you see? Do you see what happens when you don't secure [*amarrar*] your door?"

I was not keeping up.

"What happens is you get this," she said, addressing her younger half sister. "You get Zulia talking shit, excuse me, but talking shit. And a thousand other things I have tolerated until now. Let me finish my milk and we'll feed the door right now."

Next day, the 14th, we were searching for animals. The promises to San Lázaro–Babalú Ayé that had supplied us with animals in 1999 had dried up. With no one to tend to people who came by to greet San Lázaro–Babalú Ayé at his altar during the year, the community of feastgoers was fraying. Zulia had no human touch for such work. Most of the animals offered at the 2006 bembé were purchased.

Never did we search the countryside for animals when we weren't also looking for other things. Some things we knew we needed—milk, cheese, eggs, and fish. Other things we didn't realize we needed but bought because they appeared. Oier, the Angola vet with the two carts, took us to San Rafael, between Sierra Morena and Rancho Veloz on the North Circuit close to the coast. Eulalia was right; time was getting tight, but that didn't keep Isidra from asking for a detour to the beach. "Let's go down to La Panchita and see if we can't find some fish." Oier puckered his lips and cocked his head a little but made the turn toward the beach anyway. It was only a couple of kilometers.

La Panchita was a little beach with a dock onto the lagoon. A dozen small fishing boats were moored in the water, and a large government trawler was tied up at the end of the dock. A couple of desultory two-story apartment buildings with tiny windows housed personnel from the state fishing company and the Coast Guard, and their families. Isidra said that before Hurricane Kate, in 1985, the ponds on either side of the road had been full of houses on stilts. A guardhouse stood a little distance out from the dock, which was fenced off. A building held freezers for what came off the trawler. This was what the revolution called a *base pesquera,* or fishing base. There was nowhere to buy fish. Isidra went forward and stuck her head in the guardhouse.

"One hundred pesos, what do you say, Ramón?"

"For?"

"One hundred pesos for a dozen lobster tails."

"Sounds great."

"A guy named Melchor will be by the house in the afternoon. I asked him to bring four dozen."

That evening, Pica came by prompted by an invitation to join us for Eulalia's lobster tails in tomato sauce. María was her escort. Isidra never tired of staging scenes in which Pica could tell stories and talk about music. The entire detour to the fishing base, I now saw, was about this, and Pica never tired of Eulalia's *punto* [touch] in the kitchen. Pica was not a big talker, but with a little time she could be drawn out.

"Loreto and Quintina had thirteen children. I was one of the youngest, born in 1930. I was born early, at seven months. I couldn't nurse, so I was fed my mother's milk through a cotton ball. In those first weeks, I acquired four sets of godparents. One for each of four baptisms. Each time they thought I was dead. Chacha's whole Sociedad Africana came to my mother's aid as I barely hung on. I was finally baptized in the church when I was seven years old.

"I was a wild kid. I climbed trees, fell down, sprained ankles, ate grass. No one knew how to control me. Then I was mounted for the first time when I was fifteen, a couple years after these girls were born," she said and motioned to Isidra and Eulalia. "It was Oyá. Who else, with all that wildness and that loitering I did at the cemetery gate the months after I was born? I inherited Oyá from Quintina's mother. Oyá was terrible for me to bear, and I didn't like being taken by her at first. But the same thing happened to me as happened to my father, Loreto. He was the town watchman and carried a .45. He didn't like being mounted either. For him it was Changó. But little by little he got used to it and he became Changó's preferred mount at the Sociedad Africana. Eventually, I became that for Oyá. My Changó I inherited from Loreto.

"The Sociedad Africana was Chacha's thing. She founded it and she healed there. Reina Collín was the lead singer. She knew so many songs for the orisás. At the Sociedad they mostly worked on the 8th of September, Ochún's day, La Virgen de La Caridad's day, Charity's day. They would dance her up, then take her statuette out in a procession through the streets, past the church. The priest would bless her. Then they would bring her back to the Sociedad, and Chacha would take her back into the saints' room, do her thing, then the bembé would start. Sometimes we would spend four days there, sleeping on the floor at night. Chacha was always working during a bembé, working to protect us. She had a beautiful work [obra] she did to protect us against gunshots and other dangers, a ceremony involving a whole branch of bananas for which Changó needed to be present.

"She also protected us children. Loreto had lots of women. Everyone wanted Quintina's man. His lovers were always throwing witchcraft [brujería] in the yard to try to get him in love, or cause trouble between him and Quintina. Chacha kept us kids from ever eating anything we found in the front yard—not fruit, not candy. Especially not candy. She said, 'Bring it all to me.' Sure enough, Chacha could see through things and revealed that everything we brought her was worked in order to win Loreto."

Roberto was with us that evening, too, as if his conspicuous absence last year had never happened. No one even expected Máximo this year. Pica's stories drew him out.

"Chacha had a doll," he said. "It was a wooden doll the size of a grown man. She called it San Felipe. She kept it in her saints' room and dressed it in white pants and a white shirt. She fed it, and at night it would go out and do her bidding. Back then, a lot of houses had dolls like that. San Felipe was the biggest. San Felipe did what she asked as long as she fed him. If she didn't feed him, he would go out at night and look for food on his own. I've seen *chichirikues* like him more than once in the street at night. You want to run into them when they're running an errand, not when they've snuck out because they're hungry. Better just ignore a chichiriku if you see one."

"Shhh!" said Isidra.

Pica was silent for a moment and changed the subject. "In those days there was a rural guard. They were country police that went around on horseback, and they were armed. They would come after us when we had a bembé. Once, in San Rafael, between here and Rancho Veloz, where you people went today, they came after a bembé. They followed the sound of the drums, and when they were right on top of the party, they came upon an empty field. Then they heard the drums far off. They followed the sound, but again an empty field. This went on all night. Nowadays, the people in San Rafael feast Changó on the 4th of December. That is a great bembé, and San Rafael is like four houses in the middle of a cane field. The first part is straight *bembé de santo,* then they head out back to the little house where they keep the *kindembo.* There is *chamba kimbansa* and gun powder, and that part, the Congo part, they play that hard [*se juega congo duro*]. That goes on all morning from dawn until people get bored. South of here, in San Pedro, where you people went looking for animals last year, they only do straight *bembé de santo.* They don't play Congo at all."

Roberto turned the conversation back to Loreto. Loreto had been his mentor in things having to do with orisás and Congo-inspired powers. "Loreto had an Oyá stone that from year to year gave birth to other stones."

Pica corrected him. "That stone belonged to Loreto's father, Jorge Sáez. Before that it belonged to Ma' Josefa, Loreto's mother. She kept that Oyá stone in a basket made of moss, which she hung from the ceiling and covered with a mosquito net. Do you know where that stone is, Roberto?"

"No."

"Neither do I. That stone went with Loreto." Pica took a sip of water and quietly continued.

"Jorge Sáez, my grandfather," she said, "he kept snakes in his house. Enormous serpents that wriggled all over. Men kept snakes in those days. That was a Congo thing. Back then there was an old Congo who lived alone in the forest. He lived under a huge tamarind tree with its roots sunk into a pool at a bend in the river. They called him Tamarindo because of that. He was a *ngangulero congo,* and he had Congo things that would scare your pants off. He kept the worst of it hidden in the trunk of the tamarind tree. When he died, lightning struck the tree and it caught fire. In the end nothing was left of the tree or his Congo things."

"Don't talk about Congo things," said Zulia. "That stuff sits poorly with me."

Pica ignored her but quieted down. Later, Isidra accused her of shutting up Pica just when she was going to start talking about Congo things, which were the hardest things to get her to talk about.

On the morning of the 15th the feast was thirty-six hours off. Roberto was around, and Isidra and Eulalia were happy to have him.

"I'm leaving town," he said.

Eulalia teased him. "Where you going to go, Roberto? You've never left Sierra Morena. You're retired. Your house and your wife and your daughter and grandchildren are here."

"I'm moving to Santa Clara. I'm moving in with Máximo and I'm going to start a photography studio."

"Photography studio," said Eulalia. "That sounds like a good business. Have you seen the photos girls are taking of themselves these days for their *quinceañeras?* They look like they're straight out of a fashion magazine."

"Then there are the ones where they're almost naked," said Isidra. "I'm sure you want to take those, Roberto. What are those about, anyway?"

"I'm a great photographer, and I would have lots of business in Santa Clara," he said.

"And the money?" asked Isidra. "Ulises knows all about phones and computers and things like that, and the kind of camera you're talking about is not cheap. You can't just show up with a film camera and think you are going to make money." The thought of Roberto moving to Santa Clara with a film camera made Eulalia laugh.

Roberto stuttered, defending his plans. "A little camera like Ramón's Sony would do just fine. Máximo is going to front me the money. He has capital to invest." As if to preempt the critique from his sisters, he continued, "Máximo is doing really well in Santa Clara..."

Isidra's mind, which was so fast, jumped. "Then move in here. Use the living room as a photography studio. These country girls want their slutty pictures too. We'll send Zulia back to Corralillo. She can barely keep the house clean, let alone attend to people when they come by to see San Lázaro."

"Forget it," said Roberto.

Zulia, who was sitting right there, said nothing.

THIRTEEN

Oyá

ISIDRA NEEDED TO RUN TWO ERRANDS—to the cemetery and to La Corua, the bend in the river. It was late morning on December 15, and the feast for San Lázaro–Babalú Ayé would begin tomorrow night at midnight. Eulalia's deadline of the 14th for having the house all set had come and gone, and still the animals were not squared away. Isaías was not coming through with his MININT cooking pots, and countless other things had Eulalia anxious. She wanted to stay at home and move ahead with preparations, and she kept her small army of gofers, which included Justo, Yunier, and Ulises, moving. But Isidra needed her for the errands, so Eulalia joined us.

Before the sun got too high, the sisters headed for the cemetery to give Cucusa, Ma' Isidra, Chacha, and Loreto *conocimiento,* to let them know what they were up to. Roberto did not go. Celita, who had given birth by successful cesarean in January, was with us. Her new daughter was healthy, but her head was, to Celita's eye, misshapen. She had spent the year fretting about it. Those who tried to calm her pointed out that José's head, with his long, high forehead, was the same. "That is no consolation," said Celita. "They don't call him 'cucumber head' for nothing. My daughter's head is not right."

Ulises did not want to visit the cemetery and resisted his mother. He had taken up weight lifting, and this combined with his height meant he was now an imposing figure at twenty. They decided that he would remain in the house to tend the candles, which could not burn down or blow out while we were at the cemetery. An odd number of candles had to be burning at the house. We would light three at the cemetery.

The cemetery lies on the western side of Sierra Morena, on the North Circuit. It is fifty yards square. Its walls were newly painted white in 2006, as was the little building where the gravedigger kept his tools. A giant ceiba tree grew at the entrance, where it cast generous shade onto the road. The low gate opened onto a walk that bisected the cemetery with graves on one side and stacks of niches on the other. The niches are where the remains of the dead are kept. Our rounds there were perfunctory; visits to cemeteries in Cuba tend to be. Isidra recited the Lord's Prayer at the niches for Cucusa, Ma' Isidra, Chacha, and Loreto, making sure to replace the phrase "and forgive us for our trespasses/sins" with "and forgive us our debts." Isidra led us in call-and-response singing, but we kept it brief. At noon the dead would be about, and we needed to get back.

Isidra insisted Celita join us for lunch, then come with us to the bend in the river. Celita was eager to have her aunt Isidra work a cure on her daughter, Mericelia, of the kind Ma' Isidra used to do with glasses of water suspended over peoples' heads. But Isidra insisted she needed water from La Corua for any such work. She turned to Celita and said, "You don't need me for this work. You can do this yourself. Have you taken the girl to La Corua?"

Celita, who was in a glum mood, said no, and Isidra scolded her.

We should have made that trip days earlier, and Isidra had regretted not having water from the bend in the river for the various herbal *omieros* she mixed up for cleaning the house. Our trip there was as hasty as any we ever made, given that Isidra performed a convincing work of healing on Mericelia. We returned with a big bucket of water, carried the distance by Justo.

The heat was unrelenting in the days leading up to the feast. Everyone complained about it, and women walked about with parasols. In the evenings the streets were full of people who had put off afternoon errands, and the smell of charcoal cooking fires and burning garbage hung in the air. Dust and soot from the street outside were everywhere, and the house had to be mopped and the walls rubbed down every day. Zulia had a dog that Eulalia teased because it collected dust. It was mangy, nearly hairless, with tattered ears and open sores on its haunches. It was scarred all over. It kept away from people except when fed, and even then it was exceedingly cautious. Zulia had adopted it off the street and named it Miseria. The dog would sit, not lie, twitching against a wall for hours at a time.

"Can you believe that?" said Eulalia, chuckling. "Look how pathetic. It actually collects dust. Can you believe she would adopt that? And then name it Misery? Is that crazy? What is crazier, bringing this wretched thing into the house or naming it Misery? And she is calling it 'her dog.' Is that crazy?"

We looked at Miseria for a few moments then María, Pica's daughter, who was listening just then said, "That's it. Where is José? For the numbers today, I'm playing 15 and 83—dog and tragedy."

"Why don't you play 46?" I asked.

"Hunger." María deciphered it automatically. "That's a good one. Maybe I'll play all three. You should play them too."

I knew some numbers and some of their code words from hanging out with a numbers runner in Havana years before, but I never played. María played the numbers every night, like most everyone in town. She was devoted to her numbers, keeping lists of those she played and those that won. She kept the most comprehensive list of numbers and their corresponding code words I ever saw in Cuba. One night she convinced me play 35, for *mosquito,* of which there were swarms. We both won. On the 17th of December the runners "closed" the number 17, so no one could bet it. Its code word was *San Lázaro.* She never won with any number associated with Miseria. "Misery never pays," she said.

The night of the 15th the sisters hunkered down to take note of missing pieces and hash out feast priorities for the next day. They had twenty-four hours before the bembé would break open. For help they had only Zulia, who was being *ñoña,* which is to say a real pain. Agripina from Sagua hadn't shown up. Roberto was around only to gossip and bullshit, and when errands needed to be run or problems resolved, he disappeared. Celita, who could be a great help, was preoccupied with her little children. María came by to help and pulled me aside to say that the feast at the Curve was shaping up really well, with more animals than I could imagine. "That is where the promises are getting made," she said.

Ulises wanted to go out and let me know a bembé was happening a couple of blocks up the hill. He thought that if I took an interest, his mother might let him accompany me, which surprisingly she did. Isidra was annoyed that bembés for San Lázaro–Babalú Ayé had erupted onto the scene even the year of Cucusa's death. Since then they had only grown in number and size. She did not want anyone associated with her to attend those, especially the one at the Curve, because she felt it reflected poorly on the control she had over her family. But the bembé Ulises took me to was exceptional. It was a one-time event hosted by an old friend of Cucusa's. The host, Lenita, had had a mastectomy earlier in the year and had promised San Lázaro–Babalú Ayé that she would celebrate him on his day. She was not a pretender to replace

Cucusa. What Ulises wanted was to see a girl from town who had invited him to the bembé. Isidra was not naive and sent María and Justo along to keep an eye on things.

Lenita's tiny cement house was packed with steaming dancers, and the bembé had broken loose. The drummers were on fire, though I didn't recognize any of them. There was Pica, leading the chorus. María was immediately at her side singing and dancing, elated. Elégua, orisá of crossings and therefore of choices, already graced the gathering. He was mounted on a man in his thirties, muscled, with a brilliant Afro and a bushy walrus mustache that recalled the ailing Nietzsche. In Cuba men tend to keep their hair short and their mustaches neat, even when these are robust. He was shirtless, wore black shorts, and was barefoot. To please Elégua the hostess had put a red headband on his head, and this set him off with something of a Jimi Hendrix look. Handfuls of *palo muralla,* a prolific vine that grows abundantly on fences and in abandoned lots, were shoved into his shorts. Celita was dancing in the chorus, but I didn't see her. She sidled up to me still dancing and said, "He's a wild one! [*¡Está jíbaro!*]." It is true that he seemed more Congo than orisá—more wild than domesticated, more edgy than regal—but people, including the hostess, called him santo Elégua.

Oyá was mounted up on a matronly woman, or maybe it was an angry Yemayá. She wore street clothes and carried no accoutrements, so she was hard to figure out. Another orisá was mounted up on an old woman sitting in a chair, who wore a country hat and vigorously smoked a cigar as people kneeled around her—a second Elégua. The Nietzsche–Jimi Hendrix Elégua moved through the room throwing candies about. These he took as was his right from a little altar Lenita kept for him by the front door. Only he, master of thresholds, would dare take anything from there. As he went he hugged new arrivals, including us. Then he plopped down in front of the drums and sucked his thumb, mimicking a young child. Elégua is sovereign over children, childhood, and play.

We weren't in the house for more than half an hour before Elégua took a third steed, this time a youth in his late teens, muscled and handsome. His hair was short and he was clean shaven. He was an excellent dancer, and it made all the sense in the world that Elégua would want him. But Elégua took him brusquely, and Pica had to step over to settle him by putting her hands on his shoulders as she sang straight into his eyes. The chorus never stopped. The Nietzsche–Jimi Hendrix Elégua greeted the clean-cut Elégua with glee. There before him stood his selfsame other, who despite mounting a different steed was Elégua just the same. Elégua enjoyed seeing himself multiplied, and given the vitality and proficiency of his steeds, he was soon the most commanding orisá at the feast.

San Lázaro–Babalú Ayé came in hard. As he mounted a young man, he knocked him over. Pica turned to this mount, who was sitting on the floor in front of the drums. Soon the orisá was settled onto his steed and had a length of purple-trimmed sackcloth around his shoulders. Quickly, San Lázaro–Babalú Ayé was led to a room where Lenita, the hostess, and her husband waited for him. This is what the bembé was for; everything—the cleaning, the gathering, the altar making, the animal offering, the nightlong drumming, the calling, and the dancing—led to this moment. San Lázaro–Babalú Ayé claimed a mount and appeared before the gathered mass and his afflicted hostess. A look from San Lázaro–Babalú Ayé could bring hope, his touch relief, and a single word could change the way you thought about your health. He was with Lenita and her husband for a very long time. Then he emerged to bring his fate-changing touch to the chorus.

The party did not let up. Changó eventually arrived, also on a young steed. He was a man in his thirties and fit. The mounting was noticeable but smooth, more within the dance steps than breaking them. The hosts provided him with a red cotton sash. Diplomatic protocol between santo-orisá peers was breached when the two Eléguas blocked his way to the drums. Changó is master of drums and music, and as a consequence he is master of the bembé. His access to his instruments should be unimpeded. The Eléguas had taken a seat on the floor in front of the drums and were playing a game by rolling a coconut back and forth. Play was their domain, and they now claimed the living room floor as a playground and crossroads where choices would have to be made. Changó stood, legs spread with arms on his hips, to survey the affront. The Eléguas were conscious of the impasse they created; true to their trickster reputation they continued to play, sucking their thumbs, drinking aguardiente, and smoking cigars, making of point of broadcasting their conspiratorial glances. This was also consistent with Elégua's privileges. As master of the crossroads, he presides over things turned upside down, one direction becoming its opposite in the blink of an eye. He is sovereign over affronts, revolts, insurrections, and revolutions. The impasse lasted less than a minute, but in it was captured the intermeshed sovereignties of the santos-orisás. The feast was for Babalú-Ayé, but it belonged to Changó. Without the goodwill of Elégua, however, paths to it would be closed.

How do you get a pair of sovereigns who are behaving like children to not offend their peer, who wields lightning and rules over drums, parties, and wars? Do you distract them like you might children? How do you keep Changó from discharging a bolt of lightning right then and there? Do you offer him gifts to appease the offense of the scene in front of him? Each santo-orisá reposed in his sovereignty. The role of the host, or of the wise among the chorus, is to foster mutual respect between complimentary but sometimes conflicting sovereigns. This is the art necessary to achieve the intimacy and splendor of orisá community.

It was Pica who finessed the situation, flattering Changó with a couple of songs and her kind regard, while she politely coaxed the two Eléguas away with candies she had kept in hand. With music, and the prestige that came from her command of this, Pica directed their movements. Changó finally marched forward to greet his drums and drummers, blessing each with his touch.

The woman with the Oyá-maybe-Yemayá combination now added aggressive Ochún-like flirtation to her gestures. She went about with a lit cigar in her mouth saying with typical Congo intonation and fashion, "¡Hombre son hombre! [Men are men!]." Time and again she touched the glowing tip of the cigar to the shoulder of the man nearest her. Men knew to expect her and would raise their shirt sleeve for her touch. This was a typical Cuban-Congo microritual—material, painful, and casual at once. "¡Una vacunita! [A little vaccine!]," she declared. Her little vaccine, which I hoped would cure us of our toxic machismo, was to the men who received it a welcome opportunity to display and validate just that. No one refused her touch.

Ulises paid little attention to any of this and was engaged in a protracted and petty back-and-forth with the girl he had fallen in with. She invited him, he sought her, she pouted, he ignored her, she ignored him, he sought her, only to have her pout again. He grew tired, and just as he had orchestrated our outing, so he orchestrated our departure from the bembé. We left the party with Celita shortly after midnight. María remained behind with Pica as the bembé and the santos-orisás went full on. San Lázaro–Babalú Ayé, Changó, and the Eléguas only grew in stature and command.

"Don't ask me what was going on there," said Celita as we walked her home.

Ulises chuckled.

"Some of those people were from Rancho Veloz or Sagua. I see them sometimes at bembés. But that was half made up. That young Elégua, the clean-cut one, he wasn't mounted for real. That was fake."

"What did you think of the woman with the cigar, vaccinating the men? Was that Oyá or Yemayá, or Ochún? Was that santo or Congo?" I asked.

"Don't even bring that up. I have no idea what that was." She was chuckling now. "That was Congo play but orisá music. Don't ask me why Pica put up with that." Then she turned a little serious. "Did you see how much that young Elégua tried to get me to mount up? That doesn't sit well with me."

I hadn't seen it, though I was familiar with orisás actively trying to multiply themselves or bring other orisás on by physically prompting known steeds.

Ulises laughed.

"Don't laugh!" She scolded her young cousin. "You don't know what it is like to be mounted by one of the santos. San Lázaro is the worst! Go figure. I wanted to get out of my house. I left José with the kids to come find you, Cousin. I know you're after that girl. I wanted to dance a little. But that didn't give me so much as goosebumps. Go figure. The party at Cucusa's tomorrow will be good. I'll bring the kids to that."

. . .

We were sitting at the kitchen table at Cucusa's on the morning of the 16th, San Lázaro's Eve, talking over a breakfast of sweet milk and cheese. Pica was there having barely slept from the party. She was seventy-seven years old.

"How did it go last night, Pica?" I asked.

"That party didn't get good until about two in the morning, when a few people left. While you were there, the drums were going too fast [*corrían los tambores*]. The crowd was too rowdy to slow them down. It took a while, but eventually everything settled down. We didn't polish it off until 4:30. Lenita got a word with Babalú Ayé, which is good."

"What did you think of the young Elégua?" I asked, picking up Celita's doubts from the night before.

"That boy is young. He doesn't understand who he has riding up top. He just needs a few years to mellow out."

"Did you think he was for real?"

"Child," she said, "stop with your stupid questions. What you had there were two Eléguas—Congos and twins. What more do you want?"

Later in the morning, Isidra offered the earth a modest meal of rooster and pigeon under overcast skies. It was well attended by her extended family, including her brother Roberto and his grandson Boby, who rolled into town the night before. Celia did not come. Celita was there with her children, year-old Mericelia in her arms, and four-year-old Guillermo at her side. José was not. "Sleeping in," Celita said. "You can't do it all." Ulises and Anelé, who was seventeen, stood together. Zulia stayed in the house. Justo dug the hole. The meal went spectacularly, with the gathered dead of the household communicating their approval of the feast preparations. Eulalia was delighted that things were more ready than she had imagined and looked forward to putting finishing touches on the altar before the bembé broke open at midnight. Isidra was elated by what the dead communicated. Just before lunch the drought broke, and it started to pour.

After falling steadily for hours, the rain eased up, and by 10 p.m. the house was full of Isidra's kin, friends of Cucusa, and folks from town. The night was cooler, and the dust was washed away. Outside, a new state-run bar on the corner by the North Circuit was also jumping, and some of Isidra's kin went back and forth. Cyrilla, Máximo's wife, arrived unexpectedly that evening. She came in his party car and represented Máximo and their daughter, Yancie, who had paid for an enormous ram. This was the animal Máximo had owed Changó for many years now. Neither Máximo nor Cyrilla had come the year before. Cyrilla was a Sierra Morena native like Máximo, and in earlier days was an appreciated steed for Changó. In a quiet aside, Isidra complimented her as a "tremenda ngangulera" [capable of great sorcery].

Midnight and a large crowd was gathered. José and Celita were on hand with their two children. Isidra asked Pica to begin with the house prayer, then the drums broke the feast open before midnight. Folks just couldn't wait. In the first half hour a young woman in the backyard was hit by a *muerto oscuro,* one of the dangerous dead that can strike at any moment. It was MiDiana, the girl Ulises was tangled up with. She stomped around, shouted, and screamed as the dead one took her. She was perfumed and powdered and wore new Lycra shorts and a pretty tank top, but she was flung to the ground, where she writhed and groaned. The scene was annoying to the sisters, but at least it wasn't in the living room. The muerto oscuro was shaken off her by José, who knew about these things. Free of the dead one, MiDiana looked at herself covered in filth and left the house in tears.

I was talking with José and Isaías a few minutes later as if nothing had happened when a string of shouts came from inside the house. Isaías heard it first, took a drag on his cigarette, and with Hollywood flair flung it into the night. It was Zulia. "Voy," he said almost under his breath. "On my way."

The rain picked up. It poured through the roof tiles in streams. It poured down the walls. It mixed with the dirt dragged in by the many members of the chorus, and soon the floor was muddy. Pica, who was calling, seemed to revel in the conditions and sang us forward in an excited call-and-response. The drummers and the chorus never faltered, and the feast was lit.

Zulia was on the ground, facedown, in a dark blue party dress. Her hair, which she had taken time with earlier in the evening, was bedraggled. She was shouting staccato bursts into the floor. Isaías was there, but except for taking off her heels, he did not touch her. Soon, she began to crawl toward the altar in the corner of the living room, at times up on her elbows, at times lying facedown in the mud dragging her legs. Little by little she worked her way forward as the chorus let her through. "That's Oyá," said María, "and with a temper."

She lay at the foot of the altar for a minute or more. Then, with the acknowledgment of Isidra, who touched her gently on the shoulders, she stood. Her dress clung to her, soaked in mud. Her face dripped with sweat and dirt. She was one of the largest people in the room, and with Oyá, sovereign of tempests, riding her, she was enormous. Zulia placed the back of her hands against the small of her back, pulling her elbows back and pushing her chest forward, summoning the shape of wings or waves or winds, which she worked back and forth from her shoulders. She shouted staccato, rhythmic bursts accentuated by an occasional cry of anguish or ecstasy. Her Oyá was not a talker, did not "work" in the way people in town expected their santos-orisás to work. In fact, Zulia's Oyá didn't work at all. She pranced and imposed herself on the feast by virtue of her size and her shouts. The sisters did not tend to this Oyá, did not welcome it back to the saints' room, or offer it accouterments. They left her alone.

Yemayá then took a mount, or perhaps it was Ochún who mounted up. She did not remain long enough to discern. She came hard onto her steed but did not fell her. The steed was Anaís, a grandniece of Isidra's from Santa Clara who was vying to join the Cuban national volleyball team. She reeled in one direction, then another. She was one of the few people present who was taller than Zulia, but being an inexperienced mount, she was unable to bear her orisá long no matter how athletic she was. She moved through a minute or two of competent Yemayá or Ochún steps, and impressed Isidra enough to be taken back into the saints' room, where she would be dressed in the accouterments of an orisá. But this sovereign, whether Yemayá or Ochún, did not return to the party. Next I looked, Anaís was back in the living room sitting in a chair with a white kerchief in her hand, fanning herself. Orisás are not easy for their mounts to bear, and some can't stand even a few seconds with an orisá atop. Some can bear the orisá for a full minute or two. Others can bring the orisá properly on and let dance steps become the strides of a sovereign. Few have the strength and poise to carry the orisá long enough that the orisá can properly stand, speak, and preside for hours.

Elégua took a mount an hour into the opening. It was the younger, close-cropped Elégua from the night before. Then Elégua, delighted with Boby's dancing, took him as a steed too. The room opened space for the two Eléguas. The young Elégua from Lenita's was the better dancer. He was beautiful, competent, and utterly convincing. Boby's Elégua was less coherent but still much more together than the year before, when his steed was in mourning and could barely maintain his composure. At times he made movements with his hands close to the hand gestures that have become synonymous with hip-hop performance. Expected Elégua arm movements were joined by others that extend forward from the chest, fingers open, as if in mid-verse rap. Anaís's orisá made gestures like this too. Boby's Elégua tried hard to bring orisás onto the cousins of his generation, touching Ulises and Celita not to heal them but to encourage the orisás up. Celita recoiled from the effort as she had the night before.

These first santos-orisás, Zulia's Oyá, Anaís the grandniece's orisá, and the two Eléguas, Boby's included, were like the orisás at Lenita's the night before—they came on strong and tested their mounts sorely. They spoke hardly at all and gestured much. They were acknowledged, but there was not enough poise, not enough control, not enough aplomb to muster the words the chorus so badly wanted from its sovereigns of affliction and healing. The result was a start that jangled and stumbled like the mounts chosen by the orisás.

Pica sang into the first hour of the night when Changó mounted her. Pica let him mount her as she sang, and she sang to him as he mounted up. She did not stop singing while he mounted up. She was not thrown or knocked around by her sovereign. She brought him on in her words and in her dance steps, which the drummers accompanied seamlessly. Her Changó was now the lead singer at the feast, just as Loreto's Changó had been the lead drummer at Chacha Cairo's Sociedad Africana, and he carried the chorus forward in a rousing half hour of hard, straight, righteous call-and-response in which he praised himself and his orisá peers. The drummers became tighter, the chorus settled down, and the entire gathering focused on this excellent, accomplished, acknowledged sovereign. Changó moved through the crowd greeting people with hugs and bumps of the shoulder. Was there anyone who didn't know this Changó and delight in his greeting? There was bliss when

Pica's Changó approached you, the whole room repeating his words in song, then embraced you and called straight at you a song of strength, resistance, or victory, to the rousing response of the chorus.

Zulia's Oyá did not last long once Changó came into command of the feast. Neither did Boby's Elégua. Pica was far their senior and had been mounting Changó for decades before these foals were birthed. Changó claimed the full attention of the chorus, and soon the other orisás departed.

This was the kickoff, and it went on for three hours. Then the rain let up and the slaughter began. The hardest, most glorious work was the offering of the long-awaited ram for Changó. Cyrilla made sure it was properly handled and that Roberto wielded the knife. She asked me to photograph the animal before it was offered so that Yancie could see that her contribution had freed her father from his promise. We slept only after all the santos were fed, including Mariana Congo. Some of us woke only in time for lunch.

Out back, in a tree between the kitchen door and the well, Isidra ordered that the heads of the four-legged animals, two goats, and Yancie's giant ram for Changó be hung by their horns. Zulia was sitting outside, combing her hair.

"Do you see this, Ramón?" she asked.

"See what?"

"My hair. Do you see what my santo did to me last night?"

"Oyá was hard on you last night."

"She threw me down and dragged me around. I was a mess. I haven't slept. I had to bathe. My dress is ruined. I can't stand it."

I was silent.

"Look at that," she said pointing to the heads in the tree. "Can you believe that?"

"They make an impression," I said.

"How long are they going to stay there?"

"I don't know. How long should they stay there?"

"Isidra says they aren't coming down. She says they will be there when the 17th rolls around next year."

I was quiet.

"I can't take this, Ramón," she said. "How much of this am I supposed to take?"

I did not reply.

"Before you leave, this whole yard is going to stink from them. Their eyes will bloat. I'm taking them down the minute you people leave for Havana."

The second half of the feast was a resounding success, at least as far as Isidra was concerned. A hundred or more people came for meals over a few hours in the afternoon. Pica returned to sing along with Zenón, who held the call most of the night. Iván, Gonzalo, and Justo led a large group of drummers. Among them was Ulises, who graduated from mula to requinto that night. Pica mounted Changó and Oyá in succession, just like María mounted Elégua and Changó in succession.

Late in the bembé, minutes before Isidra was to move it into Congo rhythms, San Lázaro–Babalú Ayé mounted Celita. His appearance would add two hours to the orisá part of the feast. Hobbled, limping, mute, one hand paralyzed, he received a stream of people who sought his touch. Then, using pantomime, he asked for the new little girl, Mericelia, to be brought from home where José had taken her to sleep. The two, groggy father and infant daughter, were received by the sovereign of affliction and healing. He took the little girl and danced with her on his shoulder, all the while rubbing the child's head. When the time came to return the child to her father, San Lázaro kissed her forehead. He held forth for another hour.

Isidra's Congo turn never lasted long. Unlike a Congo turn I would see years later at Lázaro M.'s, hers were short lived and served more as homages to Congo styles, forces, and ancestors. Her choruses dwindled when the Congos were called, and soon the feast transitioned "from Palo to rumba," as a well-worn expression in Cuba goes. The drummers were up for a full morning of playful jamming, which they asked me to record.

We spent the 18th recovering and cleaning and prepping the house for our return to Havana. Ulises said goodbye to his girlfriend with promises of a swift return. He took his leave from his cousins, Boby and Anelé, wishing them well in the year ahead. Isidra left precise orders for how the house needed to be cleaned and the santos rinsed before they could be put away. These things Eulalia knew by heart, and she would remain another couple of days to accomplish them. The hope was that Zulia would join in the labor. Little by little, Isidra hoped to make her into a dependable caretaker of Cucusa's things. Pica and María were sad to see us go, as were Celita and José. San Lázaro–Babalú Ayé had convinced them that Mericelia should be operated on to correct her head shape. Deciding this was a great relief for Celita, who had been agonizing about the right course of action to follow. It was also the source of new worry.

Early on the 19th we were in a local 1950s Chevrolet trundling out of town. We passed the cemetery and the house at the Curve. Isidra looked out the window just then and shook her head. During the car ride back to Havana, I asked Isidra why San Lázaro–Babalú Ayé had done nothing for Fidel, who was sicker by the day. Little was known about his exact condition, only that his situation was serious.

"I didn't see Fidel at Cucusa's, did you?" She was annoyed. "The santos attend to issues at hand. They don't concern themselves with abstract problems. Did you notice that Babalú Ayé asked for Mericelia to be brought to Cucusa's even though he was mounted on her mother? You would think he could help the little girl by working on her mother. But no. The orisás want to see you, touch you, talk to you. Do you think San Lázaro isn't pulling for Fidel just because you didn't see him rub down his portrait or something? Don't be stupid. If Fidel had been with us on the 17th, you better believe Babalú Ayé would have healed him. And you would have heard that chorus *sing*. Plus, if Babalú Ayé didn't want Fidel strong and healthy, do you think he would have made it to eighty, striding as he has over every opponent? Look around you!"

It would be three years before I returned.

PART FOUR

—————

FOURTEEN

2009

DECEIT

"LISTEN TO THIS. LISTEN TO THIS. You won't believe this!" Isidra said. We were in Havana in her sunroom, where many of our conversations took place. It was December 2009, and we were preparing for a trip to Sierra Morena. It normally took us many days of running around Havana to prepare for a trip, and we often found ourselves back at her apartment between errands. It was December 9, and we were hoping for a December 12 departure for Sierra Morena, too late to prepare a bembé.

"She cut the trees down! Did you hear? She cut the trees down! Celita just called, and she says Zulia has cut down all the fruit trees in the backyard. Can you believe it? There was a *guayaba* [guava], there was an *anón* [custard apple], there was a *mandarina* [tangerine], and a *níspero* [loquat]. Those are trees Cucusa and Ma' Isidra cared for and from which we ate as children. Did you hear me?"

"Yes," I said. "It doesn't make any sense."

"Sense? It is good and crazy, and there is no explaining it. Don't even ask."

"Those aren't her trees to cut down," I said.

"They aren't her trees! They are my mother's. They belong to the house. She has no business!"

"Then . . ." I said.

"Then what? Zulia says the house is hers. She says that she lives in the house, that she cares for the house, and that the house is hers."

"You're supposed to be sharing it," I said, "so how can she say that? Is it hers now?"

"What do you think? You think the house is hers because she says it is?"

"She's lived there for like five years now? Has she claimed it legally?" I asked.

"Not yet five years. Claim? A claim. What claim? She had no right to cut down those trees so long as the inheritance issues are not worked out. Cucusa left no will, and the house has no deed. I have an inheritance claim under Cuban law. So does she. We are both Cucusa's daughters. But it was my father, Orfilio, who bought the house with his lottery jackpot. It was Orfilio and Cucusa who bought that house. She can't go cutting down trees and claiming the house unless I cede my claim to inheritance, which I will never do. Eulalia would have had to cede hers, and Roberto his, and Máximo his. Has that happened? Don't you pay attention?"

In the three years I had been away, we had kept in touch, though poorly. She didn't email, and the phone was always difficult. Ulises, who was becoming proficient at computers, had black market access to the internet now and again. We wrote one another through him. I was not up-to-date on the day-to-day in Sierra Morena.

"What about squatters' rights? Doesn't she get rights because she has been occupying the house?" I asked.

Isidra was appalled. "This is the Cuban Revolution, Ramón. We have no squatters in Cuba. The revolution sees to it that everyone is housed."

"So she lives there but has no right to change things?"

"Shhh! No rights at all. Against four of Cucusa and Orfilio's children? In the house Orfilio bought and in which we were raised? No."

"But Zulia is Cucusa's daughter, like you . . ."

"Shhh! She is Cucusa's daughter. No one says she isn't. Just because she is Cucusa's daughter doesn't mean she knows anything about how to manage that house. She never paid attention to my mother's work with her santos. She never participated. She knows nothing."

"She mounts Oyá," I said.

"Oyá, you say? Does Zulia do anything except mount up once a year?"

"But she mounts . . ."

"It doesn't matter. What we're talking about is whether she knows how to manage that house and care for Cucusa's santos. Getting all riled up once a year and writhing around on the floor shouting—that is no preparation for all the things you have to handle to host a feast for Babalú Ayé. Enough."

The next day we were back at her house after separate outings. I was looking for aguardiente, and she was out to pick up an electrical cable from one of her godchildren in Palo. My bootlegger was a government chemist with a still hidden in his backyard in the comfy neighborhood of El Vedado. He loved to talk about coils, kettles, fermentation, and distillation. Aguardiente is a rum precursor, and though he could make very good rum, his aguardiente sold better. He was excellent at his craft, and his main worry was that his several-hundred-pound black market sugar purchases would be spotted. Bootlegging is a serious offense in Cuba, not only because it challenges the government's liquor monopoly but also because botched black market hooch has led to mass poisonings. Except for his worries, he had a comfortable existence in what was a very difficult economic situation for most Cubans.

Isidra was just off a phone call with Eulalia, who was in Cienfuegos preparing for Sierra Morena too.

"Do you know what she is saying now?" Isidra asked. "She says the refrigerator I paid for and had hauled from Havana to Sierra Morena last year is hers. Did you know? That lousy Russian refrigerator of hers failed, the one she refused to trade in for the Chinese one. So I busted my behind to get another fridge and send it out there."

"What is her argument?"

"There is no argument, Ramón. She is making no argument. She just wants it. Don't you see she is incapable of having an argument?"

"But what does she *say?*"

"Eulalia says Zulia says that the house is hers, that she lives there, and that the things in the house are hers too. That is all."

I was quiet and Isidra was too, for a few seconds.

"What am I supposed to do, go in there and haul the fridge out? No, hauling out my fridge will solve nothing." She was talking to herself. "The only way to resolve this situation is to haul her out."

There came another call from Sierra Morena, this time from Celita. Isidra loved the telephone. She lived for calls from friends across town, from Eulalia in Cienfuegos, and from Sierra Morena. It was her medium, and she could spend hours in it.

"Listen to this, Ramón. Now Zulia says she is the person who lives there and she is the person who says what will happen in the house and what will not. There will be no meals to the door or to the hole this year. Can you believe that?"

"I don't think she has ever much liked those things, right?"

"Stop. This is not about what she likes and doesn't. She dislikes things she doesn't know anything about. This is about ignorance and disrespect based in ignorance."

"So, no animals offered at all?"

"She says no meals that aren't to the santos themselves."

"Why?"

"There is no 'why.' You will not get a 'why' from her. Isn't this what I was just saying, that she has no basis, no experience, no knowledge by which to run that house."

I pondered this.

"Ramón, let's be clear. Eulalia and I let her into Cucusa's house. We let her in there because Pica was tired and the house needed more care. Zulia was behaving. The deal was simple: she gets a house to live in, but in December, Eulalia and I take over. We host the bembé for San Lázaro, and she gets the house back. She agreed. Now she says no feeding the door, no feeding the earth, that these were not things Cucusa did. What does she know?"

Our days of scrounging Havana for the things we needed in the countryside were successful, and we were on the verge of our departure. It was late afternoon December 12, and Isidra had offered a rooster to the Cuban-Congo powers she kept. The *chamalongo* coconut shells indicated that the waste should be scattered on a road, not a street. "Perfect," she said, "we have a whole highway ahead of us." The ride she arranged was a van with five seats and cargo space in the back. It belonged to the Office of the Historian of the City. That the historian, Eusebio Leal, was one of the most powerful men in Cuba, that he oversaw the redevelopment of Old Havana from a squalid city center to a UNESCO-certified world tourist destination, that he controlled one of Cuba's most important companies, Habaguanex—none of this could keep his employees from moonlighting with his vans, cars, and trucks. For 60 convertible pesos [CUC], equivalent in value to hard currency, he would drive us and our load one way anytime, as long as it was dark.

Ulises was coming along, and as the three of us waited for the van, Isidra dropped some news.

"We're picking up Teodoro on the way out of Havana."

"Teodoro?" I was surprised. "He will go on a bender the minute he arrives in Sierra Morena. Don't you remember last time you took him, in 1999? He was drunk 100 percent of the time, and Zenón and Gonzalo and everyone laughed at him."

"Shh!" she said. "He has his problems and we know them. No one knows them better than I do. No one has carried the burden that is Teodoro more than I have. He would be dead if I didn't feed him. But he is the child of Emilio O'Farril, one of the greatest *paleros* Guanabacoa ever saw. How many saplings sprang from the trunk that was Tata Emilio? Teodoro has all that inside. He is a walking library of Congo things."

"Isidra, caring for Teodoro here in Havana is one thing."

"I know what you're going to say. But there are reasons to bring him."

"Like?"

"Zulia says there will be nothing but *bembé de santo* played at the feast."

"What else is supposed to be played?"

"She is saying she doesn't want us to play Congo."

I was quiet.

"Nothing Congo," she said. "No Congo turn. In my mother's house we always play Congo when we've finished playing santo. You can't close out without playing for the Congos. She says Cucusa didn't play for the Congos. She has no idea what she is saying, as if we could change something that has been done since anyone can remember, just because she says so."

"Nothing Congo, as in no Mariana Congo? Mariana Congo is evidence of Cucusa's Congo ways."

"Cucusa's and Ma' Isidra's and Ernesto Portilla's Congo ways before her. They all kept Mariana. Now you're getting it. How could Cucusa have kept Mariana and not played Congo for her? How can you feed Mariana and not play for her? Well, Zulia says she doesn't want us to feed Mariana Congo. She says the santos, yes. Elégua, yes. Ogún, yes. Changó, yes. Yemayá, yes. La Caridad, yes. Oyá, yes. Obatalá, yes, and of course San Lázaro. But Mariana, no."

"You can't feed the santos and not feed Mariana," I said. This would be the most uncouth thing a host in Sierra Morena could do, to feed some powers and not others.

"You heard me. Now you know. She says she wants Mariana out of the house. Every time she speaks, what she doesn't understand is that she is signing her own death sentence. What do you think happens if you don't feed the hole? You end up in it. What do you think happens if you don't feed the door? Misfortune comes through it. What do you think happens if you don't feed Mariana Congo? Who do you think puts you in the hole? You tell me."

"And Teodoro?"

"She wants to ban Congo, so I'm going to bring Congo."

Teodoro was sober when we picked him up. Without a doubt, the van was one of the nicest rides we ever took to Sierra Morena. The driver was a trained chauffeur, and the van was spacious. He had his own way of justifying mileage and fuel consumption, so that no one back at the shop could denounce him for moonlighting. He kept a notebook with the details of previous reports and arrangements, so his story was always consistent. The whole way, Isidra would ask him to slow down so that she could toss bits of ritual waste out the door, leaving it at major intersections, railroad crossings, and other critical points of convergence, like the entrance to a town. When we passed through the outskirts of Varadero, where Roberto was now living, we picked him up too.

We pulled up to Cucusa's, and Zulia was standing silhouetted in the door, nearly filling the double opening. The van had not stopped before Isidra was out, followed by her brother. Together they confronted Zulia. A brief exchange ensued, and she and Roberto passed through. Eulalia was inside, wiping her hands on a dish towel. Before I could begin to unload the van, Isidra was back out carrying a small bundle in her hands. Roberto was raising his voice when Ulises and Teodoro walked in and each grabbed a drum from the saints' room. We were back in the van in less than a minute. "A couple more blocks ahead," she said to the driver.

Celita and José lived three blocks away. Isidra greeted them by way of saying that five people would now be staying at their place. José loved the news, but Celita was hesitant. We unloaded while Isidra clutched the little bundle. Roberto and Eulalia soon joined us.

"Zulia says we should go back, that we can have the feast at Cucusa's," said Roberto. "The only thing she wants is for us to feed Mariana somewhere else."

Eulalia chuckled in disbelief, then thought out loud, "That might be fine."

"Listen, you two," said Isidra. "Zulia doesn't get to say what does and doesn't happen at Cucusa's feast for Babalú Ayé. It is *our* house. Who bought that house? Cucusa and Orfilio, our mother and our father. Did her father buy that house? Also, Mariana cannot be fed anywhere but where she lives, which is in Cucusa's house."

"Then you shouldn't have taken her," Roberto replied, glancing at the bundle in her hands.

"What did you want, for me to leave Mariana there alone with Zulia, who is capable of anything?"

"Then let's feed her here, and everything else happens at Cucusa's," said Roberto.

"We'll do no such thing. Don't you see Zulia then becomes the person who makes the rules about how this bembé will go? She'll have no such role. She doesn't know the first thing."

There were enough beds for everyone with Teodoro sleeping on the couch. Ulises and I shared a bed, and Isidra and Eulalia shared a bed. Celita, José, and the kids slept together. Guillermo was seven. Mericelia was three going on four. After my 2006 visit she had major head surgery and had come through marvelously. "With Babalú Ayé's blessing," said Celita. Those children were a handful, and there were times when they would not leave me alone. Mericelia handled my eyeglasses and Guillermo my camera. But even when they were exasperating, they were a distraction from the happenings of that visit, which were at times marvelous, at others infuriating, and often incomprehensible.

It was the morning of December 13. It was four days before the drums would break open the town's many bembés for San Lázaro–Babalú Ayé. We had never arrived in Sierra Morena so late. There was hardly time to stage a feast at Cucusa's, let alone try to resolve the impasse at which the siblings had arrived. Roberto was staying at his house on the main plaza, which he had closed up several months ago for opportunities in Varadero. He came by with a tirade for his sisters and daughter.

"She says she will kill me," he said. "She says I may have sorcery [*brujería*], but she has her things too. Does she know who she is talking to, the power I have? You don't talk to someone who is *padre mprenda*, who has status in Palo, in that way. With a sweep of my hand, I can have her in the grave."

"She says I have mismanaged the house," said Isidra. "That I am planning to exploit it for gain. She says I plan to sell Cucusa's legacy in a spectacle for tourists as they drive down the highway. She says she has told the cultural authorities in Corralillo that I have sold photographs of my mother's treasured things to Ramón."

"The dresser I left behind last time had a lock, and she broke into it." Eulalia was more mild and pensive, but still aghast. "She says that she'll go to Cienfuegos to denounce me to the culture authorities for collaborating with a foreigner who wants to profit [*con fin de lucro*] from our mother's house."

"This is not tourism," said Roberto. "What we do here at Cucusa's is a serious observance. If you want tourism, go up to the Curve and see what they're doing there. That's a roadside spectacle. I don't mess around. You don't mess around with Congo things."

"Well, she says she is going to denounce you to the police for the Congo things you keep in Cucusa's backyard," said Celita. "She's been saying for months that you keep a pile of bones in the backyard and that the police will come and take it all away."

"The things I keep in my mother's yard are religious items and can't be touched by the law. Have her call them. I am *padre mprenda*, and whatever she does, I can counter." Roberto was on his feet and raising his voice.

"Let her try," said Isidra, angry but seemingly amused.

Prolonged harangues ensued and took a toll on Celita. She was a gracious and attentive host to her aunts and their plans, but she seemed tired. A month before she was taken to the hospital after burning herself with hot milk. The week before she had been two nights in the hospital in Santa Clara for using a chemical adhesive to glue her dentures into her mouth. José found her collapsed in the bathroom. She had purchased the glue on the black market, and both the police in Santa Clara and the powerful MININT interviewed her to find out who sold her the compound, which was used to repair watercraft. She was still shaken from this. The raised voices wore on her. They drove Teodoro from the house, to the streets, and to the bottle.

Word of our exile at Celita and José's spread, and visitors started coming by almost immediately, each with their own bit of gossip or story to share. Pica was stuck at home, nearly blind from "sugar," which meant diabetic eye disease, but María came by with a friend from Sagua la Grande named Dayán. She said Zulia was going to host the feast whether Isidra came around or not.

Yunier, the tall and resourceful kid from previous visits, showed up. He was still dazzled by Takako a decade later. He said Zulia was threatening to go to the police to denounce the theft of the drums from the house. Justo, whom Isidra had put full-time on the task of finding animals, said Zulia had a spiritual adviser in Sagua la Grande who was helping her with the situation. Zulia called him "the messenger," and if she was stubborn, it was because he pushed her to take an all-or-nothing position.

Isidra, for her part, planned to host the feast at Cucusa's. She expected to be back in the house shortly. On the 14th she and Roberto went to Corralillo to file a complaint against Zulia for wrongful eviction. Her refusal to honor their deal regarding the use of Cucusa's house amounted to an eviction of the Ruíz Sáez siblings. They were also going to file a document with the cultural authorities in Corralillo regarding Zulia's inability to host the feast. The document would state that given her inexperience (and intransigence), Zulia would be solely liable for any public disorder resulting from the feast on December 17. The bar down the block concerned Isidra, and she cited this as an aggravating factor. As a footnote, Isidra would include a declaration that she was in the company of an old student of hers from the United States who was in town to pay his respects to San Lázaro on the 17th. This was to preempt Zulia from denouncing me to the authorities for staying in a home without a license to house tourists. Celita and José did not have the necessary permits to host me even for a night. With little effort, Zulia could get me kicked out and my hosts warned for housing me and fined if they kept me. The bureaucratic conniving led Isidra to the idea of beating Zulia to the permit for the feast. Assembling to feast African-inspired powers in Cuba requires a permit from the local police. Isidra would turn the permit into leverage. Without it, Zulia's feast would be out of order. When they returned from Corralillo, they had the permit, and it was their understanding that the police sided with whoever held it.

Roberto was happy to be back in Sierra Morena and quickly caught up on the whispers. His modernist cement house was one of the few places Isidra would allow me to go unaccompanied. At any minute, Zulia or her agents, her guy Isaías and her son Ernesto, could provoke an incident that would get me kicked out of town and sent back to Havana. The Ruíz Sáez family were in the revolutionary vanguard of the party, starting with Cucusa and including Isidra, Eulalia, Roberto, and Máximo. Their revolutionary stripes could not be questioned, so that was in our favor. Roberto and I sat on his tiled veranda.

"So when exactly did Zulia say the house was exclusively hers?" I asked.

"What do I know?" said Roberto. "She's been awful for a while now."

"Do you think it was before the 26th?" I asked. July 26 is a threshold date every year, right in the middle of the summer, commemorating the revolution's beginnings and triumph. There was a pause.

"Before," he said.

"It sounds like the police will be of help at least."

Roberto looked at me plainly. "What we need to do," he said stuttering, "what we need to do is burn her out of there."

"Burn?"

"Fire," he said, "la candela." His choice of words communicated that he was talking about using Congo-inspired forces against her. Palo, the Congo-inspired healing and harming craft he and Isidra were both adept in, is often referred to in terms of kindling, heat, and fate-shaping fire.[1] "Isidra should have done it months ago. I live here in town, so I'm not going to get into that."

"I'm pretty sure that is on her agenda," I said, insinuating that Isidra had traveled with Congo-inspired powers from her collection in Havana.

"She should have left all that back home," he said. "Now that she's here, she needs to be working in local terms, with local things. She has Mariana, and that is all she needs." He was quiet for a moment.

"Can she do it with Mariana?" I asked.

"Forget all that. Listen," he said, "there is a bend in the river, not far inland."

"La Corua," I said.

"No, the other direction, inland. In the pool lives a *number eight*. You know what I'm talking about." In Cuban-Congo parlance a number eight [*un número ocho*] is a snake [*majá*]. Even mentioning a snake can call one to you, so "number eight" is used as a cipher.

"That animal," Roberto said, leaning in, "was as long as a telephone pole when I saw it as a kid in the company of my godfather, Loreto. Even then, that number eight was more than a hundred years old. I'm seventy-one now. Can you imagine its size today?" I had to think about it to imagine it. The conversation had taken a turn, and just when I thought he would be expressing his confidence in Mariana Congo's powers, we were talking about an enormous 170-year-old snake.

"Today he must be bigger around than I could hold in my arms," he said. "He was shiny black, and his head was as big as a horse's. I will never forget the expression on its face. His eyes understood us perfectly. We offered it a black turkey right into the pool, and he did exactly what Loreto asked it to do. I have never been back or asked it to do anything in all these years, but maybe it is time." Roberto looked at me steady, with a serious expression.

"Can you remember how to get there?" I asked, not knowing what else to say. Given the tension at Celita's, a walk in the country would be nice.

"I know perfectly how to get there," he said. "But I'm too old for this shit, Ramón. Do you think you can face a number eight like that and just be calm about it? We'll be shitting ourselves. Plus, walking on river stones will kill my knees. You and Isidra go. Take a black turkey, and we'll have my mother's house cleared out in no time."

. . .

On the night of the 14th, Ulises, Justo, and I went to get Pica. She was eighty, slower and resigned to her fading vision. Isidra wanted to host her at Celita's to hear her sing. She had Eulalia fry up a fish from José's catch that day. With a little aguardiente she sat her down next to the drums Ulises and Teo had taken from Cucusa's on our entrance into town. Justo and Ulises took up a quiet bembé beat. The drums were not rousing, nor was Pica energetic, but the sound drew one person, then another, until finally there was a crowd in Celita's living room and a little bembé was underway. Zenón showed up and took a seat at the kitchen table sipping government-provisioned rum with José.

Not so long after, Zenón took up the call, easily bumping Pica out of the role. She did not have the energy to resist him and took a seat at his side. Things had been calm for a bembé until then, but Zenón lifted the energy, and in one or two songs several people were mounted, including María with a very brusque version of Changó, and Roberto with Elégua. María's Changó paced and strode with rage at the idea that Cucusa's feast would not be held and warned those present that Cucusa's house must not slip from their hands. Elégua was also irritated and denounced the abuses, the audacity, and the lack of respect displayed by Zulia. His Elégua called for a coconut, which would confirm his condemnations. Much attention was given to Roberto's Elégua, even though his voice was hard to distinguish from Roberto's everyday speech. María continued to circulate as a fuming Changó and a cousin from Sagua was mounted by Obatalá. Then José fell straight onto his face in the middle of the living room. He had been standing close to me, with a tiny plastic cup of rum in his hand, dancing calmly as the rest of the gathering got roused. He was on the floor, stiff, facedown. He laid there, groaning, spitting, while Elégua did his coconut work. José began propelling himself little by little toward the front door, where his Elégua was kept. Dancers stepped aside as he snaked past, and when he finally made it to the hinges of the door, where a candle was lit on the floor, he raised his head so that the candle would burn him under the chin. Eulalia was there to keep that from happening and to keep him from knocking his head against Elégua, in the form of a large river stone in a clay dish.

Teodoro then reappeared, drawn by the drums. He hadn't been in town in a decade, but people remembered him by the nickname Batalla, a favorite word of his that recalled his enthusiasm for scrounging up liquor and his claims to be a great Congo-inspired healer. He was recovering from a chest cold, and he had vowed to stay sober for our visit. We had barely seen him since our arrival and had heard tell that he was drinking "pharmacy alcohol." He seemed sober enough and soon took a seat at one of the drums. His flourishes and improvisations were tolerated by the musicians and chorus, but when he tried lifting the beat toward the Congo-inspired rhythms of Havana Palo, Zenón shook his head in exasperation and continued with his repertoire. Time and again the musicians ragged him for messing up the beat, and it wasn't more than ten minutes before Teodoro was again out the door. Elégua continued his rounds. He kicked the coconut gently around the house as he declaimed promised ruin for Zulia. Isidra took it all in with an air of validation. Changó praised her for her strength and determination in confronting those who would defile Cucusa's santos.

The morning of the 15th, now thirty-six hours from when the feast should break open, saw the siblings in a debate about whether to plan for the feast or cancel it. There was hardly any time left to make things happen at Cucusa's house. The preparations were too many. But Isidra insisted that the feast must happen, that the doors be open, and that people have the opportunity to encounter San Lázaro–Babalú Ayé, whether on his altar in the shape of the two Catholic figurines, or in person mounted on Celita or another steed. She thought there was still time. Her one condition for moving forward was that Zulia step aside. Roberto thought the feast should be canceled.

"She knows we have the permit. The police will take care of this," said Roberto. After having been mounted by Elégua for two hours the night before, and having slept and showered at his place, he was back at his daughter's kitchen table, his grandchildren and sisters around him. "I know the chief. He said he would talk to her."

"When?" shot Isidra. "You've seen me. No one has worked harder. I have Justo flushing animals out of people's hands as we speak, animals they had set aside for themselves. But I can't go on buying unless I know that it is Cucusa's santos that are going to eat, including Mariana Congo."

"The police will pay her a visit, and then I will tell Zulia the bembé is canceled," said Roberto, finding resolve, or maybe just clarity.

"Canceled? What are you talking about?" said Isidra. "We can't cancel the bembé and then uncancel it!"

"What do you mean, 'uncancel it'? I'm going to cancel it. As soon as the police let her know that it is up to us to call this, then I will cancel it, and that will be the end of this."

"Roberto," said Isidra now on her feet. "You cannot cancel the feast! The feast is going to happen tomorrow at Cucusa's house, and we're going to be leading it. Why cancel it when we are going to be in charge?"

"In charge? How are you going to be in charge? Do you know what I heard on my way over here? Zulia says that she doesn't care who has the permit, that it has been issued for Cucusa's house, and that is where the party for Babalú Ayé is going to be held. That is why we need the police, to let her know that when we call off the feast, she has to comply."

"She will come here," said Eulalia. "She will come here today and ask us to put this feast on for her. She knows she can't do it without us."

"She'll beg us," said Isidra, "so don't cancel anything!"

"Aunt," said Celita, "every August, José hosts a bembé here for his santo, orisá Inle, and it goes just fine. He says we should just host the bembé here. Why don't we? Let my dad cancel Cucusa's bembé and we'll host it here."

"Here? Listen, the bembé that happened here last night is not what I came all the way from Havana for. I only wanted to hear Pica sing a few old songs. I'm not here for all the rum that was passed around at this table last night, or for Pica to be falling sleep as Zenón sings a bunch of drunken chanteys. I'm here to do a serious thing, which is to feast my mother's santos, Babalú Ayé first among them. And Mariana. It will happen at Cucusa's. You will see."

Just then Pica came by escorted by María, who was recovering from multiple mountings the night before.

"Mom wants to grab you and go up the hill," she said to me.

I was happy Pica would want to go anywhere with me.

"You help her up the hill," said María. "I'm not going up there. It is early and I'm going back to bed."

Pica added, "We're going to my sister Berta's so that you can take a photograph of us, so bring your camera."

Berta lived just a few blocks away, but her street was an unpaved climb, with river stones and jagged rivulets and little crags that made the walk treacherous for someone with Pica's limited mobility and sightedness. We were going very slow when Yunier showed up and mounted Pica onto his bike rack. He got up on his pedals and used his enormous strength to zip her up the hill. Pica bounced around but held on with a calm expression.

Berta was waiting for us. She was the very image of Pica, portly, of rounded shoulders and pronounced belly, with short white hair and Loreto's square jaw, button nose, and almond eyes. She didn't have the scars climbing from her chest to her chin that Pica had, and her smile was broader and easier than Pica's. "My older sister," Pica said tersely when I complimented her warm manner. I also complimented her skirt, which was made of lined sackcloth with a purple gingham hem. It was a tribute to San Lázaro, whose sackcloth tunic is referenced in the clothes of folks throughout Cuba in December. I was especially interested in the equilateral cross that has been stitched onto the front of the dress.

"It was Quintina's skirt," said Berta. "She was my mother and Pica's mother, and the mother of eleven other children. Loreto fathered us all. As far as I know, Pica and I are the only ones who developed religiously [*que tuvimos desenvolvimiento religioso*]. Quintina was not religious, though she always participated at the Sociedad Africana. Quintina stitched the design on this skirt in 1990, when she was ninety-five. She wanted to put dogs there, too, but they were too hard for her hands then. She died in 1995, when she was 101 years old."[2]

Berta was an *espiritista,* or Spiritualist, in the mold of Allan Kardec, the nineteenth-century French founder of formal, systematic Enlightenment Spiritualism. She gathered about her a group of spirits of the dead with whom she had decades-long relationships and who mounted her in consultations. The entities she channeled spoke for yet others of the dead, who directly addressed the concerns of her clients. In effect, she channeled a spirit who channeled yet others. She showed us back to her bedroom, where she sat us on her carefully made bed. Before us was an extensive Spiritualist altar [*bóveda*] of family photos and Catholic images set on her dresser before a huge mirror.

"Don't you get going, Sister," said Pica. "He's just here to take a picture, not to learn about all the spiritual things twittering around his head."

Berta seemed delighted with anything Pica said. "By all means, take a picture of my altar. Will you take one with me in it?"

"Maybe he wants to take a picture of your altar. You two can figure that out. I want him to take a picture of *us,* like out on the veranda?"

"Fine," said Berta. "Just sit here a moment both of you and listen to what an old woman has to say. The children of Cucusa and Orfilio, they should not bother with that woman who has taken their house. We all know who she is. Those children need to approach the situation as sweetly as possible and with the best wishes possible for that woman and for the feast. What else is there to do? Fight their way in? Get angry? Shut it down? Fight her straight on? She doesn't know much, that woman, but she does know how to fight straight on. No, those children need to bathe in okra and just slide right past that bull."

I was surprised she knew as much as she did, but it made sense. She was Pica's sister, after all. But she seemed to be speaking from her own information and with an understanding independent of her sister. I was delighted to hear anyone speaking so calmly and with such assurance about a situation that was only getting worse. I could imagine her in a Spiritualist consultation, mounted by one of her benevolent dead and dispensing valuable wisdom. There was a slight change in her demeanor, though her voice remained the same.

"Let it slide. Why impede her? If you stop the bembé, don't you rescue her? Every time those children impede her, they keep her from falling. They give her an excuse for the failure she is sure to be. Don't they see the void at which she teeters? It is a void she opened for herself. Why save her from her void?"

Berta's house sat on the precipice of the hill, the last house before the steep decline. You could see the town below, sitting on its steppe, then the coastal plain and the lagoon and even the keys beyond. It was still morning, and a steady, cool breeze blew. We were quiet for just a moment, and Berta looked at us calmly.

"Shutting down the feast. They should not shut down the feast. That won't teach her anything. Only shame will teach her. If those children close the doors, if they say people can't come, then they will lose support from people in town. Everyone in town has a promise to keep with Babalú Ayé at Cucusa's house. But now there are other feasts and other opportunities. Don't close the doors. People need to greet their santo and keep their promise. Those children shut the doors, and they have less sense than that woman. Leave the doors open. Let the people greet Babalú Ayé. The people will see that that woman can't host Babalú Ayé. That is when everyone will learn. And what about him, what about Babalú Ayé? Do you think he is just going to keep to himself in all of this? Do you think he doesn't have expectations? Do you think she can meet them? So why get between her and Babalú Ayé? Do those children think they need to protect Babalú Ayé? Protect San Lázaro? Oh, he can take care of himself, and he will take care of her too. What those children need to do is follow old Elégua and his tricks. Stand aside, with one eye closed and one eye open. When she trips, they didn't see a thing. With sweetness, with best wishes, why wish her anything else?"

She smiled. Pica was falling asleep. Berta continued, "Look at me. I'm an old lady. What do I know? I have a second-grade education. What can I know? Those children all have their university degrees, and they run around with educated people like you, and they are all vanguard in the party. They will know what to do. Let the waves come and go, that is what I know, and you bob up and down. Spread honey on the waves, wish that woman the best, and let the waves pass sweetly on. Where will they crash? Look out at the sea. The sun is high now, but come back when it is low, and I will show you honey on the waves. Now, what was that about a photo? Pica, did you want us to be in it together?"

"Sister," said Pica, "I may never make it up this hill again. And you come down less and less. I want a picture of the two of us together."

"Let's go," said Berta. "Let's take it on the veranda, with the sea in background. I like the company you are keeping, Sister. He is calm and quiet. Right now that is good."

FIFTEEN

Voices of the Dead

MORNING TURNED OVER AND THE POLICE NEVER SHOWED UP. The debate about planning or canceling the bembé continued, and I communicated Berta's advice to the siblings.

"Berta. Which Berta?" asked Isidra. "Pica's Berta? Up the hill? Elégua has already said as much to me. Why do you think I fed him four-legged animals all year? So that he would speak, that's why. What did he say to me? Just that. Take a bath in *quimbombó* [okra] so you'll be slippery, and let it slide. We won't host and we won't cancel. Tomorrow I'll be at the feast, and I won't do a thing. I will sit with the chorus and wait in anticipation. And when midnight comes and she falls, she'll know I was there."

Relief was felt instantly. Tomorrow was the 16th, and at midnight the drums would sound, and we didn't have to do a thing. "When Justo comes, I'll have him take all the animals back. Let the trucks from Havana cart them off. Where is Zulia going to find animals at this late hour?"

The young people reunited in the days before the 17th. Ulises, Boby, and Anelé rambled about. Ulises was twenty-three, Boby a year younger, and Anelé a year younger than that. They seemed not much different from the little ones, Guillermo, who was now seven, and Mericelia, who was four. The children seemed oblivious to the decisions being made by their parents and grandparents, though in some ways Guillermo and Mericelia felt it more because they were emotionally entangled with Celita, who was feeling everything. Of the older kids it was Boby who was most visibly unhappy about the situation.

"They need to put this past them," he said, with flat exasperation. "Don't they see that this is about the whole town? Who cares who hosts the bembé? Who cares who lives at my great-grandmother's house as long as we play [*tocamos*] for San Lázaro on the 17th?"

"That would be overlooking a lot of insults and disrespect," I said.

"Overlook it for one week a year! You're telling me they can't put this down and see eye to eye? If they each thought about the whole town, the hundreds of people who need San Lázaro right now, who need him tomorrow, they would put it down."

"What do you think San Lázaro wants?" I asked

"Only the *oricha* can speak for the *oricha*," Boby said, using the Havana accent. "I'll tell you what, though, I wouldn't want to face San Lázaro if I were my aunt Zulia or my aunt Isidra. When that santo comes, he is going to be pissed. The santos that come to the feast tomorrow are coming for what is theirs and neither of my aunts is ready to provide."

I was talking with Boby about bembés in Santa Clara, the capital of Villa Clara Province, where he lived.

"There is a guy who sings at bembés in Santa Clara," he said. "He travels all over Cuba to sing at bembés, and everyone says he is one of the best. I brought him here. He didn't understand at all. His style, which is Santa Clara style, is pure barbs [*pura puya*]. The drums snap it open, and from then on it's just trying to one up anyone else who wants to sing. It is fun, but there is nothing there for the orichas. No songs for the orichas. It is more like Congo-style barbs than lyrics for the orichas. The singer started in on Zenón, and Zenón got the upper hand on him right away. They went back and forth to see who would outshine the other with people just watching, no chorus. That is really bad here in town. It was like rumba, but way out of place. Finally, Zenón just nailed him with some wisdom, and the guy was mounted with Changó just like that. You should have heard the chorus then! Off he went to do his santo thing. Zenón can do that to anyone he wants."

I asked Boby if Santa Clara was good for him. He had missed a chance at a college education and was now learning vocational electronics. "Where I am supposed to be but Santa Clara? Varadero? With what happened to my father? Forget it."

The good news for Isidra was that Zenón was boycotting Zulia's party. Justo was boycotting. One by one, musicians declared their intentions. The prize was Pica. Isidra knew that in years past Pica had sung at the Curve. That feast grew by the year and loomed as an alternative for people confused by the family drama radiating from Cucusa's house, or wanting to avoid it. The woman at the Curve tended to people day to day and earned their gratitude. Word was that the strife between Cucusa's daughters was freeing up musicians, and they were heading out to the Curve. But Pica was unambiguous.

"Even if the people at the Curve send a car for me," she said, "I'm not going anywhere." Gonzalo, too, said he was boycotting Zulia's feast and staying away from the Curve. Only Iván, the young drummer who was raised by Cucusa as one of her last children, was going to open the feast at Zulia's. This disappointed Isidra bitterly, and she accused him of rank betrayal.

The afternoon of the 15th went by, which by my estimation was the last possible moment we could have still pulled off a bembé at Cucusa's. Isidra had now endorsed the idea of letting Zulia flop. The calm predicted by Berta didn't last long. In the evening word came that Zulia had packed up and left. "She locked the door behind her, went to Corralillo," said Justo, who was ever in the know.

The news shook the siblings. Roberto thought they should cancel then and there. In effect, he thought it better to cancel and claim the prestige of such authority rather than subject Cucusa's bembé to the embarrassment of Zulia's failure. Isidra was baffled by his insistence. Her thoughts were immediately of taking the house back by forcing the door and occupying it. This idea alarmed Roberto so much that José again suggested that he and Celita host the bembé.

"Celita has San Lázaro. We can just give San Lázaro his goat here," he said.

"I have San Lázaro in Havana too," said Isidra. "If all I wanted was to feast San Lázaro, I would have stayed in the comfort on my apartment. I didn't come all the way here to feast anyone's San Lázaro but Cucusa's. He must eat at my mother's house."

A bembé at Celita's was rejected, but it provided an oblique counter to Isidra's idea of taking the house by force, and she stopped talking about it. Eulalia was relieved. Roberto still wanted to call it off. They decided they should *lumbrar el muerto* [bring light to the dead], which was a Sierra Morena way of connecting with the dead along the lines of what Berta did with her Spiritualist altar. Isidra had come to like María's friend from Sagua la Grande, Dayán, and she was convinced he was a competent Spiritualist medium. The idea was that we would bring light to the dead tomorrow to seek their aid in deciding what to do.

It surprised me that Isidra chose this path, and that her siblings accepted it. Such were the stakes that she was willing to consider breaking into her mother's house, which would have almost surely led to a physical confrontation with Zulia and an encounter with the police. Such were the stakes that she didn't think twice about cajoling anyone who got in her way, or writing off longtime friends as traitors. The continuation of her mother's feast for San

Lázaro–Babalú Ayé hung in the balance and along with it the continuation of her mother's memory and legacy in her community. Isidra's own prestige in town was at stake, as was her control over parts of her family still connected via the memory of their mother. Other things were at stake that I could not see, including things that maintained her power over Roberto and Eulalia.

She possessed the expertise to consult the dead on her own without the help of a stranger, like Dayán. With so much at risk, why would she choose a path that put so much in his hands? She had been around *espiritistas* and *muerteras* for decades, and she knew they could be clever, so it was not blind faith in Dayán's abilities. Of these she knew very little, so she should have been even more reluctant. Perhaps she believed a stranger would more objectively connect with the dead. Perhaps she was confident that if she did not like how Dayán communicated with the dead, she had the expertise and authority to override him. I never understood why, in the midst of the worst family crisis she had endured, she was willing to have the volition of her very ancestors channeled through him hours before the feast was to begin.

On the morning of the 16th, Isidra was jumpy. "We should be at Cucusa's right now, giving a meal to the earth. I declare that canceled. What else will I need to cancel? There is no point covering up this failure. We are stuck here, and we could make do, offer meals here, offer a bembé here, but that would only cover up our failure. The santos at my mother's house will not be fed this year, and that is a failure. The dead at my mother's house will not be tended to, and that is a failure. This is why we aren't canceling the feast, not until the last moment." Eulalia went about the morning routine, cleaning up breakfast, thinking about lunch, and worrying what the day would bring. Celita was focused on her children, and José wondered aloud whether he should go fishing. Isidra forbid it. She also forbade Ulises from going out that evening. Word that the feast at the Curve was going to be huge was on everyone's lips, and she refused to let anyone associated with her attend. She was grimly consoled that Pica, Zenón, Gonzalo, and other musicians were sitting the 17th out.

Word came around midday that Zulia had returned and opened up the house. Those with promises to keep were welcome. This news threw the siblings into near chaos as they revisited their choices and floated new plans. Isidra was in the midst of carrying on two separate arguments and setting up a Spiritualist altar when a man showed up at the back door. He was in his sixties, with his white hair clipped close and a neatly trimmed mustache. He wore dress slacks and a pressed cream shirt. He had a city dweller's hat in his hand. He spoke in a very mild voice, almost inaudible.

"I am a messenger," he said. "I'm here to sow peace."

Eulalia, who was in the kitchen just then, invited him into the living room, where Isidra sat at the table she was preparing for our Spiritualist gathering. The table was set with white lace, glasses of water, and photos of Isidra's dead, including Cucusa, Orfilio, Ma' Isidra, and Loreto.

"I am a messenger and I am here to sow peace," he said again.

Isidra regarded him, and for a moment the house was quiet. Then she jumped up and almost startled the man.

"You are messenger for who? If it is for my sister, then you are a messenger for an ignoramus. You are a messenger for a person who doesn't know what the word *revolution* means, and never has. An antisocial whose children are incarcerated and who disrespects her mother's memory. Who insults her siblings. Who lies and commits fraud. She cut down the trees, she broke her word. The orisás will have their say."

The messenger tried to speak but she shushed him, unrolling yet another list of Zulia's transgressions. The messenger tried again to speak, and again was interrupted. Isidra appeared ready to continue for some time, so he stood up and left without speaking.

"'I'm a messenger. I'm here to sow peace,'" Eulalia said, mocking him. "Did you hear that?"

"Did you see how he was dressed?" asked Isidra.

"Did you see the crucifix?" Eulalia continued. "They say she is harboring an evangelical Christian from Sagua."

"He's not from here," confirmed Celita.

"It has to be him."

"You don't have to tell me that," said Isidra. "I know who is from this town and who is not. I know every family in this town."

"They go around saying they want to sow peace," said Eulalia. "What they want is to grow their churches and sow discord against the revolution. Now you see what kind of company she is keeping!"

"They say the messengers turn you against your dead, distance you from your santos, then claim you for their churches," said Celita, who was nervous.

"Can you believe it?" said Isidra. "That is how she thinks she is going to take care of my mother's santos, by bringing a messenger around on the 17th? He's her help? I want to see him call out a song for San Lázaro. Let's see him do better than Pica. Then I want to see him feed the santos, so he can teach Zulia how it is done." She let out a sincere, genuine laugh.

Not long after, we brought light to the dead. Isidra sent Guillermo and Mericelia out to pick wildflowers and placed them on the table she had turned into an altar. Dayán was sought, and she lit a candle when he arrived. Dayán had a focused manner and an intelligent, still face. On that evening of high tension, hours before Zulia would open Cucusa's bembé, his air was welcome. He wanted to engage in a full-on Spiritualist mass, but Isidra insisted we limit our outreach to the dead to a *pensamiento*.

Dayán led us in several Catholic prayers, including the Lord's Prayer. He followed by leading us in hymns from a Spiritualist pamphlet, of which José had a copy. They were plaintive and melodic, and sometimes they seemed like prayers too. Most were too long to be sung in call-and-response, so we sang them in unison sharing the pamphlet. They intoned devout petitions to spiritual beings [*los seres*], calling them near. In the midst of these, Dayán was mounted by one of the dead he cultivated in a "spiritual field" [*campo espiritual*] about him.[1] The *muerto* [dead one] who mounted him was a "Congo" and proceeded to address each of us. He was mounted for three hours. His speech was marked by grammatical idiosyncrasies that validated his Congo roots. Roberto was incredulous and tried to interrupt him with Congo-inspired bluster, talking about *prendas* and *muertos* and *bilongos*. Dayán's muerto had the opposite effect on Isidra, who repeatedly shushed her brother.

The Congo went along, with words for Eulalia, Roberto, Celita, José, Ulises, and the children too. Justo, who was with us, shrank into a corner and was not addressed. "I don't like Spiritualist things," he said later. "Just let me drum up a bembé." The Congo's words for me were full of foreboding about my research being interrupted by sorcery.

Dayán's muerto then turned to Isidra and spoke with her for nearly an hour. "You are the head, and the body follows you. Nothing moves without you. You can't be the head without being envied. Your enemies are everywhere. Your closest relations, people in this room, could betray you."

"I'm a daughter of betrayal," said Isidra.

"Who do you trust? Don't trust anyone."

There were minutes and minutes of insinuated threats and enemies, all of which Isidra acknowledged with nods. Eulalia was implicated, and Isidra did nothing to signal that the Congo might be wrong. She seemed eager to face the worst possible prognostications. There were minutes of statements regarding Ulises, how he was a young man and ripe to be played by clever women.

Ulises was smart, and his cleverness would lead to trouble. Then minutes on Isidra's godchildren in Palo back in Havana. "Watch out for your children," the Congo said. "Your enemies will get you through your children. They will get your children to betray you." Yamilet, who had taken the refrigerator and furniture a decade ago, was also Isidra's only initiate in Ocha-Santería. Her betrayals now seemed mild compared with Zulia's.

Of Zulia, the dead one had much to say, none of it conciliatory. "She is making decisions she will regret for the rest of her life. There is no helping her now that she has chosen her path. Failure after failure has been her life until now, and failure is what awaits her."

Isidra nodded. Before the Congo's words the house had been torn by competing plans for how to deal with the start of Zulia's feast at midnight, and whether to attend. If Zulia was going to succeed, the drums would be cracking soon. Isidra agreed that she would stay put. His long consultation with Isidra was the climax of Dayán's mounting, and soon his Congo departed, leaving him slumped in his chair. José was taking us out of the Spiritualist scene with a return to the hymnbook when María arrived.

She must have been close by. She knew Dayán and the various muertos who mounted him, and she wasn't looking to join our pensamiento. She had left Pica on the stoop of an empty house a couple of blocks away and needed help with her. Had María not pointed out Pica in the shadows, I would have walked right past, so placidly was she sitting. We started Pica down the broken path back to Celita's, but María turned at the first crossing, leaving us.

"Where are you going?" I called after her, but she only waved behind her back as she quickly disappeared into the dark.

"She's going to the Curve," Pica said. "She loves that party."

Midnight arrived, and we spent the first hours of the 17th at Celita's playing the drums and singing bembé songs. Gonzalo, arguably the best drummer in town, joined us for the night, thus declaring for Isidra. She was visibly proud to have his support. Iván was rumored to be playing for Zulia, so Gonzalo's presence was a gift. He came with an informal entourage of drummers, because where he played, others wanted to play too. A chorus soon formed. Pica led us in several hours of call-and-response play. It was a small, sweet bembé. Celita was not mounted, nor José. Ulises played the drums and learned the caja. A handful of orisás joined, including Elégua, Changó, and Oyá, the last two of which were mounted serially on Pica. We played until dawn. Zenón never came. We hadn't seen Teodoro in what seemed like days.

He was rumored to be shacked up on the outskirts of town. Pica sang and danced, mounted the night through with no need of Zenón to relieve her. There was no slaughter that night.

. . .

With only a couple of hours of sleep, Isidra woke on the morning of the 17th undaunted.

"Did you hear? Did you hear?" Isidra sipped warm, sweetened, unpasteurized, local, black market milk. "She failed!"

I sipped milk and, with a lift of an eyebrow, invited her to continue.

"No one, but no one, was there for the opening at midnight. No one went to meet San Lázaro at Zulia's farce." A smile broke across her face. "Midnight with both doors open and she was sitting there by herself. The whole town was mocking her."

"It is what Berta said . . ."

"Shhh! Now you know what it means to be properly saddled up [ensillada]. The work we've been doing. Don't let anyone tell you I don't know how to work. What good has Teodoro been? He's lost with some whore a mile out of town. It was me, firm in my saddle. I know how to work."

"Is this what you wanted?" It seemed a long way from hosting the feast at Cucusa's.

"Isolation. What have I done since I arrived? Did I go knock her door down? Did I tear her hair out in the street? No. I isolated her, that is what I accomplished."

"Everyone was here last night. It was a good bembé."

"Do you see? Do you see what I can pull? Who was here last night? Gonzalo. Pica. Justo. The best, the most serious people. *That* was a bembé."

Eulalia came in from the back. "And she still doesn't want to feed San Lázaro here. We could get a goat for him and do it properly this morning."

Isidra turned. "Eulalia, we're not here to party. We're here to tend to Cucusa's things, and I will not give an animal I pay for to a santo that's not hers."

Justo was sitting by the kitchen door. "All the animals have been returned anyway. We've got a little goat and a red rooster, that's it."

"Let the trucks from Havana come," said Isidra. "That little goat can stay here with Celita and José. They can raise it up, and we'll give it to Babalú Ayé next year."

Celita, who with us, said, "Aunt, they say Zulia is going to play tonight. Last night didn't shame her one bit."

"Shame? You want shame?" said Isidra. "When six o'clock rolls around tonight and she expects a chorus, the only person who is going to be there is me. She offered no animals, she fed no santos, she fed no musicians, chorus, or mounts. Shame is that big empty house with San Lázaro looking down from his altar, and me looking on. Where will she hide in that house full of hungry santos?"

The 17th of December is a celebration throughout Cuba. The adoration of San Lázaro, either alone as the Beggar Saint of Catholic lore or coupled with Babalú Ayé, is widespread in all of Cuba. As the day approaches, people manifest the Beggar Saint in their clothing, in promises they make, and the stories of illness and healing they recount. Statues of San Lázaro are placed in windows facing the street, and in doorways. Beggars appear on the street with little statuettes of San Lázaro in their alms boxes. At El Rincón, a little town with a Catholic sanctuary and leprosarium on the western outskirts of Havana, thousands join in a procession to pay their respects to San Lázaro at his altar there. The energy in Sierra Morena was a mixture of penitence and anticipation for the bembés that the 17th engendered.[2]

I was at Pica's talking with her when María woke up. "It was a blast at the Curve last night," she said. "Great party. It was full, with tons of people and lots of orisás. They always get new steeds [caballos]. They mount up from Sagua and Santa Clara."

"We played at Celita's. Pica led us. No Zenón. Did Zenón sing at the Curve?" I asked.

"Zenón will never be caught out there."

"Will Gonzalo?"

She shook her finger tersely back and forth.

"Why not?"

"Gonzalo, I don't know. See if you can get him to talk. Zenón says it's no good."

"How can you tell if it is any good?"

María looked at me, realizing something. "Come with me now. I'll take you to a party. Justo, come."

The drums could be heard a country block from Celita's. It was Celita's grandfather, Celia's father, Lázaro M., who was hosting. His house was tiny, of revolutionary construction with cement walls and floors. A wall split the house down the middle with a kitchen and dining room on one side and bedrooms on the other. María took me by the hem of my shirt.

It was crowded and rousing. The chorus was swaying around two large bowls, one metal, one plastic. These held large stones that were covered in bright, fresh blood. A single goat's head was placed ceremoniously before them; it was the meal they had shared [*fueron convidados*]. They were Elégua and Babalú Ayé, and both ate goat. Elégua's is supposed to be a kid and San Lázaro's mature, but they can share a big one. I turned away. Lázaro M. was right in the middle of feeding his santos-orisás, and at Cucusa's this was a private affair. María gave my hem a little tug, almost preempting my reaction.

"Here everyone is invited for the santos' meal. Like at the Curve. Look how pretty."

Standing before the Elégua and Babalú Ayé stones was the host, Lázaro M., singing. Three drummers were lined up behind him, pounding out bembé rhythms on a pair of tumbadoras and a wooden box. There on a little platter alongside Elégua and Babalú Ayé was a little plaster statuette of Lazarus the Beggar, the Catholic effigy, bent over crutches, sore infested, with dogs licking his wounds. This, too, shared in the meal.

"His birthday," said María, bending me to her so I could hear. "Today is his birthday."

"Yes, it is San Lázaro's Day," I said.

"Also his," she said pointing to Lázaro M.

"On the 17th?"

"Today. He shares it with San Lázaro." She put her two index fingers together side by side to sign proximity. "Eighty-nine today."

Lázaro M. wore a pair of khaki pants cinched up at his waist, and a light purple shirt. He had close-cropped hair and a little white mustache. His skin was very light brown, light *mulato* by Cuban standards (but not *jabao*), and his eyes were blue. He stood with his feet close together without moving them even a bit as he sang up Babalú Ayé in a sweet, penetrating falsetto, calling the chorus on. Already, San Lázaro–Babalú Ayé was mounted on a woman who hobbled with a shawl of sackcloth over her shoulders and with an attendant close at hand. Babalú Ayé limped out the back door. Lázaro M. was enjoying every call, toothless, his head raised when it was his turn, his eyes appreciative of the chorus when they replied.

I was looking to see if there might be animals yet to offer when Boby spotted me and came over. He was Lázaro M.'s great-grandson, the son of

Robertico the suicide, who was the son of Roberto, Isidra's brother, and Celia M., Lázaro M.'s daughter. He took me out back into an ample yard that appeared to fade straight into the dense countryside. Babalú Ayé limped behind us. Ulises was there along with several of his generation, including Anelé. He had his arm around the romantic interest of his who had been mounted by a muerto oscuro at Cucusa's feast in 2006. I was offered a sip of government rum. That San Lázaro–Babalú Ayé was right there limping and healing people fazed them not one bit. With them was a huge man with a broken nose who had been a boxer on the Cuban Olympic team. He was eager to speak English with me. He said he could be a coach anywhere in the world if he could speak English, "even Brazil," he said. I was curious about his experience on the national team, which is storied in Olympic lore. He was just opening up when Babalú Ayé limped into the midst of our little group.

He greeted each of us in turn, and the young people were very serious with the sovereign of pestilence and recovery. For me, San Lázaro–Babalú Ayé had a big hug. We bumped shoulders. He had no words for any of us, but when he got to Ulises, he rhythmically waved his hand forward. He wanted to leave. Already he had a train behind him, and we joined it. Back into the house we went, past Lázaro M., who sang undeterred, past his satiated santos, through the chorus that hadn't flagged in the slightest, and out into the street. He needed only to turn in the direction of Cucusa's with Ulises and Boby in tow for María to stop her.

"You [*usted*] can't go that way. You [*usted*] work here."

Babalú Ayé hit his chest and again made the sign for "going," this time pointing toward Cucusa's.

"No, orisá. Orisá works where the orisá is hosted."

Babalú Ayé expressed his dissatisfaction by taking an enormous step in the direction he wanted to go. María again made her case, "If San Lázaro wants to work at Cucusa's, San Lázaro has to mount up at Cucusa's, with Cucusa's steeds."

The orisá seemed to hear this and stopped in his tracks. He turned his steed back to Lázaro M.'s without a further word, his train right behind. Once inside, his steed was met by a *babalao,* an Ifá high priest, who people said was from Havana, and who theatrically blew a puff of dry white wine on the back of her neck and a puff of air into her ears, thus sending the orisá off. The steed slumped into a nearby chair.

Back in the house, the boxer was mounted with Ogún. He was well near two meters tall and lean. His shirt was off, as were his shoes. His pants were rolled up, and a peasant's hat, like the one Elégua wears, was on his head. He had a machete in his hand. Ogún, mounted on so lovely a steed, danced with Lázaro M. in the space between the host and his santos. He gestured with his machete, artfully communicating that his prized attribute could kill and simultaneously that no harm would come to the gathered chorus. Lázaro was exhilarated as he sang Ogún forward into this full strength and nobility. This was one of the great warriors among the orisás, a rival of Changó, and who along with Elégua and Ochosi presides as sovereign-peer over the prolific depths of the forest. I lost sight of him as he marched in two or three great bounds out of the house. After a while he returned nearly covered in a creeper he had torn from the trees in Lázaro's yard. For a minute he shook like a wind-tossed bush, only to bound from the house once again, this time to vanish into the forest.

Elégua joined Lázaro M.'s feast last. First and last Elégua will be. He mounted a woman in her sixties who was wearing flip-flops, a pair of Lycra shorts, and a tube top. She was burned like Pica, with scars climbing from her chest and collarbone all around her neck and cheeks. Like the other santos who had come to Lázaro M.'s, this Elégua went right to work. He greeted the drums, greeted Lázaro M., then moved through the chorus greeting and speaking to each person present. Elégua gathered Lázaro's family around him, which in this case meant many of his great-grandsons, and communicated to them that they had to care for their elder, that Lázaro M. would not last forever, and that they had to return year after year.

In the midst of this, the Havana babalao thought he would take the call from Lázaro M. He tried to sing over him, starting a call an instant before Lázaro started his. Lázaro seemed to relish the challenge. While Elégua worked, he let the babalao have two or three calls. The calls were off the beat by a millisecond and were largely in *lengua,* or ritualized Cuban Yoruba. The chorus was immediately thrown off, and the drummers were visibly displeased. The babalao tried to impose his Havana style just as the drummers redoubled their efforts to try to shake the singer off, refusing his timing. The chorus mumbled listlessly. Even old Elégua shot him a disapproving glance. The instant the babalao could see he was losing the room, Lázaro came in with his falsetto, calling to Elégua perfectly on the beat. The chorus rallied, and in the exultation of their song they let the babalao know he could take his Havana calls back home.

In time, Elégua closed Lázaro's feast. He is the last to arrive and the one to close. These are his privileges among his orisá peers, thus he retains mastery over portals and passages. He marched out back, fetched a bucket of water, and spun through the house. Then he tossed the water onto the sidewalk outside the front door. He marched back inside and slammed the bucket upside down on the floor in front of the feasting santos, right at Lázaro M.'s feet. We lingered there for some time, sipping rum and celebrating in the company of Lázaro M., his santos, and his kin.

We were back at Celita's waiting to see if Zulia would achieve a bembé on the evening of the 17th, which was normally the climax of Cucusa's feast. Pica was there, and we were talking. "I was born in 1930. Quintina was 35. I was born premature, her thirteenth child. Then, when I was thirteen years old, I was mounted by one of the dead [un muerto]. It was the year Cucusa made her promise, 1943. That dead one sent me screaming from the house. When they finally caught up with me, I had lost a shoe. I had gone from the center of town deep into the countryside [el monte]. They never found the shoe. Pair of shoes was a big deal back then. Still is. That dead one put up a good fight for me. It was me and the dead one for a couple of years, until Oyá came and claimed me. I was fifteen. Berta took the path of the dead, into espiritismo and all that, but she was guided by a man from Havana in that way.

"Loreto had a .38. During the uprising that gave us the revolution, there were gunfights in the streets. He told us kids that if gunshots rang out, we had to hit the floor, but it never happened. When the revolution came, there was retribution against those who had been part of the police and all that for Batista, and many people were killed, but they didn't come for Loreto. Soon after, the revolution asked people to hand in their weapons. Loreto hid his .38 under a roof tile. He was the town watchman, everyone knew he had a gun, and everyone wondered if he was going to turn it in. They never came for him, and we didn't find the gun until years after he died."

Justo carried word that Zulia got the police to issue her a permit, and she was going to start at six o'clock, which was traditional in Cucusa's house. Shortly before the appointed hour, Isidra declared that she was going to walk through town to "bind up the crossings" [amarrar las esquinas]. She put on her sackcloth dress and headed out. The plan was to go along to every intersection in town. Ulises would spray aguardiente, Eulalia would throw toasted corn, and Isidra would drip honey. Justo and I would tag along. The sisters wanted Roberto to join them, but at his house Celia met us at the door. She was worn thin with a gray pall over her. Roberto was down with a fever and would not be coming out. Isidra did not greet Celia, did not ask after her situation, did not acknowledge the four years that had transpired since the suicide of her son, nor her mourning. "Let's go," she said without further gesture. Was Babalú Ayé manifesting against Roberto, dropping him with a fever? He is sovereign of illness and could have easily reached Roberto with a touch of fever. This would impede him from fighting for Cucusa's house. Or maybe Babalú Ayé was using the powers at his disposal to keep Roberto from greater harm? Or maybe it was sorcery worked by Zulia or their bygone antagonist Yamilet? I figured that given his bluster and now his bragging about the Congo-inspired powers at his disposal, maybe Babalú Ayé was keeping him from trouble. Isidra thought her brother weak.

The street was now worked against Zulia to keep people from reaching her and to keep good things from coming to her. Isidra headed for Cucusa's house. We could hear drums from a distance.

"Gonzalo," said Justo.

"Gonzalo?" said Isidra.

"That's Gonzalo playing," he said.

"Iván," said Isidra. "That's Iván. He sounds just like Gonzalo. He is a child, an ignoramus, and he has betrayed me. We knew he would play for Zulia."

"No," said Justo, "Iván is on the requinto, that's right. Gonzalo is on the caja. They are playing together. Listen now."

The house was as empty as they said it had been the night before. There were a couple of people watching through the window. The drums pounded, but there was no one to lead the call. There was no chorus. Zulia sat in a chair next to the altar, nearly alone in the room. Isidra led us into the house and to the altar, where each of us greeted San Lázaro and spent a few seconds in thought. Isidra remained behind when the rest of walked out. She knelt on the floor. In her sackcloth she looked every part the beggar Lazarus.

As we retreated, Justo asked, "Did you see?"

"I didn't look," I said.

"Why not?" asked Justo.

I was silent.

"It was him. It was Gonzalo on the caja."

"Why?" I asked.

Justo was silent.

.   .   .

A bembé erupted at Celita's on the night of the 17th. There was nothing Isidra could do to stop it, and in the end even she wanted it. It was a solid little party with strong drummers, including Ulises on the requinto and Justo on the big drum. Pica and Zenón called, and it was a source of pride to have them both. The simple desire to hear them brought out a resounding chorus and an ample crowd of onlookers. Many orisás mounted up, including Elégua on Boby. San Lázaro–Babalú Ayé mounted Celita, even though no animal had been offered and no feast held in his name. In the last three years, Babalú Ayé had looked out for Celita and her children. Mericelia had been operated on to reshape her skull, to great success. Celita was eternally grateful to the sovereign that mounted her, and each season she became a more surrendered steed. San Lázaro–Babalú Ayé worked through the night, healing the gathered crowd with the combinations of facial expressions and pantomime for which he was known when he mounted Celita. He was sought out as long as she was mounted.

Shortly before daybreak, after the bembé had dissipated, Isidra recruited Boby and I to help her feed Mariana Congo. She took Mariana from Zulia on the day of our arrival and had kept her hidden since. Mariana was for fighting, and it was inconceivable that she would not eat. It was the only meal Isidra offered that year.

When we left Sierra Morena on December 19, 2009, Cucusa had been dead a decade. Isidra's effort to continue Cucusa's feast for San Lázaro–Babalú Ayé was in disarray. The house she had shared for nine years with her extended siblings was now claimed and occupied by Zulia, her half sister. Isidra and the only full sibling she could count on, Eulalia, were in exile at Celita's house. They had become beggars indeed. Her brothers could not be counted on, Máximo being a Communist Party entrepreneur in the new economy, and Roberto was feckless. He was in town less and less, now living with Celia on the outskirts of Varadero, where their son had killed himself. Isidra's son, Ulises, was now a young man aiming for a career in whatever the new, post-1994 economy might come up with for him. Each year it was more difficult to get him to leave Havana in December. Without a permanent presence in town she would lose the house and the feast with it. Eulalia was not going to leave Cienfuegos to live in Sierra Morena, much as Isidra suggested it, just like Isidra wasn't going to leave Havana. The revolution had set them down in those cities forty years earlier, and they were home now, bustling and teeming with possibilities, though the radiant skies of Cuban socialism had fallen. How many times did I ask her why she didn't just retire back to the countryside?

Still, Isidra was determined. Zulia occupied Cucusa's house without the proper permissions from the Housing Authority, and Isidra would fight her every step of the way. The house and feast were synonymous to her, the altar and room full of santos being the common denominator. And, if our visit in 2009 showed anything, it was that Isidra was the only one of Cucusa's children capable of continuing the bembé for San Lázaro–Babalú Ayé. As an effective, imposing healer knowledgeable in her mother's protocols, she had the only real claim to that. But this was not something the Housing Authority, or the revolution, gave the slightest importance to.

All the while, other houses drummed up San Lázaro–Babalú Ayé. On the night of the 17th, Ulises snuck up to the feast at the Curve with María and his in-town girlfriend. The amount of animals offered to the santos-orisás was something to behold. The slaughter was for all to experience, like at Lázaro M.'s. There were family members and godchildren of that house that now lived in Havana and abroad, and they were back in town taking cell phone videos of everything—the slaughter, the mounted santos-orisás, everything. That was all going up on the internet. There were santos-orisás of every variety mounted. Dayán, the espiritista from Sagua who led our little Spiritualist pensamiento, was mounted with Obatalá. MiDiana, Ulises's sweetheart, was mounted by Babalú Ayé. Lots of people from Sagua and Santa Clara were mounted. Ulises was dazzled, but he was always understated. "Good party," he said. Three years later, when I would again return, it was at the Curve that we would feast San Lázaro–Babalú Ayé.

SIXTEEN

2012

PROHIBITION

ISIDRA MARKED HER YEARS OF INITIATION into Ocha-Santería every November 30 in Havana. She could not begin planning her trip to Sierra Morena until this event was concluded because it required its own elaborate preparations and expenses. Rarely would I be in Havana in time for her celebration, because my semester of teaching did not end until December. She celebrated her Ocha-Santería "birthday" by hosting a feast for Yemayá, the "keeper of her head" [*la dueña de su cabeza*]. Yemayá delights in ram, rooster, and duck, and Isidra always offered some combination of the three, along with more animals for Yemayá's Ocha peers. Animal prices in Havana went through the roof after 2010, and just "feeding her Ocha" was a major financial commitment. Her party centered on a "throne" of offerings on which she placed the likenesses of Yemayá and her peers, including Elégua, Ogún, Ochosi, Changó, Ochún, and Obatalá, all of whom ate. The offerings included baskets of fruit and trays of sweets. Her altar thrones were always well done, if modest. She would leave them up until I arrived in Havana, several days after her celebration.

Her party at the end of November 2012 was one of the few I was able to attend. It was precisely staged, modestly executed, and selectively attended. Her guests were friends from her many years in professional service, including party members and workers from various government organizations that promoted Cuban culture and in which she had worked most of her life. It was a quiet affair with people dressed nicely, and Isidra was an impeccable host. Unlike other Ocha anniversaries I had attended over the years, Isidra's party was not made up primarily of "godchildren" she had initiated into Ocha-Santería. She had only one Ocha godchild, and this was Yamilet, the half niece who robbed Cucusa's house in 1999.

The day after her party, Isidra told me that Yemayá, the keeper of her head, had spoken to her and forbidden her from traveling to Sierra Morena. Since 1999, visits to Sierra Morena were marked by family strife, and each year Isidra's November feast for Yemayá had among its motives to establish propitious conditions for her trip there. Yemayá presides over family life and is a revered ally in family fights. That Yemayá would prohibit her travel was very serious. Isidra interpreted the restriction to mean that truly perilous situations awaited her in town. There was no asking Isidra if Yemayá had provided a rationale, for the decrees of a sovereign require no explanation. Nor was there asking her if she could repeat the conversation verbatim, for such things are private, like conversations between a parent and her child. It was just a fact—she was not going.

I was Isidra's godchild in Congo-inspired Palo, and that was enough ritual kinship to extend Yemayá's prohibition to me. Neither of us would travel. Yemayá was not the keeper of my head; that was Elégua, and Elégua favors travelers. Our exchange was brief, but my claim to be a child of Elégua and thus subject to his rules failed to persuade her. But Elégua is also sovereign over disobedience and defiance, so I switched tracks. My only chance of convincing her was to appeal to the will of my dead. She had taught me over the years that the dead were the authority of last resort in African-inspired praise in Cuba, and discerning their will is most important. It is very difficult to contradict a person who speaks firmly from a place of ancestral authority, and she chose not to. Isidra tried to impede me for several days but was eventually won over to the idea of having an observer and emissary in Sierra Morena for the 17th. I was going to Sierra Morena without her, and having her help made things much easier.

That December, Isidra was mending from a significant surgery earlier in the year. She was a little slower, which for Isidra meant still much faster on her feet and in her mind than most. But she would no longer walk alone at night and warned me against it. She worried a lot for Ulises, who was twenty-seven and out a lot now, sometimes not coming home at all. She said the end-of-year atmosphere in the city the last couple of years had made people crazy and that crime was on the rise. A knife fight between gangs of local youth just blocks from her house confirmed her fears. We were walking past the corner where it happened.

"There are changes," she said.

"Have you had violence like that around here before?" I asked.

"Not since the early sixties, when I moved here. The revolution put an end to gang violence."

"There are all kinds of changes," I said. I was referring to the monumental transition from the leadership of Fidel Castro to that of Raúl, a transition that had been gradual since Fidel fell ill in 2006. Raúl assumed the presidency in 2008, and the last several years had seen more dramatic changes, such as the cutting of workers from government rolls and the decree of new self-employment opportunities to receive them. She knew what I meant, but Isidra and I rarely talked politics. She was a revolutionary who stood by her party's leaders. I was antiauthoritarian, part anarchist, part surrealist. We met on the vast, fertile, infinitely complex plain of aesthetics and ethics that is African-inspired religion in Cuba. On that ground she was unquestionably in charge.

She did not like the edge to my tone and replied, "There have been changes. We are living them. I am telling you about some of the consequences. The changes *you're* talking about we can do nothing about. They are decisions taken by our leadership for the good of the people. The ones *I'm* talking about can be addressed. Those kids need a major intervention by social workers, and then training and government employment."

"That is not the way the revolution is going," I said. "How many hundreds of thousands have been cut from government payrolls the last few years?"

"Not doctors or others in essential capacities."

"Like social workers?"

"No worker who is essential to the functioning of the revolution will be let go," she said. "If keeping kids off the street so they aren't running around knifing one another isn't essential, then I don't know what is."

"OK. Let's assume they are keeping all the social workers. What about workers who do nonessential tasks for the revolution? Drivers, mechanics, other kinds of workers?"

"Some of those are being cut."

"Aren't those the jobs a kid needs to get off the street?"

"Those are nonessential," she said, taking the hard line of her party.

"Without those jobs the revolution can't do nearly as well by those kids and the poor. If social and economic justice are the goal, aren't all jobs essential?"

"Yes, all work is essential to the revolution if you put it that way. We believe in 100 percent employment. But we are in a difficult economic moment, and we have to make choices. Anyway, those kids shouldn't need a social worker in the first place. They should have been properly brought up in the schools. What we need is more committed teachers."

"Like Ulises," I said.

"Like Ulises. He has become an educator, as his signs predicted [*según su signo*]. He teaches children how to use computers. Nothing is more important than that right now."

"I'm glad the revolution has teachers like him. Perhaps you are right. Strong teachers can take a child a long way."

In 2012 prices were rising in every part of Cuban life, and this added to her outlook. She was retired and lived off a very modest government pension paid in Cuban pesos, not the prestigious convertible pesos, known as CUCs, that were equivalent to hard currency. She had very little access to CUCs except for what Ulises gave her. Raúl had vowed to cut state-subsidized rations, and now the food on which she depended was becoming scarcer. In the official language of the revolution, goods were "freed" [*liberados*] from the ration book, which meant they disappeared from state-subsidized dispensaries [*bodegas*] and reappeared in the hard-currency stores [*las shopping*] or farmers markets at exponentially higher prices. People said about Raúl, "That man detests the ration book!" In fact, by 2012 the ration book had been cut to a shadow of what it had been before the Soviet Union collapsed in 1989, or even what it was in 2000 at the end of the crushing 1990s. Cubans were having to use precious hard currency to buy essentials like cooking oil and meat protein. Isidra felt every gram of cooking oil cut.

Almost as bad, hard currency was creeping its way into the black market. State-employed plumbers and carpenters and auto mechanics who moonlighted on the pesos black market were now asking for CUCs. Her monthly pension of a few hundred pesos was worth almost nothing in 2012, but she made the most of it.

The trip to Sierra Morena required that we scrounge for twenty pounds of rice and enough beans to eat with it. We eventually paid her dispensary guy [*bodeguero*] forty times the subsidized price for them. Those who came to him with ration books discovered that he could barely fill their quotas, but for those with money he had plenty. We spent her entire month's pension and more on the sack of rice. We repeated this for cooking oil, dry cooking wine, sugar, salt, and soap. Isidra abhorred all black market activity and routinely railed against those who abused the system, but she knew the mechanisms and had confidence to spare with her bodeguero, so when she needed a little extra, the transactions were automatic. Some things could not be had on the black market, like tomato paste, and for these we had to shop in hard-currency stores. A dozen years before, when I first met her, Isidra derided the stores and rarely entered them. In 2012 she was comfortable in them.

"There is now a CUC numbers game," said Isidra, referring to the underground lottery. "My friend Zoraida always wins something. There is never a week she doesn't win."

"Isidra, the lottery doesn't pay over the long run."

"Maybe not where you live, under capitalism. There everything is designed to cheat regular people. Here the game is only one through a hundred, and you pick one number. People win all the time. You should let me pick your numbers."

"I don't play."

"You do too. You played in Sierra Morena and won on 'mosquito' that December they were so bad!"

"I played once."

"And you won."

The numbers game had expanded in the last few months. It now included two daily Cuban peso jackpots and the new CUC numbers game. "Some people play all three." We were hurrying along to get bets in with one of the neighborhood runners, and she changed the subject.

"Zulia thinks she can steal the house."

"She has thought it was hers since 2009."

"Yes, but it is not hers. Eulalia and I, Roberto and Máximo, we all have a claim."

"She has a claim too. How can she override yours?"

"She says she is the sole owner because she has been living there for six years," said Isidra.

"Six years sounds convincing."

"Even more when Eulalia and I invited her to live there."

"Is housing law on her side now?"

"If she wasn't a cheat, it could be."

"Could be? Is there a number of years of living in the house after which she can't be evicted?"

"Under the revolution, a person is considered to reside at an address when the Housing Authority and the Rationing Authority both have them listed at the same place. Without both those things, you are not official. The revolution does regular censuses, and they expect to find you at the address they have for you."

"So does she have herself registered at Cucusa's? Is she getting her rations there?"

"What do I know? Word is she is still going to Corralillo for her rations. Which means she still has herself listed at her apartment there."

"The revolution doesn't let you have two houses, right? How can she claim to live at Cucusa's and still be collecting rations in Corralillo?"

"Why do you ask me? I don't follow her everyday affairs like she follows mine. As far as I know, she still has her house in Corralillo, so she is playing this."

· · ·

Understanding ownership, residency, and inheritance claims on property in Cuba is difficult. The revolution took apart capitalist property markets when it came to power in 1959 and replaced them with principles of universal and affordable housing—everyone is to have a roof over their head, there are no renters or landlords, and the sale and purchase of houses is controlled by the government. But, like everything else in Cuba's centralized economy, housing is subject as much to revolutionary principles as it is to baroque black market networks made possible by pervasive bureaucratic sleight of hand. In Cuba, though housing is guaranteed and affordable, people worry about it incessantly.

Owning a house has never been a simple matter since the revolution. For most of the last fifty years, houses could not be purchased outright. You came into ownership by inheritance or if the revolution gave you a place to live. During its early-1960s heyday, the revolution gave away lots of apartments and houses. They had been confiscated from landlords and those who fled the coming of Fidel Castro's 26th of July Movement. Often, tenants became owners of the very apartments they were renting. The revolution continued to give housing as people left for exile through the 1960s. Eventually, the mass redistribution ended, and the revolution didn't keep up with new construction. Massive housing blocks were raised up with Soviet help on the outskirts of the major cities, but construction has never kept pace. These days it is only the very few who are given housing—career military officers, high-level ministry functionaries, hotel managers, and internationally successful artists and top athletes.

"She has no way of getting a better house than to steal Cucusa's," said Isidra. "The revolution already gave her that apartment in Corralillo, but she doesn't like it. So she has to steal Cucusa's."

Those early "gifts" of housing were all the more valuable because the revolution suspended the sale of houses in 1960 to fight capitalist real estate speculation. Having "interest" [*interés*] in a property—an interest in its value, its upkeep, its costs, and its returns—this is something the revolution was determined to end. The revolution has denounced many internal enemies throughout its sixty-year history, but none is more pervasive than speculation, especially in real estate.

To fight it, the revolution eliminated the buying and selling of houses and replaced this with a mechanism by which houses could be traded [*permutar*]. For nearly fifty years, trades were the only way people could change their housing. But to trade you had to have. To trade you had to own a house in the housing system, either by virtue of having received a house from the revolution, by having kept family property during the revolutionary expropriations, or by having inherited. Housing trades aim to facilitate consensual home exchanges between parties, and they are overseen by the Ministry of Construction and, within this, the National Housing Directorate. This bureaucracy is famously treacherous to navigate. A housing trade in Cuba is called a *permuta*.

While in Havana in 2012, I was staying with my longtime friend Cary, who helped me understand how housing trades work. She said, "No matter what, a permuta is supposed to be a quarters-for-quarters trade. The basic rule is square footage for location." Cary lived in a small but well-located apartment in El Vedado, in the heart of Havana. She continued, "Apartments in Havana, let alone houses, will trade for entire farms outside the city. Within the city, houses on the outskirts will trade for apartments closer to the center, and the most prized houses in the neighborhoods of El Vedado or Miramar will trade for two well-appointed apartments on the neighboring streets. It is very difficult to trade into El Vedado or Miramar if you don't already live in those places."

The 2011 housing reform made it possible to sell or buy a house outside the quarters-for-quarters permuta system; for the previous fifty-two years of the revolution, the only hope of changing your housing situation was to trade. This, in order to stop speculation.

"Why look for a permuta?" Cary explained. "The reasons to enter into a permuta are many, but start with the fact that hardly any new housing has been built in Cuba since the collapse of the Soviet Union. Twenty-some years. No new housing is built in city centers. Young people and their parents have no housing to aspire to except under the most limited of programs. If they are not willing to serve years as members of a self-help construction brigade, their only hope is to strive for a house-giving job. Climb the ladder for twenty years in a ministry. Otherwise, they are stuck at home with their parents. The kids get married and have kids, and now their living space just won't do, so their only hope is to *permutar* somewhere bigger, in a worse neighborhood, or out of the city. This has happened to neighbors around here over and over.

"I have neighbors who the revolution awarded an apartment to when they were a young couple in 1963. A nice two-bedroom apartment in a good building here in El Vedado. Now, in 2012, they live with their two grown children, their spouses, and their children, all three generations living in the same apartment. This happens all over Havana. You've seen how rooms are divided, then divided again, and the high ceilings customary in Havana are turned into lofts. To get out of this situation, the entire family traded their plumb location for two apartments and then traded one of those for two again. Total three apartments far from the city center. If they hadn't lived in El Vedado, they would have been stuck. You've seen the way apartments are divided into warrens in the bad neighborhoods. Those people have no choice." There are a thousand reasons for this basic permuta scheme to play out, including marriage, the birth of children, divorce, the marriage of children, the birth of grandchildren, plans to emigrate, death, or the need for cash.

Cary told me the permuta system has never been as far from cash as the government's disdain for it would imply. The system exists to ensure that living quarters are traded for living quarters; sometimes, however, people have quarters but want money. Similarly, those who would like to move have no quarters to trade but have money. Cash is illegal in the system but handled under the table. "Happens all the time," said Cary. "You still need a ton of luck to find a permuta partner willing to part with their property, but a lot of cash often sweetens the deal." These kinds of trades are obvious to the government notaries and inspectors who control the permuta machinery, and these functionaries are paid under the table to move the sketchy trade through the system with all official seals in place. Thus helped by the very people tasked with keeping speculation out of the system, a cash-infused transaction comes to rest as an official quarters-for-quarters trade in the archives of the National Housing Directorate.

This basic example, in which quarters are critically short and money saturates a system meant to keep speculation out of housing, is in one way or another a precursor to most exchanges. It transmogrifies into countless shapes, some of which boggle the imagination. A property owner dies and leaves no will, heirs contest one another for the house, and now you have a truly baroque situation. Housing is one of the higher-stakes sectors of Cuba's sprawling black market economy. If sales of basic foodstuffs at prices above those set in the ration books are the bass drum of Cuba's vast black market sprawl, then the cash-garlanded permuta system is the piccolo, probably inaudible to someone hearing the great cacophony of the informal Cuban economy for the first time. To finally hear these notes is to experience a shudder at the extent of deceit in Cuba's daily exercise of socialism, a trembling all the more astonishing because it makes utter sense within the convoluted logic by which the rest of Cuba's black markets run.

This was the state of affairs in Havana for more than fifty years. Early in the 1990s, I knew a couple who lived in a studio apartment in a dingy building on an even more dingy street in dingy Centro Habana. Their place was several floors up, the elevator having burned out long ago. The apartment was one large room with a tiny kitchen and even tinier bathroom. The saving grace was a balcony that opened onto the street. Then again, that street was Águila at the intersection of Monte. A more soot-covered vista is difficult to find in Havana. The room doubled as bedroom and living room. They had been divorced for four years and had a ten-year-old daughter who lived with them. She slept with their daughter in the bed, while he slept on the floor. They shared the refrigerator but not meals. She was quiet and serious, and their daughter resembled her. Her dream—and it was unusual in those years for residents of that dingy part of Havana to still have any dreams—was to be a hotel maid as the revolution turned to tourism for survival after the fall of the Soviet Union. He was a garbage man who had stopped working and now flipped whatever he could find on the local black market—in those days, bread, meat, and cheese. He had beaten her before and threatened to beat her again. Neither would leave the apartment for fear of losing their claim. They had been waiting for a permuta since before their divorce, but no permuta partner, no matter how desperate, would trade quarters to move to Águila and Monte. A little money to sweeten their escape would have made all the difference. As it was, the only hope either of them saw for their broken cohabitation was for him to leave Cuba, floating off in an inner tube. This was his dream, the last one she shared any part of. It came true in the summer of 1994, when a mass exodus erupted on the Havana waterfront.

At the other end of the Havana housing spectrum lived Cary's friend Tania. Hers was a three-bedroom apartment on the tenth floor of a highly coveted building (with working elevator) on 23rd Avenue in El Vedado. She routinely received cash-laden permuta invitations, but starting in 2011 the limited deregulation of the housing sector led to direct cash offers. Between then and 2015, Tania's apartment jumped in speculation value from 10,000 to 30,000 in hard currency, be it US dollars or euros. Most of her offers came from Europeans married to Cubans, though recently she received her first inquiry from a Miami-based investor who would be represented in the permuta system by relatives in Havana.

• • •

Isidra and I were still talking about the impasse with Cucusa's house. "Could Zulia sell the house in Corralillo and claim Cucusa's as her only residence? The new housing law allows her to sell."

"Before last year she could not have done that. Raúl's housing reform allows her to do that now. Now she can sell for cash. But she will not sell her house in Corralillo while her son Ernesto needs a place to live."

"Can she give the house to Ernesto?"

"She could. There is something called a *dejación,* whereby she could officially leave him the house without selling it."

"That would free her up to claim Cucusa's as her sole residence," I said.

"Yes, but only if she is the sole inheritor."

"Which she can't be because Cucusa had eleven children," I said.

"Eleven children. But my mother left no will. The law in this case makes all of us inheritors."

"So how can she become a sole inheritor?"

"By being the sole inhabitant. Just because a person who owns a house dies doesn't mean their relatives from across the island now get to come live in the house of the deceased. The people who lived in the house with the deceased, if they are on the ration book, continue to live there. They inherit the house."

"And the others?"

"Lawsuits for years."

"So she has to establish residency at Cucusa's by leaving her house to her son and squatting there? For how long?"

"No squatting in Cuba. There is no such thing. If there is an empty building or apartment, it belongs to the revolution. The revolution distributes all housing. Houses, apartments, everything. If they think a house is too big for the number of people who live there, they can divide it in two. If they think your housing is unsafe, they can condemn it, tear it down, and move you across town. If you occupy a house that isn't yours, or live somewhere you are not registered, eventually a social worker will come, or a housing inspector will come, and you will have to leave. You establish residency by getting yourself put on the ration book at a particular address. Once you do that, then you have a claim to the house."

"How do you get yourself put on the ration book at a specific address?"

"Your questions never stop. There are lots of ways, none of them easy. If the revolution gives you a property. If you're born there. If you marry in. If you are adopted in. There are other ways. This is why I won't allow Ulises to be at my apartment with women. He gets a woman pregnant and he goes crazy and puts the baby at my address. The mother gets in too. Now I have not only Ulises living here but a woman and a baby. Forget it. Haven't I been explaining this?"

"So has Zulia gotten herself put on the ration book?"

"Anything she has done is fraudulent, so it doesn't matter. As long as she hasn't officially left the house in Corralillo to her son with a *dejación,* then nothing of what she is doing in Sierra Morena is legal. Her years living there don't count. Any attempt to get put on the ration book doesn't count. Saying she is the sole inheritor to the house is without any basis. Not even if she had my dead on her side would she succeed."

"What about you, how can you claim your inheritance given the house you own here in Havana? The revolution says you can't have two houses."

"Now you can. Since November of last year, when Raúl changed the law, the revolution says you can have two houses as long as one is in the city and the other in the countryside or the beach."

"So you can claim your inheritance and keep your house in Havana."

"I can claim it and she cannot. I am legitimate, she is not."

We finished our discussion as we arrived at the door of the numbers runner. The runner recommended 25, for "house," and 77, for "war."

Isidra was now all in on my solo trip, and between the food and goods we had gathered, including a mattress, a Russian washing machine, and a fifty-gallon water barrel, a car would no longer do. The car we were giving up was a 1980s Peugeot supermini driven by a young man who lived in the same alleyway [*solar*] as one of the neighborhood numbers runners. He inherited the car from his father, a merchant marine, before he could drive. He was one of two surviving quadruplets whose mother, a nurse, had abandoned as an adolescent when she sought asylum in Angola at the end of an official Cuban medical mission abroad. In theory she was going to get him a visa and a ticket to Angola, like she had his surviving quadruplet sister, but they never came and the calls were rare when I met him. He lived with his grandmother and subsisted from chauffeuring despite being dangerously hesitant behind the wheel. The 80 CUCs he would have earned from my trip to Sierra Morena would have been all he needed to make the end-of-year special. He was obsessed with FC Barcelona soccer and could not wait for the weekly black market flash drive of digital media [el paquete], for which he paid CUCs and which always included Spanish league highlights.[1]

· · ·

Isidra was squaring a van rental. "It is crazy out there. The money people are asking."

"How much?"

"You don't want to know. More than 100 CUC one way. Not a chance we're going to pay that."

"Is it a good van like last time, from Eusebio Leal?"

"We're not going to pay it. People are hiking up prices. It is greed, pure greed. End of year makes people crazy."

"End of year?"

"Everybody wants to party, everyone wants to put on a show for their family and their girlfriends and lovers. The CUC stores add to the hysteria by putting out new things, and the resellers drive kids nuts. This is not an easy economic moment for us. You can see why some thoughtless kid would pick up a knife."

"The CUC shopping stores belong to the revolution," I said. "Can't they turn it down a notch?"

"The revolution has its plans and strategies, but social problems are not solved from one day to the next. These kids have gone crazy, and I wouldn't be caught out after dark. Everyone knows someone who has been mugged. You're a foreigner. Everyone knows crime against foreigners is harshly punished. But just last week a couple of girls from Europe had their camera stolen outside the stadium down the street."

"So, the van driver is also end-of-year crazy."

"Another form of mugging. Don't trust anyone right now."

Preparing for my departure took more than a week. It was December 10, and Isidra started to seriously consult her "things" [cosas]. She consulted with her Yemayá, which had spoken so lucidly regarding this trip already, and she consulted with her Palo things.

The good news was that Yemayá was now on board with my travel and said that for my trip to be safe and successful, we had to make two pilgrimages: one to La Merced Catholic church in Old Havana, to let our dead know about our plans, and another to El Rincón, where Havana renders homage to San Lázaro–Lazarus the Beggar on the 17th. Her Congo-inspired things, for their part, required that Ulises and I go to the east of the city to visit with Teodoro and his Congo-inspired things. Teodoro's house in Guanabacoa, which had been his father Emilio's and where the Quita Manaquita society had lodged for decades, collapsed in a storm in 2010. The last two years, Teodoro had been living on the far eastern fringe of Havana in a government barracks along with his formidable collection of Cuban-Congo things, many of them inherited from Emilio. By the time I left on December 13, Isidra had laden me with healing packets, protection packets, and packets of ritual waste that her things said must be disposed of on the way to Sierra Morena, even indicating particular intersections in town.

In the hours before a van arrived, Isidra loaded me with prohibitions: I was not to go out at night. I was not to drink with José. Drinking with José would get me into trouble. I was not to take a lover, no matter how tempting. "Those country girls will shake you to pieces. We'll never get you out of there!" For fortitude, I was to go to La Corua on my first morning in town to dip my feet in the pool and sing praises to Yemayá. "You go there with Celita and the kids and sing all the Congo songs you know. Sing the ones you know from Sierra Morena. Yemayá will know I sent you." I was not to speak to Zulia or go within a block of her house. I was not to speak to Isaías, her guy. I was not to speak to Gonzalo or Iván, my once-upon-a-time drum teachers whom she accused of betrayal back in 2009. "Traitors!" I was not to go anywhere with Zenón, and I had to be careful of what he said. He was a sorcerer [brujo] and infantile to boot. "Don't give Zenón any money. Don't give María money either. If you want to help Pica, give it directly to her." I was not to go to the feast at the Curve, even if María and Pica were going. "That party is a scam. The woman who hosts it will relish having you there. Don't shame me by going." I was to advocate a bembé at Celita and José's on the eve of the 17th, and at midnight I was to read a statement she had prepared. It invoked all the dead of the Sociedad Africana and promised that Babalú Ayé would provide for a feast at Cucusa's soon. If Celita and José refused to host, then I was to spend a quiet evening at home with them and their kids. To attend any other feast for San Lázaro–Babalú Ayé was understood to be a betrayal of her cause. Even Lázaro M.'s feast was forbidden. Finally, I had to remember that Cuba was suffering a terrible drought and I was not to flush any toilets. "Every toilet in Cuba is clogged. Always use the outhouse!"

The van that took me to Sierra Morena on the night of the 13th belonged to a state-run company that provided security for shipping containers around the port. The driver was assigned to the second in command at the company, and their trips took them all over Cuba. Like van drivers the city over who worked for government companies and ministries, he kept records of fuel allocated against fuel used, miles planned against miles actually traveled. Spare fuel was siphoned and sold on the black market, spare miles were built into a buffer he could apply to his moonlighting, even for a long trip like the one to Sierra Morena. "No problem," he said. "When my boss's mother died last year, we drove from Havana to Jibacoa, the far eastern tip of the island, overnight, fourteen hours straight. It was dangerous like you can't believe, going through the mountains in the middle of the night. But we made it in the morning. I had so many miles written into the records that we were able to hide that trip too. No problem!"

The driver was easy about the drop of packets here and there as we rolled down the North Circuit. A worked coconut was dropped at the cemetery gate outside Sierra Morena. A packet of goodies for Elégua was dropped at the first corner we came to in town. A treated egg was broken on the corner of Celita and José's block. Isidra had sent a bottle of herbal water [omiero] with which to purify their house, and it wasn't until we had mopped from top to bottom that we could properly greet one another.

SEVENTEEN

Lázaro M.

IT WAS DECEMBER 14, 2012, WHEN I WOKE AT CELITA'S HOUSE.
José was smoking out back, and the kids had gone to school. She was delighted
to host me and wanted to hear about Havana.

"Why didn't my aunt come?"

"Yemayá told her not to," I said.

"Did Yemayá speak at her Ocha birthday?"

"Yemayá spoke the day after."

"So no one was mounted at my aunt's party? That isn't how Yemayá spoke?"

"No. It was after. When she was divining with shells."

Celita made a tiny gesture with her lips. "What about Ulises? Why didn't
he come?"

"Ulises is earning money. He couldn't leave Havana for even a couple of
days."

"He teaches computers to kids at the elementary school close to my aunt's.
Is he making his money on computers too?"

"Something like that. He can fix them, both hardware and software."

"That must be good money in Havana."

"That and cell phones. I think Ulises is selling those now too."

"Those aren't being sold in Havana shopping stores yet, are they?"

I was quiet.

"Does he have a girlfriend?"

"Hard to tell because his mother won't let him have anyone over. He is
away from home a lot these days."

Celita was silent for a moment. "His mother is afraid he's going to bring a
pregnant girl home, then she'll have to share her apartment."

Guillermo, who was now ten, was spending more time away from the house, too, on school and baseball, both of which he was quite good at.

"You should hear Guillermo on the drum. He likes it. He likes the bembé his father throws every year for Orisá Inle. You should hear him."

Mericelia was now seven and a huge handful. "She says she wants to be a child of Oyá. Can you believe that, Ramón?"

"Pica is a child of Oyá."

"Oyá is not easy to bear. I don't know if I want that for her."

"Is any santo easy to bear?" I was thinking specifically of Celita's San Lázaro–Babalú Ayé.

"No. But you'll see. She's a very clever child. *Smart* . . ." She paused then. "You won't find my father here, Ramón."

"Where is Roberto?"

"He is living in Matanzas. He moved there about a year ago. Before that he was living in Varadero, remember?"

"I remember we picked him up outside Varadero when we came last time. And your mom, Celia?"

"My mom is with him. They went through hell when my brother died, but they stayed together."

"What is he doing in Matanzas? Photography studio? That is what he was going to do with Máximo's help."

"That was when he was planning on leaving my mother. You know he is *padre nganga* in Palo. He is working as an assistant [*mayordomo*] to a big palero in Matanzas. He is busy every day."

"Matanzas is getting touristy. Does he treat Cubans or tourists?"

"He tells me it is people who work in the stores and hotels in Matanzas and Varadero. To keep them safe from envy."

I was quiet.

"Tourists too."

"So now it is just you to carry your aunt's battle here in Sierra Morena," I said.

"My father was never much help, Ramón, to tell you the truth."

"I'm sorry your parents are gone, Celita. Our children are the same age. Having your parents far away is hard."

"He's making a lot of money. Sometimes they pay CUC."

"Congo things are supposed to be cheaper. I've never heard of Congo things in CUC."

"Everything is changing, don't you see? But don't worry, here in town you barely have to pay anything for Congo things."

"Zulia must be happy."

"That my father is gone? If you want to, you can see that as a victory for her. Who cares what she thinks. She is impossible to understand."

"People here in town must be getting used to her living at Cucusa's."

"People here don't talk to me about her, so I wouldn't know."

I was quiet.

"People here want a party, Ramón. They would love to have Cucusa's party back. That was the only party for Babalú Ayé many of them ever knew. The other parties aren't the same."

"How?"

"Cucusa's party was straight out of Chacha's Sociedad Africana. Chacha authorized that party. It was the only party she ever authorized. After Chacha died and her house burned down, Cucusa's party for Babalú Ayé was what we had left. People loved Chacha's parties, and they also loved my grandmother's."

"Your grandfather Lázaro M.'s party is like Cucusa's, no?"

"Not at all. It is a small party, without Pica or Zenón."

"Same orisás, though."

"Not entirely. Same orisás, different mounts."

"But they work the same. They come to help. They talk."

"They work, it is true. But Cucusa's party was a town event. You only ever saw my aunt Isidra's version of it. My grandfather Lázaro's party is small, like a family event. At Cucusa's the orisás worked for the whole town. It was like Chacha's Sociedad—the whole town. Now that happens at the Curve."

"Is the bembé at the Curve like Cucusa's?"

José was now in the doorway.

"The party at the Curve is bigger," he said. "You'll see. We're going to take you."

"To the Curve?"

"That is where we have been going recently," said Celita. "It is a good party. You need to go if your book is going to be any good. You can't live in the bubble my aunt has made for you. You won't believe all the animals they give. More than I have seen given anywhere—even when José hosts his bembé for orisá Inle and we give double the animals."

I was quiet.

"A lot of people mount up," said José. "A lot."

"Same people as here in town?"

"Some."

"How else is it different?"

"The music is different," said Celita. "It's easier to get mounted up."

"It isn't bembé music?"

They were both quiet a moment. "It is a bembé," José responded.

"But the music is more Spiritualist," said Celita. "People around here like it. You'll see."

José agreed with a bob of his eyebrows. I remembered the seriousness he lent the Spiritualist work we did in 2009.

"Listen, Ramón," said Celita, seemingly recalling a moment in our conversation just passed. "Congo drums were played in town last night. Didn't you hear them? People say they were meant for you."

"For me?"

"That they were played at Zulia's. To impede you or harm you."

"I thought Zulia was repulsed by Congo things. She sent that evangelical messenger last time."

"My aunt Zulia knows no bounds, Ramón. If playing Congo is going to get her what she wants, she'll do that. She doesn't want you in town."

"Well, here I am."

"That is because my aunt Isidra is a mighty sorceress [*muy bruja*]. Do you see? Do you think you'd be here if it weren't for all the things she did for you?"

"I would not be here if it weren't for everything she did for me in Havana. No way."

"You know what I mean."

"We don't know it was Zulia," said José, a little annoyed. "Justo says it was Zenón. If it was him playing [*jugando congo*], it was to give Ramón cover."

"Cover?"

"From Zulia, from anything people are going to send your way."

"Speaking of which, do you think you'll have any problems because I'm staying here? Zulia could denounce you for not having a license to host me."

"I guess in Havana there are fines if you don't have a license and host a foreigner," said Celita. "I've never heard of that here. This is a small town. Everyone knows you're here, and everyone knows José, from the police to the MININT people at the base, to the MININT people in Corralillo. What are they going to do?"

"Kick me out, send me back to Havana, and fine you," I said.

José spoke up. "I know you say that you've been flushed out of the countryside by MININT before. You said that was in Bayamo back in 2000. Twelve years is a long time for people to get used to foreigners traipsing about everywhere. It won't happen here."

"And the fines?"

"Let it go," Celita said, almost laughing. "What is going to happen to us? Do you know how many times José has been fined? For fishing, more than once; for running numbers, more than once; for making water tanks without a license too. It can't get any worse than this life we lead, Ramón."

Celita not only felt responsible for my well-being and comfort while in town, but also wanted my work to succeed. During that visit she accompanied me everywhere and filled the role of research assistant, the first and only time I ever had such help. On the 15th, Justo took up his spot in the chair outside the kitchen door. He escorted us to Zenón's. I had a set of songs transcribed from recordings I made in 2006. I had checked these with Isidra in Havana, and I wanted him to comment on the lyrics to see if she and I had gotten them right. Also to see if he could interpret the ritual language when it appeared, whether Ewe or Fon, Yoruba or Congo.

"My mother was Ingo," said Zenón. "She was Chacha's adopted daughter. I learned bembé songs from her. Ingo inherited the call from Reina Collín. She kept a file all about La Sociedad Africana. When I finished my military service, I had nothing. School gave me nothing, the military gave me nothing. I returned home and that file saved me. I would not be a *bembesero* without it."

"Did you play last night?" I asked.

"Didn't hear a thing last night. No one played."

"They say you played Congo drums and that you meant to hurt or help me."

Zenón looked straight at Celita. "Don't listen to Celita and José, Ramón. They're excitable."

"You didn't hear anything?"

"Nothing."

Celita didn't debate him, and Justo, who was the source of the Zenón rumor, looked away.

"Take a listen to these songs," I said. I handed him an MP3 player with headphones.

"You and Isidra have this about 70 percent. Let's go over this word by word." His interpretations of lyrics diverged from hers, just like his translations of specific words. His vision of the role the orisás played in peoples' lives was simple and sweet. "The orisás exist to care for people," he said. "They always look out for us. Even Oyá."

"Why would Oyá be any different from the others?"

"Oyá is hungry. Hunger will take the best person and turn them into a wolf. Oyá is hungry for life, like a wolf. She wants to eat us all up. It's not for nothing that she keeps vigil at the cemetery gate."

"Her gate is always open," I said.

Zenón's teaching style was not rote. Learning from him meant asking about a side comment or detail; then his response was an anecdote or allusion. What knowledge he offered was embedded in a web of stories and songs that he associated as he spoke. There was no line to follow, only stories and songs. It was narrative teaching and required apprentices willing to spend years listening in order to become good singers and storytellers. My shorthand attempts to make learning more systematic in order to suit the ends of scholarly ethnography were hopeless. His mode was story-within-song-within-song-within-story, which he practiced without getting deeper or closer to answering my questions. He could connect a single detail to a dozen others, and the choices he made might never be repeated. A three-day visit to town would not get me far.

I had been especially proud that Zenón was willing to officially enroll in my study following university research guidelines and signing a consent form. He laughed at the gesture. Later, as we wrapped up what I thought would be the first of many sessions but that was our only real conversation, he said, "Tell them, those people who want to know who I am, tell them my Congo *prenda* has twenty-one dolls, twenty-one human figurines, men and women. Tell them that everything you learn from me is what my twenty-one dolls tell me to tell you. I should have signed twenty-two times, once for me and then for each of them!"

Later, Celita was impressed that Zenón had spoken to me at all.

"He is very private. He doesn't have anyone he teaches about the things you want to know. He had a teacher, but they don't talk anymore."

"Who was that?"

"It is my grandfather, Lázaro M. Grandfather is the only one in town besides Pica who can teach Zenón anything."

"What happened?"

"Don't ask. You'll never see Zenón at his party. It is a shame."

"Did you notice what Zenón said when I asked him if he had played Congo last night? He said no, that he was asleep early."

"He's a mighty sorcerer, Ramón. No one in town knows what he knows. I think he likes you, so that is good."

I was quiet.

"Be careful with him and your book," she said. "Zenón makes things up. You can't trust anyone you talk to."

. . .

Pica had lost her sight by 2012. I paid her a visit at her home, and she was in a glum mood.

"No one has invited me to sing on the 17th," she said.

"The people at the Curve didn't invite you? That's impossible."

"Well, they invited me. But I can't be walking along the highway in the state I'm in."

"Haven't they offered to pick you up?"

"Not this year."

"Are there other parties? Will you sing at Lázaro M.'s?"

"I might go there. I don't usually go to Lázaro's."

"Zulia isn't going to host anything at Cucusa's?"

"How could she, that poor thing. They say she can't sleep at night because the dead in Cucusa's house keep her up. She is there alone now. Ernesto and Isaías fled months ago."

"Fled?"

"Fled the dead that were driving them all crazy."

"Ernesto was never quite together," I said.

"Don't underestimate those dead," Pica snorted.

María was with us just then and added, "They are driving Zulia crazy. That is Cucusa and Ma' Isidra and Loreto and Orfilio. Did you hear what happened with Roberto when he moved to Matanzas?"

It was like María to gossip where Pica preferred discretion.

"You know what he kept in that little shed back of Cucusa's yard. She said she couldn't stand having his Congo things back there. It is his mother's house, not hers. It's his shed, not hers. But she said she couldn't stand it, that his Congo things made her nervous, and that if he was going to Matanzas, he had to take them with. So he says he is not moving a thing, that his things have their home and that their home is at Cucusa's. Well, she says she is going to go back there and turn those cauldrons upside down and dump them out so that everyone can see what is in them."

"When was this?"

Pica sat quietly with rice in her hand to feed the animals that came and went from the yard.

"About a year ago," said María. "She said the police would see exactly what is in there. Is that crazy or what?"

I nodded in appreciation of the story, and of Zulia's tenacity.

"Can you believe she would do that?"

"Things like what Roberto kept in that shed shouldn't be kept in town anyway," said Pica. "Congo things belong properly tucked away in a tree in the forest [el monte] or in a briar tangle in the bush [la manigua]. Congo things need to be outside with the dead, so they don't get lonely."

"So, Zulia chased him out?" I concluded.

"He took his Congo things with him, yes. But we'll see who chases who," said María.

"Isn't Isidra running out of options?" I asked after a silence.

They were both quiet.

"Do you know who Isidra's mother was?" asked Pica.

"Her mother was Cucusa," I said.

"And her grandmother?"

"Her grandmother was Ma' Isidra," I said.

"Ma' Isidra was Cucusa's mother, correct. Do you know who Ma' Isidra's mother was?"

I was quiet, but María responded. "Kimbito."

"Kimbito had seventeen children," Pica continued. "Seventeen is San Lázaro's number. All of them lived. Ma' Isidra had thirteen. All of them lived. Ma' Isidra had two twin births, and all of them lived. Then Cucusa had eleven, not all of them lived. That girl of hers died, then she almost lost another, so she made her promise to Babalú Ayé."

"Yes," I said.

"Did you know that when Isidra came out of Cucusa, she had the bag around her? I saw it. I was eleven years old. It was all the way around her."

"Those kinds of births are rare," I said. "In cultures around the world, children born like that stand out."

"You see," said Pica. "When Isidra was little, when Kimbito died, when her great-grandmother died, I remember because I was seventeen when Kimbito died. Little Isidra and the other kids were afraid to go near the body. It was laid out at home, and we were keeping vigil. Loreto told them, 'There is nothing going to hurt you about Kimbito. Go on, grab her thumb, see for yourselves.' None of them dared but little Isidra. She walked right up and took Kimbito by the thumb, held it until the grown-ups got uncomfortable. Loreto asked her to let go." She wasn't ten years old, maybe six years old.

Pica paused. "There was the time we were down the road at the thermal baths. That was when they were just muddy puddles. I hear they've gone and cemented them in and that the water is clear now. Well, back when they were puddles, they were famous, and half of it was because of the mud. The owners let us local people bathe even though we were Black folks. One day, they tell us María Josefa Sánchez was there. She was the astrologer for one of those magazines before the revolution."

"*Bohemia?*" I offered.

"*Bohemia.* They say the revolution kept it going. Doesn't come around here. She did the zodiacs, and they told us the whole country followed her. There she was, lying in the mud. We were too afraid to approach her. But Isidra wanted to know her fate, so she just walks right up and asks her to read her palm. Isidra must have been ten or eleven. The astrologer said she would make her life as a dancer. Now, you see who you are dealing with?"

I wanted Pica to listen to the songs I had worked on with Isidra and Zenón. I gave her an MP3 player with recordings from previous field visits. Like Zenón, she answered questions by association, in her case always to other songs. One song was interpreted by another, and that by another. Songs were her only explanations. There was simply no final interpretation, no sure meaning for any given word or verse. Trying to draw positive, homogenous, incontrovertible, or repeatable knowledge from her songs was absurd to her. She either laughed or tired easily when I insisted on lingering with a phrasing or vocabulary term. She didn't like starting and stopping songs. On the few occasions I was able to bring her around to something she had interpreted earlier, she was likely to contradict herself. Time and again, it was clear to me that she was working with multiple interpretations at once.

She also complained that Zenón appeared on the recordings too much, and that I should have made a different selection for her that featured her more.

"He's a yard rooster. He croaks. He is as dumb as a rooster too. Listen to him here on your recording. Here he is in full-on bembé, and he's using a song that you should use only when you're killing animals. It's a sacrifice song that he is singing as a party song. Did he explain that to you?"

"No."

"Listen to your godmother Isidra more than to the yard rooster. She has a chance of knowing something. She gets it from her mother and grandmother.

Ma' Isidra was a very special healer [*curandera*]. She attended to maladies that doctors could not cure, fevers that wouldn't go down, and problems with the nerves that no pill could help. Isidra-granddaughter has paid attention and has been respectful."

"Mother, look who is here," said María, motioning to an arrival at the door.

"I can smell him," said Pica before being told it was her nephew Aneas. "I can't see him anymore, but I bet he looks like Loreto." He did, same almond eyes and button nose, same jaw.

"You're interviewing my aunt Pica," said Aneas. "She is a good one to interview. She paid attention to my grandfather Loreto. But good luck. She's clever as a fox. I've never gotten anything out of her." He took a seat with us. He was in his fifties and energetic. "I'm an atheist," he said.

María interrupted, "He's an atheist, but you should see the saints that mount up on him! [*pasa tremendo santo*]."

"I'm an atheist," repeated Aneas. "Only atheists can be true revolutionaries. Ramón, I can see you are an atheist from a league away [*a la legua*]. Who isn't? You need to understand what an atheist is. An atheist is not a person who does not believe in God. No, an atheist is a person who lives by proof. That is what Marx meant by materialism. That is why you are interviewing my aunt, for proof. It's all science. Same as you, when I see a santo mounted up at a bembé, I need no further proof."

Aneas was cheerful and had a ready smile. His mind was a mixture of revolutionary rhetoric and African-inspired cosmology.

"Ideas never die," he said. "The mind wants ideas, concepts. They live so long as individuals choose to live them in their own particular way. That is why the world belongs to the young."

This could have come straight from the passages penned by Fidel Castro over the last years of his life and faithfully published as "Reflections by Comrade [*Compañero*] Fidel" in the Communist Party paper, *Granma*.

Aneas continued, "I play the drum, saints mount me. That doesn't mean I am not an atheist. It just means I have a different mission to complete. The orisás rule. Their domain is the whole world—forget about anything else!"

· · ·

Celita had been following along as I visited with Pica and Zenón and thought we should check in with her grandfather. Lázaro M. was 92 years old in 2012 and was preparing his feast for San Lázaro–Babalú Ayé on December 17, which was also his birthday party.

Lázaro was happy I had returned to town and happy to talk. He didn't look a year older. "Arará songs are different from bembé songs," he said. "There are lots of them, but if you don't know the difference, you can't tell. Arará songs are in *lengua*. Bembé songs are mixed, but mostly in Castilian. Most people think the Arará songs are just old bembé songs too difficult to sing."

"Which do you like better?"

"They have their virtues. An Arará song is the most beautiful thing you can hear. But the chorus can't follow you, and if you sing three in a row, the energy drops. Bembé songs, everyone knows them, so you can really get the room heated up. Who doesn't love that?"

"But the young people aren't learning the old songs, Grandfather," commented Celita.

"They aren't. What are we to do?"

"Grandfather, I have been seeing a woman. She is short and very dark, and she has a basket on her arm."

Lázaro listened to his granddaughter as she described two dreams.

"Could it be my great-great-grandmother?" she said.

"Kimbito?"

"Did my great-great-grandmother carry a palm frond basket on her arm?"

"That is why they called her Kimbito," said Lázaro. "Because she went around with a basket of *quimbombó* [okra]."

"Isidra says Kimbito is a Congo name," I said.

"That too," said Lázaro.

"Was she little, like that?" asked Celita, marking a height with her hand, "and very dark?"

"That is her," said Lázaro, as if seeing her.

"She is coming to me a lot, Grandfather. She is always present. I saw her in the house this morning."

"Let her come, Granddaughter. She won't do you any harm. She was a hell of a flirt and a great dancer."

"Lázaro," I asked, "before Cucusa did it, who feasted Babalú Ayé?"

He thought for a moment. "Town was different then. There were lots of people here before the revolution. We had Spaniards from Galicia [*gallegos*], and we had Chinese people. The Liaos owned a bar in town. They lived near where you like to go with Isidra, by the bend in the river. They weren't the only Chinese in town. There were Cantonese people too. Now, Consuelo la Gallega owned the pharmacy. The Galicians had important businesses. They would loan money and then people had to go to Camagüey to work the sugarcane harvest [*la zafra*] to pay it off. The Caballeira brothers ran their shop that way, and there were others. All these people left town not too many years into the revolution.

"One person who never owed them anything was Tomasa Sánchez. She was older than Cucusa. She was a Black woman, big like a tank. She owned the nicest house in town, there by the church. Her husband was Juan Guillén, but the money was hers. She had stocks in Havana banks. She had maids. She was church godmother to half the kids in town, including the Liao kids. She was your aunt Isidra's church godmother. We had a church, but not a priest of our own. When he came to town he would have breakfast at Tomasa Sánchez's house. When the revolution came, Tomasa died soon after in a hospital in Havana. Go figure. Her adopted son—who was white-white, more white than you, Ramón, none of your red—he died a week later in a car accident. Well, back then, Tomasa offered the feast meal in the house of old Eusebia. It was a feast for Babalú Ayé. Eusebia's was a selective house, and no part of the feast was open to the public. Eusebia and Tomasa made the invitations. There were other houses too. But Cucusa's feast was different. Anyone could join the part of the party for Babalú Ayé that wasn't the meal for the saints."

"What do you think about the party at the Curve?" I asked.

"Haven't been out there. My granddaughter here seems to like it. You should go. But don't miss mine. I'm cracking open at dawn on the 17th."

"Happy birthday," I said.

"May the dead bless me," he said with a smile in his eyes.

The evening of December 16 everyone was waiting for midnight. María came by to say she would be leaving Pica at home and heading for the Curve around eight o'clock. Boby showed up. I asked Celita and José if they ever hosted a bembé for San Lázaro–Babalú Ayé. They had no interest. "Not unless my aunt is here," said Celita. There was no question of where we would be spending the midnight hour, and José found it entertaining that the three of us would be disrespecting Isidra by going to a feast she had been denigrating since at least 1999.

"You're going to be the real disappointment," he said. "She no longer expects much from Celita and me. What are we supposed to do but go to the best party in town? You, on the other hand, you could stay home with Pica and make recordings. What does Isidra say about the Curve? 'Those people are frauds; those people are hucksters.' It seems to me you are in a bind." He laughed but understood my dilemma. He also understood exactly why the Curve was important for me to attend.

"Where is Zenón going to be?" I asked.

"Apparently there is a little vigil [*velada*] for San Lázaro up on the hill tonight."

"Will he sing?"

"Not at that sort of thing."

EIGHTEEN

Two Bembés

WE WENT TOGETHER TO THE CURVE, Celita, José, and their kids, Guillermo and Mericelia, María and I. The house was on the west side of town, just beyond the cemetery, which the children ran past in one breath. It was a big cement house with a tall wall. Just inside the front gate was a little wayside shrine in the shape of a tiny chapel, complete with a figurine of Lazarus the Beggar behind a glass door. There he was in his tattered purple tunic, with his crutches and his dogs, announcing to anyone who might wonder that this was the place. A driveway led all along the wall to the back. The house had a long veranda along the driveway. It was a modern 1950s structure in a town full of clapboard houses. People were gathered at the back.

We were two hours early. Even so, a crowd was gathered. In a covered carport, a more than life-size statue of Lazarus the Beggar stood surrounded by an elaborate offering. The statue depicted an emaciated Lazarus on crutches, dressed in a loincloth and covered in sores. A small pack of dogs crowded around him, licking his wounds. If the little statue at the roadside was discreet, this statue displayed the Beggar Saint in his wounded, wretched magnificence. Lights in purple and green surrounded the figure. Flowers, plastic and fresh cut, were placed around, and at his feet were tray upon tray of sheet cakes, raw-sugar macaroons, and other homemade sweets stacked high with merengue. At the back of the lot, half a dozen goats, as many rams, and tens upon tens of roosters and hens were on hand for what was sure to be a long slaughter. A small cage held a hutia, a muskrat-like rodent prized as a meal by some of the orisás and the dead.

An hour passed, then two, and still the crack of the drums waited. Celita cordially introduced me to the hostess, Katia. She was a small, sixty-something white woman who easily communicated sympathy with her eyes and furrowed brow. Her daughters, who like her were white-white by Cuban standards, were at her side. Most of the people in attendance were white and looked like poor folks from the countryside, *guajiros,* as Cubans call "peasants" or "farmers." The family was busy getting the last things ready, but before she turned away, Katia said, "Give my regards to your godmother. I would not be alive if not for Cucusa."

At midnight, December 17, the drums broke the boredom and tension of the crowd with the requisite songs for Elégua, orisá of beginnings and thus first among sovereigns. The chorus was weak given how many people there were on hand, especially for the Elégua songs, which were among the more popular in town. There were plenty of people watching. At Isidra's or Lázaro M.'s feast, with the right twenty people you could have a roaring bembé. If you didn't sing and dance, you were headed for the sidewalk. Here, a hundred or more farmers could barely raise their voices. The dancing was shuffled. The drummers were young men who didn't get much time at the drums back in town, or they were folks from Sagua la Grande or Santa Clara.

The Elégua likenesses were brought forward and placed on the ground in the center of the gathering. There were ten or more figurines, all different but predominantly made of fist-size conch shells. I assumed these were the Eléguas of family members and Katia's godchildren. Katia's husband, the man of the house, was a white-reddish man in his sixties. He had an entourage of white sunburned men who accompanied him and helped him stage the offering of each animal, though it was one of Celita and José's neighbors, Julio, who wielded the knife. Julio was a large man, Black by Cuban standards, and steady in his privileged role. He was the grandson of Digna Sáez, sister of Loreto Sáez and for many years the prime mount for Yemayá in Chacha Cairo's Sociedad Africana. Julio offered two goats to Elégua, who consumed the meal through the gathered figurines.

The chorus should have been rousing by now. Songs to Elégua should have been at the top of our voices, but we were flat. The singer was in part to blame. He was an enormous white-white man who wore a Florida Panthers hockey jersey, Miami Dolphins baseball cap, and sweat pants rolled up to his knees. Sharp tennies. He was young, in his twenties, and handsome. Given his size, his voice projected poorly, and his tone was not great. But he knew lots of songs and soon muscled his way into calling the first part of the feast. His name was Hendry. He was from Rancho Veloz, one town east toward Sagua la Grande.

It was a bad start, and for an hour we dragged through what should have been exalted praise for Elégua. Little by little more folks arrived from town, and sometime around 1 a.m. a significant portion of Lázaro M.'s family showed up. Boby was among them. He was Lázaro's great-grandson. Boby was a little drunk and looking for a woman who was supposed to be at the Curve. The dancing picked up, and the chorus was more responsive.

The Elégua songs concluded, and things moved on to Changó. María, who was doing more socializing than singing or dancing, said "Just you wait, when they play for Changó and offer him up his rams, lots of people will be mounted." The Changó figurines were similar to one another, likely made by the same hand. Each featured a large conch shell and a pair of bulls' horns. Three rams were brought forward. Majestic Changó ate lavishly. Julio was efficient, but a large male ram is no small feat to offer, and each animal required a gang of men to lift and hold. The drums were rousing and the chorus more energetic, but only a couple of people received Changó on their backs. One was the singer, Hendry.

He was a big man, nearly two meters tall and a meter wide, muscled in a gym-workout kind of way. His Changó was colossal, all of that body charged with the authority and potential of the fate-shaping sovereign of distilled masculinity. His strides were immense, the ax-wielding movements of his arms massive. His interpretation of Changó seemed a little formal, like someone who learns salsa or tango in the ballroom, but his size carried the performance. How could a body like that not please Changó? With it he would shake the earth, bring thunder, emit searing lightning, and shake the kingdoms of fate. Hendry's Changó would hold forth for the next four hours, at times dancing, at others consulting, at others singing. He sang while mounted, and this resembled orisás at Isidra's feasts, like Pica's Changó and Oyá.

Hendry's Changó spoke. This is essential in orisá healing, in that the words from the orisá break fates open and show new vistas. Orisás are masters of potential. Their words electrify a congealed present and push it toward a future on the precipice of becoming different. Theirs is the realm of transformation. Their words are often cryptic, uttered in broken Spanish, which demonstrates to the listener that African forces and ancestors inspire the speaker. Orisá utterances are considered semiprivate; when an orisá speaks to a person, those close by pretend to pay no heed. Those spoken to hang on these utterances; though it may be indecipherable, orisá speech is always prized.

Changó, dressed in hockey jersey and sweats, spoke as clearly as if he were not mounted. Occasionally, a broken word would come in here and there, but as the mounting extended from minutes to hours, those dropped out. Another discomfiting thing was that Hendry's Changó spoke to the crowd, often to no particular person, and held forth in soliloquies. Who was he talking to? He was more like a hip-hop–era sovereign addressing an audience than an orisá ready to vitalize the life of individuals in a participatory chorus. When another singer tried to take the call from him, he responded with barbs rather than wisdom songs and in nearly normal speech, inflected only enough to assert that it was an orisá speaking. This mode of speech would have been out of place at Isidra's or Lázaro M.'s feasts, but Katia and her gathering seemed to expect this Changó and loved him.

María and I stood together appreciating the scale of the feast—a couple of hundred people and the chorus each moment tighter. She was wearing a beadwork ring I had picked out for her in Mexico City. It was a frilly design in purple and black, perfect for San Lázaro. She made a point of bringing it close to her face to express her appreciation for it. She seemed to get lost for a second in its glittering surfaces, then suddenly she was bowled over with Changó mounted up. María was a proxy for Pica, and having her present elevated the feast. That Changó would choose to mount María at that moment was an honor the orisá bestowed on Katia's gathering. He was not present long, and when he dismounted, María was barely winded.

The singing was shifting, led by Hendry's Changó. To the call-and-response and the driving beat of bembé songs, a yearning lyricism was added from time to time, until the songs were as much Spiritualist hymns as were they bembé praise songs. The chorus met this shift with approval, and their unison and volume expressed their affinity for the church-like arias. Their energy drove Changó forward.

José seemed for many years to have a special love of Spiritualist hymns, and the energy and devotion of the chorus brought Orisá Inle onto his back. Like the last time I had been in the presence of his Inle, this time he was also woeful. José's Inle seemed to belong more to the realms of Cuban-Congo praise than orisá praise. His Inle was especially wretched for the chorus to bear. They clearly appreciated more approachable orisás, like Hendry's Changó. José fell hard, and only a quick hand in the chorus spared him a grievous blow. Now he moved forward as a snake, slithering along the broken cement of the driveway toward an objective I could not discern. His shirt was off, and he pushed himself along with only his toes, leaving his arms and hands dragging listless at his sides. His cheeks ground into the cement. The chorus parted to let him pass. Hendry's Changó danced above.

Inle slithered through the crowd, and I lost sight of him. Celita and the children paid no special attention and danced as part of the chorus. María emerged from somewhere in the house, where she had been offered water and a washcloth. It was time to feed San Lázaro–Babalú Ayé. The gathered likenesses were bowls of river stones black with previous blood meals. No statuettes of the Catholic Beggar Saint were fed. The first goat was lifted and its blood directed onto the stones when Celita collapsed. María broke her fall, quickly slipped her shoes off, and got her back on her feet.

San Lázaro–Babalú Ayé is hard to bear. The first impression is that this orisá is violent with his steeds. He twists their bodies into the shape of his withered and tortured limbs. One cannot convincingly bear the orisá of affliction without bringing on his limping body and his atrophied extremities. He is covered in sores. Celita bore him agonizingly. He knocked her over, and while prone she writhed. Up on two feet, she limped. But the most evident sign of her anguish was her inability to speak. Her santo healed but was mute.

In the same instant that San Lázaro–Babalú Ayé twists his mounts into a tortured likeness of himself, so too does he elevate them. No one who mounts San Lázaro would refuse his torments, for they are the source of his authority. His sovereignty as orisá resides in having hideous wounds to overcome. His is the power to determine exceptions to the inevitability of illness. He displays his lesions and abscesses to incarnate them and announce, with his gestures, the horrors that he can overcome. He rises from his pestilence. San Lázaro–Babalú Ayé occasionally mounts up regally, composed and noble as the orisá peer he is. He thereby demonstrates to all those gathered that the calm luxury of a healthy body is also his. Celita's Babalú Ayé always mounted her as a wounded wretch, and he tested her harshly. But there, among the farmers and the Spiritualist songs, he spoke for the first time.

Babalú Ayé stood up and people flocked to him. First, a worried-looking mother with a bewildered-looking child, then an older woman clearly relived to have San Lázaro–Babalú Ayé so immediately at her side. Soon, the line to speak with the santo of despair and overcoming grew long. In each encounter, Babalú Ayé had things to say, as if to make up for all the years this mount of his had been mute. His words were decisive. Those who received them showed pensive relief. Like Changó, Babalú Ayé began the night peppering his speech with a broken word each sentence or two. But shortly into his appearance these terms vanished, and the orisá simply spoke Spanish in a voice identical to his steed.

Yemayá, La Caridad–Ochún, and Elégua were all atop multiple mounts, in multiple iterations. There were orisás on only one mount, too, like Ogún and Obatalá. Celita carried the only San Lázaro–Babalú Ayé, and this made her presence as important for Katia's feast as that of Julio or María or the attendance of Lázaro M.'s family.

The children were growing tired. Inle had slithered off with their father. Celita was an hour into what would become a three-hour mounting by San Lázaro–Babalú Ayé. Guillermo wanted to go home, though he had promised his mother he would not go by himself. She dreaded him walking past the cemetery in the dark. Mericelia was in my lap. The truth was, it was I who needed looking after. At about 3 a.m., with animal offerings continuing strong and many people mounted and Hendry the hip-hop Changó still in the lead, I asked Mericelia, "How long will it last?"

"All night," she said, blasé and wishing for her bed. "Just wait for the Congos."

The kids and I were becoming sleepy when singing erupted at the front of the house. It was call-and-response in the Cuban-Congo style. Short Spanish verses were met with short replies. It is a more staccato, punctuated kind of music, and after a few verses it is unmistakable. I had spent a decade writing about Congo-inspired community and craft in Havana, but "things Congo" had eluded me in Sierra Morena. I had begun to think that unless I lived long term in town, moving there with my family, perhaps, I would never be included in a Congo-inspired scene except for the final turns Isidra gave to her feasts. A drum had been moved up near the road, and a portion of the chorus had moved with it.

The scene surrounded the little wayside shrine to Lazarus the Beggar. A circle of people two to three deep surrounded this. Celita's San Lázaro–Babalú Ayé was there in the middle. With her were three men mounted by Congo powers. Two Congos mounted the bodies of Black men, while one mounted a squat, white-white man. The three were engaged in a confrontation. Calling songs for the scene was Aneas, Pica's atheist nephew. With his calls, which included little goads, he prodded the two Congos to shake open the little shrine. The hairy white-white Congo opposed them with all his girth. Celita's San Lázaro–Babalú Ayé ignored them as she touched and spoke to those who gathered around. She did nothing to impede the Congos. In fact, her continued healing seemed to encourage them, as if the guest of honor, San Lázaro–Babalú Ayé, in not impeding them licensed their play.

Now the two Congos were picking at the metal frame that kept the glass on the shrine. The little beggar inside was tipped over, and the candle was snuffed out. The white-white Congo tried through an infantile pantomime to impede the others, who were mischievous and irreverent. This is a Congo prerogative, to come from the forest and ignore the rules of a house, or a feast, or even the orisás. Congos heed their own sovereignty, which is that of the trembling forest and the undulating sea of the dead. The effort to stop the two Congos was terrible to see. The white-white Congo's infantile gesturing, his crude pantomime, and his hypermasculine gesticulations were futile.

He did not touch the other two. He could not speak, so he groaned and gargled. His face was a series of clefts in the thick flesh lying over his head. Brows impinged on eyes set deep in cheeks, which sagged over his nose, itself teetering over pendulous lips. He was shirtless and barefoot, with his pants rolled up to his knees. He had been an animal handler earlier in the feast and part of the entourage of the man of the house.

Children impersonate orisás and orisá mounting. They do it in out-of-the-way spaces while feasts are underway, or they do it in the days after feasts they have attended. They are playing, and often there is a mirror involved. They do a sweet and satisfactory job at impersonating the impersonations they might publicly perform in the future. The white-white Congo was subpar by the standards of these performances, and it was astonishing that he was able to command a presence at all.

The Congo dead are monumental like the orisás, joyful, exuberant, and terrifying at best. The movements of their bodies, the dance they knit together as they test the limits of how a body can move, communicate ancestral authority and a shared history of forceful struggle. Song and gesture combine to affirm communal investments in these dangerous, mischievous powers. The cheerless blundering of the white-white Congo denigrated the performances of the others. I was starting to wish San Lázaro–Babalú Ayé would dismount Celita, because things teetered on the precipice of the absurd. José reappeared about then, Inle now dismounted, and he and María watched from a safe distance. Either of them could have made a significant intervention in the scene. The man of the house appeared at José's side and implored him to get San Lázaro off Celita, to "erase" her, but he simply replied, "Let Babalú Ayé do his work."

Receptacles that contain orisá likenesses command respect. They help people associate with the sovereigns and are understood to harbor mysteries best left untouched. Only experts in the protocols of the santos-orisás, or the protocols of a particular Congo-inspired receptacle, should attempt to handle them. But this is what the Congos were after in the little shrine. They were sovereigns, and no rules or protocols could impede their rooting out the mysteries of that little shrine. Katia and the man of the house looked on quietly, she with a dying light in her eyes while he fumed. Katia had no voice of her own. She did not sing, and the only way to tone down the scene unfolding before her was to sing it down. Even if she could sing, she was no match for Aneas, who held the call against all comers. He was having a marvelous time. Zenón or Pica might have outsung him, but this was not their scene. The white-white Congo stomped off, and Katia watched, sad rather than angry. The two Congos shook open the shrine and meddled with the things inside. San Lázaro–Babalú Ayé, who was keeping tabs on them, called for a young rooster, and the owners complied. San Lázaro–Babalú Ayé used the bird as a hand broom to brush those who came forward. The orisá of pestilence then handed the animal to the two Congos, who tore off its head and fed the little statue of the Beggar in the shrine.

Cucusa's Catholic figurines "ate," as did Lázaro M.'s, as had Chacha's in the Sociedad Africana. They were as relevant a manifestation of the orisás as were the river stones in their shallow bowls. The Congo powers decided it was time for the figurine in the roadside shrine to be fed. It was intolerable, to them, not to feed San Lázaro–Babalú Ayé there. To leave it out of the meal meant hosting something other than a bembé. Maybe they also sought to supercharge the secrets held by the little shrine or to introduce new secrets to it. To the hosts this was a sacrilege. They did not see that in the instant of desecration, the Congos were also inducting the little santo into the order of the orisás and the Congos, elevating it to new relevance and potential.

They should have been grateful, except that anytime unfamiliar forces are brought into contact with materials under your care, it is best to know what was done and how to either dissipate or maintain this work. Those Congos were not very communicative, and the hosts did not know if along with the meal other things had been done to their shrine. The Cuban-Congo world is especially open to inversions of absolute values on a continuum. What in one instant seems unambiguously benevolent in the next becomes terrifyingly dangerous. The good becomes the bad, only to become glorious again because of this. The Congos knew this, of course, and their choice to raid the shrine and alter its contents was an assertion of their sovereignty, which is never far from the priorities of play, mischief, and transgression. Once those Congos broke into the shrine, its keepers could never know exactly what had been planted or empowered there. They did know that once fed, the little Beggar would now want to feed at all subsequent feasts. In the meal they forced at the little shrine, the Congos also suggested that the life-size figure of Lazarus the Beggar at the back of the house should eat too. If she disliked the turn offered by the two Congos, Katia's response would involve attempts to neutralize the meal and thus, eventually, reclaim her shrine.

This was begun almost immediately, as Hendry's Changó moved in to challenge Aneas for the call. Aneas himself shifted his calls "from Congo to santo" to let everyone in earshot know that he had handed over the call without having lost a test of Congo wisdom. With the call in his hands, Hendry's Changó turned the song toward orisá-inflected words to disorient the Congo-inspired chorus, causing the scene to quickly sputter out.

Back at the scene of the slaughter, the house was preparing for a climax event, which they called "the meal for the Indian" [*la comida al indio*]. María sidled up and said "the man of the house has an Indian," by which I understood that one of the beings in his Spiritualist field [*campo espiritual*] was a Plains Indian warrior, or chief. Such entities are common in Spiritualist life.[1] "The Indian is fed last," she said to me, "and the offering is very beautiful. You'll see."

The man of the house sat shirtless on the ground. A little plaster likeness of a muscular, shirtless man with buckskin breeches, a beaded breastplate, and a headdress of eagle feathers stood immediately before him, ready to be fed. The chorus transformed seamlessly into a Spiritualist mass, circling around him. They sang to the beings [*seres*] and spirits [*espíritus*] in the darkness, calling them to the light. As the offering was prepared, perhaps it was the hutia, Celita arrived from somewhere in the house, her Babalú Ayé dismounted.

She collapsed into a lawn chair in the carport next to the life-size statue of Lazarus the Beggar and was swarmed by her children. They were concerned for her and implored her to leave. It was after 4 a.m., and both wanted badly to be home. Celita was barefoot and grimy, covered in filth and sweat. Dirt and blood caked her blouse and hair. Dirty merengue frosting punctuated the grunge. Her jeans, which had cost her hard-currency CUCs and of which she was very proud, were destroyed. She could not speak. Mericelia found a kerchief, and together we tried to get her cleaned up. Julio, who had led the slaughter all night long, came into the carport and asked if she had been sprayed with dry cooking wine [*vino seco*]. She herself answered, by shaking her head. He proceeded to find a whole bottle, which he then blew in mouthfuls over her shoulders, her back, her arms, her front, then her feet. "Good," he said, addressing the children. "Don't use water. It offends San Lázaro. Ochún was revolted by his sores, so she threw water at him. No more of that." The wine made it easier for us to clean her.

The Indian mounted the man of the house as his likeness was fed. The mounting was brief, a buck forward and a grunting from his steed; then he sat ramrod straight, his arms high across his chest. It was a Plains Indian cliché, but common in Spiritualist images. The look on his face was one of shock, his eyes wide open. His family and many who remained at that late hour gathered around, never letting the Spiritualist hymns flag. A feathered war bonnet in the style of Plains Indian people was brought forth as the Indian's attribute, along with a cigar. The bonnet was too small for the steed, and what could have been compelling costuming appeared as the prop it was. He stood and made a Plains Indian war cry straight out of 1940s Hollywood by tapping his open palm on his mouth. He pounded his chest and blew on his cigar. His entourage of white-white men flanked him, holding rum and more cigars for him. He reached out to be greeted, and people came forward to bump shoulders with him. To each he offered a treasured word from the realm of courage and ancient nature from which he hailed. When it was my turn, he thumped his chest and offered me a sip of rum. "¡Saluda cacique! [Hail the chief!]," he demanded. I did. Just then, a man in his entourage was mounted by an Indian, then another. The three Indians then sat cross-legged in a circle facing one another while the chorus formed a conga line around them and the call became a bembé-like praise song for the Indians, "¡Qué lindo es el indio!" The scene was unlike any bembé I had experienced when Hendry, no longer mounted by Changó but now by one of the dead from his own Spiritualist field, busted through the conga line around the Indians and started a sexually explicit commentary. Those present just then found this hilarious, and he proceeded to command the scene as a licentious clown. A Spiritualist song to send off the dead was intoned, and soon the Indians were gone, leaving their mounts slumped on the ground where they sat.

Day was breaking, and Lázaro M.'s feast was soon to start. Boby and the rest of his family had returned to town hours before, while the Congos destroyed the shrine. The children and I were ready to leave the Curve, but Celita was nodding off, insisting that she and the children be driven home in a car. The feast should have been over, except there were drummers and singers sufficient to keep things going and bembé songs that leaned toward rumba were being called. I walked back to town alone. The early light on the giant ceiba tree that grew at the cemetery gate was reassuring, and I paused to ask Cucusa what she thought of all this. She said I should hurry along.

. . .

Lázaro's was in full swing. The house was packed and the bembé jumping. Gonzalo was on the big box, where he commanded the music. The chorus was brimming and tight. Old Lázaro stood in the middle of his kitchen and held forth. It was his birthday, he was ninety-two, and with all the strength in his diminutive frame he called to San Lázaro–Babalú Ayé. His voice was clear and sweet and high, and even the hard songs with lots of Arará (Ewe and Fon) words were followed pretty well by the chorus of his kin. The head of a goat lay at his feet before his compounded San Lázaro likeness, which was a large river stone accompanied by an Elégua stone and a little statuette of Lazarus the Beggar. Blood glowing almost orange soaked everything. The killing had just happened, right at sunrise, they said. How I would have liked to see the ninety-one-year-old kill that goat with the help of his grandsons and great-grandsons. It was now out back, butchered and in a pot.

Boby and his male cousins surrounded their great-grandfather. He called out songs to the orisás, Elégua before his peers. Boby took up the snap-stepped dance of the master of the boundary and the limit, and soon he was mounted. The Elégua he brought on was clearly his. I recognized it from feasts past, but now everything about him was more precise, deliberate, and practiced. After many years, Boby was becoming a mount Elégua could count on. His was still very much a Santa Clara Elégua, choreographed down to his sharp steps, but his appearance atop Boby was acclaimed at this party. He went about, greeting each person in his path, giving sweet lengthy hugs almost unbecoming of an orisá. He listened to the petitions of those who approached him, and between pantomime and a few theatrically accented words, he spoke to their needs. The energy in the room turned excited to reflect Elégua's virtues—openness, courage before change, and a willingness to embrace the play of chance. Lázaro M. reveled in his great-grandson's orisá and laughed as he sang him forward. His kin presented themselves as ready mounts for other orisás to come.

María showed up a little after eight, straight from the Curve, where she had closed down the rumba.

"Mom is going to kill me."

"Pica doesn't mind if you have too much fun, does she?"

"When she hears what she missed! She would have loved the party last night. She'll want to hear every word, but just watch, she'll be grumpy."

"Did you like it?"

"Like it? Did you see everything that went on there? The santos never stopped!"

"Did you see that Celita's Babalú Ayé spoke?"

"Nice and clear," she said, and twisted her lips for a second.

"Too clear?"

"Everyone wants the santos to work. Babalú Ayé works. Her Babalú Ayé is coming along. He always works."

"What about Hendry?"

"Worked like crazy."

"Too much?"

"Maybe."

"What about the Spiritualist part?"

"I liked that," she said. "Could have been more."

"I found the Indians hard to believe," I said.

"I liked them. I like Indians when they come."

Like his feast I attended in 2009, Lázaro was almost the sole singer. When another caller chimed in, it was only for six or seven verses before Lázaro returned to the call, refreshed. Orisás coursed through the gathering: at least two Eléguas, a Yemayá, a Changó, but no Babalú Ayé. Celita, Lázaro M.'s granddaughter, had just arrived home from the Curve and was getting into bed, bathed and sore.

Six hours almost to the minute of having offered San Lázaro–Babalú Ayé his goat, Lázaro moved to close the feast. Many of the santos-orisás were departing, disoriented mounts looking about wondering what had happened. Boby was getting his legs back under him, but other orisás were just arriving. A tall, thin woman, with scars all up her neck, was praising Elégua with dance solos. She was one of the mounts Elégua chose at this feast three years ago. She was reddish, and her skin carried yellow tones, but not so much as to be called *mulata* here in town. Her face was long and her eyes low and sad. She wore hot pink Lycra shorts, and the colors of her orange, red, and pink striped blouse were picked up perfectly by her skin. Elégua mounted her just as Lázaro was going to close.

Elégua greeted Lázaro with regard and feigned horror. How could he close the feast just then, just as Old Elégua showed up? "Heh!" shouted Elégua in proud dissent.

Lázaro was tired, as were Boby and his cousins and uncles. Everyone had been at the Curve, no one had slept. Lázaro continued with the closing, half a dozen calls to chill out the feast. The chorus of neighbors and friends, however, was still strong. The crowd, to triumph over the will of their host, joined with Elégua in moving the energy back toward the party. To each of Lázaro's calls they replied with optimistic vigor. Lázaro insisted, motioning to one of his grandsons to fetch a bucket of water. Elégua appealed directly to the drummers to continue, to redouble their efforts. Elégua had come to work, and he wanted to do it to music. How else? He began his rounds by checking in with one and then another of the chorus, who were caught between a host wanting to close things down and an exalted guest wanting to keep things going. Elégua intercepted the bucket.

"Eh!" He said, with a smirk of disregard across his mouth. "Eh!"

Elégua wanted this bembé to last. He wanted it to go on, running, and burning, and shaking. What he said with his grunted protest was "Let's play! Come on! We've just started. Let's play a little longer! Did the mounts at the Curve exhaust me, Old Elégua? I exhausted them! Come on, a little more play for Old Elégua!" Elégua marched out the back door and put the bucket down then returned to continue healing those gathered. He had the chorus on his side and also the musicians. Lázaro relented with a change of lyrics and called directly at Elégua. Elégua worked and worked and no one went untouched.

When the time came to finally close it down, it was Elégua who took matters into his hands. He had Lázaro's young men season up the bucket of water as he stood over them. This he spun about the house and tossed it into the street, returning in full laughter, cackling, as he slammed it down with a bang. Reminding us all of the conflict a little earlier, he said laughing, "What were you thinking? I open *and* close! How do I control the opening? Only I can close it!" He departed in an eruption of laughter as his mount buckled, spent.

I left Lázaro M.'s by way of a conversation with Gonzalo and Boby. Gonzalo wanted his picture taken, "So there is a nice picture of me on my casket." He was relieved that Lázaro's feast gave him a place to be on the 17th. "Zulia failed to bring a feast together, so now I drum here. But Iván still goes there, even if he doesn't play."

"Why?" I said, perplexed by the allegiance of his son-in-law to a failed feast.

"That boy was raised by Cucusa. He spent more time with her than with his mother. Even as a child he was a great drummer. Cucusa made him promise he would never be absent from her feast."

"And you, Gonzalo," interjected Boby, "why do you still go there?"

"I go to play along with Iván a little, so that he doesn't have to go it alone. Simple reason, right? Where is the betrayal in that?"

Boby pondered this. "This is bullshit," he said. "Why are we being made to take sides? Whose idea is that? My aunts are fucking this up royally."

"That there is no feast at Cucusa's?" I asked.

"That and everything else. That Gonzalo is an exile and Iván is a traitor. That Zulia has run my grandfather out of town. That my aunts Isidra and Eulalia don't come to town now."

Gonzalo and I were silent.

"I went over there," said Boby after a pause.

Gonzalo made an almost undetectable gesture of revulsion.

"I went over to negotiate with her. To propose a truce."

I looked at him with raised brows.

"But I was too drunk to talk by the time I got there. So I only asked her if she'd let me see the santos, and she let me in."

"Were they fed?" I asked.

"No. There was nothing for them but a candle she had lit. At least there was that."

"She doesn't know how to care for them, simple as that," said Gonzalo.

"Can you live like that, without feeding your santos?" I asked, interested in Gonzalo's thoughts. As far as I knew, he kept no santos, nor did he host a feast.

"No. No one can. If you keep santos in your house, you must feed them. They will punish you if you aren't caring for them properly."

"So she's stuck?"

"Stuck."

"Doesn't need to be," said Boby. "One week! Why can't they get along for one week?"

He was aggrieved, and in his eyes I recognized some of the pain of his Elégua the first time I had seen him mounted up.

Zulia's failed feast meant the collapse of Cucusa's house. Isidra was in self-exile in Havana, together with Ulises, Yemayá, and her Congo things. Roberto, once one of Sierra Morena's leading revolutionary figures, was in Matanzas, assistant to a palero. Eulalia was in self-exile in Cienfuegos. Celita was the obvious choice to take on the feast. She was Cucusa's granddaughter and a mount for San Lázaro–Babalú Ayé. Instead, she was a mount at the Curve. That feast had grown since Cucusa's death and showed no signs of getting any less popular.

The contrast between the Curve and Lázaro M.'s bembé was arresting. The Curve seemed all chaos and nervous excitement, while Lázaro's feast was concise and compact. Each was a bembé, excessive and unleashed. Lázaro's feast seemed to lead to glory, while the feast at the Curve flirted with catastrophe.

Lázaro's M. knew perfectly well the orisás to be expected, and he handled them with care. He knew the Ewe and Fon (now become Arará) and Yoruba sources of bembés like few others. He knew that the height of a bembé was a pleased orisá diligently at work to heal the gathered chorus. His party embodied a paradox I often ponder when thinking about bembés, which is that festivals, while seeking to heedlessly burn up as much as possible, also seek to "recover" from this outpouring, and not only recover but also emerge from the festival wreckage transformed for the better. The recovery from utter festival was one of the gifts of Lázaro's feast, and of Cucusa's, and Chacha's before that. From the release, from the spilling of energy and resources, perhaps only because of it, the feast could create new vistas.

Lázaro's feast, though unleashed, was "contained" in the sense that the surrenders he made were preempted and prepared for. Preparation allowed for greater intimacy between feastgoer and santo-orisá in the moment of contact. The transgenerational connections at his feast maximized ancestral recognition in that elders could garland santo-orisá performance with anecdotes and stories of mounts past. Lázaro's feast promised fluidity and depth of understanding. Preparing for the orisás, selecting their mounts, calling knowledgeably and joyfully in the rural, Arará-inspired style [*Ará Oco*], these practices staged the possibility of collective surrender—of those who sing, of those who drum, of those who dance and receive the orisás on their back. Surrender was the experience from which fate-changing encounters came. It was the intimacy from which new days were born. His preparations and expectations, which like Isidra's were modest compared to the Curve, made it possible for public intimacy to refract through the feast, intensifying it and amplifying it. His preparations were his command. His expectations led to collective energy that was a little tighter a little longer, so that it could *do* things before it was lost. In the lasting intimacies of his feasts, Lázaro achieved transformations in the lives of his kin and guests. This was his joy.

A group large or small can raise the roof in a deep, joyful bembé. The energy of the group is what moves santos-orisás. They in turn handle this energy as only sovereigns can. Their grace is to direct the energy of the gathering onto individual devotees. They do not keep this energy for themselves;

though they may waste it, they do not do so selfishly. As sovereigns they could toss the collective energy to the wind without a thought of sharing it with those who adore them. But they don't. Rather, they waste it productively, not for themselves but for those gathered in the chorus. This is why in the morning, mounts for the orisás do not remember. They have kept nothing for themselves, nor do they expect a return for their work.

At the Curve, astonishing things happened. First, it was great fun. I wish I could have laughed with and played with the musicians and Aneas, the singer, as the Congo powers tore the shrine to pieces. I wish I could have appreciated the meal they gave to the little statue in the shrine. I wish I could have exulted in José's excruciating Inle drama and Celita's similarly protracted mounting by San Lázaro–Babalú Ayé. Or in Hendry's casual, jocular Changó. Or in the *indio* scene at the end. They were each forceful and unleashed. These mountings were what the hosts and the gathered crowd of white-white farmers wanted, even though they could not control them. Their credulity lent the Curve its grandeur.

New styles of bembé praise were taking shape at the Curve. Ewe, Fon, and Yoruba-inspired melodies and lyrics that held the center of the feast at Isidra's or Lázaro M.'s were casually replaced by Spiritualist hymns, for which the drums never missed a beat. Spiritualist protocols that at Cucusa's bembé were kept to the hours before the drums broke things open took the bembé at the Curve by storm. The slow, melodic, church-like Spiritualist hymns found their way into, around, and through country Arará melodies and rhythms, traveling on the improvisational genius of singers and drummers, some of whom were mounted. The ease with which the hymns interlaced with the already-mobilized bembé energies was the source of both beauty and dismay.

In its openness and profligate recombinations, the party at the Curve was too much for Katia and her family. They did not have enough knowledge of the music, and neither Katia nor the man of the house drummed or sang. Without command of music, which they could have had with the help of people like Pica or Zenón, they lacked the means by which to direct the santos-orisás and the Congo-inspired powers. As that party spun out, it was not lost on me that we had all left Pica at home.

Similarly, the public protocols and sovereign decorum that distinguished the gestures and comportment of the santos-orisás back at Lázaro's feast were missing at the Curve. Katia's steeds were not sufficiently experienced to carry sovereign personages like Elégua, Changó, and Oyá in all their dignity. Without them, the social forces unleashed at the Curve landed in the hands of clumsy mounts, and they were as likely to heal as they were to harm through reckless indifference to the chorus or the hosts. Without the decorum of sovereigns, the orisás were less predictable and less accountable. In some cases, orisás selfishly grandstanded, apparently more focused on their performance than in working for the afflicted. In the case of the Congo dead, they violated the integrity of the house itself.

Sovereigns, be these the orisás, the Spiritualist dead, or the Congo dead, are limited by rules that guarantee each their power. These keep sovereigns from uttering or doing anything truly devastating. But Spiritualist and Congo sovereigns, like the *indio* and the Congo powers who destroyed the shrine, are bound by their rules less tightly than are the santos-orisás by theirs. These were the powers unleashed at the Curve, and thus a feeling of risk and unintended consequences was palpable there, if not excruciating at times. It spread through the chorus time and again, and by unsettling the chorus, it limited the healing that could happen. The bembé at the Curve unleashed raw powers, untamed not by virtue of being Spiritualist or Congo, but by virtue of being unbounded by a singer capable of intoning the rules by which they would grow and subside. It was a great party, but the place got trashed.

The Bembé at the Curve, though more open, though larger and more lavish, made less of a difference. It moved through fewer people with its unresponsive chorus and unexpected orisás. The energies of sovereign transformation that the feast put into motion were likely to be gobbled up by the very orisás they enabled. Blasting wildly into the night, they escaped without a chance to change the situations of those in attendance. Unexpected, the energies failed to make the connections the chorus so eagerly sought. Those who enjoyed the energy in full were those who were mounted. Without obligations, their santos-orisás and Congos were loose with their power. At times, the bembé became a spectacle monopolized by a single orisá rather than a participatory theater for the healing of all. At any moment, it could become a display of individual improvisational prowess at the cost of diminishing the collective making of orisá and Congo prestige. As such, it accomplished only partially what it set out to do, which was to heal those gathered.

When I returned to Havana, Isidra was exultant. On the 18th, Yamilet, the half niece who lived next door and had a decade earlier been her greatest antagonist, called to propose a negotiation. Zulia, now her neighbor, was impossible, and Yamilet wanted to join her Ruíz Sáez aunts and uncles in their fight to remove her from Cucusa's house. Isidra considered this an immediate dividend of my trip. She was pleased that her ability to change situations traveled so fluidly through me. She loved the photos on my phone and the stories I had to tell. She was displeased, however, that I had not read the speech she had prepared for me to give at midnight on the 17th. She was very unhappy that I had gone to the bembé at the Curve against her explicit instructions, and that so many others in her family attended as well. But she listened intently to my firsthand descriptions of that feast, which confirmed her suspicions about it, and she considered her previous denunciations proven true. She dismissed out of hand the opportunity to negotiate with either of her antagonists.

PART FIVE

NINETEEN

———

2014

DESPAIR

IT WAS THE NIGHT OF DECEMBER 12, 2014. I was back in Cuba after two years. This time Isidra was allowed to travel to Sierra Morena by her Yemayá and Congo powers, and we were waiting for our ride. Scouring Havana for supplies took longer than expected, and we were behind schedule. Arriving the night of the 12th would be our tightest timeline to date, just four full days to prepare the feast for San Lázaro–Babalú Ayé. This did not deter Isidra, who had ambitious goals. In Sierra Morena little had changed: Zulia remained in control of Cucusa's house, but she was unable to host a proper feast for San Lázaro–Babalú Ayé. This was the opening Isidra needed to continue her struggle for control over Cucusa's house, feast, and legacy. We would begin our stay with Celita and José, but Isidra had every expectation of a triumphant return to Cucusa's in time to host the bembé on the eve of December 17.

Our ride was another Peugeot supermini hatchback from the 1980s. These cars were never officially imported into Cuba, but a number of them returned with merchant marines who found space for them in the holds of government ships. Fifteen years after the collapse of the Soviet bloc, they were weathering better than the Russian Lada and Moskvitch models imported in huge numbers in the 1970s and 1980s. The kid at the wheel was from Sierra Morena, and he had come all the way from town to pick us up. He said he came empty and that every time he took someone to Havana from Sierra Morena, he returned empty.

"Not my thing to pick up people looking for rides at the bus station. Too dangerous, being end of year and all. You're sure to get ripped off, or robbed, or killed for your car."

Isidra had hoped for a 2000s-era Japanese van or a 1950s American boat, but a little French hatchback from the 1980s was what she got. We packed it to the roof. The kid didn't mind the load or her punctiliousness. She offered to work his car so that we would be protected during the trip, and he was cheerfully indifferent. He had inherited the car from his father when he committed suicide three years earlier. His mother had arthritis that kept her from walking. "Work it however you want, as long as you pay me," he said. "That's the protection I need."

We settled into silence, watching Havana fade out as we drove east. We passed within walking distance of the Quita Manaquita praise house, where we had spent so much time with Teodoro in 1999–2000 learning what we could about Cuban-Congo praise. It had collapsed in 2010. Teodoro still lived in the government barracks where I had visited him two years before.

"It is good you decided not to bring him," I said.

"Don't say another word. The binge he's been on. If you had not arrived, who knows how long it would have lasted."

"He looked terrible."

The driver interjected in his sunny manner, "I'm going to play 49 as soon we get to town."

"What does 49 stand for?" I asked, surprised by how the numbers game can insert itself into any conversation in Cuba.

"Drunkard," said the driver. "Also ghost."

"That is unfortunately appropriate," I said.

"Then go ahead and play 83," added Isidra.

"Tragedy," said the driver.

Isidra then prompted the driver. In a society with strict government control of information, even in the days of rife black markets in digital content, prompting was an art form. "They say there are eggs in Sierra Morena."

"Nope. No eggs. Gone, vanished," he said.

"They're missing here in Havana too," said Isidra.

"Yup. Looked for them," said the driver. "In town they said I'd find them for CUC in the shopping stores, but nope. If I had found them, I would have filled the trunk with them. Then you would have been screwed." He smiled.

"Where are the eggs?" I asked with a prompt so unartful, it came out as a question.

"Where are they ever?" asked the driver in reply.

"With the state," I said, knowing this could easily sound negative, but he had prompted me back. His was the kind of simple question that opens doors if people want to speak critically about the revolution. Eggs were perennially a portal for turning conversations against the revolution. In fact, in 2012 a ring of workers and administrators in the government poultry company was busted for stealing eight million eggs. We didn't know this at the time. The government didn't report it until 2015, when the prison sentences were announced. Still, my barbed suggestion was the kind of statement that elicited rebukes from Isidra. To preempt her, I asked, "What is the number for 'egg'? I'll play that when we get to town."

"Sixty," said the driver. "I hope you brought tomato paste. No tomato paste in town either. I hope you brought some of that."

Before I could ask the number for "tomato," Isidra directed her conversation to me. "Imagine if we had brought Ulises? We wouldn't have room for any of this!" She had tried to get him to come until the last minute, but he held her off. "He doesn't sleep at home anymore," she said.

"A woman," interjected the driver as if he were figuring out a mystery. "Nothing keeps a man from his mother like a woman will."

"You saw him in his room," she said to me. "He stayed because you were in town, but he is never home."

"He told me he was staying in Havana because he had work," I said. Ulises was now nearly thirty and selling cell phones at a market fair the government had opened for street artisans who had previously crowded around Old Havana's cathedral. Going to Sierra Morena would cost him 200 CUC in losses at least, this being end of year and business being brisk. He was maintaining Isidra now, so she had zero leverage over him.

"If he would spend two nights a week, I would appreciate that. I'm not a young woman anymore. I'm seventy-four."

There was a pause as we slowed down in Jovellanos, and all of us looked about for signs of life in that sleepy town.

"You met the prosecutor," Isidra began after a long silence.

"He seemed nice," I said. She had introduced me to a retired prosecutor who lived a couple of blocks from her. He was about her age and had worked in the civilian courts all his life. Together they had worked up a brief against Zulia and the housing authorities in Corralillo. Isidra would present her case while we were in town.

"With his brief, they'll run for the hills. Zulia, the housing people, everyone," she said.

"Seems like a very smart person," I said.

"You've got to be smart when dealing with people like Zulia," she said. "Now you know who I am and how I will take this fight to many fronts."

"Tell me how Pica died," I said. This was one of the pieces of news Isidra dropped on me without wanting to elaborate.

"Ask Celita when we get there. What can I say?" With an answer like that, it was pointless to ask about the even more shocking news that María, her daughter, died three months to the day after Pica.

"It would be nice to see them," I said, using the plural.

"Forget about that. You can't want things you can't have."

I wondered how she would manage without them. The mother-daughter pair mounted five santos-orisás between them and had been the backbone of Isidra's feasts in town. I pondered this for some time, but when I found a way to pursue the topic, she was asleep.

We were unpacked and talking in the kitchen at Celita and José's. Eulalia had preceded us by two days. The exile from Cucusa's house continued, now in its fifth year. Celita was delighted to have her aunts in town, and plans were afoot to host a bembé at their house.

"Hold up," said Isidra. "I didn't come all this way, packed like a sardine in that miserable car, to host a feast here."

"Aunt," started Celita.

"Shh!" Isidra interjected. "This town hates her, you know that, and I have cards to play."

"The whole system is activated against Zulia," said Eulalia enthusiastically, referring to the local Committee for the Defense of the Revolution and the police. "Her and her family."

"That may be," said Celita, "but you can't just walk in there anymore, Aunt. That is her house now."

"Her house?" Isidra stood up. "Because she has lived there for nine years? A squatter and a cheat? I have been moving things in Havana, and I will move things in Corralillo. Don't think she has anyone fooled."

"Aunt, people in town think it is her house, and you can't just march in there to host a bembé. Look at the date."

"Well, she may have convinced you and everyone in town, but she hasn't convinced me," said Isidra. "I'm here to fight for that house. I'm here to host a bembé for Babalú Ayé in Cucusa's house. Forget it if you think I'm here so you and José can have one of your bashes."

We had arrived late on the 12th, just four days from when the bembé was to begin. On the morning of the 13th, Isidra was up while it was still dark, waking up the house ahead of the roosters while she sang and divined. In a day bag she had brought Mariana Congo, which she had taken from Cucusa's house in 2009 and now kept in Havana. She had unwrapped the white kerchief and was throwing Mariana's clam shells for insights into what lay ahead. Celita and Eulalia were at her side, a disoriented but attentive chorus. José and the kids, Guillermo and Mericelia, stayed in bed. Years past, I would have been up with Eulalia and Celita, but I wasn't called, so I stayed in bed.

As I listened to Isidra grow louder and more determined, I appreciated her divination with Mariana Congo. Isidra's consultations with the coconut disk *chamalongo*, which accompanied her Congo things, were treacherous. There were only four chamalongo, and they were as likely to speak negatively as affirmatively. When they spoke affirmatively, Isidra tended to check the answer. Mariana Congo had five clam shells for divining. They tended to fall affirmatively more often than negatively, the fifth shell apparently tilting things in benign directions. The affirmation she got from Mariana calmed Isidra; her tone was milder than when she used the chamalongo. She was less likely to doubt the results of a throw or seek confirmation with another throw. Mariana Congo made her feel confident, and the outcomes for the rest of us were easier. It was decided that Isidra's work with the legal brief in Corralillo could not be undertaken until she greeted La Corua, the pool at the bend in the river that had something to do with Mariana's powers.

After breakfast, Isidra and Eulalia made short rounds around town, and I was alone with Celita. It was Saturday and her kids were out playing. José was at work.

"I'm sorry about Pica," I said.

"Everyone misses her."

"And María," I said. "I'm sorry about her too."

"No one can explain it, Ramón. No one can talk about it. Both of them are gone."

"What happened?"

"María's adopted daughter inherited the house, sold everything inside, sold the house to a *guajiro* from out toward San Rafael, then left town. The man now says the house is impossible to live in, that it's full of the dead, and he wants his money back."

I looked at her, hoping for more.

"Her daughter just vanished, and no one knows where she's gone. Took the money and ran." She made a hand gesture common in Cuba that means "took off."

"What happened to Pica?"

"Ramón, this is not easy. What do you think? Pica died of diabetes, and neglect."

I was silent.

"María could have cared for her better, you know that. We all wanted Pica better cared for. She was our library and our light. María's girl was only in it for herself. María didn't see how bad it was getting and didn't do what she should have."

"And María?"

"María?"

"What happened?"

"You'll have to ask Zenón or Gonzalo, who were at the bar with her when she died. I need to not think about it. I need to focus on Guillermo and Mericelia through the 17th. And José. He can't fish anymore, so he is working as a cook down at the food kiosk at the beach."

"But he was cleaning a ton of fish when we arrived last night. We had fish for breakfast."

"There is a little harbor at the end of the beach. Some commercial fishermen gave those to him, praise San Lázaro. Sometimes he goes out with them. He is good on the boats. But his inner tube and his gear are gone. They took it from him, and next time they'll fine him 1,500 Cuban pesos. The days of people just going out are over, for now."

"Zenón and Yunier too? No one is fishing?"

"They closed it down. That big beautiful lagoon, and we're not allowed to fish. Too many lobster tails go from these towns along the coast to Varadero, where little private restaurants buy them to feed tourists who escape from their all-inclusives. You said there were no police checkpoints last night. You'll see, on your way back to Havana, it isn't so easy. They'll search you just on the other side of Corralillo."

"I'm sorry for them. Fish is a special food, and fishing clears your head."

"How we need that here," she said.

Mericelia was around with friends. She was eight years old and a bold little kid who led her neighbor friends around.

"Did you hear about my other brother, Alejandro?" said Celita.

"No," I said as I thought about her brother Robertico's suicide, nine years before.

"He fled last week."

"How?"

"A speedboat from Miami picked him up somewhere along the coast here."

"Anelé's dad?"

"Along with his new wife. He didn't tell Anelé or her mother. They found out when he called them from Miami. Anelé is heartbroken."

"He could have taken her too," I said as I pondered the relationships in play.

"There is no knowing if she would have gone."

"I'm glad they made it."

"He worked in Varadero and got into trouble like Robertico did." She spoke about the beach enclave that had become the primary destination for all-inclusive tourism in Cuba. Varadero nourished the fantasies of countless Cuban youth and sent rays of opportunity hundreds of miles into the countryside in all directions. "Varadero is killing us," she said.

I thought her verdict applied to tourism in Cuba in general.

"I hope he does well in Miami," I said.

She looked worried, as if imagining that strange world. It made Varadero and its temptations seem insignificant by comparison. "I'm glad he chose to flee. I hope he sends Anelé money. She is pregnant, did you know?"

Just then the sisters came in.

"We're waiting for Esteban from Sagua la Grande," said Isidra. "He's supposed to be here soon, and we need his voice for the offering at La Corua."

Esteban had been a pupil of Isidra's in her days teaching "folkloric" music and dance, in the early sixties. He credited her with kindling his interest in the African inspirations of his family when the revolution was moving in other directions. He owed her a lifelong debt, and in the absence of Pica his voice would be essential if we were going to have any chance of hosting a bembé.

"When he gets here, it will be your job, Ramón, to walk him down to the river. You know the way. He is almost blind now."

Esteban and I made it to the river ahead of Isidra and her party, which included Eulalia, Celita, and the kids. I had led him over rough terrain and through thickets of *marabú,* even through sagging barbed-wire fences, all while holding his hand. Esteban was a decent singer of bembé songs and other styles, like Congo barbs. His voice was deep and grizzled, at once powerful at its core and wheezy at the edges—a rough baritone. In my experience he had been a minor singer who always deferred to Pica and Zenón. A shady little ledge where the river had carved away the bank at La Corua offered us a place to sit and wait.

"Esteban," I started, "you are from Sagua la Grande, to the east. Is the music the same there as here?"

"No. Sagua has its own music, and it influences the towns around it."

"But not this far west?"

"No. Sagua style comes this way only as far as Quemado de Güines."

"Doesn't reach Rancho Veloz?"

"No. Rancho Veloz and Sierra Morena are different."

"What about to the west of Sierra Morena?"

"To the west you have Arará city music. Cárdenas is the center of that."

"Not Matanzas?"

"Matanzas is its own phenomenon. It has lots of Arará music, but not only. Matanzas has to manage the influences from Havana."

"So, Sierra Morena and Rancho Veloz have their own style?"

"That is what I'm saying."

"What would you call it?"

"Ará Oco. Raw bembé."

"What happens from Sagua la Grande going the other direction, to the east?"

He paused and thought. "Things get complicated. Things get more Spiritualist the farther east you go."

"Whiter too?"

"That too."

The sky was blue with little downy clouds. It was a lovely morning to be down by the river.

"Can a singer bring on an orisá?" I asked. "I have seen callers direct their calls at particular people in the chorus. Can a singer make someone mount a santo?"

"A singer can't call a santo down [bajar un santo]. Only santos decide when they are going to take a mount."

"Can a caller help?"

"Orisás are the ones who call the shots [el orisá manda]. Sometimes a mount will feel the orisá coming on and resist. A singer sees this. You can help the mount along so that they let the santo up."

"So you can do something as a singer."

"If the mount resists the saint, you can tickle a little."

We sat at La Corua for some time. The opposite shore was higher where the river bent out. Our side was all river stones underfoot, the same stones kept as santo-orisá likenesses and fed during bembé slaughters. An almost imperceptible breeze came from the forest. The river was shallow except where we sat. Where the river came from I did not know, but we sat just a few kilometers from the sea. Isidra called it a place of "two waters," meaning it was fresh water that intermingled with the sea. La Corua connected the realm of La Caridad–Ochún, patroness of love and all things sweet, including fresh water, with the realm of Yemayá, mother of the sea. La Corua was ever full, even when the rest of the river ran dry. Its considerable depth was eerie and signaled to people that it was a place propitious for contact with Congo-inspired powers, which are closely aligned to expansive, vibrant nature.

Esteban was napping when Isidra arrived singing to Ochún and Yemayá, the two patronesses of that place. Eulalia, Celita, and the kids followed, offering a minimal chorus. She was there to feed one of her Congo powers called Batalla, which she had received as a gift from a woman in San Rafael down the road many years ago. Batalla was along as on trips past, to help us do what its name designated. She also had in mind to feed a "guide" of her Mama Chola, a feminine Cuban-Congo *prenda* used in Palo healing back in Havana. Mama Chola has affinities with the orisá Ochún. A "guide" is some part of the larger collection of substances called a prenda, or "jewel," in Cuban-Congo life.[1] Whereas a prenda is usually a heavy thing, requiring more than one person to lift, a guide is a portable portion that retains its powers. It can also communicate back to the mother prenda. Feeding her Chola guide at La Corua would strengthen it for the days ahead. When she returned to Havana, it would also refresh the Mama Chola to which it was linked. Batalla wanted to eat young rooster; the Chola guide wanted to eat a yellow hen.

Batalla was fed first. "He eats like Elégua, but Congo," Isidra said. "Sing, Esteban."

A young rooster was swept over each of us as Esteban led us in a simple call-and-response of Congo songs. Without much ado, which is Cuban Congo style, Isidra tore the young rooster's head free and poured its blood on Batalla. The carcass was laid next to it. She put her Chola guide half into the water and squatted down close to it. She brought the hen down so that it was almost touching the water, then lowered herself so that she could whisper to it. She spoke to it for half a minute, leaving with it her wishes and fears. She did not cleanse us with this animal. With her fingers, she pulled feathers from under its neck and set them in the water around the Chola guide. In an instant, the tiny breeze caught these and sent them sailing across the surface of the water, which appeared perfectly still. Sunlight caught the feathers, and for a few seconds they were a tiny fleet running before the wind. Minnows pecked at these, leaving tiny rings in their wake.

"Don't tell me sorcery isn't pretty," said Isidra, laughing.

Esteban kept the calls going, and she plucked more feathers until the pool was covered in them. She then pulled off the hen's head and fed her Chola guide, letting drops of blood fall directly into the pool, thus feeding it too. When the hen could give no more, she flung it into the pool, where it made a dreadful, though hardly incongruent, addition to the work she had just accomplished.

With the meal "directo a La Corua," and Batalla and her Chola guide properly fed, she could now assert herself in town. We were back well before midday to avoid the dead that would be about in the forest at that hour.

On the 14th, Eulalia was confident about their case and explained it to me over a lunch of fried fish and cold rice. "Cucusa has eight heirs. Three of them have ceded their inheritance rights to Zulia. The other three have ceded their rights to me. Two parties of four. All of that had to be certified and notarized."

"How long did that take?"

"Since last you were here. Two years."

"Why did Isidra and Roberto and Máximo cede you their rights?"

"Because I am the only one of us who doesn't have a house. The revolution doesn't allow a person to have two houses. I have never had one of my own." She lived in a room in Cienfuegos, in the house of two men who were her dear friends.

"I thought you could own two houses now," I said referring to Raúl Castro's housing reforms of 2011. "Couldn't Isidra claim Cucusa's house as a country house, while keeping her apartment in Havana?"

"It will be easier if I claim it. I have never had my own housing."

"So you want to live here?"

"We'll see about that. This is less for me than for Cucusa's santos. They need a room of their own. For now, Zulia and I are the sole heirs. We need to establish my right to half of Cucusa's house."

"Half? Does Isidra know you are willing to settle for half?"

"Until we can prove Zulia broke the law, and bribed, and lied like she has, asking for the house to be split is our best option."

"Split? How is a house split?"

"The Housing Office splits the house. They come out and measure and decide where the wall is going to be built, how the yard is going to be divided, and where a new door will go if it is needed.

"But Isidra wants the whole house."

"And she will eventually get it. But first we have to split it."

"Who is going to get the well in the backyard?"

"Zulia cut down all those trees. The house is falling apart. She has proved herself a poor caretaker of the property. We have documented everything. Yamilet next door, who has caused us so much trouble, now says she can't stand Zulia. She's cooperating with us. We're going to fight so that we get the well."

"With Yamilet on your side? After everything that happened in 1999?"

"She has her role to play."

I pondered all this, wondering why Isidra had said nothing to me. "The house has two front doors, so that helps," I said.

"It is a big house. It should be easy to split. The revolution split practically every house in town over fifty years, so I don't expect any problems. Our part will be for Cucusa's santos, so they can have a room where they are safe and cared for. Isidra has her case to make in Corralillo."

"With the brief?"

"The Housing Office in Corralillo is corrupt. Did Isidra tell you that the file on our mother's house is missing? Coincidence? That is what Isidra's complaint is about. It is laid out in the brief clear as day. Corruption in the housing office with Zulia at the heart of it."

"How long will that take?"

"It will take forever. First they will divide the house. Then, when we prove our corruption case, Zulia will be evicted, or jailed. At that point we'll ask for the house to be joined back together. This is the path to follow, with Elégua's blessing."

We spent the 14th planning and wondering about whether to buy animals. Everything was slow. Roberto and Máximo were out of the scene for good. Justo came by but was ornery and in little mood to help his cousins. Yunier kept his distance. Zenón had not come by. José, who was always a great help, spent his days at the kiosk and helping commercial fishermen.

On the morning of the 15th the sisters headed to Corralillo, the municipal seat where the housing bureaucracy had offices. Their plan was to march in and request the file on Cucusa's house. When this failed to appear, they would let drop the prosecutor's brief. They also planned to talk to the chief of police in Corralillo. The chief in Sierra Morena had snubbed Eulalia the day she arrived in town. She went to their mother's house, of which she was a coproprietor, but Zulia refused to let her in. So she filed a complaint with the police, but the chief mocked her and told her to just barge inside. Eulalia, who was seventy-two, with the stature of a stalk of grass, was deeply offended.

"They're crazy," said José when they were well down the road.

"Shh!" cautioned Celita. "Don't let the children hear you."

"They're never going to get that house, or half of it. People here in town are pissed at Isidra for the way she is handling this. Half her family is pissed at her."

"My aunt is strong."

"Strong and crazy. You can't win a fight like this from Havana or Cienfuegos, not by burning bridges here in town."

"Do you think any of this can happen by tomorrow?" I asked. We had thirty-six hours to prepare a bembé.

"Not a chance," said José. "She's asking me to run out and buy animals for Elégua and San Lázaro for a feast at her mother's house. I'll get the animals, but it isn't going to happen at Cucusa's. The party will be here. Count on it."

"Sounds right," I said.

"Sounds right? Do you remember what I said when you left here last time?"

"No."

"I said, 'Enjoy Pica because she won't be here next time you come.'"

"I don't remember that," I said. "But you didn't say anything about María."

"Who could have guessed that!"

"How did María die?"

"She died on the three-month anniversary of Pica's death. People said she showed up at the bar to dance herself to death, and that is what she did. Danced until she collapsed."

"Was she mounted by Changó?"

"No."

"Were you there?"

"No."

The sisters returned from Corralillo exultant. The police chief said he would pay a visit to Zulia tomorrow, on the 16th. Isidra understood that she would practically have a police escort when she returned triumphantly to her mother's house on San Lázaro's Eve. She would be just in time to sweep the place and rinse off the santos before the bembé started. More importantly, they got the Housing Office to admit that the file for Cucusa's house had been stolen and to recognize that Zulia was not a sole heir. Eulalia's claim would be acknowledged. This was tremendous news.

"This morning we had nothing. Now look. You can't steal a house from me!" said Isidra.

Eulalia smiled. "You should have seen her!" she said, coaxing her sister.

"You should have seen me! One woman at the Housing Office thought she could play the dope, the other took the hard line. Neither of them was going to lift a finger for us. Then I pulled out the prosecutor's brief. I started reading it straight to them. You should have seen them jump! Even the dopey one!" Isidra paced back and forth with a broad smile, relishing the event.

"She pulled Cucusa's house from the brink!" said Eulalia.

A look of mischief crossed Isidra's face. "Zulia thinks the house is already hers, with all her lies and tricks. Just wait till she gets this news!"

"We'll tell her when the police chief lets us in tomorrow!" said Eulalia.

Then Isidra's manner changed.

"Celita, look at this place. Look at the mess you live in."

Celita slumped. Her aunt's shifts were notorious.

"It is a miracle I can stay in this place at all. I am an old woman. I need basic conditions. You shouldn't let the children onto your furniture like you do. Why do you think it is falling apart? And you complain about the dirty walls? Do you think they learn when you don't discipline them?"

"Aunt, why don't we talk about something else."

"Because disorder breeds disorder. Are those children more likely to turn out like me or like Zulia? Did Cucusa let us up on the furniture like that?"

The reference to Zulia visibly troubled Celita, but it was the suggestion that she was not living up to her grandmother's standards that hurt. She went to complain, but Isidra continued.

"Why did you sell that big goat you were supposed to keep for me? Didn't you think I would be back and that Babalú Ayé would need to be fed? Why don't you think? This revolution schooled you in its finest schools, trained you as an engineer, sent you to Bulgaria for seven years, for you to be this scatterbrained? What happened to the engineer?"

"Aunt . . ."

"And don't think I haven't figured out that you are keeping up a relationship with Zulia. Even if it's just to greet her in the street. Do you think you are the only person I talk to? I may live in Havana, but I am a phenomenon in this town. There is nothing you can do that I'm not going to know about. Like how the heads of my drums got busted. Weren't you supposed to keep them and not let them be touched? I know all of that. But you're a bigger fool if you think Zulia won't take advantage of your little 'hellos' and 'good evenings.' If you offer them, she'll turn your prayers against you."

Celita was trembling.

"Cry," said Isidra. "Go ahead. See how much that helps us get the animals we need tomorrow night."

Celita was her favorite target when she unloaded, and none of us ever spoke up to stop her. None of us could deny her language was severe. But neither could we deny that there was usually truth in the things she said— sound warnings and incisive observations. Eulalia believed this more than anyone. Isidra's harangues were one of her modes of extending into the world by amplifying her volition. She refused to show pity, ever, and to accept pity would have been the worst. She refused, also, to acknowledge the debt implied in gifts, which she understood to be deserved by the merit of her labor and prowess.

The plan when we woke up on the morning of the 16th was to prepare everything for the return to Cucusa's. Isidra set me to chasing down the few remaining birds to be offered. José thought we could find them not far from his workplace, near the beach. It seemed an awful long way to go for two roosters, but the trek would get us out of the house for a few hours, which is what he was angling for. He was also angling for some fried fish and rum, and we had a bit of each by the time we were returning back to town—without the birds. Zulia was lounging at the bar down from her house, where María had died. She looked at us and made a little smirk before she returned to exaggerated nonchalant conversation.

The police chief from Corralillo never showed up. Afternoon arrived, and our chances of cracking open the bembé at Cucusa's at midnight faded. Isidra put on a brave face. There would be no bembé, she said. Rather, we would host a *velada,* a small soiree for San Lázaro at Celita's.

TWENTY

Sovereigns of Affliction

WORD SPREAD THAT ISIDRA'S ATTEMPTED FEAST at Cucusa's house was not going to happen. Isidra had managed to introduce a sense of suspense to town life that made for a couple of days of exciting talk. Now people turned their attention to the feast at the Curve. Lázaro M., who normally didn't begin his feast until daybreak on the 17th, was moving his start up to midnight, thus filling Cucusa's slot and as a consequence keeping his many kin from attending at the Curve. Cucusa's family, led by Celita and José but including the branch of the family connected to Lázaro M., also stayed away from the Curve. Without María or Ulises to sneak over to the party, I spoke to no one who attended at the Curve that year.

Midnight of December 16 crept into view, and the scene was pathetic. Eulalia and Isidra, along with Celita, had shaped up the house. Celita had not recovered from her aunt's relentless scolding and kept despondent airs. José was asleep with the kids. Esteban sat quietly in a corner. Our most loyal helper, Justo, had marched off the day before. Yunier had never come around. A sheet cake and the dozen meringues Celita had ordered days before were never made. "The eggs have vanished! [¡*El huevo está perdido!*]" was one of the most heard refrains that December. "Get me the eggs and I'll make you the meringues!" the self-employed pastry maker said in her defense when Isidra scolded her. A drunk woman whom Isidra accused of being a spy for Zulia persisted in hanging around Celita's door and was now inside, nodding in a chair.

A little before midnight, Boby showed up from Santa Clara. He was now a lineman for the government electrical utility and was in the company of a couple of his coworkers. They were drunk but cheerful.

Isidra greeted them cautiously. "I can't have drunks at this little party," she said. "We won't disrespect San Lázaro tonight!" Boby, repelled by this curt reception, turned on his heels and walked out the door. He could see that though we had drums, we had no drummers, so no bembé would happen at Celita's. The bembé at his great-grandfather Lázaro's was about to start.

At the stroke of midnight, Isidra gathered our motley little group, and with a rattle in hand she led us in the prayer that opened the feast at Cucusa's. Pica's memory lingered close to this song.

"Bamba luca!" began Isidra. She was declarative and defiant, a far cry from the modesty Pica usually showed.

We replied with a percentage of her energy, "Bamba luca."

"Bamba luca!" insisted Isidra.

"Bamba luca," we replied weakly.

"Bamba luca lubeya," added Isidra, her voice rising.

"Bamba luca lubeya," we replied.

"Bamba luca," she sang.

"Bamba luca," we replied.

"Bamba luca lubeya," she finished.

"Bamba luca lubeya," we replied.

How far were we from the last time I had heard that prayer called at Cucusa's house? Isidra and Eulalia were in their sixth December of exile, each year more ignominious. Every year the plan was to return the feast to Cucusa's house, and each year the house became more closed. Despite the successes in Corralillo the day before, the fight for the house was lost in bureaucratic entanglements with no sure way forward. The police could not be counted on. Roberto never came from Matanzas, and his and Celia's children were more scattered by the day. Máximo was no longer coming around in December. Pica was dead and María was dead. The feast at the Curve, which Isidra had denounced for fifteen years, was thriving. More and more houses in town now hosted feasts for San Lázaro–Babalú Ayé in the space once occupied by Cucusa's party alone.

Determined, Isidra took up the drums. She sat behind the big box, put Eulalia on the *requinto,* and asked me to play *mula* on Tata Emilio O'Farril's little *tambor de brujo,* which she had brought along from Havana. You know you've hit rock bottom in Sierra Morena when an anthropologist from North Carolina is one of your starting percussionists.

"Sing, Esteban," she said.

We played along, half-heartedly, with Isidra animated, trying by force of will to make this more than an exercise in papering over the humiliation of exile and defeat. Twenty minutes into this, when it was time to give up,

Zenón appeared at the door with a couple of young men. We had yet to see him on this visit. People said he was in the countryside taking care of a sick brother. He was exceedingly polite, formal almost, in his entrance. He greeted each of us with feigned formality.

"You've come, Zenón!" Isidra struggled to contain herself. Her act of determination had paid off just in time. "Go on, sing!"

"I'm not here to sing. I heard this was just going to be a little vigil [velada], no drums. My brother is sick. I'm tired. My throat is dry. I just came to greet all of you and show my regards for Babalú Ayé."

"You can't come here and not sing, Zenón! Come on," Isidra said, trying to keep it cheerful.

"These people," he said referring to Celita and José, "they skipped my party for Changó on the 8th."

"Well, they aren't hosting this party." Isidra started to get emphatic. "This Cuban you see standing here talking to you is the host. Don't drag me down because these people dissed you!"

"And what about you and Ramón? Why didn't you come from Havana for my party? I invite you every year."

"Sing, Esteban! Show Zenón that we're serious. Ramón, get Zenón what he wants."

Once the little gourd of aguardiente was in his hands, Zenón sang as if he couldn't stop himself. He loved the clean distillation of the Havana chemist who made our aguardiente. I was replaced on the *mula* before he even started. After his first couple of calls, José and the kids were up. Our replies to his calls were anemic and visibly disappointed him, so he turned to one of the men who had come with him and said, "¡Trae mi tumba pa'ca! [Go, bring my crew!]." Mericelia read the scene perfectly and was at my side, holding my hand. I was delighted with the turn of events, but she was downcast. I prompted her with a little furrow of my brow. "I hope my mother doesn't get mounted," she replied and pouted off.

In minutes the house was full of musicians. They were led by an enormous man who was Roberto's unrecognized, illegitimate son. Boris had been coming around the last few Decembers, since Roberto and Celia's departure for Matanzas. He was the spitting image of his father: his height and the reddish hue of his skin, his broad shoulders and the way they sagged, his nose, his lips, even something of his despondent air. Over the last couple of years, he and Celita, his half sister, had developed a rapport. The crew at his back was warmed up and ready to go, pulled away from the party at Lázaro M.'s. Zenón had not stopped singing the whole time, and he kept calling while he directed me and others to get the furniture out of the house. With room to dance, the chorus jumped to life.

Celita—who had been frazzled all day, whose misery under Isidra was more marked by the hour, whose father and mother had moved away just as her little children were getting old enough to appreciate their grandparents, whose one brother was dead, and whose other brother was newly in exile—was mounted just like that. She was dancing precipitously close to the little altar her aunts had built for San Lázaro–Babalú Ayé when he mounted her, and she fell abruptly to the ground [*la tumbó*]. His vehemence was unmistakable. Her fall was caught by no one. No longer was María around to provide the knowing hand just in time. She lay on the ground, now on her side with one hand on her hip and the other reaching for the drums as she bucked. San Lázaro–Babalú Ayé, sovereign of affliction and relief, was with us now.

She was helped to her feet by those close to her, and she carried San Lázaro–Babalú Ayé with the anguish of an afflicted beggar. San Lázaro–Babalú Ayé was in her body, on her shoulders, bent and burdened. He limped, and his fingers were curled in pain. His head was thrown back, his mouth a grimace, and tears streamed down the cheeks of his steed. Sovereign of affliction and keeper of unremitting wretchedness, San Lázaro was perfectly at home on her. What more apt a steed than this one for the master of the open sore? The afflictions of San Lázaro–Babalú Ayé are those of the body—of its diseases and pains. But Cubans will also tell you that San Lázaro–Babalú Ayé presides over affliction itself, be this physical, emotional, or other. He is sovereign over suffering, including that of the broken spirit. Eulalia realized the violence of Celita's fall and was soon at San Lázaro's side. She removed Celita's shoes, and brought a burlap sack to throw over the orisá's shoulders. A purple sash was tied around San Lázaro's waist, and a cigar was brought for him to smoke.

The chorus responded. A crowd formed around San Lázaro–Babalú Ayé, and Zenón reveled. He drove us forward with calls for him, songs now sung directly to the beggar-saint master of suffering and orisá of healing. More orisás were soon to come, and Isidra prepared their accoutrements.

The house was overflowing now, as if this party had been going for hours, as if the town had expected it for days. Boby appeared at my side.

"Say something, American!"

"Say something, Boby!"

"I need this," he said, looking on as the bembé picked up steam. He was buzzed and looked appreciative.

"Aren't we taking energy away from your great-grandfather Lázaro's?"

"This is the only place to be now. Zenón will call them all down. I need a minute with Babalú Ayé."

I furrowed my brow.

"Heart attack."

I shook my head in disbelief.

"Heart attack. Happened at work. I got hit by a live current, and it gave me a heart attack." He nodded slowly, matter-of-factly. "Let me get up close to my aunt and her santo now. Let's see if Elégua will let me."

His santo wouldn't. Babalú Ayé was cleansing a woman who wore her distress plain for all to see. He was deep into attending to her, to working his healing, and the feast circled around them, exalted. Boby took to dancing. His dancing improved year by year, and the chorus made room for him to move. Thus is an orisá's sovereignty first affirmed by a gathered chorus. Elégua, master of his head, appreciated his movements and gladly accepted the invitation to mount up.

Boby's mounting was less calamitous than in years past. His dancing was better, more in step with his Elégua, so that his orisá's ride was more seamless. The fit between mount and orisá had become comfortable, such that Boby appeared to bear lightly the immense weight of the sovereign of portals and play.

The chorus was delighted with Elégua and so was Zenón, who now sang for him. Eulalia and Isidra were ready for the orisás to come; this was the role in which they thrived. Had they expected their little vigil to become a full-on bembé? It didn't matter now. They received Elégua with agreement and appreciation. They took his shoes and placed a red-and-black cap on his head. They gave him a cigar, hooked a crook of *guayaba* over his arm, and offered him a little gourd of aguardiente. This last did not fail to draw Zenón's notice, who motioned to the sisters for a similar dram.

Boby's Elégua was "less wild [*menos jíbaro*]," José observed. His steps were more assured, so his transition from an orisá who dances to an orisá who attends to the afflicted was more convincing. From the whirlwind of dance, its powers for mimicry and its glories of evocation, he emerged as a fully embodied sovereign, upright and observant, crackling with potential that could be felt like a current. Boby's Elégua was unique in that he retained some of his dance moves as he worked among the chorus, like large, decisive steps made on tiptoes, and an alert cleverness communicated by searching movements of his head. His Elégua persona was self-assured, strong, and ready.

Babalú Ayé and Elégua attended to the gathered crowd, offering their advice and vision to those who suffered disease, worry, and treacherous passages in their lives. These afflictions often braid around one another, so the appearance of Babalú Ayé and Elégua was propitious. Celita had been at it for some time, so the voice of her orisá had slipped from the muzzled [*bozal*] speech expected from santos-orisás to her everyday voice. If you were attending Cucusa's feast, or even earlier, Chacha's feasts at the Sociedad Africana, you wouldn't know what to make of such plain speech. Had you been Chacha Cairo or Loreto Sáez, you might have swept such an orisá off their mount. But Celita was beloved by the chorus and the gathered onlookers. Elégua, for his part, reflected the attributes of his mount, including a playful streak and propensity to flirt.

The two sovereigns met in the middle of the room. The chorus made way for them, and the drummers added energy. Zenón provided the calls the chorus needed to take the bembé higher. Mounted on steeds that were aunt and nephew, the two santos-orisás communicated recognition and respect for one another with a formal embrace, bumping shoulders. San Lázaro–Babalú Ayé held a bundle of ritual waste from his cleansings—bits of coconut, torn cloth, and the shredded leaves of a vine with which he rubbed the afflicted—wrapped in brown paper. In his hands he held the disease, pain, and misfortune of those he had treated. Such waste was safe only in his hands. It could not harm him. Just before, San Lázaro–Babalú Ayé had decided the bundle needed to be disposed of far away, at the base of an ancient tree. But, hobbled as he was, he could not walk there himself. He turned to Elégua, master of the passage, trailblazer, and sovereign in the forest, to carry it for him. Only the master of the path could safely carry the waste. Babalú Ayé motioned for Elégua to take the load and go far.

This was not a request Elégua cared to receive. He was enjoying himself mightily. He had gotten a few more gourds of aguardiente, and his cigar burned bright. He captivated many in the chorus with his healing gestures and words. As master over the crossroads, he was also the sovereign of transformation and play. He was comfortable, the music played to his liking, and the bembé was just getting to be fun. He made a dissatisfied face.

No force at the bembé could resist San Lázaro–Babalú Ayé, but Elégua shook his shoulders and turned to the side, finding delight in the person nearest to him. He stepped away from Babalú Ayé but then stopped, as if reconsidering his peer's request. He would have to leave the feast, and the night was cold. San Lázaro–Babalú Ayé had somehow gotten a set of chamalongo coconut shells in his hands, and before the sovereign trickster could march away, he threw the four coconut shells at Elégua's feet. Two up, two down, affirmative. San Lázaro–Babalú Ayé drew the attention of the crowd to the result. Elégua was outdone and feigned displeasure. With his left hand he plucked the package from San Lázaro–Babalú Ayé and headed for the door. Isidra was waiting for him there with a lit candle. With his right hand he took this and held it on his left shoulder, thus illuminating the limb that held the accursed waste. The misfortune and illness he carried were isolated on his left side. He took a quick look around and, mischievous as ever, caught my eye. He commanded me to follow.

In a moment we were out the door, not running but bounding off the veranda, down the steps, and across the small yard into the street. I was not the only person he caught with his sharp scan of the room. With us came the scarred woman who mounted Elégua at Lázaro M.'s in years past. Justo, who was milling around outside, followed at a short distance. Nocturnal perambulations by orisás were a feature of Cucusa's and Chacha's bembés. Santos-orisás sometimes sojourned outdoors to complete their works. Such outings were rare during the revolution, but Pica's Oyá had once escorted Isidra to the cemetery. Elégua turned toward the forest where the dead, in their vegetative profligacy, would absorb the load of affliction with ease. The forest edge was half an hour away, toward La Corua. I braced for this when Elégua stopped in his tracks.

We came to the first crossroads, and, being the ruler of such places, Elégua felt he could stop and ponder the situation. He sat down in the very center of the crossing. He put the candle and the packet on the ground between his legs. He tugged at his pant leg to express that at the crossroads he wore the pants. He tapped his chest with his right hand and threw it forward. His expression was one of smug defiance as he asserted his sovereignty. He sat down with the package between his legs and brought the candle to eye level, so he could look through the flame. This was his counter-chamalongo, and he pondered what he saw there for several moments. The dead communicate through flames, and it was they who gave him the affirmation he needed. He opened the package of waste and began to rummage through it.

None of us disputed Elégua's utter right to make the exception he did. This could only be done by a power such as he, orisá of movement, transport, and portage. Orisá of the limit, the rule, and the transgression. Now in his domain, what had been Babalú Ayé's became his to command exclusively. He sat in the middle of the intersection, smoking a cigar. He gestured for Justo to come over and handed him a handful of raw coconut bits taken from the bundle. Again using signals, he instructed Justo to distribute them at the four corners to secure the crossroads. His immunity to the substances extended to those he deputized. Then he stood and proceeded to disperse the contents of the bundle, in all their impurity, horror, and revulsion, around the perimeter of the crossing.

Every crossroads is a portal, a potential point of contact between the living, the dead, and the santos-orisás, a point of contact between the painfully congealed present and the undetermined future.[1] Elégua established such a point, and into it he poured the illness and despair San Lázaro–Babalú Ayé had collected. Through the portal Elégua opened at the crossing, they were swept into the vast, amorphous flows of the dead that underwrite life itself. The dead, seething with energy, absorbed the danger. Left behind were but a few leaves and bits of cloth indistinguishable from the surrounding land. Elégua had no doubt that his work with the sacred waste had achieved righteous ends, and in conclusion he jumped up and danced his way back to the bembé. Before we could reenter the house, well water had to be tossed over our heads—a basic precaution to shake off any misfortune clinging to us, Elégua's helpers.

Two Changós had joined the feast. One was Boris, Roberto's illegitimate son. He looked enough like Roberto to be mistaken for him. He was a big man and an obvious mount for Changó given his reddish skin and projected masculinity. As far as anyone could remember, this was his first time being mounted by an orisá at a bembé in Sierra Morena. His aunts embraced his Changó and were delighted to receive the greetings of the orisá of thunder, sovereign of the drum. Their embrace was lasting and otherwise impossible in their everyday lives. His Changó was a little hesitant, which he tried to cloak with brusque movements and gestures. He was efficient in his exchanges with those gathered and quickly moved through the room greeting the chorus and attending with pantomime gestures to the special cases brought to him.

The other Changó was tiny. He mounted a little woman named Cléo, who was perhaps eighty years old. She was starting to show the frailty of her age. But with a red-and-white striped satin cap and a piece of red satin over her shoulders that Eulalia had provided, she was as credible a Changó as Boris. Cléo's Changó worked hard, spending careful time with those who approached her. She would take her hands and pull down on her cheeks below her eyes to emphasize that she was about to speak from a place of vision. Then she would take two fingers and point them above a person's head, to say that what was seen was from a great distance, in the sky or on the horizon. Her counsel was delivered in a thick *bozal* voice. Changó's advice is prized in situations of struggle and open conflict. On the back of this aged mount, who became ancestral before our eyes, the orisá of conflagrations was wise and gentle. His healing was widely sought.

Little Cléo was accompanied at the bembé by her sister, similarly octogenarian, maybe her twin. She was mounted by La Caridad–Ochún, sovereign over sweet delights, including romance and erotic intimacy. Mounted on such a steed, Ochún was poetry. What had that body felt in its day? What had it sought, without regret? What did it promise in its embrace of sensuality for the young? Lavish sensuality and erotic love—Ochún ruled over these things and extended them freely to those who sought her without shame. A length of yellow satin was placed over her shoulders, and she spent the next hour standing in place, swaying to the music and dispensing her powers to those who approached her. Changó and Ochún coincide in involved tales of romance, rivalry, and betrayal not unfamiliar to many of us gathered in the chorus. To have them present on such sweet steeds was a great event. The two sisters, mounted side by side, presided for more than an hour.

Just then, I was tapped on the shoulder. Next to me was a skinny man with sunburned olive-white skin, a farmer acquaintance from years back. He reached for my shoulder and brought his head in close, to talk over the din of the feast. "Oye Ramón," he said. The smell of alcohol was strong, so I pulled back, but he repeated himself, louder. "¡Oye Ramón! El bloqueo se acabó." He looked at me as seriously as he could with his eyes swimming. This was the most ridiculous thing I could have heard at that moment, that the embargo imposed by the United States on Cuba was over. I turned away from him, but he grabbed me, holding gently onto my arm. "It's over," he said. "We're friends now."

I looked at him.

"Obama and Raúl," he said, "like this," and touched the lengths of his index fingers together to show how close.

Two hours into the bembé, Zenón stopped singing and walked out to the backyard. He had just handled a tricky situation. A young woman had trouble managing the orisá that tried to mount her, or perhaps it was a *muerto oscuro,* one of the unformed, obscure dead. She writhed on the floor and yelled. The chorus did their best to ignore her. They had orisás to please with their voices and dance. After minutes she was subdued, and then José tried to sweep away whatever was mounting her, to no avail. The situation became annoying, and people started appealing to Zenón for relief. He ignored the struggling woman and focused on the orisás present in the house. Finally, when the situation grew intolerable, Zenón walked over to the helpless woman, sang directly at her, and easily cleared away whatever was mounted on her. The exhausted steed sat stunned in a chair. He asked for a little cold water to blow behind her ears, and he was done. Isidra pursued him straight out the door.

"I'm done!"

"You can't be done," she replied. "This is just getting going."

"This was supposed to be a little vigil, not a full-blown bembé. I'm tired."

"There are orisás mounted up in there! You can't leave them without music."

"My throat! I can't sing because of my throat," he said, extending a little plastic cup.

"What you need is Pica to keep you straight! Less than a year without her, and you've gotten spoiled."

"I do miss her at things like this," he said, with an almost rehearsed seriousness.

"Don't we all," said Isidra. "You have to do this on your own now, and I know that is not easy."

"What I was saying! Now you know what I'm worth."

"But I won't let you get drunk. First sign of drunkenness and I will personally escort you out!"

Zenón was back to singing when Caridad was mounted by Elégua. She was the mother of the young woman he had just cleared. Caridad was tall and fit. She was a longtime ally of Isidra's in the struggle with Zulia, a source of information and a channel for communications. Her steps were lovely, and her Elégua mounted up as she danced. Boby's Elégua had departed, and this left his red-and-black cap and crook available. Caridad's Elégua was a talker with a convincing "muzzled" [bozal] accent that people found especially attractive. Her santo-orisá was very direct, looked people in the eye, and in two or three words declaimed on situations they confronted.

Three hours into the impromptu bembé, Zenón switched the music. The drummers needed but a single word to know things had gone from "santo to Congo." The verses were shorter, and the "tongue" was Congo inflected, though predominantly Spanish. The ethos of this music is to communicate unmitigated potentials, such that forcefulness, even ferocity, are suggested. This is reflected in the drumming, which is more direct, and the dance, which is energetic and undecorated.

Caridad, who was mounted by Elégua, switched right along with the music. Without having her Elégua dismount, without "erasing," she changed straight into "Congo." The power she now bore was no longer Elégua, but it resembled him in its potentials. Elégua's cap was removed and his crook hung up, while a red sash was tied around a bicep to accent her physical strength. Cléo's Changó switched to Congo, while her sister's Ochún and Boris's Changó dismounted, leaving their steaming steeds to cool off in the backyard.

The Congo power that mounted Caridad set about protecting the house against ill will by way of a work at the door. Her work took some time and involved a variety of substances, including a candle, aguardiente, cascarilla chalk, and vines brought from the backyard. The chorus was thinner now, but those who remained closed around the working Congo as if to pick up power by simply being close. Zenón's calls urged her to proceed.

A "Congo" turn signals the intensification of a bembé. Congo-inspired forces push things out of their frames and routines. They burst out and ramble through stuck or stagnating situations, and those who need more than the santos-orisás can provide will remain to face the Congo dead. This requires some courage, because Congo powers can be brusque, and their counsel can lead down frightful paths. A house with the expertise and confidence to host the Congo powers could provide openings to otherwise irremediable situations. Congo turns are intense for those who join them, and the excitement of invoking such dangerous forces is often felt as joy.

But a Congo turn also marks the beginning of a bembé's end. Bembés are not meant to turn "back to santo." I only ever witnessed such a reversion at the Curve two years earlier, when the Indians were praised after Congo powers trashed the shrine for San Lázaro. In the case of bembés like those of Isidra and Lázaro M., the Congo turn is an invitation to turn things up and inside out, harder, more aggressive, extensive as well as intensive. It is jarring and more masculine. It is a call to spend what remains, to push it to the limit and beyond, be this your strength as a dancer, your endurance as a drummer, or your voice as a caller.

A feast with energy yet to give after a Congo turn will switch to rumba, and the musicians who want to keep going do so under the banner of having a good time at a remove from the fate-shaping powers a bembé generates. Or, in the case of bembés in Sierra Morena, people who want to keep going find another feast to join. Because Zenón did not attend Lázaro M.'s feast, he wanted a rumba to erupt right there and then But most everyone headed around the corner to Lázaro M.'s.

Isidra's little vigil erupted into a full-blown bembé, took a Congo turn, and eventually sputtered out. She had animal offerings for San Lázaro–Babalú Ayé and Mariana Congo. Boby, whose Elégua had dismounted before the Congo turn, remained behind to help his aunt with the discreet slaughter. San Lázaro–Babalú Ayé was fed using Celita's collection of river stones. He ate frizzled rooster. Only a handful of us were present. It wasn't until dawn that we were done, and Boby and I left to join his great-grandfather Lázaro's bembé.

Sunrise on December 17 and Lázaro M. was ninety-four years old. His family was gathered for his bembé to San Lázaro–Babalú Ayé. It was the best gift he could imagine. Boris, who mounted Changó the night before, caught me on my way in.

"Listen, *compadre,* is it true?"

"Do tell," I said. "You mean the stuff people are saying about the embargo, Obama, Raúl, and all that?"

"That too. But they say I was mounted by Changó at Celita's last night. Is that true?"

"It is. Your Changó was good."

"That is what my cousin says, but I don't remember a thing."

"The only thing that happened with your santo that you should know about is that no one took off your shoes for a long time. Changó probably wanted to be barefoot."

"I heard that. My cousin also says I didn't talk."

"Your Changó didn't talk, that is correct. But your Changó had good hand signs. Everyone understood you."

"My cousin says another Changó spoke to me. Is that true?"

"Cléo was mounted with Changó. I didn't see her Changó speak to yours."

"She told me that 'an orisá works through speech, not signs.' A good santo talks." Boris said this half asserting, half performing the realization of it.

"Your Changó was excellent. The chorus loved him, and he worked hard."

Lázaro M. sat on a simple chair in his kitchen. His party had been going all night but really picked up at daybreak when the people who left Celita's showed up. His Babalú Ayé stone, its attendant Elégua stone, and his little Catholic figurine of Lazarus the Beggar were on the ground before him. They were flanked by some bottles of aguardiente, of which he held a full glass. A plate of toasted corn kernels was near his feet. The stones and the figurine had been fed goat and roosters sometime earlier. Their heads and feathers adorned the scene. Three drummers were right behind him, where they could fit in that tiny house. The chorus crowded around. He called from the chair, and the response was vivacious.

Caridad, who a few hours before had been mounted by Elégua and then serially by one of the Congo dead, was mounted by Elégua again. She moved through the chorus and the surrounding onlookers in the backyard, the foyer, and the street. Lázaro's younger brother, himself in his late eighties, was mounted by Babalú Ayé. He was a little drunk, but his orisá was welcome, and the work he did was well received.

Eventually, Lázaro M., too, turned his feast to Congo. He was soon engaged in a playful back-and-forth with a younger man, perhaps in his fifties. Congo play often takes the form of callers competing in a display of knowledge, and they went back and forth trading Congo verses with the chorus responding to each. The point was to keep going, to know more calls and display more knowledge and cleverness, to outlast your rival. A repeated call was an admission of surrender, then another caller stepped in to continue the competition. Lázaro's calling was playful, sung with a smile on his face. There was never any question of who would prevail. Then Aneas, Pica's nephew, stepped in. His smile and demeanor were as joyful as Lázaro's, and I recalled the mischief he presided over when the Congos took apart the shrine at the Curve two years before. Lázaro and Aneas went back and forth, performing a sweet rivalry that elevated them both. Each of them played for fun but also for keeps, and the chorus and drummers egged them on. Their songs referenced Dahomey, slavery, and slave revolt, and with knowing irony they mocked white institutions, like slave ownership and the Catholic Church.

Lázaro called, "No cuero, no cuero / Allá Dahomey no cuero!"

We responded, "No cuero, no cuero / Allá Dahomey no cuero!"

Lázaro called, "No whip, no whip / There in Dahomey there is/was no whip!"

Aneas called, "Congo llama congo / como congo llama congo!"

We responded, "Congo llama congo / como congo llama congo!"

Aneas called, "A Congo calls a Congo / how Congos call Congos!"

Lázaro called, smiling, "Rezando estaba / Yo vine pa' tu fiesta!"

We responded, "Rezando estaba / Yo vine pa' tu fiesta!"

Lázaro called, "I was praying / but I came to your party instead!"

Aneas called, "Palo su-su, Palo rayaya / Yo quiero ver la conga que se llama siete saya!"

We responded, "Palo su-su, Palo rayaya / Yo quiero ver la conga que se llama siete saya!"

Aneas called, "Palo su-su, Palo rayaya / I want to see the conga they call 'seven skirts'!"

Lázaro called, "A la vuelta, a la vuelta / Caballo tumba el amo!"

The chorus responded, "A la vuelta, a la vuelta / Caballo tumba el amo!"

Lázaro called, smiling, "At the turn, at the turn / The horse will buck his master!"

Aneas kept up, and called, "Mañana es Domingo / Yo pongo mi corbata!"

The chorus replied, "Mañana es Domingo / Yo pongo mi corbata!"

Aneas called, "Tomorrow is Sunday / I'll put my tie on!"

In the midst of their encounter, Boby was mounted by a Congo power. The Congo that took him resembled his Elégua, but in excess. He threw his limbs against their sockets and spun too fast in the space he had. He arched his back and extended his chest forward, threw his head back, and cried. His eyes rolled back in his head and tears streamed down his cheeks. He strode forward, then back, spun, and shouted. Lázaro and Aneas kept singing. The Congo power groaned and threw his mount down, grinding his face into the ground. It took a group of his kinsmen to subdue him.

The mounting was consistent with the Congo turn. When situations are irreversible, when forces are stacked high against one such that change is impossible, when horizons are closed, then Congo powers come into play. They extend where the orisás are reserved, they spill out where the orisás are contained. They unleash forces and overload situations, forcing them to change. Congo forces always seek an outside beyond the constraints of a given situation.

The first "situation" they bring their forces to bear upon is the bodies of their steeds. The human body, its flesh and bones and skin, is not exempt from this push. In fact, it is the matter immediately to hand on which a Congo power will test its strength. If it must, a Congo will tear apart the body of its mount in its search for the outside. The disregard Congo powers show for the bodies of their mounts is a disregard for what family, and society, and history have to say about how a body should be ordered, constrained, and cared for. It is a disregard that seeks a future when flesh might be organized into something other than "a body" that can be enslaved, contracted, indebted, and otherwise bound to labor. A future where flesh will be less easily shackled to regimes of labor, be these forced, coerced, or poorly compensated by a nation-state. A future when flesh is unrestrained, expressive, and capable of immediate discharges.

Congo powers seek an outside to society too. Their insurrection at the boundaries of social conventions is often staged as play. Their path out is one of mischief, subversion, and unflinching tests of strength against those forces that would contain them. They are contemptuous of the reassurance that social limits provide. They run away from regimes of all sorts and aim for the forest [*el monte*], where they become yet more vital and decisive in the company of the dead that throng there.

With the help of kinsmen attendants, Boby's Congo power was eventually composed enough to move through the crowd. "His Congo" worked with those in the chorus brave enough, or desperate enough, to seek the abrupt and frightful solutions that Congos will propose. Lázaro M. and Aneas continued until Boby's Congo burned himself out. They were the last two standing, and that playful bout, too, soon burned out. The chorus lost dimension and eventually died out.

Lázaro M.'s feast was tight and compact and burned bright. The physical proximity into which it stacked its emotional and artistic potentials generated significant social light and heat. At his ninety-four years, he looked forward, not behind. His ninety-four years were praised, but it was the days ahead for which his bembé prepared. He overflowed with life and led his feast in overflowing, in letting go of complaints, resentments, and investments. As "historical" as the bembé was with its cultivation of African-inspired potentials and invocation of ancestral virtues, including the struggle for dignity against a slave regime, it was always forward looking. The bembé extended eagerly toward the future when Lázaro sought health, life, and pleasure for himself and those gathered. The orisás and the Congo dead were invited to help him prepare for and welcome the future, which extended no further than a year, when San Lázaro–Babalú Ayé, and Lázaro M.'s birthday, would be celebrated again.

Word later on the morning of the 17th was that the bembé at the Curve was a hit and that Zulia's was a flop. Bembés for San Lázaro–Babalú Ayé were still expected later that afternoon and into the night, back at the Curve and other places. I ended up at one in the tiny living room of a house that backed onto Cucusa's yard, a house that had been divided and subdivided over the course of the revolution. Such division was the future of Cucusa's house. The party was more of a youth gathering than a scene set to praise the orisás. There were three drummers, though, and the music was more like Lázaro M.'s than the Curve's. The chorus and drummers addressed themselves to a painting of Lazarus the Beggar on one wall of the room. A few sheet cakes and a bowl of roasted corn kernels rested on the floor there. It overflowed with young people who danced untidily but effusively. Couples danced. The host, Angela, was giddy. In the midst of it all was Zenón, calling song after song, and he was not disappointed in the response from his chorus.

Iván, who mingled outside the party, said he would eventually take a turn at the caja. "This party is not what Cucusa's used to be, or even a shadow of it. I imagine you think it is bad. This time of year used to be my happiness. You can't imagine how I waited for it and enjoyed it. What a shame." He looked at me wondering if I could understand, then his manner became more upbeat. "I'm a better percussionist than when I tried to teach you. Will you stay for a while?"

I was sitting on my bed back at Celita's, trying to fight off sleep and write in my journal. The house was quiet, and the kids were laughing in the living room. They took aunt Isidra's drums and started a mula beat, which was met by Guillermo on the requinto. Some kids from next door were over, and they took up a song for Yemayá. By the time I got up, they were having a grand time, mimicking their elders in their bembé songs and dancing, impishly mocking them. Mericelia, the ringleader, was really hamming up the arm movements of Yemayá. Their laughter was excited. She was a fresh little kid, so she let a wave run from her shoulders to her toes as she teetered back on one foot, arm thrown across her eyes, only to be faithfully caught by those dancing with her. Her simulation of Yemayá taking her mount was met with an uproarious response. The adults chased them off.

Later I commented to Mericelia that her Yemayá was almost believable.

"That wasn't Yemayá," she said, teasing me for my ignorance but also a little disappointed. "That was Oyá." It was the santo-orisá Celita said she had preference for, the sovereign of harbinger winds and tumult. "I guess I wasn't that good," she said thoughtfully.

An hour before we were to leave for Havana, Isidra launched a little expedition to the bend in the river. She had a bundled-up soup bowl meant as a meal for La Corua.

"When I was little girl," she said as we stood by the riverside, "I once came here early on the 17th with Pica, who was mounted by Oyá."

We lit a candle on a stone by the shore, and without more than a few calls of her favorite Yemayá war song, Isidra sent the bowl spinning into the pool. It sank quickly.

"She was waiting for it," she said.

Our departure was imminent. Isidra's disposition toward Celita was softer now, though hardly sentimental. Her goodbye from Eulalia was perfunctory.

She was moving on. She thanked no one and rather expected gratitude as we took our leave.

The house for which she had worked so hard remained closed to her. Her brothers were scattered and disconnected. Pica and María were dead, and would-be allies, like Gonzalo and Iván, no longer spoke to her. Zenón was her last resource, along with Celita and José, who by themselves could throw a formidable bembé. But Cucusa's feast was now usurped by many pretenders, some old, some new. She spent the visit in contemptible exile, but she left for Havana confident that her struggle for Cucusa's feast was righteous, and that we had been successful, despite falling short, in advancing her cause. She was pleased.

EPILOGUE

———

2018

RECOVERY

ON SEPTEMBER 9, 2017, THE DAY AFTER SIERRA MORENA'S many bembés for La Caridad–Ochún, Oyá brought her wrath. Hurricane Irma came ashore as a Category 5 storm just to the east of Sagua la Grande. It lumbered west, grinding the coastline as it added the houses of Sierra Morena to its deadly mill of roof tiles, fence posts, and treetops. Rescuers fought their way down the North Circuit for more than a week to reach Sierra Morena and the towns beyond. It was a monstrous storm, among the worst in Cuba's awe-inspiring history of such events.

A year later, when I returned for the first time since 2014, I expected to find things still in ruins. I expected Irma to be all anyone wanted to talk about, and I was prepared for the visit to be largely about the storm and its aftermath. Celita and José lost the roof of their house and everything they owned, just like many of their neighbors. Fifteen months later they were still waiting for pieces of roof to be delivered by the revolutionary recovery effort. But they were remarkably unfazed.

"We didn't have anything in the first place," said Celita with a comic expression. I wondered if her smile and the lines in her eyes wouldn't turn to grief in an instant, so I listened more than probed.

José was even more dismissive of the devastation. "Once we get the roof back on, we'll be back where we started—nowhere." Fishermen managed to shelter some of their boats in the surrounding mangroves, and a few came through in salvageable condition. José recruited family in Havana to help him buy one of these. Keeping his boat in working order was all he wanted to talk about in 2018.

The rest of town appeared in remarkably good shape—shabby and run down but hardly worse than in 2014. Two changes stood out: The bar down the street from Cucusa's house had grown in importance as a place to gather and socialize, especially for the older set. It was there that I ran into Lázaro M. and a sizable crowd of his male kin preparing to celebrate his ninety-eighth birthday. The other was that younger people, like Guillermo and Mericelia, converged on the town center, where a Wi-Fi hot spot had recently been installed by the government. True, to access the internet you needed hard currency, and young people had little of that. Still, the hot spot signaled gradual changes underway since my 2014 visit, but perceived anew since the death of Fidel Castro in 2016. That death was awaited and prepared for, and his passing was without political fallout. In Sierra Morena the revolution trundled onward, except now everyone seemed to at least have a cell phone, if not a connection.

Isidra had victories she was eager to show off, and she could not be bothered with too much talk about the storm or changes since Fidel's death. Most important was that over a few years, Yamilet had been moving toward a reconciliation. By 2015, Isidra accepted her entreaties and forged an alliance with her once life-and-death antagonist.

"Children," said Isidra. "Children will drive you to face the truth time and again. Yamilet's oldest is in a delicate situation with his health. She has put him through the course of revolutionary medicine to no avail. Only Babalú Ayé can help him now. Skin condition—his specialty. That is why she has come around. Where is Babalú Ayé going to respond to your pleas better than here, at Cucusa's altar?"

With Yamilet on Isidra's side, Zulia was soon at her wit's end. Eulalia had proceeded with the plan to have the revolutionary housing authorities split the house, but in 2016, Zulia preempted the process. Zulia had Cucusa's house literally cut down the middle. The half she claimed was demolished and replaced by a drab cement structure. Both Zulia's new house and what remained of Cucusa's once stately red-tile, clapboard ranch house survived the storm. They stood side-by-side, with a narrow passage between them. Isidra was elated, even in defeat.

"Look at the bunker she built herself. Ten years of lies are revealed to the whole town. She never cared about Cucusa, her santos, or her bembé. All she wanted was a house. Selfish. They say the things you make reflect your soul. Now we see what is inside Zulia. A paranoid, selfish, sick individual. Look at the fence, the way it hugs the house, even the veranda. If you had a lot half the size of Cucusa's grand old house, would you have built yourself a cage?"

The half Isidra and Eulalia now occupied was what had once been the room devoted to Cucusa's santos. Zulia had not spared it rough handling in the course of the demolition, and it badly needed attention to the roof. Back of the house, Zulia had kept the well; Isidra and Eulalia got the latrine. A fence separated the two yards.

"We were able to legally enter at the end of 2016. When we broke the seals, we found she had abandoned Cucusa's santos in the part of house she had bricked off, so they were waiting for us. Then she left us the whole altar except for one of the two figurines of San Lázaro. She took the one that was prettier, not the one with the longer history. Ignorance incarnate. In 2017 we were able to have a bembé for San Lázaro, but imagine how barebones—half a house with no electricity three months after the storm."

Eulalia was now at her side, the titular owner of the house. The prosecutor who had helped her with a brief in 2014 was also with her, as was one of her Palo godchildren who was a proficient carpenter. Celita and Yamilet worked as a pair ready to help their aunts as they prepared the bembé. Then there was me, the anthropologist she kept on hand to document her "struggle and traditions." Missing were her brothers.

We organized the bembé for San Lázaro–Babalú Ayé in record time. Two goats were needed, she would skip the ram for Changó this year, and the rest of the orisás would be fed roosters and chickens. There was also Mariana Congo. Isidra was remarkably quick in gathering the animals she needed, with the exception of the young goat for Elégua. Typical to have Elégua impede your progress. Eventually, the little goat was offered by Iván, the last child Cucusa raised and one of Sierra Morena's superb drummers. Isidra had accused him of betrayal for a decade. That offering was the beginning of a reconciliation that would conclude with Iván and Gonzalo leading the drums at the bembé for San Lázaro that year. Zenón sang at the opening and also for the bembé after lunch on the 17th. With the three of them under her roof, Isidra could claim to have the tightest musicians of any bembé in town. It was a significant victory over the upstarts, especially the pretenders at the Curve.

By Isidra's all-or-nothing standards of years past, there was much to want, like all of Cucusa's house and having Zulia routed back to Corralillo. But, given the obstacles to surmount, the bembé on December 17, 2018, was a success. Many people attended, including friends of Cucusa's who had stayed away from Zulia's attempts at a feast over the years. The chorus was solid if not rousing, and the sovereign santos-orisás mounted up in abundance.

Yemayá, La Caridad–Ochún, Oyá, and Changó all made appearances on able mounts. Elégua came atop Boby, who had come to Sierra Morena for his great-grandfather Lázaro M.'s bembé and birthday party. He was pleased to dance and offer himself as a mount at Cucusa's house, especially because his great-grandfather had promised Babalú Ayé he would "keep things quiet" that year.

San Lázaro mounted Celita near the end of the bembé on the 17th. Anyone in the chorus who needed him was touched by his healing hands. Mothers brought their children to be cleansed by his burlap and purple satin shrouds. Finally, the sovereign of affliction and healing turned his attention to Yamilet's eldest.

"Little by little," said Isidra as we roared back to Havana on the bed of a charcoal truck she had arranged with the help of the prosecutor. "You don't see orisás in Havana work like Celita's Babalú Ayé. You can see our accomplishments. You see the work that yet needs doing. Yamilet had to come my way, of that I was certain. Zulia will go her way too. None of this is destiny. It is hard work. That and selfless devotion—to Cucusa, to Chacha, Ma' Isidra, and Kimbito, to Loreto, and to their santos and to the orisás. You say you need an ending for your book? Do it with these words: Oyá may be the wind, but Yemayá is the sea."

NOTES

PREFACE

1. My interpretation of santo-orisá praise draws on the work of the French philosopher Gilles Deleuze. Deleuze draws on Nietzsche, also important to my interpretation, to provide avenues into writing about drama and sensation, two important aspects of santo-orisá praise. Gilles Deleuze, *Nietzsche and Philosophy,* trans. Hugh Tomlinson (New York: Columbia University Press, 2006).

2. This insight into religious life is owed to Talal Asad's work in *Genealogies of Religion* (Baltimore: Johns Hopkins University Press, 1993), itself part of a conceptual genealogy that travels through Michel Foucault back to Nietzsche.

3. Throughout this text, I have grappled with the utility and nonutility of bembé praise scenes. This concern is inculcated by the work of Georges Bataille, and I credit it with providing me with many insights into religious and social life. Georges Bataille, *Theory of Religion,* trans. Robert Hurley (New York: Zone Books, 1989).

4. Todd Ramón Ochoa, *Society of the Dead: Quita Manaquita and Palo Praise in Cuba* (Berkeley: University of California Press, 2010); Kristina Wirtz, *Ritual, Discourse, and Community in Cuban Santería: Speaking the Sacred World* (Gainesville: University Press of Florida, 2007); Jalane Schmitt, *Cachita's Streets: The Virgin of Charity, Race, and Revolution in Cuba* (Durham, NC: Duke University Press, 2015).

5. Readers familiar with my previous work may have noticed that I am here using the term *Congo,* with a *C* rather than a *K.* In general, scholars who treat the language, resources, and inspirations of BaKongo people in the New World use the term *Kongo* to qualify or describe them. This is done to distinguish the people from the geographic entities known as Congo and the Democratic Republic of Congo. But the people who informed this book and who taught me so much use the term *Congo.* I find it forced to translate the Spanish *Congo* to the English *Kongo* for the sake of scholarly convention. This is especially the case when the term *Congo* appears in dialogue. For the sake of this book, I will stick with *Congo* and hope that

in future writing it will be easier to adhere to the scholarly use of *Kongo,* with which I agree.

6. Ochoa, *Society of the Dead,* 10.

1. THE RING AND THE ALTAR

1. For a synopsis of major storms in Cuba from 1750 to 1958, see Luis Enrique Ramos Guadalupe, *Huracanes: Desastres naturales en Cuba* (Havana: Editorial Academia, 2009).

2. Santa Bárbara and Changó share affinities on the West African side of the Cuban cosmos. For Changó's place of honor in West African–inspired praise in Cuba, see David H. Brown, *Santería Enthroned: Art, Ritual, and Innovation in an Afro-Cuban Religion* (Chicago: University of Chicago Press, 2003), 191–95.

3. Samuel Decalo, *A Historical Dictionary of Benin* (Metuchen, NJ: Scarecrow Press, 1987).

4. Laird W. Bergad, Fe Iglesias García, and María del Carmen Barcia, *The Cuban Slave Market, 1790–1880* (Cambridge: Cambridge University Press, 1995). See also the Slave Voyages database, https://www.slavevoyages.org/voyage/database.

5. Brown, *Santería Enthroned,* 15.

6. Bergad, Iglesias García, and Carmen Barcia, *Cuban Slave Market.*

2. LA SOCIEDAD AFRICANA, 1880–1940

1. Ramos Guadalupe, *Huracanes,* 95–96.

2. For a history of slave emancipation in Cuba and the *patronato* system, see Rebecca J. Scott, *Slave Emancipation in Cuba: The Transition to Free Labor, 1860–1899* (Princeton, NJ: Princeton University Press, 1985), 139–41.

3. Aline Helg, *Our Rightful Share: The Afro-Cuban Struggle for Equality, 1886–1912* (Chapel Hill: University of North Carolina Press, 1995), 193–226.

4. Helg, *Our Rightful Share,* 107–16.

5. For a sustained reflection on gender performance in African-inspired praise in Brazil, Cuba, and Haiti, see Roberto Strongman, *Queering Black Atlantic Religions: Transcorporeality in Candomblé, Santería, and Vodou* (Durham, NC: Duke University Press, 2019).

6. For a comprehensive study of La Virgen de la Caridad del Cobre, see Schmitt, *Cachita's Streets.*

4. 1999: RETURN

1. Lydia Cabrera, *La laguna sagrada de San Joaquín* (Madrid: Ediciones Madrid, 1973). See also Hippolyte Brice Sogbossi, *La tradición Ewé-Fon en Cuba: Con-*

tribución al estudio de la tradición Ewé-Fon (Arará) en los pueblos de Jovellanos, Perico y Agramonte, Cuba (Havana: Fundación Fernando Ortíz, 1998).

2. Sogbossi, La tradición Ewé-Fon en Cuba. See also David Brown, Santería Enthroned (Chicago: University of Chicago Press, 2003), 74, 77, 141, 320n35.

7. SLAUGHTER

1. For a reflection on human attitudes toward ingestion, see Georges Bataille, Theory of Religion, trans. Robert Hurley (New York: Zone Books, 1989), 39–40.

2. An excellent handling of food, cooking, and cuisine can be found in Elizabeth Pérez, Religion in the Kitchen: Cooking, Talking, and the Making of Black Atlantic Traditions (New York: New York University Press), 2016.

3. For ritual identification between the animal sacrificed and the deity sacrificed to, see Marcel Mauss and Henri Hubert, Sacrifice, Its Nature and Functions, trans. W. D. Halls (Chicago: University of Chicago Press, 1981), 31–33.

8. A BEMBÉ FOR SAN LÁZARO–BABALÚ AYÉ

1. I am reminded of the phenomenon of simultaneous attraction and repulsion lodged at the heart of sacred experience, and this is described by Bataille and Deren: Georges Bataille, "Attraction and Repulsion I: Tropisms, Sexuality, Laughter and Tears," in The College of Sociology, 1937–1939, ed. Denis Hollier (Minneapolis: University of Minnesota Press, 1988), 103–12; Bataille, "Attraction and Repulsion II: Social Structure," in College of Sociology, 1937–1939, 113–24; Maya Deren, Divine Horsemen: The Living Gods of Haiti (Kingston, NY: McPherson, 1983), 247–62.

2. Exemplary in this regard are Kristina Wirtz's two ethnographies based in Cuba's eastern city of Santiago de Cuba: Ritual, Discourse, and Community in Cuban Santería and Performing Afro-Cuba: Image, Voice, Spectacle in the Making of Race and History (Chicago: University of Chicago Press, 2014).

9. 2005: LOSS

1. Ochoa, Society of the Dead, 21–40.

10. A HOLE TO FILL

1. Antonin Artaud, The Theater and Its Double, trans. Mary Caroline Richards (New York: Grove Press), 1958.

2. Artaud was an early theorist of affect, following Nietzsche. Their interest in affect, affectation, and being affected was elaborated later by Gilles Deleuze and Félix Guattari. For example, Gilles Deleuze and Félix Guattari, *A Thousand Plateaus: Capitalism and Schizophrenia,* trans. Brian Massumi (Minneapolis: University of Minnesota Press, 1987), 158–60.

14. 2009: DECEIT

1. Ochoa, *Society of the Dead,* 279n9.
2. For Congo themes in the New World, see Robert Farris Thompson, *Flash of the Spirit: African and Afro-American Art and Philosophy* (New York: Vintage Books, 1984), 103–11.

15. VOICES OF THE DEAD

1. Diana Espirito Santo, *Developing the Dead: Mediumship and Selfhood in Cuban Espiritismo* (Gainesville: University Press of Florida, 2016), 210–11.
2. For the island-wide adoration of Lazarus the Beggar, which is epitomized in the town of El Rincón on Havana's western fringe, see Laciel Zamora, *El culto a San Lázaro en Cuba* (Havana: Fundación Fernando Ortíz, 2000); Eduardo M. Bernal Alonso, *Rincón y la peregrinación de San Lázaro: Raíces de una centenaria tradición cubana* (Havana: Editorial José Martí, 2011).

16. 2012: PROHIBITION

1. Scholarship on *el paquete* and the informal circulation of digital media in Cuba has been emerging over the last decade. Ted A. Henken, "Cuba's Digital Millennials: Independent Digital Media and Civil Society on the Island of the Disconnected," *Social Research: An International Quarterly* 84, no. 2 (Summer 2017): 429–56; Anna Cristina Pertierra, "If They Show *Prison Break* in the United States on a Wednesday, by Thursday It Is Here: Mobile Media Networks in Twenty-First Century Cuba," *Television and New Media* 13, no. 5 (September 2012): 399–414.

18. TWO BEMBÉS

1. Espirito Santo, *Developing the Dead,* 181–88. See also Michael T. Taussig, *The Magic of the State* (New York: Routledge, 1997), 33–40.

19. 2014: DESPAIR

1. Ochoa, *Society of the Dead,* 10–12.

20. SOVEREIGNS OF AFFLICTION

1. Thompson, *Flash of the Spirit,* 110.

BIBLIOGRAPHY

Artaud, Antonin. *The Theater and Its Double.* Translated by Mary Caroline Richards. New York: Grove Press, 1958.

Asad, Talal. *Genealogies of Religion.* Baltimore: Johns Hopkins University Press, 1993.

Bataille, Georges. "Attraction and Repulsion I: Tropisms, Sexuality, Laughter and Tears." In *The College of Sociology, 1937–1939,* edited by Denis Hollier, translated by Betsy Wing, 103–12. Minneapolis: University of Minnesota Pess, 1988.

———. "Attraction and Repulsion II: Social Structure." In *The College of Sociology, 1937–1939,* ed. Denis Hollier, translated by Betsy Wing, 113–24. Minneapolis: University of Minnesota Pess, 1988.

———. *Theory of Religion.* Translated by Robert Hurley. New York: Zone Books, 1989.

Bergad, Laird W., Fe Iglesias García, and María del Carmen Barcia. *The Cuban Slave Market, 1790–1880.* Cambridge: Cambridge University Press, 1995.

Bernal Alonso, Eduardo M. *Rincón y la peregrinación de San Lázaro: Raíces de una centenaria tradición cubana.* Havana: Editorial José Martí, 2011.

Brown, David H. *Santería Enthroned: Art, Ritual, and Innovation in an Afro-Cuban Religion.* Chicago: University of Chicago Press, 2003.

Cabrera, Lydia. *La laguna sagrada de San Joaquín.* Madrid: Ediciones Madrid, 1973.

Decalo, Samuel. *A Historical Dictionary of Benin.* Metuchen, NJ: Scarecrow Press, 1987.

Deleuze, Gilles. *Nietzsche and Philosophy.* Translated by Hugh Tomlinson. New York: Columbia University Press, 2006.

Deleuze, Gilles, and Félix Guattari. *A Thousand Plateaus: Capitalism and Schizophrenia.* Translated by Brian Massumi. Minneapolis: University of Minnesota Press, 1987.

Deren, Maya. *Divine Horsemen: The Living Gods of Haiti.* Kingston, NY: McPherson, 1983.

Espirito Santo, Diana. *Developing the Dead: Mediumship and Selfhood in Cuban Espiritismo.* Gainesville: University Press of Florida, 2016.

Helg, Aline. *Our Rightful Share: The Afro-Cuban Struggle for Equality, 1886–1912.* Chapel Hill: University of North Carolina Press, 1995.

Henken, Ted A. "Cuba's Digital Millennials: Independent Digital Media and Civil Society on the Island of the Disconnected." *Social Research: An International Quarterly* 84, no. 2 (Summer 2017): 429–56.

Mauss, Marcel, and Henri Hubert. *Sacrifice, Its Nature and Functions.* Translated by W.D. Halls. Chicago: University of Chicago Press, 1981.

Ochoa, Todd Ramón. *Society of the Dead: Quita Manaquita and Palo Praise in Cuba.* Berkeley: University of California Press, 2010.

Pérez, Elizabeth. *Religion in the Kitchen: Cooking, Talking, and the Making of Black Atlantic Traditions.* New York: New York University Press, 2016.

Pertierra, Anna Cristina. "If They Show *Prison Break* in the United States on a Wednesday, by Thursday It Is Here: Mobile Media Networks in Twenty-First Century Cuba." *Television and New Media* 13, no. 5 (September 2012): 399–414.

Ramos Guadalupe, Luis Enrique. *Huracanes: Desastres naturales en Cuba.* Havana: Editorial Academia, 2009.

Schmitt, Jalane. *Cachita's Streets: The Virgin of Charity, Race, and Revolution in Cuba.* Durham, NC: Duke University Press, 2015.

Scott, Rebecca J. *Slave Emancipation in Cuba: The Transition to Free Labor, 1860–1899.* Princeton, NJ: Princeton University Press, 1985.

Slave Voyages database. www.slavevoyages.org/voyage/database.

Sogbossi, Hippolyte Brice. *La tradición Ewé-Fon en Cuba: Contribución al estudio de la tradición Ewé-Fon (Arará) en los pueblos de Jovellanos, Perico y Agramonte, Cuba.* Havana: Fundación Fernando Ortíz, 1998.

Strongman, Roberto. *Queering Black Atlantic Religions: Transcorporeality in Candomblé, Santería, and Vodou.* Durham, NC: Duke University Press, 2019.

Taussig, Michael T. *The Magic of the State.* New York: Routledge, 1997.

Thompson, Robert Farris. *Flash of the Spirit: African and Afro-American Art and Philosophy.* New York: Vintage Books, 1984.

Wirtz, Kristina. *Performing Afro-Cuba: Image, Voice, Spectacle in the Making of Race and History.* Chicago: University of Chicago Press, 2014.

———. *Ritual, Discourse, and Community in Cuban Santería: Speaking the Sacred World.* Gainesville: University Press of Florida, 2007.

Zamora, Laciel. *El culto a San Lázaro en Cuba.* Havana: Fundacion Fernando Ortíz, 2000.

INDEX

Abuelito José María, 21

affect, xvii, xviii, 302n2

affliction. *See* healing work; San Lázaro-Babulú Ayé

African-inspired praise. *See* Arará cultural resources; Congo-inspired praise; Palo (Congo-inspired praise)

aguardiente, 6–7, 11, 56, 78–79, 85, 87, 96, 104, 114, 139–40, 147, 149, 186–87, 194, 279, 288

Albertina (Chucha) Portilla (Ma' Isidra's daughter), 25–26, 32, 34, 39, 47

Allada, 9–10, 14, 52

alms, 140

altars (to San Lázaro), 7–9, 52–53, 62–65, 79–80, 90–91, 98–99, 110–11, 150–51, 164, 196, 243, 250–51, 280

Angola, 120–21, 127, 134–35

animal offerings, 90–100, 126, 146, 150, 214–15, 245, 251

Ará Oco, 52, 257, 270

Arará cultural resources, xvii, 9–10, 52, 240–42, 253, 257–58. See also *bembés;* Congo-inspired praise; praise; *santos-orisás*

Artaud, Antonin, 139, 301n1, 302n2

Asad, Talal, 299n2

Asojano, 11. *See also* Babalú Ayé; San Lázaro-Babulú Ayé

atheism, xv–xvi, 38, 44–47, 86, 105, 128–29, 162–67, 204–5, 239

babalao, 77–78, 210–11

Babalú Ayé, 281–82; alternative names of, 11; calls for, 108–11, 152–53, 209; feeding the earth for, 73, 275; gifts for, 91, 142, 207–8, 240–41, 275; healing work of, 175, 181, 191, 209–11, 214, 249, 254, 281, 295; mounts for, 108–9, 152–55, 247–49, 251, 280–81; promises to, 55, 59, 199, 237, 279, 297; sovereign domains of, 9–10, 36–38, 103, 120, 128, 132, 281–83; speech of, 212, 247, 254, 283; stones of, 98, 209, 288. *See also* San Lázaro-Babulú Ayé

BaKongo, 14, 16, 299n5. *See also* Congo-inspired praise

Bataille, Georges, 299n3

Batalla (substance), 56, 68, 122, 271

Batista, Fulgencio, 18–20, 42–43

Bay of Pigs invasion, 43

becoming, 85, 131, 148–49, 173, 245

bembés: breaking open of, 83–89, 101, 142–50, 176, 244; calling praise songs and, 84–87, 94–99, 101–5, 108–10, 112, 128, 140, 142–50, 162, 176–77, 194–95, 201, 257–59, 289–90; choruses of, 15, 29–32, 38, 79, 84–90, 101–5, 108–14, 142–58, 172–81, 195, 200–201, 206–14, 244–59, 267–71, 280–92, 296–97; definition of, 10–11; drumming and, 38–39, 156–59, 244; feasting and, 55–56, 62, 76–82, 90–100, 249–51; healing and, 26, 32–34, 62, 104–11, 120, 132, 152–55, 173–81, 195–99, 214, 234–35, 245–59, 281–84, 297; the hole for, 77–79, 137–40, 145, 176, 187–89, 203;

bembés (continued)
   lengua and, 87, 146, 211, 240–42, 286;
      local styles of, 201, 256–58, 269–70;
      policing of, xvi, 18–19; as praise element,
      xiii–xiv, xv, xv–xvii, xvii; preparations
      for, 57–66, 68–70, 76–82, 120–23,
      131–41, 164–65, 175–76, 185, 263–64,
      273–76, 296–97; Cuban Revolution
      and, 43–47, 166–67; slaughters and,
      90–100, 126, 146, 150, 214–15, 245, 251;
      Sociedad Africana and, 13–33. *See also*
      healing work; praise; *santos-orisás*
black markets, 45–46, 51–52, 56–57, 59–60,
   187, 192, 219–20, 223–24, 264–65, 268
Brazil, 10
bundles (Congo-inspired substances), 24,
   34, 67, 98–99, 122, 150, 179, 189, 193–94,
   196–97, 214–15, 266–67, 296

Cairo, Guadalupe, 13, 17
Cairo, Tomasa, 11. *See also* Chacha
caja (drum), 38, 89, 93–94, 114, 142, 157–58,
   206, 253
campana (bell), 158
Castro, Fidel, 7, 42–43, 80, 156–57, 181,
   217–18, 239, 295
Castro, Raúl, 42, 217–18, 285–86
Catholicism: Cuban Revolution and,
   44–45; saints of, xiii
CDRs (Committees for the Defense of the
   Revolution), 43–45, 53–54, 74, 266
Centella, 113
Central African cultural resources, xvi,
   xvii, 16. *See also* Arará cultural
   resources; Congo-inspired praise
Chacha (Tomasa Cairo), 232; adopted
   daughters of, 33; Cucusa's feast and, 30;
   death of, 47, 136; La Virgen de la Caridad and, 27, 166; San Lázaro-Babalú
   Ayé's *bembé* and, 36; shadow of, 66;
   Sociedad Africana and, 13–33, 36, 38–39,
   42, 165–66, 234, 244; status of, in Sierra
   Morena, 11, 25
chance, 138–39, 253. *See also* Elégua *(orisá)*;
   numbers game
Changó *(orisá):* animals for, 57, 62, 81–82,
   93, 98, 100, 105, 113–14, 176, 179, 216,
   245–46, 296; *bembé* appearances of, 26,

128; calls for, 102, 104, 245; mounts for,
   15, 17, 19–20, 23, 33, 36, 38–40, 62,
   87–89, 102–5, 114–15, 128–29, 140,
   151–52, 165–66, 173–74, 178, 180, 195,
   206, 246–47, 258, 284, 287–88; Ogún
   and, 29–30; sovereign domains of, 15,
   18–19, 36, 38, 65, 87–89, 102–4, 173–74,
   300n2
charada china, 5. *See also* gambling
China, 161–63
choruses, 15, 29–32, 38, 79, 84–90, 101–5,
   108–14, 142–58, 172–81, 195, 200–201,
   206–14, 244–59, 267–71, 280–92,
   296–97
Chucha Portilla. *See* Albertina (Chucha)
   Portilla
cleansing, 26, 69, 79, 108, 136–39, 153, 272,
   281–82, 297. *See also* animal offerings;
   San Lázaro-Babulú Ayé; *santos-orisás*
Cléo, 284, 287–88
cockfighting, 5–7, 11, 38, 41, 56, 77
"color" (and Cuban racialization), 5–6,
   27–28, 62–63, 74, 238, 243–44, 254,
   270. *See also* Cuba
Comisión Africana, 32, 38–39, 47
Communist Party of Cuba, 44, 47, 61
company cars, 4
Congo (people), 13–14, 16, 299n5. *See also*
   BaKongo
Congo (region), 13–14
Congo-inspired praise, xvii, 17–18, 23–24,
   34, 56, 66–67, 75–76, 113, 174–75,
   188–91, 193, 214–15, 227–28, 236,
   248–51, 258, 266–67, 271–72, 287, 290,
   299n5. *See also* Ocha-Santería; Palo
Congo substances, 16, 65–68, 188–89, 271,
   284, 287. *See also* bundles (Congo-
   inspired substances); *prendas;* stones
   (Congo-inspired substances)
Conjunto Folklórico de Cuba, 44
containment, 290–91
coolness (as characteristic), 23–25, 69–70,
   78, 139, 149
Corralillo, 4–7, 15, 37, 52–56, 77, 115, 121, 168,
   191–93, 221–26, 233, 267, 273–78, 296
Creole, 13, 17, 27, 75. *See also* "color" (and
   Cuban racialization); Cuba
Creole cuisine, 91, 150

crossing and crossroads, 31, 36, 68, 84–86, 95–97, 129, 172–73, 212, 282–84

Cuatro Vientos (Palo power), 56, 68, 75–76

Cuba: African heritage in, xiii, xvi–xvii, 9–10, 12–15, 18–21, 27, 34, 44–45, 87; Angolan intervention of, 120–21, 127, 134–35; "black decade" of, 45–46; black markets in, 45–46, 51–52, 56–57, 59–60, 187, 192, 219–20, 223–24, 264–65, 268; Chinese trade with, 160–63; currency in, xv–xvi, 163, 188, 219, 227, 264; *embarcaciónes* from, 125, 224–25, 268–69; independence of, 20–22, 27; masculinity in, 156–57, 174; numbers game in, 5, 56, 75, 171, 219–20, 264; property and inheritance in, 3–11, 40–41, 48, 53–54, 74–75, 115–16, 185–86, 190–94, 214–15, 220–27, 230–31, 265–66, 272–75; racialization in, 5–6, 14–15, 18, 21, 27–28, 44–45, 63, 74, 238, 243–44, 254, 270; Raúl Castro's succession and, 218–19, 225–27; revolution in, xv–xvi, xvi, 7, 42–43, 71–73, 105; San Lázaro in, 8–9; slavery in, 9–10, 12–14, 20–22, 34, 52, 87; Soviet support for, 45, 72, 120–21, 160, 219, 221–24, 263–64; Special Period of, 55, 162; tourism and, 46, 120–21, 123, 127–28, 141, 149–50, 188, 224, 268–69; U.S. embargo on, 285–96. *See also* CDRs (Committees for the Defense of the Revolution); *specific ministries*

Cuban Revolution: atheism of, 38, 44–45, 47, 86, 105, 128–29, 162, 166–67, 204–5, 239; Castro's persona and, 156–57, 218–19; CDRs and, 43–45, 53–54, 74, 266; cockfighting and gambling prohibitions of, 56; description of, 41–44; food rations and, 59–60; property rights and, 186, 221–27, 230–31, 272; reforms of, 264–65

CUCs (currency), 219–20, 227, 231–32, 264–65

Cucusa (Vicenta Petrona Sáez): altar to San Lázaro-Babalú Ayé of, 5, 7–9, 37–38, 40–41, 62; children of, 34–35, 37–41, 220; cockfighting and, 6–7, 35–36, 77; Congo substances and, 24; death of, 5,

11, 47, 55, 111–12, 135–36; as host of San Lázaro-Babalú Ayé, 10–11, 25, 30, 33, 36, 42, 44–45, 232, 241; as owner of house, 3–11; parents of, 24–25, 34; Cuban Revolution and, 44–45; shadow of, 66, 236; as Yemayá's mount, 17, 34

cultural resources: Central African, xvi, xvii, 16; West African, xvi, xvii. *See also* Arará cultural resources; Congo-inspired praise; Ewe; Fon

curve (house on), 115, 128, 135–36, 150–51, 171, 191, 201, 214–15, 228, 232–33, 236, 241–52, 254–55, 257–59, 278, 287, 291, 296–97

dancers: mounting of *orisás* and, 39, 85–88, 107–8, 144, 177–78, 281–82. See also *bembés; santos-orisás*

dead, the: consultations with, 202–4, 217, 228, 283; offerings to, 78–79, 83, 133–34, 137; preparations for, 64–70. See also *muertos oscuros*

December 17 (San Lázaro's Day), 11, 13–14

deeds (to property), 3

dejaciónes, 225–27

Deleuze, Gilles, 299n1, 302n2

denunciations, 189–92, 233, 260

Digna Sáez (Ma' Josefa's daughter), 16–17, 26, 32, 39, 47, 244

drummers: breaking open of feasts and, 84, 101, 142–52, 176, 200, 206, 244, 277–78; Changó as sovereign of, 19, 38, 102–4; improvisation and, 115, 159, 195; roles of, 114–15, 180; *santos-orisás* and, 14, 157–59; the slaughter and, 93–94; tumbadoras and, 83–84

eggs, 264–65

Elégua *(orisá):* animals for, 55–56, 99, 134, 144–45, 209, 216, 296; calls for, 101–4, 142–50, 244–45, 253, 255; family disputes and, 85–86; mounts for, 31, 33, 39–40, 85, 94–97, 113–14, 140, 144, 147–48, 151–52, 172–73, 175, 178–80, 195–96, 211, 214, 247–48, 253–55, 281–82, 286–87, 297; sovereign domains of, 30–32, 36, 39, 68–70, 84–86, 95, 97, 101, 147–48, 172–73, 211–12, 217, 244, 253, 282–84

El Niño de Atocha (santo), 31
El Rincón, 228
El Vedado, 186, 221–25
emancipation, 12–15, 18, 20–21, 27, 34, 87
entanglement, xvii, 31, 112, 150
Ernesto Portilla, 24–25, 34, 189
Esteban, 269–72, 278–79
Eugenita (Chacha's daughter), 33
Eusebio Díaz, 41
Ewe, 9, 14–16, 87, 146, 234, 253, 257–58
excesses and exuberance, 45, 99, 257, 290.
     See also Congo-inspired praise; praise

fate, xv, 11, 14, 33, 37, 96, 102, 111–12, 130,
     139, 173, 193, 238, 245, 257, 287
feasts. See *bembés*
feeding the earth, 77–79, 137–40, 145, 176,
     187–89, 203
figurines, 8, 19, 75, 243, 250, 280, 288
fishing, 59, 125–26, 136, 164–65, 203, 234,
     268
Fon, 9, 14–16, 87, 112, 146, 234, 253, 257–58
forces, xvii, 19–24, 56, 99, 112, 132–33, 180,
     193, 245, 250, 258, 287–91
Foucault, Michel, 299n2

gambling, 5, 35, 40–41, 75, 171, 219–20
Genealogies of Religion (Asad), 299n2
Glasnost, 45
goats, 55–56, 91–94, 99–100, 134, 144–45,
     209, 246–47, 254
Gobierno Sáez, 29–30, 32, 38–39, 47, 93,
     161–62
Gómez, Máximo, 22
Guattari, Félix, 302n2
Guevara, Ernesto "Che," 42

hard currency, xvi, 46, 56–57, 62–63, 163,
     188, 219, 264, 295
Havana: African cultural resources in,
     xvii; El Vedado neighborhood of, 186,
     221–25; praise scenes of, xvi, 19–20, 26,
     55, 76–79, 112, 206, 216–17
healing work: Babalú Ayé's, 175, 181, 191,
     209–11, 214, 249, 254, 281, 295; *bembés*
     and, 26, 32–33, 104–11, 132, 152–55,
     173–81, 195–99, 214, 234–35, 245–59,
     281–84, 297; Palo and, 56, 67–68,

75–78. *See also* Congo-inspired praise;
     santos-orisás
heat (as Palo property), 23–25, 78, 193
Horizonte plantation, 13–14, 21–22, 34
house of Cucusa: CDRs and, 43–44;
     cleaning of, 131–32, 137, 170–71;
     cockfighting ring of, 35–36, 56, 77;
     Cucusa's ownership of, 40–41;
     descriptions of, 38–39, 52–53, 90–91;
     family disputes over, 47–48, 185–87,
     194–203, 205, 207–8, 214–15, 217,
     220–22, 225–27, 265–66, 273, 278–79;
     feeding of, 164, 170–71, 189–90;
     Orfilio's purchase of, 36–38, 186; Palo
     protections for, 56, 68–70; Pica as
     caretaker of, 115–16; revolution and,
     44–45; splitting of, 272–73, 291–93, 295
Housing Authority, 214–15, 220–21,
     272–75, 295
Hurricane Irma, 4, 16
Hurricane Kate, 4, 16, 165
Hurricane Michelle, 4

Ifá, 77–78, 112, 210
import and importance, xvii, xvii. *See also*
     affect; Congo-inspired praise; praise
in-between spaces, 86. *See also* crossing and
     crossroads; Elégua *(orisá)*; thresholds
indenture, 14, 28. *See also* emancipation;
     slavery
Ingo (Chacha's daughter), 33, 87, 104, 159,
     162, 234
initiations and initiates, xvii, 20, 55, 76–77,
     116, 206, 216–17
Inle *(orisá)*, 197, 231, 246–49, 258
inversions, 250. *See also* Congo-inspired
     praise

jabaos, 62–63
John Paul II (Pope), xvi, 47, 80, 105
Jorge Sáez, 15–16, 20, 22, 38, 47, 167
José María Sáez, 21
Juan Guillén, 241
Juan Sáez *(muerto)*, 129

Kardec, Allan, 198
Kimbito Sáez, 13, 17, 20–21, 26, 32, 47,
     237–38, 240

Óko (orisá), 73
Old Dahomey, 9–10, 14, 52
Orfilio Ruíz, 3, 5–6, 33, 35, 40–41, 236
orisás: animals dedicated to, 55–56,
    59–62, 69, 80–83; Catholic saints'
    relation to, 37; definitions of, xiii;
    dismounting practices and, 39, 41,
    86–87, 97, 104, 110–11, 210, 282, 286;
    mounting practices and sovereign
    domains of, 38–40; slaughters for,
    90–100. See also santos-orisás; specific
    orisás
Otilia Sáez, 28–29, 32, 39, 47, 161–62
outside, the, 291. See also containment;
    inversions; mischievousness and
    mischief
overflow. See excesses and exuberance
Oyá (orisá): bembé appearances of, 26;
    mounts for, 20–21, 23, 25–26, 34, 39, 42,
    86–87, 104, 106–7, 111–13, 140, 145–46,
    151–52, 172, 176–79, 186, 206, 212, 283;
    Ogún and, 30; Pica and, 165; sovereign
    domains of, 20, 25–26, 31, 106, 111–12,
    234–35, 292
Oyo, 9–10, 14

Palo (Congo-inspired praise), xvii, 15–16,
    21–22, 24; bembé preparations and,
    79–80; healing practices of, 56, 67–68,
    75–78; muertos and, 41–42; powers of,
    16, 24, 34, 56, 66–67, 90–98, 122, 167,
    209, 247, 250, 288; prendas and, 271. See
    also Congo-inspired praise
Papo Angaríca, 77–78
paquete, el (digital content), 227, 302n1
pensamientos, 137, 205
Perestroika, 45
permutas, 222–24
Pica Sáez (Loreto's daughter), 20, 23, 32, 47,
    56, 58–59, 65–67, 75–77, 79, 84;
    blindness of, 236; as caller, 84, 87,
    94–95, 98–99, 101–2, 128, 140, 142–50,
    158–59, 172–74, 176–77, 180, 194–99,
    201–2, 205–7, 214, 250; as Changó's
    mount, 87–89, 102–3, 114–15, 178, 180,
    206; childhood of, 165–67; the curve
    and, 150–51, 236; death of, 265–68, 274,
    293; as Oyá's mount, 106–7, 113, 165–66,

180, 206, 231, 283; Sociedad Africana
    and, 159
play, xvi, 19, 31–32, 40, 97, 106–7, 113–14,
    172–75, 206, 248–56, 281–82, 289–91
police, 59, 80–81, 111, 166, 191–96, 200, 212,
    273–76, 278
potential, 28, 55, 67, 77, 85, 99, 110, 114, 146,
    150, 245, 250, 281–91
praise: affect and, xvii, xviii, 302n2; animal
    slaughter and, 90–100, 126, 146, 150,
    214–15, 245, 251; Catholicism and, 7–8,
    27, 31, 37–38, 44, 112, 198, 205, 289;
    combination of cultural resources and,
    xvi, 16, 66–67, 79–80, 90–98, 102–3,
    106, 112–14, 116, 138, 148–49, 154–55,
    163–64, 167, 174–75, 179, 188–89,
    204–5, 209, 233, 247, 250–60, 286–87,
    260; definitions of, xv; initiations and
    initiates in, xvii; Ocha-Santería and,
    xvii, 19–20, 26, 55, 76–79, 102–6, 112,
    206, 216–17; official sanction and, xvi;
    Palo and, xvii15–16, 21–24, 41–42, 51,
    56, 66–68, 75–80, 90–98, 112, 122–25,
    209, 247, 250, 288; quotidian nature of,
    xv–xvi; religion's relation to, xv–xvii;
    Cuban Revolution and, 38, 42–47, 86,
    105, 128–29, 162, 166–67; Spiritualism
    and, 70, 76, 137–38, 198–99, 202–5, 212,
    215, 233, 246, 251–52, 254, 258, 270. See
    also specific African traditions
prendas, 67, 271
property disputes, xiv, 3–11, 48, 53–55,
    61–62, 64–65, 115–16, 185–94, 214–15,
    220–27, 230–31, 265–66, 273–75

Quintina (Loreto's marida), 18, 129, 197–98
quinto (drum), 38, 114–15, 157
Quita Manaquita society, 228, 264

racialization. See "color" (and Cuban
    racialization); Cuba
rams, 91–92, 95–97, 105, 113–14, 133–34, 138,
    176, 179
Rationing Authority, 220–21
"Reflections by Comrade Fidel" (Castro),
    239
refrigerators, 54–57, 62–63, 160–63, 187
Reina Collín, 33, 104, 159, 166, 234

steeds. *See* mounting (by *santos-orisás*)

stick workers. *See* Palo

stones (Congo-inspired substances), 16, 66–67, 90, 94–98, 167, 209, 247, 250, 288

superabundance. *See* excesses and exuberance

surrender, 257

Takako Kudo, 51, 58, 62–64, 69, 83, 192

tangles, xvii, 30–32, 112, 150

temporality, xvii, 10, 17, 64, 85, 102, 104, 109–15, 157–58

tenant rights, 3, 186, 225, 266. *See also under* Cuba; property disputes

theater of cruelty, 139

thresholds, 19, 30–32, 40, 68, 84, 94, 106, 114, 172, 193. *See also* crossing and crossroads; Elégua *(orisá);* in-between spaces

time, xvii, 10, 17, 64, 85, 102, 104, 109–15, 157–58

Tomasa Sánchez, 241

tourism, 46, 120–21, 123, 127–28, 141, 149–50, 188, 191, 224, 268–69

transgression, 250, 283. *See also* inversions; mischievousness and mischief; outside, the

transportation, 189–90, 219–20, 226–29; hired cars and, 4, 51–52; state-organized hitchhiking and, 52

tumbadoras, 83–84

26th of July Movement, 7, 42–43, 221–22

Varadero, 3, 51, 120–21, 123, 125, 127, 149–50, 269

Virgin of Charity, 8, 27. *See also* La Caridad-Ochún *(santo-orisá);* La Virgen de la Caridad del Cobre

vitality, xv, 67, 73, 150, 173, 246, 291. *See also* bembés; healing work

West African cultural resources, xvi, xvii. *See also* Arará cultural resources

Yemayá (orisá): animals for, 99, 216; *bembé* appearances of, 26; counsel of, 217, 228, 230; gender of, 23; mounts for, 14, 16–17, 33–34, 39, 129–30, 132, 136–37, 151–52, 172, 177, 244, 247–48; songs for, 66; sovereign domains of, 14, 16–17, 25, 31, 36, 68, 130, 270–71, 292

Yeyo Cairo, 35

Yoruba people, xvii, 14–16, 56, 87, 112, 116, 211, 234, 257–58

Founded in 1893,
UNIVERSITY OF CALIFORNIA PRESS
publishes bold, progressive books and journals
on topics in the arts, humanities, social sciences,
and natural sciences—with a focus on social
justice issues—that inspire thought and action
among readers worldwide.

The UC PRESS FOUNDATION
raises funds to uphold the press's vital role
as an independent, nonprofit publisher, and
receives philanthropic support from a wide
range of individuals and institutions—and from
committed readers like you. To learn more, visit
ucpress.edu/supportus.